ADVANCES IN GENDER RESEARCH   VOLUME 7

GENDER PERSPECTIVES ON HEALTH AND MEDICINE: KEY THEMES

EDITED BY

MARCIA TEXLER SEGAL

Indiana University Southeast, Indiana, USA

VASILIKIE DEMOS

University of Minnesota-Morris, Minnesota, USA

with

JENNIE JACOBS KRONENFELD

Department of Sociology, Arizona State University, AZ, USA

2003

ELSEVIER
JAI

Amsterdam – Boston – Heidelberg – London – New York – Oxford – Paris
San Diego – San Francisco – Singapore – Sydney – Tokyo

ELSEVIER Ltd
The Boulevard, Langford Lane
Kidlington, Oxford OX5 1GB, UK

First edition 2003

Library of Congress Cataloging in Publication Data
A catalogue record from the British Library has been applied for.

ISBN: 0-7623-1058-8
ISSN: 1529-2126 (Series)

♾ The paper used in this publication meets the requirements of ANSI/NISO Z39.48-1992 (Permanence of Paper).
Printed in The Netherlands.

CONTENTS

GENDERED PERSPECTIVES ON MEDICINE:
AN INTRODUCTION
Marcia Texler Segal and Vasilikie Demos with
Jennie Jacobs Kronenfeld   *1*

SITUATING EPIDEMIOLOGY
Beth E. Jackson   *11*

GENDERING THE MEDICALIZATION THESIS
Elianne Riska   *59*

"BIG PHARMA" IN OUR BEDROOMS: AN ANALYSIS OF THE
MEDICALIZATION OF WOMEN'S SEXUAL PROBLEMS
Heather Hartley   *89*

THE CONTINUUM: SOMATIC DISTRESS TO MEDICALIZATION
IN WOMEN WITH BREAST CANCER: THEORETICAL AND
EMPIRICAL ASSESSMENT
Erica S. Breslau   *131*

INTERSECTIONALITY AND WOMEN'S HEALTH: CHARTING
A PATH TO ELIMINATING HEALTH DISPARITIES
Lynn Weber and Deborah Parra-Medina   *181*

"WE'RE NOT A PART OF SOCIETY, WE DON'T HAVE
A SAY": EXCLUSION AS A DETERMINANT OF POOR
WOMEN'S HEALTH
Colleen Reid   *231*

RARIU AND LUO WOMEN: ILLNESS AS RESISTENCE
TO MEN AND MEDICINE IN RURAL KENYA
  Nancy Luke   *281*

ABOUT THE AUTHORS   *323*

INDEX   *327*

GENDERED PERSPECTIVES ON MEDICINE: AN INTRODUCTION

Marcia Texler Segal, Vasilikie Demos with
Jennie Jacobs Kronenfeld

This is a volume about gender, health and medicine broadly defined. It is based on the now widely-held assumption in the sociology of medicine that medicine and health are social constructions and that gender is an embedded part of them (see Lorber, 1997). The essays reveal that embedded with gender in the institution of medicine are race, class, and sexuality. Taken as a whole, the volume offers a critique of exclusively biomedical approaches to personal and public health and calls for more sociological input and qualitative research to help us understand aspects of health and illness. Among the recurrent themes in the seven essays are the medicalization of personal and social problems, the commodification of healthcare, and questions of agency, responsibility and control.

The proportions of women and men in various medical and allied health fields fluctuate creating an imbalance in the relative power that women and men have in research, diagnosis, health policy and treatment. The health-related concerns and access to alternatives to address those concerns vary widely. The vocabularies that we use to discuss health-related issues and the ways in which we define what is relevant to our health and well-being are bound by gender as well as race, class and sexuality.

Medicalization refers to the definition of a particular set of circumstances as biomedical in nature, in need of research by scientists trained in biology and medicine and treatment by a physician or other medical practitioner, typically with drugs or other forms of medical technology. Examples of medicalization

Gender Perspectives on Health and Medicine: Key Themes
Advances in Gender Research, Volume 7, 1–9
Copyright © 2003 by Elsevier Ltd.
All rights of reproduction in any form reserved
ISSN: 1529-2126/doi:10.1016/S1529-2126(03)07001-2

are menopause and attention deficit/hyperactivity disorder (ADHT). In the case of menopause these circumstances might be considered a normal part of aging and therefore not "treatable," or in the case of ADHT, behavior within the normal range of childhood variation or an educational problem requiring alternative teaching methods. Instead, they are currently treated by physicians with prescription medications. (See, for example, Horwitz, 2002, for a recent discussion of the redefinition or medicalization of many behaviors and reactions to social conditions or events as mental *illness*.)

When circumstances are medicalized they tend also to be treated as "private troubles" rather than "public issues" to use C. Wright Mills' (1959) oft-quoted words. Individuals and their families are made responsible for complying with the course of treatment prescribed, and any possible part played by the broader community is ignored. A current pattern, popular since the identification of the Type A personality (a stereotypically western, masculine set of traits), with heart disease, is the identification of behavioral or genetic medical risk factors. (See, for example, "Measuring Behaviors that Endanger Health" on the United States Centers for Disease Control and Prevention website.) Once these are identified, individuals are considered responsible for their own health. Social factors and public policy that might contribute to or alleviate the problem are ignored. As Cockerham (2000) has pointed out, a person's life chances are often largely determined by their socioeconomic status, age, gender, race, ethnicity and other factors that shape health lifestyle choices. Obesity is an example. Poor diet and eating habits place one at risk for obesity which further puts one at risk for heart disease, diabetes and other ailments. That poor diet and eating habits are more common in some segments of the population than others – indicating a social structural determinant of obesity – is likely to be overlooked by the dominant paradigm of health. This extends beyond medicine, to pubic health, the focus of several of the articles in this volume.

As several of the essays in this volume point out, identifying risk factors and placing responsibility on the shoulders of individuals is a neo-liberal approach to health and wellness. It can be problematic when it detracts from the possibility that we will recognize and rectify social circumstances that impact people's health (Barbee & Little, 2003). It may lead to blaming the victims of life – and health-threatening conditions, as has been pointed out in research in medical sociology for over 20 years, as well as in newer material that discusses neo-liberal approaches to health (Kronenfeld, 1979). As our authors also note, however, medicalization can have the effect of denying people, especially women and the poor, agency and control.

Once the medical profession takes over, people become patients. They no longer define their symptoms and cannot control their course of treatment except by failing to comply with the prescribed regimen. Girls being treated for anorexia nervosa, for example, may refuse to reach their prescribed "target weight" as a way of maintaining control over their lives (Gremillion, 2002). Finally, whole social movements have been built around the desire to have a set of circumstances medicalized or de-medicalized. Advocates for those suffering with Gulf War and chronic fatigue syndromes sought medicalization as a form of validation and in order to obtain research and treatment (Williams, 2000). Gay men, lesbians and their advocates sought to have homosexuality de-medicalized to remove a stigma and provide acknowledgment that treatment was not needed. Parents of children with behavior problems are ambivalent about whether medicalization is the best approach (Stolberg, 2002).

The papers by Heather Hartley, Colleen Reid and Nancy Luke are data-based. Those by Beth Jackson, Elianne Risku, Erica Breslau, Lynn Weber and Deborah Parra-Medina are largely theoretical. Each of the authors, however, points indirectly or directly to the importance of using qualitative methods in researching health and health care.

It is obvious from all the statistics available (see, for example, the statistics on the distribution of chronic diseases on the United States Centers for Disease Control and Prevention website) that health and wellness are unevenly distributed in our society. The statistics, however, allow only a partial view of peoples' well-being. The authors in this volume and its forthcoming companion, that focuses more closely on reproductive health, argue that a more complete understanding of a population's health and health care needs is possible only through the use of qualitative research methods. Such methods are sensitive to the voices of people seeking health care. Particularly with respect to less privileged groups such as poor women, qualitative methods permit us to learn how people define health-related issues, when, where and how they seek treatment and the barriers that they perceive. Their comments go beyond the narrow confines of the medical establishment to issues of access to information, recreational facilities, and childcare. We cannot eliminate disparities in health and wellness without placing the issues in a broader context.

Healthcare is commodified. As David A. Rochefort states in his review of a recent book on the subject: "The transformation of the U.S. health system has alienated patients, incensed organized medicine, and given private entrepreneurs a profitable new area for financial investment" (2002, p. 228). Heathcare is marketed, bought and sold, no longer implying or requiring a traditional relationship of trust between healthcare recipient and healthcare provider. In fact, one way that some medical sociologists have suggested to reconceptualize the older concept of the doctor-patient relationship in the new millennium, given the impact of managed care, is as a buyer-beware, consumer protection model, in which recipients of healthcare can no longer assume that the provider of care will have the best interests of the consumer as a major concern. As with other commercial transactions, recipients of care must be their own advocates for quality and appropriate care (Kronenfeld, 2001). Managed care intervenes to lower costs in ways that may have unanticipated consequences for patients and the system. Treatments are often focused on new drugs and technology-based. They save time but drive costs. Drugs can be prescribed even without a clear idea of the problem as with psychotropic drugs for various anxiety disorders or when there really is no problem as with performance enhancing drugs or cosmetic surgery. As Erica S. Breslau explains in this volume, the potential exists to short circuit diagnosis. We need to ask to what extent the somatic symptoms experienced by some breast cancer patients are symptoms of the disease, symptoms caused by the treatment or symptoms reflecting the stress the patient is under.

In "Situating Epidemiology," the first essay in the volume, Beth Jackson provides a feminist critique of epidemiology, "the basic science of public health (p. 11)," and by implication, modern medicine. Jackson traces the history of epidemiology as a public health history, and identifies several periods of epidemiology, particularly as they apply to Canadian health care. She critiques current epidemiological research as positivist, microbiological, quantitative, and universally-oriented and maintains that the neo-liberal tendencies of the 1990s and the early 21st century and its individual statistical approach to health overlooks specific sub-populations of people.

Looking to Nancy Krieger's (1994) proposal for an eco-social epidemiology, Jackson argues for "re-situating epidemiology" more in line with an earlier conception of public health, one that takes a broad-based population approach. She further points to the importance of using a multiplicity of methods to collect data about health care and of locating "truth claims" within a social context, informed both sociologically and biologically. Jackson concludes,

> But if scientific knowledge is social knowledge (Longino, 1992, 1996), then biological knowledge does not have a primary stability, and despite a realist commitment, we can neither assume a truth of biology that is 'covered over' by misdirected or inadequate investigation, nor that there is a significant distinction between biological and social facts. If ecosocial epidemiology is to be fully informed by feminist locational epistemologies, it must leave open the possibility that the 'truth' of the biological world is just as elusive and fragile as that of the social.

In "Gendering the Medicalization Thesis," Elianne Riska reviews the history of the thesis from its emergence in the 1970s and analyzes that history with respect to the part gender has played in it. Riska identifies three gendered periods of medicalization. Officially the first period, just prior to the 1970s, was a gender-neutral period; actually, it was a time when studies were conducted primarily on men, work on hyperactivity in children focused on boys, Type A Personality was basically associated with the risk of heart disease in men, and alcoholism was treated as a men's disease. The second period began in the 1970s as feminists began identifying an over-medicalization of women, and liberal feminists pointed to the practice of medicine as patriarchal with women treated offensively as stereotypes by the male-dominated medical profession. The 1990s ushered in the third period, a time in which men have been medicalized. The development of viagra has led to the "viagricization" of men's health and a concern with penile health and sexual potency, and with a rise in men's concern with body image.

Riska argues that beginning in the 1980s, medicine has been increasingly reductionist driven by efforts to contain health care costs and a focus on genetically-based risk factors for disease. Similar to Jackson, she points to the effect of neo-liberal economics, and notes that health and medicine is viewed as an individual problem with the consequence that many people are marginalized by the dominant health care system.

R. W. Connell (2000) has noted that such masculine practices as automobile racing, drinking and using drugs are bad for men's health. Yet, he rejects defining men as victims in the same way women are defined as victims. All women are subjugated to masculinity, but men have more power than women. Men's power points to the complexity of gender equity. Some men – those who have the opportunity and the desire – practice hegemonous masculinity, dominate over other men, and have access to health care. Thus, working class gay men find themselves more isolated and vulnerable in dealing with HIV-AIDS than middle class gay men, and research on HIV-AIDS was delayed because of its initial association with a subordinated form of masculinity, gay manhood.

Riska sees the completion of the gendering of the medicalization thesis, as a path to the recognition of diverse health care needs. In line with Connell (2000), she argues that the feminization of medicalization victimizes all women, but that its masculinization does not do the same to all men. Pointing to not one but many masculinities, Riska notes masculinity represents both health risks and privilege, and urges a more complex view of medicalization taking into account multiple masculinities and the impact of race and class on gender in health care.

Heather Hartley, also, considers the medicalization thesis as it relates to gender. Her focus is on the critical role of pharmaceutical companies in the medicalization of sexuality. In "Big Pharma in our Bedrooms: An Analysis of the Medicalization of Women's Sexual Problems," Hartley focuses on women and "female sexual dysfunction." She notes that "androgen deficiency syndrome" has been identified as a health condition without the substantiation of interest-free research.

Hartley argues that the marketplace success of viagra and the medicalization of men's sexuality has prompted the pharmaceutical industry to attempt to achieve similar success with women's sexuality. Based on her participant observation at conferences on sexuality, interviews with key researchers, and analyses of various documents ranging from scholarly journals and FDA reports to newspaper articles, Hartley demonstrates the enormous power pharmaceutical companies have in controlling the definition of a medical condition and the marketing of therapy to deal with it. She details how the proliferation of research centers unrelated to universities has made it possible for pharmaceutical companies to better control the publication of adverse research findings, and how researchers both in and out of universities failing to obtain research funding from the FDA become obligated to the pharmaceutical companies that do provide the funding.

In "The Continuum: Somatic Distress to Medicalization in Women with Breast Cancer," Erica S. Breslau through a theoretical and empirical assessment considers the problems generated when somatization is medicalized. Somatization is the physical symptom manifestation of distress, an inability to cope. Breslau notes that somatization has been recognized as a number of conditions including Chronic Fatigue Syndrome, but that it is unspecified in dealing with breast cancer.

Breslau explains that because many of its symptoms can mimic the symptoms of breast cancer, somatization is difficult to treat. At the same time, she is critical of the biomedical approach to somatization and its medicalization. In breast cancer patients, particularly, medicalized somatization results in the application of high tech expensive therapies controlled by insurance companies and physicians, and a loss of control over care by the patient. Breslau's argument for research on somatization in breast cancer patients is compelling. Such research would make possible more accurate diagnoses in breast cancer patients and appropriate non-medical low-cost treatments.

In her study of Jewish and African-American women who were mothers in the 1930s and 1940s, Jacqueline S. Litt (2000) uses an "intersectional" approach. She demonstrates that medicalized motherhood is not only a gender issue, but, also an ethno-racial one. Their racial and social class situations meant the women found themselves on the margins of the white-dominated patriarchal medical system.

Lynn Weber and Deborah Parra-Medina's and Colleen Reid's papers explicitly focus on the "intersectional" concerns of Jacqueline S. Litt. Weber and Parra-Medina continue a critique of the biomedical approach to health in their article, "Intersectionality and Women's Health: Charting a Path to Eliminating Health Disparities." Turning their attention to the consequences of health for race, gender and class, Weber and Parra-Medina call for an intersectional approach to eliminating disparities in health and health care that is similar to the arguments Jackson makes about re-situating epidemiology. They identify a number of problems with the individually oriented biomedical model of health, and observe that race, class, gender and sexuality are treated in varying ways in biomedical research. Thus, discrimination is acknowledged in race studies and sometimes mentioned in gender research, but never mentioned with respect to class. They note, also, that the American ideological meta-narratives of race and gender as ascribed are embedded in research as is the meta-narrative of the American Dream with its focus on equality of opportunity and class as achieved.

Weber and Parra-Medina observe the "downstream" biomedical model focuses on the individual thereby ignoring group processes, and on the distribution of variables in a population at the expense of explaining how these are experienced in individual lives. They note that no one is totally oppressed and no one is totally oppressing, and argue for using an "upstream" model of health in which the intersection of race, gender, class and sexuality power is taken into account. In such a model patterns of dominance are seen as a "matrix of power" not a dichotomy.

Weber and Parra-Medina, also, point to methodological weaknesses of the biomedical model of health. They are critical of quantitative studies stating that these do not get at relational aspects of power. In addition, they are critical of the treatment of less privileged members of the population noting that research is funded by dominant members of the population whose interests drive the research. In order to even obtain information about less privileged members, an "over-sampling" is conducted and sample results are compared with population "norms" thereby treating the less privileged members as deviants. Thus, in addition to using an intersectional upstream model of health research, similar to the public health model discussed in Jackson's paper, Weber and Parra-Medina advise using qualitative research methods. They argue for using Patricia Hill Collins's (1986) concept of the "outsider within" – the individual who has intimate inside knowledge of a situation, but who is prevented from full participation in it, thus allowing a detached observation – as a critical source of knowledge. Just how powerful such an approach can be is demonstrated by anthropologist Susan Greenhalgh in her recent autoethnography, *Under the Medical Gaze: Facts and Fictions of Chronic Pain* (2001).

Colleen Reid is in agreement with Weber and Parra-Medina. In her article, "We're Not a Part of Society, We Don't Have a Say": Exclusion as a Determinant of Poor Women's Health," Reid agrees with Weber and Parra-Medina's implied argument for public health and explicit call for qualitative health research and, consequent, equity. Using qualitative research techniques, working in a women's collective as a project manager and doctoral researcher, Reid explores the effect of exclusion on poor women's health in Canada. She finds that although there is universal health care in Canada, the system is two-tiered and poor women are invisible and stigmatized. Poor women face lack of access to health care resources, the discriminatory attitudes of health care professionals, and differential health care services. As a result of feeling excluded, poor women experience shame which is manifested by low self-esteem, depression and a number of other conditions.

Reid, similar to Jackson, Riska, Breslau, Weber and Parra-Medina, makes a good argument for using qualitative research methods in studying health. Such techniques go to the complexity of health and health care, providing insight into the needs of populations generally overlooked by the health care establishment. As are the other contributors to the volume, Reid is critical of the dominant market-driven health care system with its focus on individual responsibility, and in addition, she points to the global consequences for the underprivileged as neo-liberal health care spreads throughout the world.

In the last article, "Rariu and Luo Women: Illness as Resistence to Men and Medicine in Rural Kenya," Nancy Luke demonstrates the relevance of such ideas as "situating knowledge," medicalization, and somatization to easing tension for women while maintaining social order in rural southwestern Kenya. Rariu, an illness associated with reproduction, is manifested by a pain in the lower abdomen, a heaviness that can prevent birth. It is reported among the Luo women in western Kenya.

Luke describes the social construction of rariu from symptoms to diagnosis and treatment. She explains that the Luo are a patriarchal group in which bride wealth is a critical feature of marriage. Luo women have little power. Men control them sexually as well as non-sexually. Their patrilocal residence pattern means that women having moved into the homes of their husbands as wives are on the margins of family and household life. The children of divorced or separated Luo women belong to the home of their husbands or the patriarchal home. Women are controlled by threat of divorce or separation and by beatings.

Luke argues that Luo women use rariu to resist patriarchy indirectly. Rariu provides respite for women from their sexual and other duties, and an explanation for failure to conceive. Women seek treatment for rariu from an herbalogist or *nyam-rerwa* who provides personal help rather than the impersonal western bio-medical health care system. Women most likely to have rariu are those least educated and empowered. Observing that urban Luo women are more empowered than those in rural area, Luke notes that Luo women living in cities consider the condition a part of rural traditional life. Thus, rariu as a somatized condition is tied to a particular social context. The Luo women, however, unlike western breast cancer patients, have the option to turn to traditional medicine and reject western medicine.

ACKNOWLEDGMENTS

The editors wish to thank Katherine D. Wigley of the Indiana University Southeast Institute for Teaching and Learning Excellence, for technical assistance, and Martha Garcia for her usual thorough and thoughtful job in preparing the index to this volume.

REFERENCES

Barbee, E. L., & Little, M. (2003). Health, social class and African American women. In: E. Disch (Ed.), *Reconstructing Gender: A Multicultural Anthology* (3rd ed., pp. 553–568). Boston: McGraw Hill.

Cockerham, W. C. (2000). The sociology of health behaviors and health lifestyles. In: C. E. Bird, P. Conrad & A. M. Fremont (Eds), *Handbook of Medical Sociology* (5th ed.). Upper Saddle River, NJ: Prentice-Hall.

Collins, P. H. (1986). Learning from the outsider within: The sociological significance of Black feminist thought. *Social Problems, 33*(6), 14–32.

Connell, R. W. (2000). *The men and the boys*. Berkeley: University of California Press.

Greenhalgh, S. (2001). *Under the medical gaze: Facts and fictions of chronic pain*. Berkeley: University of California Press.

Gremillion, H. (2002). In fitness and in health: Crafting bodies in the treatment of anorexia nervosa. *Signs, 27*, 381–414.

Horwitz, A. V. (2002). *Creating mental illness*. Chicago: University of Chicago Press.

Krieger, N. (1994). Epidemiology and the web of causation: Has anyone seen the spider? *Social Science and Medicine, 39*(7), 887–903.

Kronenfeld, J. J. (1979). Self care as a panacea for the ills of the health care system: An assessment. *Social Science and Medicine, 13A*, 263–267.

Kronenfeld, J. J. (2001, July–September). New trends in the doctor-patient relationship: Impacts of managed care on the development of a consumer protections model. *Sociological Spectrum, 21*, 293–317.

Litt, J. S. (2000). *Medicalized motherhood*. New Brunswik, NJ: Rutgers University Press.

Lorber, J. (1997). *Gender and the social construction of illness*. Thousand Oaks, CA: Sage.

Mills, C. W. (1959). *The sociological imagination*. New York: Oxford University Press.

Rochefort, D. A. (2002). Review of the book institutional change and healthcare organizations: From professional dominance to managed care. *Contemporary Sociology, 31*, 228–229.

Stolberg, S. G. (2002). Preschool meds. *New York Times Magazine*, November 17th, 58–61.

United States Centers for Disease Control and Prevention website: www.cdc.gov

Williams, S. (2000). Chronic illness as biographical disruption or biographical disruption as chronic illness: Reflections on a core concept. *Sociology of Health and Illness, 22*(1), 40–67.

SITUATING EPIDEMIOLOGY

Beth E. Jackson

No layer of the onion of practice that is technoscience is outside the reach of technologies of critical interpretation and critical inquiry about positioning and location; that is the condition of articulation, embodiment, and mortality (Haraway, 1997, p. 37).

... questions of knowledge and method can rarely be answered satisfactorily in abstraction, before the fact. Rather, these questions have to be addressed locally, in piece-by-piece analyses of specific instances of knowledge-making ... (Code, 1995a, p. 43).

INTRODUCTION

Epidemiology is often described as "the basic science of public health" (Savitz, Poole & Miller, 1999; Syme & Yen, 2000). This description suggests both a close association with public health practice, and the separation of "pure" scientific knowledge from its application in the messy social world. Although the attainability of absolute objectivity is rarely claimed, epidemiologists are routinely encouraged to "persist in their efforts to substitute evidence for faith in scientific reasoning" (Stolley, 1985, p. 38) and reminded that "public health decision makers gain little from impassioned scholars who go beyond advancing and explaining the science to promoting a specific public health agenda" (Savitz et al., 1999, p. 1160). Epidemiology produces authoritative data that are transformed into evidence which informs public health. Those data are authoritative because epidemiology is regarded as a neutral scientific enterprise. Because its claims are grounded in science, epidemiological knowledge is deemed to have "a special technical status and hence is not contestable in the same way as are say, religion

Gender Perspectives on Health and Medicine: Key Themes
Advances in Gender Research, Volume 7, 11–58
Copyright © 2003 by Elsevier Ltd.
All rights of reproduction in any form reserved
ISSN: 1529-2126/doi:10.1016/S1529-2126(03)07002-4

or ethics" (Lock, 1988, p. 6). Despite the veneer of universality afforded by its scientific pedigree, epidemiology is not a static or monolithic discipline. Epidemiological truth claims are embodied in several shifting paradigms that span the life of the discipline. Public health knowledges and practices, competing claims internal and external to epidemiology, and structural conditions (such as current political economies, material technologies, and institutions) provide important contexts in which certain kinds of epidemiological knowledge are more likely to emerge.

The aim of this paper is neither to establish nor dispute the veracity of any particular epidemiological knowledge claim, but to render accountable those claims, to situate them in the particular historical, political, and social conditions that define "what counts" as data, evidence, and truth. I propose that by subjecting epidemiology to the scrutiny of a feminist epistemological lens, we can illuminate the contexts of that knowledge, and why and how it changes. Equipped with that analysis, we are better positioned to evaluate emergent paradigms of epidemiology.

To what do we refer when we speak of epidemiology? In the 20th century, epidemiology has been concerned with the distribution and determinants of disease in human populations (Tannahill, 1992), but the definition of epidemiology has changed over time. Hippocrates is often recognized as the first epidemiologist, having introduced the words "epidemic" and "endemic" in his teaching over 2,000 years ago to distinguish between diseases that "visit" communities from those that "reside in" them (Buck, Llopis, Najero & Terris, 1988; Lilienfeld & Lilienfeld, 1980). The term "epidemiology" was first recorded in Spain in the late sixteenth century and did not reappear until the beginning of the eighteenth century, in *Epidemiologia Española*, a book written by the Spanish physician Don Joaquin de Villalba (Buck et al., 1988; Terris, 1987). Several notable individuals subsequently conducted what are now known as "epidemiologic studies" before a distinct discipline emerged, but France is credited as its birthplace, "the anvil of epidemiology, where it was first hammered into shape" (Lilienfeld & Lilienfeld, 1980, p. 28). Epidemiology thus emerged as "the science of public health" in several locales over the course of several centuries, and since its emergence as a distinct discipline, it has undergone a number of transformations, each of which constitute a different "movement" or paradigm (Susser & Susser, 1996a). The first of these, referred to as the era of "sanitary statistics" or "traditional epidemiology" prevailed through to the first half of the 19th century; the second, "infectious disease epidemiology" (which marks the beginning of "modern epidemiology") predominated from the second half of the 19th century through the first half of the 20th century; the third era or movement, "chronic disease epidemiology" (also known as "social epidemiology" or "risk-factor epidemiology") has occupied the last half of the 20th century (Pearce, 1996; Susser & Susser, 1996a). Within the last decade, a new paradigm has been proposed to lead us into the 21st century: "ecological" epidemiology (which is expressed differently as "eco-epidemiology" or "ecosocial epidemiology" (Krieger, 1994; Pearce, 1996; Susser & Susser, 1996b)). We are urged by some historians of epidemiology to not only focus on what and when developments occurred in the discipline, but why and how – because "men and methods make epidemiology, not statistical significance levels, nor computers, nor inferences, as important as these are" (Lilienfeld & Lilienfeld, 1980, p. 37).

In the following pages, I offer to the reader a situated history of the paradigmatic shifts in epidemiology. My construction and analysis of this history is guided by a series of questions that attempt to locate each paradigm in its historical, political, and social terrain:

- What were the intellectual conditions in which each paradigm/"movement" of epidemiology took shape and flourished? That is, what have been the prevailing paradigms of knowledge-production in science and medicine, and of disease causation/dispersion? What structures and organizations were formed to support and promulgate these paradigms?
- What were the concomitant prevailing paradigms of public health, the parent/partner discipline of epidemiology?
- What were the political-economic conditions in which these intellectual traditions took shape?
- What is the relationship between the "knower" and the "known" in each of these historical movements of epidemiology?
- What were the technologies (material, literary, and social) that supported each movement of epidemiology? That is, what instruments were used for producing evidence, what were the means of communicating that evidence, and what were the conventions for evaluating evidence or knowledge claims? (Haraway, 1997)
- What is the nature of data, evidence, and findings in each version of epidemiology? What *counted* as data/evidence/findings, and how were these produced?
- Who/what are the subjects constituted by epidemiology in each of its incarnations? Who are the knowers? Who/what can be known?

These questions are informed by the insights of feminist epistemologists (specifically, Barad, 1996; Code, 1995a, b; Haraway, 1991, 1997; Wylie, 1991, 1992a, b) who oppose foundational, positivistic accounts of knowledge, and attend to how political and historical conditions shape its construction. Thus, in my account of epidemiology, I review prevailing theories of disease causation, public policies, and methods of producing and interpreting data within each era, paying particular attention to the concurrent, influential paradigms of public health knowledge. It becomes clear that the "pure" science of epidemiology is a dream; it is "contaminated" by its existence in a real world of knowers, who make and contest claims from particular, invested and complicated positions. Equipped with this insight, we might embrace the opportunity offered to us by the emergent movement of ecosocial epidemiology. We might envision/re-vision a "situated" epidemiology, guided by an approach to scientific knowledge that demands we take our complicated positions into account.

In the next section, before embarking on the history of epidemiological paradigm shifts, I shall review briefly some feminist critiques of foundational epistemologies. I then consider alternative, "locational" epistemologies, which provide a compass for charting the course that epidemiology has taken over the last four centuries, and may take in its future.

FEMINIST CRITIQUES OF FOUNDATIONAL EPISTEMOLOGIES OF SCIENCE

Public health practices of risk assessment are based on the assumption that we can discover, measure, and control *all risk*, with the requisite skill and expertise (Gabe, 1995). This expression of positivist-empiricist science, informed by Enlightenment principles of progress and human mastery over nature, rests upon a correspondence theory of truth. First, it assumes a true and stable reality in which "facts" have an independent and passive existence. They hang like apples on a tree, waiting to be harvested by the observer-scientist. Second, it assumes that scientific theories and measurement accurately mirror reality, transparently disclosing to mute observers the "nature of nature."

The ideal of positivistic objectivity suggests that through the exercise of reason, a knower can "transcend particularity and contingency" to get at the "truth" (Code, 1995a, p. 24). Unsullied by the specific conditions of the knower's (and object's) existence, knower and knowledge are thus detached from any political interests. The researcher becomes simply another instrument; scientists and their methods are presumed to be neutral conduits through which facts pass from the natural (unmediated) world to the social world of knowers.

This version of positivist-empiricism closes off conversation about what and how we can know, and denies responsibility for the knowledges that we create. Facts (e.g. "risk factors") are presumed to "speak for themselves" both as "data" and as "findings" (Code, 1995a); but I concur with Code that there are no dislocated truths – "research is legitimated by the community and speaks in a discursive space that is made available, prepared for it" (Code, 1995a, p. 43; see also Longino, 1992).

LOCATIONAL EPISTEMOLOGIES

Does Code's position imply that the only alternative to a transcendent positivist empiricism is radical relativism, where all knowledge claims are equal? No. Code, Wylie, Haraway, Barad and others, have provided feminist alternatives to positivistic knowledge-production practices *and* to radical relativist alternatives. Code (1995a, b), who supports a "mitigated relativism," urges us to "take subjectivity into account" and to denaturalize naturalized epistemologies; Wylie (1992a, b) recognizes that data and evidence are theory-laden, but maintains that reality resists theoretical closure; Haraway (1991) calls for "situated knowledges" and an "embodied objectivity" to engage with an active reality; and Barad (1996) offers a position of "agential realism" that challenges the context-independence of knowledge claims. All of these accounts attempt: (a) to preserve the idea that objects of knowledge are "real," with real effects, and (b) to maintain the possibility of credible, justifiable knowledge of that reality, *without* lapsing into foundational objectivism, or radical, "anything goes" relativism.

Taking subjectivity into account is a crucial first step in this challenge. It requires us to acknowledge how and where knowing subjects are situated in social relations and practices, and to identify whose interests are served by certain constructions of knowledge. Looking forward to the history of epidemiology in the pages ahead, we might ask: Whose interests are served by a single-cause model of disease that allows risk to be embodied by/in "suspect" individuals who can be contained and separated from an "innocent" community? Whose interests are served by a multiple-cause model of disease, that emerged in response to the reduction of infectious disease in the West, and the chronic diseases of affluence? What interests are served by an epidemiological model supported by "lifestyle" health promotion, that shifts attention away from publicly funded health care services and downloads responsibility for health care to individuals? We will see how various paradigms of epidemiology reaffirm positivist-empiricist science: "facts" and "evidence" are believed to exist outside the observer – both "germs" and the "determinants of health" have an existence apart from the scientist who "discovers" them.

According to Code, taking subjectivity into account requires "acknowledging that 'facts' are always infused with values, and that both facts and values are open to ongoing political debate" (Code, 1995a, p. 42). Wylie concurs, asserting that "(D)ata and evidence are radically constituted (. . .) richly 'theorized' constructs" (Wylie, 1992a, p. 275). But these assertions do not imply a move to relativism. Code, Wylie, Haraway and Barad reject the idea that the positivist view from nowhere should be replaced by a relativist "view from everywhere" (Haraway, 1991, p. 191), because "both (views) deny the stakes in location, embodiment, and partial perspective; both make it impossible to see well" (Haraway, 1991, p. 191), and both deny responsibility for the truth produced. Haraway contends that taking our "partial perspective" into account enables us to see "objectively" because this opens up, rather than denies, the question of accountability for knowledge-production; it brings into full view the positionality of knowledge claims, replaces knowers and knowledge in their contingent localities, and exposes the neutral observer as a myth.

The alternative to positivist objectivity or to radical relativism is what Haraway calls "situated knowledges" and Code calls "mitigated relativism" (1995a, p. 53): knowledge is always located in specific circumstances, and the *validity* of the knowledge produced rests on clearly locating its production. Consequently, scientists must provide an account of how data or "facts" are constructed as credible "evidence," to situate the knowledge they produce.

Central to situated knowledge is a commitment to accounting for a reality "out there" that we *can know* (Code, 1995a). But this is not a fixed universe; it is an "active" reality that resists our cognitive manipulation. Still, not any account will do. Wylie tells us that while data is neither stable nor given, "it is by no means infinitely plastic. It does, or can, function as a highly recalcitrant, closely constraining, 'network of resistances' " (Wylie, 1992b, p. 25). Haraway's embodied objectivity also imagines a reality that is active and involved, rather than inert and abstract. Reality does not wait passively to be discovered, nor does it transparently speak for itself. Objects of knowledge are social "boundary projects" that are the result of the interaction of knowing subjects with material reality in local conditions. Taking Wylie's notion of "recalcitrant data" a step further, Haraway describes the world as a "material-semiotic actor" which is not only assigned meaning by subjects, but which *generates* meaning in its interaction with knowers. In this relationship, we must acknowledge that the distinction between the (active) subject and (passive) object of knowledge blurs. We are encouraged to remain open to surprises that remind us reality is not fully under our discursive control. Similarly, Barad, a theoretical physicist, describes an "agential reality" that challenges the clear distinction between subject and object assumed by positivist-empiricist science. Whereas positivist science presumes that measurement is neutral, or at least that the effects of measurement can be separated from objects of observation, Barad contends that measurement "is an instance where matter and meaning meet" (Barad, 1996, p. 166). Because there is no clear way to attribute the qualities that we observe either to objects or to the agencies of observation (i.e. the instruments of measurement and the observer), we cannot conclude that there is an inherent distinction between subject and object. "Hence, observations do not refer to objects of an independent reality," but to "phenomena" (objects and agencies of observation together) (Barad, 1996, p. 170). In other words, our observations refer to "our participation *within nature*," that is, to agential reality (Barad, 1996, p. 176). Agential realism re-situates theory in measurement practices, and locates both within social contexts.

Barad notes that when we make scientific observations, we introduce a *socially constructed* division between the object observed and agencies of observation. This division helps us to measure and understand certain qualities of the phenomena *in a specific context*, denaturalizing observation processes and creating a situated and local knowledge of the object. *Competing* accounts of reality describe different "cuts" between objects and agencies of observation; that is, they describe different phenomena. For example, certain apparatuses (microscopes) produce a particular "result" or understanding of disease-causation (disease is caused by single agents – germs). Other apparatuses (multi-causal statistical modeling) produce another understanding of causation (i.e. disease is produced by a complex interaction of biological, environmental and social factors). The second conclusion may seem to emerge from "better" knowledge (or at least, more data) but neither is "incorrect" – they simply describe different phenomena. Scientific concepts are not context-independent truths; rather, they obtain their meaning from particular means by which we mark the distinction between objects and agencies of observation.

The feminist epistemologies outlined above challenge us to interrogate the conditions under which epidemiological knowledges are created. They provide means to situate changing knowledge claims about disease and examine the contexts in which data about risk and health are assumed to be self-evident.

TRADITIONAL EPIDEMIOLOGY AND "SANITARY STATISTICS"

Ordering the Universe

You are to be in all things regulated and governed, said the gentleman, by fact. We hope to have, before long, a board of fact, composed of commissioners of fact, who will force the people to be a people of fact, and of nothing but fact (Dickens, 1998, p. 9).

The underlying logic of epidemiology evolved from the scientific revolution of the 17th century (Lilienfeld & Stolley, 1994). Early modern science was premised on a rejection of supernatural influences; challenges to traditional religious authority; a detached rationality that could deduce the truth of experiences and phenomena in the material world; and a belief in human progress. Many scientists of the time who, like Descartes, took "great pleasure in mathematics because of the certainty and the evidence of its arguments" (Descartes, 1637, 1641/1993, p. 4), believed that the order of the universe could be expressed in mathematical relationships; and if the physical world was subject to such principles, then so must be the world of biology. Mathematical astronomers brought this certainty to the technology of the "life-table" (which provided "age-specific probabilities of death" in a population). They applied the mathematical "laws of mortality" that governed the movements of planets, to human beings. Edmund Halley (after whom the famous comet is named) created the first life-table in 1693 (Lilienfeld & Lilienfeld, 1980, p. 29). Subsequently, the "development of biostatistics throughout the 18th century was premised on the notion of natural laws of mortality" (Lilienfeld & Lilienfeld, 1980, p. 29). Unabashed reverence for Enlightenment scientific principles continued well into the 19th century, as demonstrated by the comments of Stephen Smith, founder of the American Public Health Association, in his Presidential Address to the First Annual Meeting in 1873:

> The science which we cultivate, and which this Association is organized to promote, discarding the traditions of the past and the teachings of false philosophies, interprets the laws that have been set for the guidance and control of man's earthly existence by the exact demonstrations of a true physiology. This science of life reveals to us the stupendous fact that man is born to health and longevity, that disease is abnormal, and death, except from old age, is accidental, and that both are preventable by human agencies (cited in Terris, 1985, p. 33).

Scientific societies and professional associations were founded to support the works of "men of science" (rarely women), and permit communication of information among members. The writings of Francis Bacon (who was keen to subdue unruly nature with scientific laws) were the inspiration for the Royal Society of London, established in 1662. One of its first members was John Graunt, whose *Natural and Political Observations Mentioned in a Following Index and Made Upon the Bills of Mortality* was a pioneering epidemiological study of mortality and morbidity in human populations. He collected Bills of Mortality in London and in the rural community of Hampshire to derive inferences about mortality and fertility, make distinctions between causes (acute vs. chronic disease) and identify urban-rural differences. Having constructed statistical tables from this data (not unlike the "life-tables" produced three decades later), Graunt advocated that each country "prepare similar tables so that they could be compared to construct a general law of mortality" (Lilienfeld & Stolley, 1994, p. 24). Three hundred years later, Glass (1963) remarked:

> ...the most outstanding qualities of Graunt's work are first, the search for regularities and configurations in mortality and fertility; and secondly, the attention given – and usually shown explicitly – to the errors and ambiguities of the inadequate data used in that search. Graunt did not wait for better statistics; he did what he could with what was available to him. And by so doing, he also produced a much stronger case for supplying better data (cited in Lilienfeld & Stolley, 1994, p. 24).

The drive for "better data," closely associated with the belief that the universe (and the human affairs within it) could be controlled "by enumeration and classification," was satisfied by an "avalanche of printed numbers" produced by amateur and bureaucratic statisticians (Hacking, 1990, p. 2). Statistics in the West were motivated by "a desire to improve society by applying reason to facts" (Hacking, 1990, p. 45). As French statisticians like Adolphe Quetelet advanced mathematical technologies, the application of these methods to health and disease was refined and extended. But by the mid-18th century, epidemiology in France declined, and London became the centre of activity for the discipline (Lilienfeld & Stolley, 1994). Although France had originally provided fertile ground for epidemiology to develop because of a vibrant interest in public health,[1] it lacked "one essential component needed for epidemiology to develop and flourish [–] the existence, maintenance, and utilization of vital statistics, i.e. population-based statistics" (Lilienfeld & Lilienfeld, 1980, p. 37). England, on the other hand, had a substantial vital statistics system in place: the London Bills of Mortality had been produced since the 1500s; the English military had kept detailed records of troop mortality since the late 1700s; and life insurance companies compiled statistics on subscribers since the 1800s (Hacking, 1990; Lilienfeld & Lilienfeld, 1980).

The Miasma of Disease and the Health of Populations

But "what prompted a statistical approach *to disease* in the first place," what data was considered relevant, and what findings and explanations were produced by analysis of these data? (Hannaway, 1980, italics added). In the late 1700s, the Société Royale du Médicine in Paris collected data to attempt to quantify the current definition of "epidemic," to expand understanding of this phenomenon beyond "a disease affecting a large number of people with the same symptoms at the same time." The prevailing paradigm of disease causation was miasma theory: natural climatic and environmental phenomena such as atmospheric conditions (including the presence of foul odours), weather, and topography are related to the occurrence of disease. Over time, more sophisticated atmospheric and meteorological instruments became available. Consequently, "(a)s the science of the atmosphere became quantified, so did 18th century epidemiology. (. . .) It was believed that if sufficient data was collected and analyzed some 'natural' laws of epidemics would emerge behind the apparent contingencies of the weather and the ailments of the populace" (Hannaway, 1980, p. 40).[2]

The quantification of disease was also fueled by "(t)he early modern political philosophy of mercantilism (which) stressed the need to measure the strength of the state by assessing levels of health" (Porter, 1999, p. 49). James Lind's 1753

"Inquiry into the Nature, Causes, and Cure of the Scurvy" demonstrates the close link made between a state's political-economic power and the health of its citizens:

> The subject of the following sheets is of great importance to this nation; the most powerful in her fleets and the most flourishing in her commerce of any in the world. (...) I flatter myself that it will appear from the following treatise that the calamity (of scurvy) may be prevented and the danger of this destructive evil obviated (...) (Buck et al., 1988, p. 20).

The health of the population emerged as a "policy objective" which required methods to manage and coordinate rising birth rates, increasing longevity, public health, housing and migration (Foucault, 1990), all of which had a profound impact on the state. This spurred the development of techniques for exercising control over populations. Demographic surveys, economic tables measuring distribution of wealth, calculations of mortality, all marked the beginning of an era of "bio-politics" (Foucault, 1980, 1990) in which repressive methods of control (symbolized by the sovereign's power to impose death) were replaced by constructive methods (where bodies and populations were carefully regulated) (Foucault, 1990; Gastaldo, 1997). The need to address demographic change and to coordinate its relationship to production with more sophisticated mechanisms of power prompted the concept of the "population," "with its numerical variables of space and chronology, longevity and health, to emerge not only as a problem but as an object of surveillance, analysis, intervention, modification, etc." (Foucault, 1980, pp. 171–172). Individuals and the populations they comprised were now viewed as resources which must be managed and efficiently utilized (Gastaldo, 1997). This management was "an indispensable element in the development of capitalism" (Foucault, 1990, p. 141). Epidemiology, thus employed as a technology of bio-power, was intimately linked with not only biological and mathematical science, but with the political-economy of the state.

Sanitary Statistics and Social Reform

The scientific and statistical revolutions that shaped epidemiology were concurrent with political and economic changes in Europe and North America. In 18th century France, the Revolution eliminated many dated medical beliefs (and those who held them) and created an opening for new theories such as the public hygiene movement. The analysis of social conditions and how they affected the spread of disease became the central focus of this movement. Influential leaders of the post-Revolution Parisian school of medicine (who were active participants in the public hygiene movement) included the "fathers of modern epidemiology," such as Pierre Charles-Alexandre Louis, Louis René Villermé, and Adolphe Quetelet

(Lilienfeld & Lilienfeld, 1980). Louis was a renowned teacher and advocate for the use of statistics in medicine (a practice he called "la méthode numerique"); he had many prominent international students, including William Farr, who spread the method to England, Switzerland, and the U.S.

The first half of the 19th century was marked by a movement of "sanitary statistics" that documented the effects of the dramatic reorganization of production and explosive urbanization of the Industrial Revolution (Susser & Susser, 1996a). The devastating living conditions that were created by these changes motivated and shaped the work of both French and English epidemiologists. Social reformers such as Louis René Villermé, William Farr, and Friedrich Engels used vital statistics and other data to document the deterioration of health among the working classes. In *A Description of the Physical and Moral State of Workers Employed in Cotton, Wool and Silk Mills* (1840), Villermé described the conditions he found in several French factories, and revealed his social justice concerns:

> Horrible indigence, destitution, depravity, and marked degradation have been documented in Lille, as well as many workers who are poorly sheltered, poorly dressed, ill-nourished, pale, thin, and exhausted from fatigue in the Haute-Alsace. However, most of these workers, who have been given the odd and expressive epithet of 'white negroes' (. . .) deserve the compassion of respectable persons in view of their good qualities and the cause of their misery (Buck et al., 1988, p. 33).

However, many reformers, convinced that individuals were responsible for their own happiness, were ambivalent about poverty; not all were motivated by social justice. One of the primary aims in some quarters of the early public health movement was to keep the working population healthy and avoid insurrection that might be fueled by their disastrous living conditions (Petersen & Lupton, 1996). Reformers like Edwin Chadwick and Dr. J. P. Kay avoided the moral questions of poverty by insisting that high mortality in cities was caused not by deprivation, but solely by "effluvial poisons." They also proposed solutions that, with frightening familiarity, have enjoyed renewed support in the late twentieth century: relief should be withheld when it did not "encourage industry and virtue"; harsh working conditions, poor sanitation, labour unrest and vice would all be solved in a society guided by the tenets of free trade (Terris, 1985, p. 24). Chadwick authored the *Report on the Sanitary Condition of the Labouring Population of Great Britain* and was Secretary of the Poor Law Commission responsible for the draconian Poor Law of 1834.[3] The Poor Law was seen as "an insurance of life against death by starvation, and of property against communistic agitations" (William Farr, cited in Terris, 1985, p. 26). Chadwick promoted sanitary reform "so that workers would live long enough to attain 'steady moral habits' " (Terris, 1985, p. 25) and become immune to the "anarchical fallacies" that inflamed assemblies of labourers.

Most of the studies by sanitary physicians and public health reformers focused on the slums of England, France, Germany, Scandinavia and the U.S., and the evidence collected was largely undifferentiated by disease. The findings presented were mostly overall morbidity and mortality rates; it was not until 1839 that William Farr used specific classifications of diagnosis for national mortality statistics (Susser & Susser, 1996a). Large-scale public sanitation projects (better sewage/drainage/water systems, garbage collection, housing, public baths) comprised the bulk of the public health responses or "treatment" strategies. Public health advocates believed that these strategies would not only reduce morbidity and mortality, but poverty as well; the former was accomplished, but the latter was not (Susser & Susser, 1996b).

Early epidemiology and "sanitary statistics" emerged in a revolutionary landscape. Scientific revolution, industrial revolution, political revolution, and increased international trade fundamentally transformed societies through the 17th to 19th centuries. Dominance over nature and the inevitability of human progress were key themes in the language of science, repeated in the crusade to reduce rates of mortality and morbidity in populations. Scientific societies and professional associations (such as the Royal Society of London, the Société Royale du Medicine, the London Statistical Society, and the London Epidemiological Society) were established to support the work of physicians, statisticians, scientists and health reformers, creating a body of "experts" who produced the evidence to support theories of public health and the policies that followed from them. These expert "knowers" were separated from the "known" (the objects of study) by virtue of their detached rationality; knowers and known were discrete, fixed entities. Scientific principles of objectivity demanded that knowers be "modest witnesses" to the realities they observed (Haraway, 1997). They were ego-less, invisible; they inhabited the "unmarked category," the "culture of no culture," where facts are established unproblematically and with the authority of transcendental truth (Haraway, 1997). The miasma theory of disease was partnered with a sensitivity to the impact of environmental and social conditions. It prevailed in the context of a paradigm of public health "primarily directed at controlling filth, odour and contagion" and concerned with keeping the working population healthy, productive and content with their lot (Petersen & Lupton, 1996, p. 2). The role of statistics in this crusade was central. Considered "the science of social reform," statistics "promised to defuse party passion and to substitute for rhetoric, certainty based upon the accumulation of irrefutable facts. (. . .) The science of statistics would discover the principles of legislation and administration" (Eyler, 1980, p. 5).[4] Statistics also promised to increase the credibility and accuracy of medicine by applying the positivist methods of the "higher" (physical) sciences (Eyler, 1980).[5] *Data* about *individuals*, produced by the technologies of "life-tables," surveys (e.g. censuses), vital statistics, advanced mathematical calculations, and even atmospheric instruments, were consumed as *evidence* about *populations*. These "sanitary statistics," were disseminated in reports to members of scientific and professional societies, and were produced, analyzed and stored by state bureaucracies (e.g. England's Registrar-General's office), creating a "public record" of the health of the population. The remedies prompted by this knowledge tended toward large-scale sanitation reforms, rather than individual treatment. Although these statistics and reforms distinguished different classes (of disease, of citizens, of "deserving" and "undeserving" poor) the primary subject of early public health and epidemiology was the "population."

INFECTIOUS DISEASE EPIDEMIOLOGY

Germ Theory and Infectious Agents

The era of "sanitary statistics" was brought to a close by advances in microbiology and the development of germ theory. In 1840, Jacob Henle published a treatise proposing that a major cause of disease was tiny organisms; John Snow suggested in his work on cholera between 1849 and 1854 that the disease was transmitted by innoculation of morbid material, most likely through contaminated drinking water; in 1865, Louis Pasteur demonstrated that an epizootic affecting silkworms was caused by an organism; and eventually, in 1882, Robert Koch, a former student of Henle's, established that tuberculosis was caused by mycobacterium. Together, these men were the symbolic founders of a new era of "infectious disease epidemiology" informed by a new paradigm (Susser & Susser, 1996a). "Contagionism" displaced "miasma" as an explanation for the occurrence and spread of disease; "socially neutral biologic agents – the microbes" were now the focus of the public health campaign (Buck et al., 1988, p. 8).

Germ theory was characterized by "the narrow laboratory perspective of a specific cause model – namely, single agents relating one to one to specific diseases" (Susser & Susser, 1996a, p. 670). The laboratory model, a contemporary incarnation of the Enlightenment scientific method, promoted a parsimony of explanation that precluded "fuzzy" social causes. Both the scientists in their white cloaks of invisibility, and the germs upon which they focused their attention (and microscopes) were unmarked by social location or condition. Bacteria and viruses were indisputable and unproblematic foes. With the question of the *cause* of disease answered, the central epidemiological question remaining was how the disease *spread*. Late nineteenth and early twentieth century epidemiologists responded by tracing the 'point-contact spread' of infection; i.e. from which individuals did the cases of the disease become infected with the epidemiologic agents? In this manner, it might be possible to find out which individual brought the disease into the community so that contacts between this individual, those already infected, and uninfected persons in the community could be minimized (Lilienfeld & Stolley, 1994, p. 30).

Public health strategies shifted from improved public sanitation to limiting disease transmission through the use of vaccines, isolating those affected (by various means of quarantine), and treating infected individuals with chemotherapy and antibiotics (Susser & Susser, 1996a). In the latter half of the 19th century, Acts of Parliament were introduced in England to contain infectious diseases at the level of the individual; these Acts included the Vaccination Acts, regarding the compulsory vaccination of children in their first year of life, and the Contagious Diseases Acts, requiring the compulsory examination and possible isolation of women believed to be prostitutes. Laws in the later part of the century, directed at controlling those infectious diseases that had created high morbidity and mortality within local communities, were the most powerful of this public health legislation. "Under the Local Government Act of 1875, MOHs (medical officers of health) were granted powers to remove sufferers of such diseases from the community and place them in isolation or fever hospitals, as 'nuisances.' " (Porter, 1999, p. 134). The requirement to notify local MOHs of individual cases followed in an Act of 1889. "The preventive methods of the Acts were based upon a bacteriological model of disease causation. Notification identified the location of an incidence of infectious disease and the possibility of immediate isolation" (Porter, 1999, p. 135).[6] The epidemiology of populations and environmental factors, and the social dynamics of disease (the focus of miasma theory) were thus "replaced by a focus on control of infectious agents" (Susser & Susser, 1996a, p. 670; see also Lilienfeld & Stolley, 1994). In other words, the new "subject" of epidemiology was the germ, and the individual who carried it.

The Death of Social Causes

With the advent of germ theory, epidemiology came to be seen as derivative rather than a science in its own right (Susser & Susser, 1996a). The biomedical hierarchy placed identification of disease-causing organisms and the prevention of infection at the apex, while social-environmental variables (and those researchers who studied them) fell in importance and prestige. Nineteenth century advances in the design and application of field surveys, the construction of national systems of vital statistics, and statistical analysis of large samples, were barely maintained in the era of infectious disease epidemiology (Susser & Susser, 1996a). This is not to suggest that no other epidemiological theories were present. There were still debates about the types of causal factors (biological or social) that could be linked to disease patterns in populations (Krieger, 1994). Among others in the British social medicine movement, Major Greenwood (founding member of the Social Medical Association and Professor of Epidemiology and Vital Statistics at the interdisciplinary London School of Hygiene) continued in the early 20th century to emphasize social and occupational conditions that correlated with disease in populations. Greenwood defined epidemiology as "the mass aspects of disease, where not the sick individual but the group, the herd, is the unit of observation" (cited in Terris, 1987, p. 318). Later he elaborated the distinction between clinical medicine and epidemiology:

> The physician's unit of study is a single human being, the epidemiologist's unit is not a single human being but an aggregate of human beings, and since it is impossible to hold in the mind distinctly a mass of separate particulars he forms a general picture, an average of what is happening, and works upon that (cited in Terris, 1987, pp. 318–319).[7]

In the U.S., Joseph Goldberger's and Edgar Sydenstricker's research established a relationship between poverty, nutritional deficiency, and the incidence of pellagra in the rural South. But the work of Greenwood, Goldberger and Sydenstricker "ran against the tide of belief" in epidemiological theory (Susser & Susser, 1996a; also see Krieger, 1994). The current was strongly in favour of individual explanations of and responses to disease, over macro analyses of the impact of more broadly defined, unwieldy "social" and economic variables.

It was not only scientific advances in microbiology that swelled the tide of "biological individualism" (Krieger, 1994). Decisions regarding institutional funding and the training of public health researchers provided structural support for infectious disease epidemiology. For example, a strong preference for a biomedical approach led to the first U.S. School of Public Health being founded at Johns Hopkins University, instead of the more sociologically-oriented Columbia University (Krieger, 1994). The momentum of germ theory and the specific cause model, in teaching, research and practice, continued into the first half of the twentieth century, until the threat of infectious disease, at least in "the developed world," began to subside.

CHRONIC DISEASE/RISK FACTOR/SOCIAL EPIDEMIOLOGY

Disease Models: Black Boxes and Empty Webs

In industrialized nations, mortality attributable to chronic disease had overtaken infectious disease mortality by 1945. Peptic ulcer, coronary heart disease, and lung cancer were now described as epidemics. The complexity of chronic disease necessitated a departure from the specific-cause model of germ theory; accordingly, germ theory was replaced by more elaborate models of "host, agent and environment." Two dominant metaphors represented multiple-cause models of disease: the "black box" and the "web of causation" (Krieger, 1994; Susser & Susser, 1996a). These conceptual tools inspired epidemiologists to take into account complex interrelationships among multiple factors in causal models of disease.

The "black box" represented a self-contained system/unit whose inner workings and processes are hidden from view. In its application to causal modeling in epidemiology, researchers focussed less on specifying particular relationships between single causes and events, and more on demonstrating a relationship between exposure to some factor and a disease outcome. "This paradigm related exposure to outcome without any necessary obligation to interpolate either intervening factors or even pathogenesis (although not all neglected such interpolation)" (Susser & Susser, 1996a, p. 670). Faced with having to explain chronic diseases of unknown origin, epidemiologists favoured this approach, conducting exploratory descriptive studies to establish the distribution of disease and identify potential risk factors. Early studies seldom relied on complex statistical analysis (Susser & Susser, 1996a).

The "web of causation" was introduced in 1960 by Brian McMahon, Thomas Pugh and Johannes Ipsen in the first formal epidemiologic textbook produced in the U.S. The "web" challenged the persistent tendency of epidemiologists to think in terms of single agents that caused discrete diseases, and invited them to embrace a more sophisticated view that accounted for complex interrelationships among causal factors (Krieger, 1994). The metaphor of the "web" made use of a persistent logic of interconnection that, in the 1950s, became increasingly popular in a variety of scientific disciplines, especially cybernetics and ecology (Krieger, 1994).

One criticism levelled at the "black box"/"web of causation" approach to disease causation is that while these models address causal complexity by considering interrelationships among a variety of factors, there is no account of how particular components or "strands" in any "web" are chosen for consideration (or excluded). Syme and Yen (2000) describe the epidemiologist's choice of "risk factors" as "typically heuristic: If a social factor predicts a disease occurrence, use it; if it does not, exclude it" (p. 372); the theoretical foundations of the concept and its relationship with other concepts are glossed over. Susser and Susser (1996a) are more blunt: "the problems selected for investigation were the chronic diseases that most visibly threatened the public health, and the groups that were most studied were those at manifest risk – namely, middle-aged men" (p. 670). The influence of gender and class were rarely acknowledged as complex social (rather than individual) variables in the "web of causation"; their *effect on the research process* was invisible to most observers. Krieger (1994) thus asks of the "web of causation": "Has anyone seen the spider?" (p. 887). The absence of this allegorical arachnid conceals the *theoretical and political* origins of the choices employed in the causal model-building at hand.

Furthermore, despite taking into account a wide variety of potential causes, the web tends to focus on those believed to be "closer" to the illness under investigation – these typically represent biological causes of disease *in individuals*, and/or "lifestyle" risk factors, both of which permit intervention at the individual level (Krieger, 1994). The web also fails to distinguish between determinants of disease in individuals and in populations. Different research questions are required to investigate each, and have different implications. For example, asking why any particular *individual* has a disease (like peptic ulcer), emphasizes individual susceptibility and interventions targeted at "high risk" individuals; this is different from asking why some *populations* experience high levels of peptic ulcer while in others it is rare, which emphasizes population exposures and the need to improve the health status of the whole population (Krieger, 1994). Finally, the multiple cause model ignores *historical* accounts of changes in disease patterns in a population over time. These aspects of multiple-cause models point to a theoretical foundation of "biomedical individualism" which is persistently reductionist, distilling questions about disease incidence in populations to questions about occurrence in individuals, and further, to questions about individual biological susceptibility and/or malfunctioning (Gordon, 1988a; Krieger, 1994; Pearce, 1996). We are returned to the "socially neutral microbes" that captured the spotlight when contagion/germ theory came on the epidemiological scene.[8] According to Krieger, the "web" model of causation did not challenge the biomedical or individualistic orientation of germ theory – "(w)hat it opposed were simplistic interpretations of the doctrine of 'specific etiology' " (that is, single-cause models of disease causation) (Krieger, 1994, p. 892).

Ideologies, Politics and Institutions

Terris (1987) traces the geographical origins of chronic disease epidemiology and its evocative metaphors to Britain and the U.S., where local ideological commitments and available material resources created the conditions for its emergence. In Britain, the growth of labour and socialist ideology among health professionals "created an intellectual climate concerned with the societal causes of social problems" (Terris, 1987, p. 321). Social hygiene and social medicine, committed to exploring the links between the living conditions of different social classes within a population and their corresponding health status, were well-developed in Europe in the early 20th century. In Britain in particular, there was a strong tradition of interdisciplinarity that shifted attention away from individualistic and biological explanations for disease. In addition, there was important collaboration with state health departments, which made records, staff, and monetary resources available for compiling epidemiological data (Terris, 1987). Similarly in the U.S., federal, state and local public health departments provided the source of much epidemiological research. The post-World War II affluence of the U.S. enabled federal leadership in epidemiological research to expand and continue, while state health departments made important contributions to the advancement of non-infectious disease epidemiology through such initiatives as widespread cancer control programs (Terris, 1987).

Building upon holistic models of health and the framework of social medicine developed in the first half of the 20th century, the discipline of sociology inserted itself into epidemiological discourses more clearly than ever before. The term "social epidemiology" appeared for the first time in the title of an article published in the *American Sociological Review* in 1950; the author of that article, Alfred Yankauer, later became the editor of the *American Journal of Public Health* (Krieger, 2001). Nearly 20 years later, in an address to the American Sociological Association, Leo Reeder defined social epidemiology as the "study of the role of social factors in the aetiology of disease," essentially "calling for a marriage of sociological frameworks to epidemiological inquiry" (Krieger, 2001, p. 669). The success of that "marriage" is questionable; although the partners have clearly had an impact on one another, their communication needs work (see, for e.g. Syme & Yen, 2000).

Despite the legacy of social medicine in the emphasis on chronic disease, the political environment of the 1950s did not permit a large-scale investigation of the social determinants of health. Post-war McCarthyism and Cold War tensions squelched academic discourse that put social inequality at the centre of analysis (Krieger, 1994). Consequently, most epidemiological research was premised upon biomedical and individual-level theories of disease causation, "in which population risk was thought to reflect the sum of individuals' risks, as mediated by their 'lifestyles' and genetic predisposition to disease" (Krieger, 1994, p. 890; see also Pearce, 1996).

Promoting Public Health

The tension between individual- and social-level accounts of disease was mirrored in the public health paradigm that was dominant when chronic disease emerged as a focus for epidemiology. The "new" public health that began to take shape in the mid-20th century shifted away from infectious disease prevention, and toward health promotion. From the 1950s to the mid-1970s, public health policy emphasized health education, and improving citizens' knowledge was a central theme in the decades that followed. School-based education programs were the first intervention method, followed by more broadly-based population education via national and mass media campaigns.

Canada was a global leader in the new public health. The 1974 Lalonde Report ("A New Perspective on the Health of Canadians") introduced the term "health promotion" to the lexicon of public health. The report was a response to both political and economic pressures. Political pressure came from feminist, environmental, and social justice groups that challenged biomedical approaches to health and how the health care system operates. Economic pressures were encapsulated in three main health care system crises: (1) medical interventions (measured by increasing medical expenditures) were not improving the health of the population (measured by overall life expectancy); (2) the increase in medical expenditures in the 1960s and 1970s created budget crises for the federal and provincial governments; and (3) chronic conditions were not being improved by medical interventions, but knowledge about prevention was increasing (Labonté, 1994). The Lalonde Report made one of the first attempts to alter public perception around the link between health and medical care, by maintaining that health does not result solely from access to health care services, but "from an interplay of determinants from four health field elements: human biology, lifestyles, the environment, and health care" (Labonté, 1994, p. 74). Although the Lalonde Report moved away from a narrow bio-medical "treatment" focus to more holistic view of health, it also offloaded responsibility for increasing health costs from service providers and governments to individuals, especially those with "unhealthy lifestyles" (Labonté, 1994). Lifestyle-focused health promotion implies that humans are rational actors whose behaviour can be modified by interventions of information, that all individuals have access to this information equally, and that individuals make critical choices that are little influenced by their social location or the structure of society (Badgley, 1994; Kronenfeld, 1979).

The Lalonde Report was followed over a decade later by the federal document "Achieving Health for All: A Framework for Health Promotion" (otherwise known as the Epp Report). The Framework presented three challenges for achieving health in Canada: reduce inequities in health, increase prevention efforts, and enhance coping with chronic disease and disability. It proposed three mechanisms for addressing these challenges: self-care; mutual aid, and healthy environments. Together with the Ottawa Charter on Health Promotion, the Epp Report balanced the Lalonde Report's emphasis on lifestyle and behaviour with an enhanced social model of health, which once again pointed to health determinants that lay outside the health care system. Although what became known as "community health promotion," increasingly politicized around structural determinants of health, appeared to have a relatively explicit project of citizen empowerment (Labonté, 1994; Robertson & Minkler, 1994), some analysts contend that the focus of health promotion through the 1980s remained on individual responsibility (Raymond, 1989). In this prevailing "paradigm of definition,"

> populations are screened for behavioral risk factors; specific rates reflecting the distribution of risky behaviors are calculated and targeted populations are exposed to interventions designed and carried out with the intent of influencing high risk populations to change their health-related behaviors and thereby reduce their risks. (. . .) (B)ehavior-change initiatives are introduced on a large scale as community-based and health promotion-disease prevention interventions (Raymond, 1989, p. 285).

Echoing Krieger's (1994) critique of chronic disease epidemiology (where population risk simply reflects the sum of individuals' risks), Raymond argued that health promotion in this paradigm was simply a "variation on clinical interventions on a mass scale" (Raymond, 1989, p. 285). By treating behaviour as if it simply issued from isolated individuals, this type of health promotion ignored the ecological context in which health is achieved or compromised. Strangely, in the midst of concern about a broad range of health determinants, individuals and their attitudes and behaviours remained the subjects of public health interventions.

The Science of Health Promotion

Epidemiology has been "widely recognized as an important scientific foundation for health promotion" (Tannahill, 1992, p. 86). Pearce notes that the shift from infectious disease epidemiology to chronic disease epidemiology "involved not only a shift in the object of study (from germs to other sources of disease) and a recognition of multiple causes, but also the development of new techniques of study" (Pearce, 1996, p. 680). Early on, in the face of unknown origins of chronic disease, epidemiologists "resorted to straightforward descriptive studies of disease distribution and exploratory sweeps" for possible risk factors (Susser & Susser, 1996a, p. 670). As time passed, these early methods gave way to advanced statistical analysis of large data sets in order to test *causal* hypotheses generated by descriptive data. Since the end of World War II, the use of computers to store, manage, and analyze large data sets has continued to grow (Krieger, 1994). With breathless respect, Susser and Susser (1996a) describe how statistical technologies continued to refine epidemiological knowledge and provide the scientific evidence essential for public health:

> Epidemiologists began to explore in depth the subtleties of confounding, misclassification, survivorship, and other such issues. This labor is represented in the elegant and unifying concept of the four-fold table and the case-control and cohort designs (. . .) (p. 671).

Not all epidemiologists are so thrilled with this development, however. Pearce (1996) complains that "traditional" epidemiology has become not only unfashionable, but maligned:

> One is left with the impression that 19th-century epidemiologists used ad hoc methods that have now been placed on a sounder foundation through recent developments in methods of study design (e.g. the theory of case-control studies), data analysis (e.g. logistic regression), and exposure measurement (e.g. new molecular biology techniques). (. . .) These methodological developments have been paralleled by, and have reflected, a shift in the level of analysis from the population to the individual. Most modern epidemiologists still do studies in populations, but they do so in order to study decontextualized individual risk factors, rather than to study population factors in their social and historical context (p. 679).

What kind of data have been produced by these new statistical technologies, and how have they been interpreted as evidence? Data are frequently obtained from a variety of sources that are unrelated to epidemiological research (e.g. death certificates, hospital discharge reports, general household surveys, medical practice records, etc.). Data may also be generated specifically for cross-sectional or longitudinal epidemiological studies, where a representative sample of the population is surveyed at/over a period of time. The descriptive statistics used to document the distribution of disease in communities have remained similar to early "life-tables," describing the quantity of certain diseases, incidence (cases/population over a period of time), and the distribution of diseases according to characteristics of time (rates and trends), person (socio-demographic variables), and place (geographic area).

In the tradition of viewing epidemiology as the "basic science of public health," health promoters have used epidemiological data to identify and quantify illness, and to design and assess prevention strategies (Tannahill, 1992). Descriptive data are frequently used to imply causal relationships; accordingly, "the resultant catalogue of categories of ill health and risk factors is directly translated into 'health promotion' programmes" (Tannahill, 1992, p. 97). This is a problematic move. First, association between variables does not signify causation. Second, epidemiological research typically lacks sophisticated social analysis and treats complex variables like gender, race, and class as "singular attributes of individuals

(...) rather than characteristics of a society or social system" (Bird et al., 2000, p. 8; also see Syme & Yen, 2000). This has profound effects on the application of epidemiological data in public health programmes: "The end product is a series, indeed a hotch potch of disease- and risk factor-based initiatives" (Tannahill, 1992, p. 97). McKinlay (1997, 1974) is highly critical of these "downstream endeavours" that respond superficially to "almost perennial shifts from one health issue to the next" without considering the "upstream" political and economic forces that create disease and illness (p. 520).

When lists of diseases and risk factors are "translated into targets for achievement" (Tannahill, 1992, p. 98), statistical data are viewed as an uncomplicated means by which "better health" can be measured, and as a tool to manage the process of meeting public health objectives. Pearce (1996) charges that "Epidemiology has become a set of generic methods for *measuring* associations of exposure and disease in individuals, rather than functioning as part of a multidisciplinary approach to *understanding* disease in populations" (p. 682). These methods have been critiqued for producing "a vast stockpile of almost surgically clean data untouched by human thought" (Smith, in *The Lancet* editorial, 1994, p. 429). Persistent positivist goals of prediction, control and progress in the practice of chronic disease epidemiology remain clear. Large quantities of (decontextualized) data are presumed to create better knowledge.

Given the Cold War chilling of discourses focusing on social determinants of health; the economic pressures to contain health care expenditures and the consequent emphasis on efficiency, individual prevention and lifestyle change; and the persistence of the biomedical influence on public health research and practices, the subject of epidemiology between the 1940s and early 1990s was still the individual (and/or that individual's "risk factors"). Despite the rhetoric of "empowering communities" and "social determinants of disease" the focus of epidemiology remained on what has been variously called the "bottom-up" Pearce (1996) or "downstream" approach (McKinlay, 1997, 1974) to understanding the disease process. This reductionist, positivist model fragments complex processes into component parts and focuses on the smallest unit of analysis possible. It then uses these bits of information to develop a theory of higher-level mechanisms. "One current example is molecular epidemiology, which attempts to understand disease at the molecular level and then ultimately to use this knowledge in public health policy (e.g. by screening populations for individual susceptibility to specific carcinogens)" (Pearce, 1996, p. 681). In the early to mid-1990s, the chorus of objections against epidemiology's chronic reliance on the gold standard of the randomized clinical trial and its microscopic approaches to understanding the health of populations reached a crescendo. A new paradigm of "ecological" epidemiology was emerging on the horizon.

ECOLOGICAL AND ECOSOCIAL EPIDEMIOLOGY

The Emergence of a New Paradigm

At the close of the 1980s, there was a call for a clearer partnership between public health and epidemiology:

> It is natural for those of us concerned with prevention and promotion to focus on initiatives and efforts which benefit as many persons in as equitable a manner as possible. (. . .) It is appropriate that the fields of public health and prevention continue to explore research methodologies and approaches in support of health promotion by adding to its armamentarium the public health strategy of behavioral epidemiology (Raymond, 1989, p. 281).

Raymond envisioned an epidemiology that extended its reach beyond traditional identification of behaviours that are linked to disease (e.g. smoking with lung cancer), to a study of the *distribution and determinants* of those behaviours causally linked with disease (e.g. who smokes, why they smoke and what interventions might prevent them from smoking). The former focus had led to a mechanical listing of risk factors (Tannahill, 1992). The latter approach, Raymond believed, would pursue "a social-ecological paradigm" that draws attention to the "psychosocial and social ecological antecedents" of health-related behaviour (Raymond, 1989, p. 284). Whereas conventional public health and epidemiology are "atheoretical," social-ecological epidemiology must be based on "sound theoretical frameworks" (Raymond, 1989, p. 285). Theoretically informed research designs and multivariate statistical techniques could contribute "to the development of health promotion out of science rather than ideology" (Raymond, 1989, p. 285). "Good science" would be a prophylactic against politics. Raymond was not alone in his concern that the chronic disease paradigms of the "black box" and "web of causation" produced a purely technical epidemiology, one that was simply a "set of practices and methods" rather than a theoretically grounded knowledge oriented towards public health objectives (Raymond, 1989, p. 285; see also Krieger, 1994; Pearce, 1996; Susser & Susser, 1996a; Syme & Yen, 2000).

Susser and Susser (1996a) predicted that the next paradigm shift in epidemiology would come as a result of two forces: (1) a transformation in global health patterns; and (2) new technology (p. 671). First, the HIV pandemic provided evidence that the previous "black box" paradigm could not adequately address epidemic control. Despite widespread agreement on the causal organism and critical risk factors, and despite the fact that prevention is theoretically possible, many countries face devastation by AIDS. Public health practitioners, medical sociologists, and even epidemiologists have argued that analysis of individual-level data is not sufficient for predicting at what level of organization intervention and prevention efforts should be directed.

Second, new technologies in biology and biotechnology (e.g. genetic recombination and imaging) and in information systems (e.g. the global communication network and information networks) have paved the way for a new approach to epidemiology. Advanced biotechnologies now enable epidemiologists to develop more knowledge of disease at the micro(scopic) level. The mapping of the human genome, for example, has allowed for specification of the role of heredity in disease, and advances in imaging technologies facilitate diagnosis and interpretation of physiological function. Susser and Susser (1996a) see tremendous potential (if not a panacea) in these technological advancements:

> The potential contribution of these advances to epidemiology is an exquisite refinement of the definition and measurement of susceptibility, exposure, and outcome. (. . .) We can be confident that new techniques, properly applied, can help dig epidemiology out of the slough of marginally significant risk estimates (p. 672).

It seems we've just been lacking the right tools (shovels?). For their part, advanced information technologies have made vast databases available to the task of understanding and controlling disease. Susser and Susser (1996a) describe how new data resources can be exploited:

> Information networks can provide instant access to – and enable the continuous assemblage of – existing stores of vital statistics and other relevant health and social data across the world. (. . .) Stores of data can be mined to describe distributions across societies, to make comparisons of strata and groups nationally and internationally, to generate test hypotheses, and to serve as sampling frames (1996a, p. 672).

Their excitement is apparent. Clearly, these data are seen as an important public health tool for developing and applying population-level interventions.

Chinese Boxes and Fractal Objects

Susser and Susser (1996b) and Krieger (1994) have proposed new metaphors for the conceptual paradigm that infuses this emergent epidemiology. Susser and Susser suggest "Chinese boxes"; Krieger imagines a fractal object. Both images are multidimensional and dynamic, and invoke "literal – and not just metaphorical – notions of ecology, situating humans as one notable species among many cohabiting, evolving on, and altering our dynamic planet" (Krieger, 2001, p. 671). However, important differences between these models exist.

For Susser and Susser (following Raymond, 1989), the goal for an emergent paradigm of epidemiology is to apply new technologies and techniques to multiple levels of analysis, and the "Chinese boxes" metaphor allows for this application. The Sussers' "Chinese boxes" metaphor represents the underlying causal principle of "ecologism" which they claim is characteristic of the biological sciences. This principle replaces that of "universalism," which is ubiquitous in the physical sciences (as well as in earlier orientations towards epidemiology) and limited by its attempt to provide universal causal explanations for events in the physical world, without proper regard for context. Susser and Susser (1996b) assert that while a universalist approach may be appropriate for entities that are not alive, or for very micro levels of analysis, "universalism is not universally applicable" – "above the level of molecules, no biological entity can conform entirely to universal laws because of the overarching contexts and the interactions between levels within a biological structure" (p. 675). Ecologism, on the other hand, attends to local circumstances and "to the bounds that limit generalizations about biological, human, and social systems" (Susser & Susser, 1996b, p. 675). Consequently, the Sussers use a biological "systems analysis" to explain interrelations among social structures or phenomena at a single organizational level, and/or at multiple levels. Their analytical strategy strongly echoes the sociological theory of structural-functionalism. A system is defined by factors that are related in some coherent way (through structure or function). Each system is self-contained in the sense that it has its own limits, and can be understood within those limits. The coherence of the relationship between factors comprising a system "implies a degree of persistence and stability" (Susser & Susser, 1996b, p. 675). But change also occurs in systems, and because intrasystemic factors are interrelated, change in one part of the system will affect other parts. In turn, whole systems are related to other systems which may exist at the same, or different levels of organization, such as at the molecular level, the individual (bodily) level, the social level, and the universal level. This is where the metaphor of "Chinese boxes" is most illustrative.

The relationships among systems may be imagined as a "conjuror's nest of boxes, each containing a succession of smaller ones" (Susser & Susser, 1996b, p. 675). Within this "hierarchy of scale and complexity," (Susser & Susser, 1996b, p. 675), each "box" represents a different level of organization (e.g. molecular, or societal); each successive level of organization contains the simpler level(s), and is intimately linked with them. Within each level or "box," relatively bounded structures (e.g. nations, cities, communities) are "characterized by lawful relations that are localized to that structure and can be discovered" (Susser & Susser, 1996b, p. 675). These "laws" are generalizable to other, similar structures at the same level of organization. Thus, the lawfulness (and orderliness) of reality, and the generalizability of that lawfulness – both prized by positivist science – are preserved in this ecological paradigm. The defining characteristic of this paradigm is that it addresses *relations within and between* different systems. In its application, "eco-epidemiology" would analyze outcomes and determinants of health at different levels of organization: at the macro, or broad contextual level (potentially drawing upon the technologies of new information systems) and at the micro, or in-depth level (using the new molecular and genetic technologies of biomedicine). The preventive strategies suggested by ecological epidemiology would then focus on level of organization where intervention would be most efficient and effective (Susser & Susser, 1996b).

The "Chinese boxes" metaphor is compelling in its attempt to account for multiple determinants of health at different levels of biological and social organization. It encourages epidemiologists to literally "think outside the (black) box" – but epidemiologists may be trading a single black box for a "conjuror's nest" of boxes that are ultimately just as limiting. The Sussers employ a biologically-grounded functionalist theory to remedy chronic disease epidemiology's biomedical individualism. But by doing so, they invite a critique that parallels Krieger's query about the "web of causation's" absent spider: now we must ask, where is the missing magician? A description of system functions does not imply causal explanation, and cannot fully explain system changes (Bottomore, 1972). Sharing this limitation of structural-functionalism, the Sussers' model does not adequately account for the distribution or exercise of power within and between the systems it describes. By insisting that we can enumerate the "discoverable laws governing social entities" at any level of organization, it reinstates the very universalism it hopes to displace, and denies the complex politics of geographies, economies, and intimate social relations.

In an alternative response to the limitations of chronic disease epidemiology, Krieger (1994) and Pearce (1996) (who does not explicitly apply the language of "ecology") similarly envision a more contextual epidemiology that incorporates a causal analysis of disease at the population level. Recognizing that explanations of disease causation reflect the level of analysis which is undertaken (e.g. individual, intermediate, or population levels), Pearce (1996) contends that "any meaningful analysis of the causes of disease in populations must integrate the individual-biologic and population levels of analysis without collapsing one into the other or denying the existence of either" (pp. 680–681). Pearce (1996) explains that epistemological approaches to understanding disease causation occupy two main categories "that mirror wider scientific debates in recent centuries": the "bottom-up" approach, which is "inherently reductionist and positivist"; and the "top-down" approach, which is "inherently realist" (that is, it acknowledges that phenomena have an external and independent reality, but "differs from positivism in that the object of scientific inquiry is not patterns of events but rather the underlying processes and structures that cause these events to occur") (p. 681). The "bottom-up" approach, rooted in an individualistic clinical tradition whose gold standard is the randomized clinical trial, focuses on the lowest level of analysis (individual components or factors in a process) to build knowledge at higher levels of analysis. Alternatively, the "top-down" approach starts at the population level, focusing on the social structures and processes that create the conditions for poor health. From a "top-down" perspective, the "cause" of disease is located in mechanisms that are internal to populations and that "operate dialectically, rather than involving regular associations between externally related independent objects" (Pearce, 1996, p. 681).

Pearce recommends mediating this tension by resituating epidemiology as the science of public health, and thereby reinstating the primary goal of epidemiology as understanding and preventing the cause of disease in populations (1996, p. 681). As a consequence epidemiology should focus on determinants of health and disease at the population level, in order to put the etiology of disease in a social and historical context. This would permit strategic response at the appropriate level of intervention (population and/or individual). Pearce advocates a multidisciplinary, multimethod epidemiology to understand the determinants of the health of populations in their local contexts.

Similarly, Krieger proposes an "ecosocial" epidemiology, informed by theory that "embraces population-level thinking and rejects the underlying assumptions of biomedical individualism without discarding biology" (Krieger, 1994, p. 896). Krieger (1994) recommends replacing the metaphor of the spiderless "web of causation" with a combination of two metaphors: "the continually-constructed 'scaffolding' of society that different social groups daily seek to reinforce or alter" and "the ever-growing 'bush' of evolution" (p. 896). Together, these link the social and biological "potential and constraints of human life" (Krieger, 1994, p. 896). This metaphorical structure of scaffolding and branches, existing at all levels of organization from subcellular to societal, repeats indefinitely like a fractal object. Population-level epidemiologic profiles would reflect the "interlinked and diverse patterns of exposure and susceptibility" that result from the dynamic interconnections between social and biological factors (Krieger, 1994, p. 896). Krieger claims that this fractal metaphor retains the complex dialectic between the social and biological, does not erase agency, and includes the impact of history. Neither the individual nor the social is reducible to or obscures the other. Any given portion of the fractal structure represents "one set of possible epidemiologic profiles produced at a particular time by a particular combination of social structures, cultural norms, ecologic milieu, and genetic variability and similarity (among humans and among other organisms in the region)" (Krieger, 1994, p. 896). Consequently, this model requires multi-level causal analysis of disease causation and dispersion. Because these levels are inextricably linked, they must *all* be considered in any explanation for disease at any given level. The fractal metaphor does not offer a universal explanation for disease causation; rather, it poses a series of questions ("about social structure, cultural norms, ecologic milieu, and genetic variability" (Krieger, 1994, p. 897) that must be addressed in the analysis of any particular case. Both population level factors and individual agency and accountability are preserved in this analysis.

Krieger maintains that an ecosocial model of epidemiology would situate the health of individuals and populations in an ecological context, encouraging a more "global" view of how the health of humans is interconnected with that of the earth and other species that inhabit it. Furthermore, an ecosocial model would highlight both the social production of health and disease *and* the social production of science. This position acknowledges that hegemonic world-views and scientific authority influence the research questions scientists ask, the theories they develop, the data they collect, the methods they employ, and their interpretation of evidence (Krieger, 1992, 1994). By accepting that science is inherently both objective (because reliable data is produced by commonly accepted research methodologies) and subjective (because values influence how and which questions are asked) epidemiologists can avoid confusing scientific assumptions for the world "out there" – a trap which frequently befalls those adhering to a biomedical approach (Krieger, 1994). According to Krieger, an ecosocial epidemiology is a better epidemiology – more precise, because it would interrogate the social origins and effects of categories like "race," class, gender, sex, and age. It would "end the practice of obscuring or misclassifying agency" (Krieger, 1994, p. 899) through a critical assessment (if not rejection) of frequently employed epidemiological terms like "lifestyle" and "environment" – it would relocate the spider in the web, the architect in the scaffolding.

NEW PUBLIC HEALTH(S)

Population Health

A new public health paradigm accompanies the emergence of ecosocial/ecological epidemiology. Population health, the successor to health promotion, emerged in response to persistent international demands to focus on social and structural de-terminants of health. By 1992, there were three formally established research units devoted to building knowledge on the social determinants of disease: the Canadian Institute for Advanced Research (CIAR) was founded in 1982 in Toronto, and its Program in Population Health was launched in 1987; the International Centre for Health and Society was established in 1991 at University College in London; and the Society and Health Program, a joint undertaking of the Harvard School of Public Health and the Tufts-New England Medical Center, was launched in 1992 in Boston. In 1993, the influential Leeds Declaration was presented at a conference of the Nuffield Institute of Health at the University of Leeds; it laid out ten principles for action for population health research and practice in light of "the role and limitations of epidemiology as generally practiced today" (Dean & Hunter, 1996, p. 745). The first principle addressed the need to focus research "upstream," that is, on the social structures and processes that cause illness, rather than on individual risk. The Declaration also emphasized the limitations of quantitative research methods, and the persistent undervaluing of qualitative methods. It also demanded that the importance of lay knowledges be recognized, and recommended that participatory research become an integral component of public health research. The Declaration further called for research to focus on what enables people to remain healthy, even in the most adverse conditions (Anonymous, 1994; Young, 1998). Although population health (or the "social determinants of health" perspective, as it is known in the U.S.) is defined by an "upstream" focus, it continues to be dominated by quantitative, population level research. In what follows, I shall focus on the work of the CIAR, as the publications of its Program in Population Health have remained the most influential documents steering the population health agenda (Hayes & Dunn, 1998).

In the late 1980s and early 1990s, the CIAR and its Population Health Program developed the empirical and epistemological bases of a population health framework and analysis. The Population Health Program has pursued two related interests: (1) measurement of health at a population level and the development and improvement of data systems "to permit us to know with more precision how our health is evolving and what factors are affecting it" (Evans et al., 1994, p. xi); and (2) understanding the role and strengths/limits of the health care system as a means of improving health. The first of these objectives demands a clear definition of "health," but proponents of population health seem to vacillate on their endorsement of a suitable definition. The World Health Organization's Constitution (1948) defines health as "a state of complete physical, mental, and social well-being and not merely the absence of disease or infirmity" (cited in Young, 1998, p. 1); this was later reformulated (in a 1984 health promotion document) to refer to "the extent to which an individual or group is able on the one hand to realize aspirations and satisfy needs, and, on the other hand, to change and cope with the environment" (cited in Young, 1998, p. 1). Both definitions describe a comprehensive notion of health that goes beyond narrow biomedical limits and "negative" formulations that emphasize disease or disability. Presumably, this is a direction that would be favoured by population health enthusiasts. Because societal and structural causes of ill health on a population level fall outside the conceptual boundaries of a disease-focused and individualized definition of health – the social context of "lifestyle choices," for example, are not taken into account – population health researchers urge us to conceptualize health and its determinants more broadly. Yet, population health proponents dismiss the broad WHO definition of health as "rather unhelpful operationally" and essentially meaningless: it is "everything, and hence nothing in particular" (Evans, 1994, p. 24). In an attempt to strike a balance between too narrow and too broad a definition, the CIAR program paradoxically reverts to the assumption that "health is the absence of disability or disease" (including both subjective experiences of illness by "patients," and objective diagnoses of disease or injury by clinicians) (Evans, 1994, p. 24). Such a "thin" definition is justified by the claim that this concept of health can be represented through quantifiable and measurable phenomena: death or survival, the incidence or prevalence of particular morbid conditions" (Evans & Stoddart, 1994, p. 29). They argue that what appears to promote the absence of disease or injury, probably also promotes that which is contained in "more comprehensive definitions of health" (Evans & Stoddart, 1994, p. 29). Thus we are returned, by a rather circuitous route, to an individualized, disease-focused measure of health, despite the apparent intentions of eco-epidemiology.

The emphasis on "population" in population health is explained as follows. The persistent correlation between a nation's wealth and the health of its population, *and* the correlation between equitable distribution of that wealth and health status, suggests that poor health is not simply a matter of basic deprivation. Rather, there is a continuous gradient across socio-economic classes with regard to morbidity and mortality; in other words, there tends to be a difference in health status between *each* stratum of wealth in a society (rather than a difference in health status only between "low-" and "high-wealth" strata) (Evans, 1994; Hertzman et al., 1994; Mustard & Frank, 1994). The fact that this gradient applies to most major causes of death in turn suggests that whatever underlies the gradient of health affects the basic "host response" to a wide range of diseases. Consequently, the relationships among social status, coping, stress, and health must be examined at a population level rather than at the level of etiology of specific diseases. Accordingly, proponents of population health recommend that governments avoid "counter-productive" programmes aimed only at the poor or most disadvantaged, because these will not directly address the "true" determinants of health, and will only negatively label impoverished or disenfranchised groups. Running counter to in-fectious disease and chronic disease epidemiological paradigms described above, Mustard and Frank (1994) assert:

> The notion of a continuous gradient of under-achieved human potential and health status helps the policy maker to find the balance among narrowly targeted policies and programs aimed

only at 'the tail of the distribution' versus more broadly based approaches which recognize the importance, in aggregate, of deficits in health and personal development among the majority of the population. (p. 41)

The CIAR's concern with efficient use of social resources is implicit here. The cost of that efficiency clearly falls on the "tail of the distribution" (more specifically, those people whose health needs exceed the "average").

Population health proponents take particular aim at resources directed to health *care*: "health in human societies (as opposed to the course of individual cases of illness) is powerfully influenced by a nation's wealth creating capacity and the distribution of wealth – much more so than by provision of medical care" (Mustard & Frank, 1994, pp. 10–11). In fact, they assert that increasing resources allocated to health care may even *diminish* the overall health of a population. "Inappropriate and increased expenditures will act as a drag on a modern economy, reducing overall efficiency and competitiveness for global trade and decreasing the capacity to create wealth" (Mustard & Frank, 1994, p. 11). In the United States for example, the health care system is a major consumer of resources, leaving less "for investment in new capital or research – *true* wealth creation" (Mustard & Frank, 1994, p. 30, italics added).

A Critical Response

Although the CIAR version of population health has substantial currency (Hayes & Dunn, 1998; Robertson, 1998; Young, 1998),[9] it is countered with critique from an historical political economy of health perspective.[10] Poland et al. (1998) raise several concerns: they criticize the "undertheorized, (...) oversimplified" relationship between wealth and health; they demonstrate how the claim that health care is only weakly linked to population health is vulnerable to conservative interpretation in the interests of the restructuring and retrenchment of welfare state programs; and they illuminate the limitations of the CIAR's implicit social theory (a "modified pluralist interest group perspective") (p. 786; see also Labonté, 1995; Robertson, 1998).

First, there is "an absence of human agency" in population health, and in the accounts from which it draws its supporting evidence (Poland et al., 1998, p. 788). From a population health perspective, improvements in living conditions occur as a result of the "natural" workings of the capitalist market, rather than because of intervention by public health advocates, the working classes, or the women's movement. The gradient effect of wealth on health does not take into account the explicitly social origins (e.g. racist and sexist discrimination; capitalist relations of production) of the health effects of social location. For example, the first Whitehall study of British civil servants, upon which the notion of a "gradient effect" is largely based, neglected to include women at all, and yet its results are generalized to the "population" (Kaufert, 1999). Moreover, Poland et al. (1998) contend that the CIAR provides neither direction for how to stimulate the economy to greater wealth, nor insight into how that wealth will be translated into population health. Instead, the CIAR model is one of "trickle down" health (p. 790). But the promised "trickling" has not happened, amidst "the rolling back of the welfare state in order to support corporate and middle class tax cuts and deficit reduction" (Poland et al., 1998, p. 790).

Second, the call to improve the accountability of health care professionals and to expand the definition of "good medical practice" to "include concepts of cost-effectiveness" (Mustard & Frank, 1994, p. 32) fits neatly with current neoliberal policies of fiscal restraint. Meanwhile, the recent restructuring and de-funding of the health care system has a significant and disproportionate impact on women and people at the lower end of the socioeconomic scale. For example, when public expenditures on health care are cut back, when access to hospitalization and institutional care are reduced, when care is shifted from institutions to private households, and when health care services are contracted out to private companies that protect their profit margins by employing non-unionized workers, women bear most of the burden, both as recipients of care, and as paid and unpaid care providers (Armstrong et al., 2001).

Finally, Poland et al. (1998) raise a concern reminiscent of Krieger's (1994) quest for the missing spider in the "web of causation" model of chronic disease epidemiology: "are each of the factors noted (in Evans & Stoddart's 1994 model) of equal importance as a set of determinants of health?" (p. 791). They note that genetic and biological factors figure prominently, while the "social" is packaged into a single box, implying that other factors are *not* social, nor affected by the social. Other factors are decontextualized: "inequality" is treated as a statistical variable rather than "an explanatory category in social analysis," and the use of the term "population" in "population health" suggests that national populations are homogenous categories, stripping communities of complex social relations (Poland et al., 1998, p. 791; see also Labonté, 1995). There is a misplaced emphasis on biological, genetic and psychological mechanisms that purportedly explain the relationship between social class and health, while there is an inadequate explanation for how economic inequalities are created and sustained. Consequently, the CIAR analysis depicts the social problems of (economic) deprivation and inequality as biological or psychological pathology, and discourages/limits an interrogation of macro social forces that may account for inequity. And in the present, the state of the health care system must be understood in the context of conservative political movements, globalization, and the dismantling of the welfare state (Poland et al., 1998). Without a complex and nuanced analysis of how the health care system reached its current condition, the CIAR cannot make credible recommendations for change. The theoretical assumptions at the foundation of the CIAR's "highly truncated and largely implicit" social analysis are "hidden behind a veil of ostensible 'objectivity' that accompanies empiricist quantitative epidemiology" (Poland et al., 1998, p. 792). Empirical (presumably "neutral") data stand in for committed argument. Consequently, the CIAR model's politically ambiguous pronouncements are left open to becoming a justification for conservative policies of retrenchment. "The 'invisible hand' of economic growth and prosperity – central to CIAR's model of health determinants – replaces the analytical critiques of capitalism, patriarchy and non-ecological industrialism raised by social justice, feminist and environmental movements" (Labonté, 1995, p. 166).

FORGING "FACTS" AND EVIDENCE

The "eco-epidemiology" espoused by Susser and Susser (1996b) and the "ecosocial epidemiology" proposed by Krieger (1994) and Pearce (1996) are aligned with different visions of public health. The Sussers' emphasis on the importance of new technologies in microbiology and statistical analysis, and their functionalist model of "conjurer's boxes" (which lacks an analysis of social power), best fits the CIAR version of population health. Krieger's and Pearce's concern with assigning responsibility for pathogenic (or, health-promoting) social structures is more closely aligned with an historical political economy of health. Accordingly, each combination understands the nature of data and evidence differently. While "eco-epidemiology" and population health demand (and produce) universalizing, decontextualized statistical data, "ecosocial epidemiology," informed by a critical political economy of health, calls for data produced by multiple methods that preserve diversity and local knowledges.

POHEM, the System of Health Statistics, and the Health Information Template

The necessity to adopt an interdisciplinary, multi-method approach to research on the health of populations has been widely acknowledged (for e.g. see Anonymous, 1994; Dean & Hunter, 1996; Krieger, 1999; Popay & Williams, 1996). Regardless, positivistic scientific methods continue to set the standard, especially in epidemiology: "Contemporary epidemiology is characterized by heavy reliance on mortality or a specific disease as the outcome 'health' variable and on experimental design as the optimal form of research investigation" (Dean & Hunter, 1996, p. 746).

Michael Wolfson, a senior official in Statistics Canada and affiliate of the CIAR, is a key figure in the creation of conceptual models that direct data production from a population health perspective. According to Wolfson, "reliable and valid data" are a powerful and important means to understanding the determinants of health, the conduct of institutions and individuals in the arena of health, and the effective management of these institutions (Wolfson, 1994, p. 287). He defines "data" and "information" as follows:

> By data, we mean elements of description, numerical or otherwise, of things, people, places, and events. By information, we mean the ordering and interpretation of data to impose or extract meaning. For example, the enumeration of one's activities over the past week constitutes data. These can then be interpreted as employment or unemployment, and then further aggregated with other similar data to generate an estimate of the Canadian unemployment rate (p. 314).

Wolfson complains that health care information tends to be fragmentary, unreliable, misleading, and (at its worst) false. Most available data on health refer to "input" (the resources consumed by health care) rather than "outcomes" of particular interventions at the individual level (changes in health status). This impedes "quality assurance" projects and "outcomes management" in the health care system. Conversely, at the population level, there are inadequate national data to determine accurately what is the health status of the population and whether it is improving or worsening. Citizens and politicians are thus distracted from recognizing and addressing the *real* concerns of health, and health policy is instead focused on crisis management. Wolfson proposes three strategic developments in health information systems to address these concerns, and to meet the goals of population health: (1) developing an overall index of population health status; (2) merging administrative and self-report data; and (3) creating a template or framework for health information (Wolfson, 1994, p. 294).

Wolfson claims that the development of a reliable measure of overall population health status can correct the "outcomes" data gap – population health status "could be measured by regular surveys and summarized in one overall index like the GDP or the CPI"[11] (1994, p. 290). Politicians and public sector administrators could use this "aggregate index of population health" in combination with administrative data (reported by hospitals and health care professionals) to guide policy and develop programmes. The construction of such an index begins with measuring *individuals'* health, preferably averaged over some time period (e.g. a year), and permits a calculation of an average health status index for the entire population, comparable to "average family income" (Wolfson, 1994). The data collected for this index must be multivariate (addressing a broad range of domains/factors), multilevel (focused on individuals and their external environments), micro (individual-level data), and longitudinal (so that individual life paths can be analyzed and long-term lagged effects identified) (Wolfson, 1994). Wolfson's POHEM (population health model) thus takes the individual as the smallest unit of analysis, and follows each from birth to death.

> POHEM generates a representative sample (say one hundred thousand) of such complete life paths, including information not only on risk factors and disease, but also on health status (on several different dimensions). Health-status-adjusted life expectancies for each individual are then aggregated by POHEM to produce population health expectancy, or PHE (Wolfson, 1994, p. 299).

Although Wolfson (1994) recognizes the PHE index would "inevitably require simplifications of concept and measurement" (p. 291), he insists that the benefits of focusing decision-makers on appropriate objectives outweigh the drawbacks. He also recommends that the index should not be subjected to standards higher than those set for other useful and widely accepted indices such as the CPI and the GDP. "After all, economic statistics are far from perfect in their designed purposes, and much less so for their actual uses in the public arena. Yet no one suggests that we would be better off without them. The best should not be the enemy of the good" (Wolfson, 1994, p. 291).

The diversity and complexity of all this data requires a coherent organizing framework. This framework would provide much-needed theoretical guidance for strategic planning, and data collection and management.

> Data and facts are not like pebbles on a beach, waiting to be picked up and collected. They can only be perceived and measured through an underlying theoretical and conceptual framework, which defines relevant facts, and distinguishes them from 'background noise.' The framework acts as a filter, determining which observations must be attended to and which can safely, often unconsciously, be ignored. It is a map of the territory, and plans can only be made and actions taken on the basis of maps, not on the totality of all possible information about the territory. (The trick is to choose the right map for the purposes at hand.) (. . .) This process is clearly illustrated by the System of National Accounts, whose development and elaboration was guided by Keynesian macroeconomic theory (Wolfson, 1994, p. 309).

To accomplish this task, Wolfson proposes a "System of Health Statistics" (which originated in conceptual work aimed at supplementing the United Nations System of National Accounts). "Such a system of health statistics, and its associated template, could become for health information what the System of National Accounts is for economic information" (Wolfson, 1994, p. 289). He argues that if health policy is to extend beyond health *care* policy, and is to address the broad determinants of population health, then the appropriate statistical systems must be in place to provide the foundational data to inform that policy.

In the early 1990s, informed by the System of Health Statistics, Wolfson and others developed a Health Information Template, wherein population data are organized into three domains: Individual Characteristics; External Milieu; and Health-Affecting Interventions. The microdata comprising Individual Characteristics arise from observations about individuals, "but describe a population" – in other words, these microdata are used to generate a picture of an "average" member of the population/sub-group within a population (Wolfson, 1994, p. 310). The External Milieu includes "physicochemical" environments, sociocultural environments, economic environments, and health system environments (physical structures of hospitals, numbers of health care professionals, etc.). Health-Affecting Interventions, which prevent the External Milieu from exclusively shaping the health of populations, include both individual level interventions (e.g. surgery) and collective interventions (e.g. health and safety regulations, or funding for medical diagnostic equipment) (Wolfson, 1994, p. 311). Wolfson (1994) argues that one of the benefits of the template is that it is not hierarchically organized, which "means that our thinking about health information need not be (implicitly) constrained from the outset" (pp. 312–313). Furthermore, the template provides a means "to link the development of health information to policy modeling applications," much as the System of National Accounts data is used to inform macroeconomic policy and forecasting models (Wolfson, 1994, p. 313).

The System of Health Statistics and the Health Information Template recommended by Wolfson produce data and evidence compatible with Susser and Susser's (1996b) model of eco-epidemiology. The System of Health Statistics (a multi-level causal model) produces multivariate data which are interpreted as evidence for the "laws" that operate at each level of organization (from individual life-course, to population health). The universalism of these laws of eco-epidemiology (and the statistics which provide evidence for them) inevitably gloss over the intricate complexities of local conditions and politics. It is crucial to illuminate the epistemological assumptions at work here, because these conceptual models and the tools that produce evidence to support them are presented as objective instruments that produce neutral facts. But these models and instruments do not stand apart from their particular socio-political contexts and they have specific (invested) effects.

Wolfson's definition of data clearly assumes that data are in themselves neutral, and have an existence separate from processes of interpretation and analysis (which produce "information"). Description and meaning are separated here; the agencies of observation (Barad, 1996) are presumed to be apolitical, and the resulting description is therefore presumed to be unbiased. However, Marilyn Waring's critique of the U.N. System of National Accounts data (which relies on measures such as GDP) shows how the process of data *collection/creation* affects the "information" outcome (Waring, 1988, 1999). In Wolfson's example of employment statistics, he fails to acknowledge that how one defines "activity" or "employment" shapes both the data and the information produced. For example, if unpaid caregiving for family members (performed mostly by women) counts as work-related productive "activity," the impact on our conceptions of "employment" (and who is deserving of employment benefits) is profound. Nevertheless, despite acknowledging that a System of Health Statistics "will not be methodologically ideal" (Wolfson, 1994, p. 295), Wolfson aspires to the standard of admittedly problematic CPI and GDP aggregate indicators, ignoring serious critiques of these indices and how they are calculated (see for e.g. Waring, 1988, 1999).

Wolfson (1994) contends that a framework for gauging population health "will require agreement on a standard set of measures (i.e. concepts and definitions) of health status, and will thus provide a common basis for analysis in many other areas such as quality assurance, technology assessment, and community health" (p. 300). However the assumption of conceptual consensus does not attend to the operation of power in the measurement process, nor does it adequately acknowledge the complexity and fluidity of lived experience. Questions like "what constitutes a population?," and "is the 'widely accepted' disease-oriented definition of health adequate?" are not raised in Wolfson's account of how indices of population health are to be constructed. "Populations" are presumed to be homogeneous categories. Difference and diversity complicate matters statistically, so they are effectively erased: "For epidemiologists and statisticians, the aggregation of data, or their adjustment for age or sex, are simply routine procedures" (Kaufert, 1999, p. 125). The consequence is that while the POHEM appears to admit some detail into the calculation of population health expectancy (PHE), in the end, an "average" unit still stands for the whole. Hayes (1994) notes:

> In the CIAR analysis, evidence is taken from various contexts, but presented as though factors identified within specific populations are generalizable to all humans. This universalizing tendency runs roughshod over differences between the populations in such dimensions as ethnicity and culture, gender relations, social networks, power, as well as differences in topography and the physical setting of relations, as distributed across spatial and temporal dimensions. The individuality of human experience (...) is denied by the 'person x' attitude of the analysis (p. 127).

Hayes does not object to a population perspective (nor do I) – it is important to have an overall understanding of group differences in order to identify structural inequalities; consequently, we "must deal with aggregates of information" (Hayes, 1994, p. 127). Rather, his concern (and mine) is about an undertheorization of "the local" in the framework for generating and interpreting data: "various manifestations of social relations give rise to differences in meaning and interpretation of action within localized cultures, as well as differences in routines and activities – differences that are under-appreciated" in the population health perspective and in the Sussers' eco-epidemiology (Hayes, 1994, p. 128). In an attempt to gain the "objectivity" of distance from individual particularity, eco-epidemiology and population health consider individual data to be important only from the standpoint of providing enough information to generate a statistical measure of the "normal," and from that position, local idiosyncracies are erased.

Finally, Wolfson comments on the role of theoretical frameworks in guiding data collection. The beginning of his statement, "Data and facts are not like pebbles on a beach..." (1994, p. 309) suggests he acknowledges the social construction of facts, and nowadays it may be only a "straw positivism" that would claim the context-independence of data (although some expressions of positivistic method come surprisingly close). Regardless, his distinction between "relevant" facts and "background noise," and the notion that the latter "can safely, often unconsciously, be ignored" is troubling (Wolfson, 1994, p. 309). "Safely ignored" for whom?[12] It makes sense to focus our attention on specific concerns, lest we be overwhelmed by "information overload," but we must be careful not to assume that all facts have the same status: "we'll look at a bit at a time, and get to the others when an appropriate problem comes up." That assumption ignores how facts are politically charged. It ignores (not so safely) how the "trick" of "choosing the right map for the purposes at hand" (Wolfson, 1994, p. 309) is a political trick that does not, left to its own devices, provide an account of how "the map" or "the purposes at hand" come to be defined.

Wolfson should not bear the brunt of this criticism alone, because he builds his model on a foundation upon which many others have laboured. Stolley (1985) has stated unequivocally that epidemiologists should strive to "separate emotion from fact, faith from evidence" (p. 39). He invokes Bertrand Russell to guide epidemiologists through "turbulent times":

> In the welter of conflicting fanaticisms, one of the few unifying forces is scientific truthfulness, by which I mean the habit of basing our beliefs upon observations and inferences as impersonal and as much divested of local and temperamental bias as is possible for human beings (Russell, cited in Stolley, 1985, p. 42).[13]

More recently, Savitz, Poole and Miller (1999) have taken pains to distinguish (and distance) the science of epidemiology from public health, which "can be seen as an ideology, a profession, a movement, or a set of actions, but not as a single scientific discipline" (p. 1158). In their view, the science of epidemiology is aligned with objectivity, rigorous rules of research, hypothesis-testing, and "the generation of accurate and useful information" (Savitz et al., 1999, p. 1158). Still faithful to Popperian principles which hold significant weight in some epidemiological circles (see Buck, 1975; Susser, 1986), Savitz et al. (1999) acknowledge the tentative nature of all scientific knowledge. But rather than exposing the political nature of science, this model asserts that knowledge (as theory) survives only when subjected to tests of universality, simplicity, and precision (Susser, 1986). A mixture of science and activism "threatens the validity of epidemiologic science" and creates "impassioned scholars who go beyond advancing and explaining the science to promoting a specific public health agenda" (Savitz et al., 1999, p. 1160). Ideally, they claim, public health policy decisions, ethics, and attention to local particularities are outside the purview of epidemiology; "The product of research is information," not social action (Savitz et al., 1999, p. 1160). Scientists do science; the implications of the "objective" knowledge produced are left to policy makers, into whose decisions morality and politics intrude.

Local Understanding vs. Universal Measurement

Pearce's (1996) and Krieger's (1994, 2001) visions for a new epidemiology, building on and expanding a political economy of health,[14] provide an alternative to the universalism of eco-epidemiology. What kind of data and evidence must be produced to support *ecosocial* epidemiology? Pearce (1996) calls for developing a multidisciplinary *understanding* of the cause of disease in complex populations, as opposed to simply measuring statistical associations among exposures, diseases and individuals. Data should therefore be created by multiple methods that can capture the historical and social contexts of disease: "it is essential to understand (. . .) the importance of diversity and local knowledges rather than only searching for universal relationships" (Pearce, 1996, p. 682). Strategies such as randomized clinical trials based on an experimental model, where processes are extracted from their ecological context, are inappropriate for this task. Krieger (1994) focuses her attention on a gap in epidemiological theory, and with Pearce (1996) criticizes the discipline for being taught and viewed "as a collection of methods to be applied to particular problems involving human diseases and health" (Krieger, 1994, p. 899). Krieger advocates moving beyond a micro biological focus, in order to attend to the social context of disease and public health. In her commentary on the construction of public health information, Krieger (1992) objects to the regular omission of social class data, the persistent treatment of race and sex as essentially biological variables, and the exclusion of the effects of racism, classism and sexism. It is essential to acknowledge that scientific knowledge is political, because "which theories we rely on, which questions we ask, which studies we conduct, which data we believe are worth obtaining, and which data we even recognize when confronted with unanticipated findings: this is where values enter and worldviews leave their indelible mark" (Krieger, 1992, p. 422).

This is a profoundly different position from that taken up by Wolfson (1994) when he describes how theory provides the guidance that allows us to distinguish between "relevant facts" and "background noise." Krieger (1992) demands "better data," produced by self-reflexive and critical science. These data would emerge from the theoretically informed questions posed by Krieger's fractal model: How do population level variables such as social structure, cultural norms, ecological environments, and genetic variability affect the health of a population? And how are social accountability and individual agency concurrently implicated? The data produced would allow us to clearly locate the scientist(s) in the evidence.

With eco-epidemiology, ecosocial epidemiology, and the new public health paradigm of population health, we seem to have returned full circle to concepts and principles first identified in the era of sanitary statistics. Once again, the official subject of epidemiology is the population; as before, detailed data about *individuals* (from genetic constitution to daily habits) are consumed as evidence about *population* health. This is especially true in the case of population health and Wolfson's System of Health Statistics. The (oft-unacknowledged) political terrain in which population health and eco-epidemiology has taken hold (i.e. the decline of the post-World War II welfare state and the concurrent rise of a neo-liberal ideology of fiscal restraint) (Shields & Evans, 1998) has been profoundly influential. As critics of the CIAR framework have pointed out, population health is susceptible to a neo-liberal interpretation, in which a focus on broad determinants of health has been used to justify cutbacks and restructuring in the health care system, both of which have disproportionate negative effects for women and their health; this has occurred at the same time as neo-liberal policies of restraint have created greater economic inequities and weakened the "social safety net" (Poland et al., 1998). Population health and eco-epidemiology are both open to these interpretations precisely because they start from the assumption that data are neutral, and scientists are objective. Politics are seen as external to the business of scientific knowledge production. Accordingly, positivistic science continues to be the standard against which this knowledge is measured. The universalism of eco-epidemiology contrasts with the particularity and positionality of ecosocial epidemiology, where diversity and local knowledges are integral to understanding health and disease. There are continuing disputes about whether a "top-down" or "upstream" approach (focusing on macro, structural variables) or a "bottom-up," "downstream" approach (focusing on micro data which are combined to generate a picture of the population) is most suitable for creating knowledge about the health of populations (McKinlay, 1997, 1974; Pearce, 1996). Ongoing developments in material technologies (genetic research, advancements in information systems) support the hegemonic "bottom-up" approach – disease risk is increasingly measured at the microscopic level, and population health proponents champion increasingly sophisticated and extensive databases for storing information about individuals' health. Thus, knowledge about health and disease still rests in the hands of a cadre of expert knowers, including epidemiologists (of various stripes, from social to clinical), genetic researchers, health economists, and "total quality" managers/assessors.

SITUATED EPIDEMIOLOGY?

Epidemiology is a dynamic form of knowledge production that has passed through three major paradigm shifts in its modern history: "traditional" epidemiology or sanitary statistics; infectious disease epidemiology; and chronic disease/risk factor/social epidemiology. These paradigm shifts have occurred in the midst of complex conditions – political and social revolutions, advances in material technologies, and changes in public health policies and practices, to name a few. Epidemiology has been exposed as an "impure science." Despite the hopes and claims of those who subscribe to the independence of the scientific enterprise and the truths it produces, epidemiology has not been insulated from external (or internal) pressures (Epstein, 1996). In the present, we are witnessing the emergence of a fourth paradigm – "ecological epidemiologies" – and can see how epidemiological knowledges are contested, from within and without the discipline. Feminist locational epistemologies provide us with rich questions to pose to the history of epidemiology, and offer useful tools for building this newest paradigm. When we situate past knowledge claims about disease, we see that positivist-empiricism, liberal-humanism (and neo-liberalism), biomedical individualism, and historical political economies map out the discursive space in which epidemiologies are created. We have seen shifts from concerns with social and environmental causes of disease (not without some blame attached to the poor who were afflicted), to single-cause, infectious models of disease, where the "neutral" germ was a truth that was purportedly independent of the observer or the instruments that measured it. But once those germs were brought under control in the affluent West, we saw a return to multiple-cause models of disease that once again attempted to address its social context, even as data collection and intervention remained at the level of individual agents. As pressure to contain "costs to taxpayers" continued to intensify in the 1990s and in the new century, there have been more urgent calls to turn attention (and government funding) away from costly medical interventions and towards the efficiencies of disease prevention. Once again, the health of the population is the focus of epidemiology. Data about individuals, produced by advanced statistical technologies, is interpreted as evidence about population health status. This "neutral" evidence can then be used to measure the efficacy of public health initiatives. The epidemiologist vanishes.

What possibilities exist for a "situated" epidemiology? What if the fourth era of epidemiology were guided by embodied objectivity? I believe that Krieger's (1994) proposal for an "ecosocial epidemiology" comes closest to this vision. Rejecting the spiderless "web of causation," Krieger advocates for more accountability in the production of epidemiological knowledge. She takes subjectivity into account by acknowledging that the process of scientific research, from formulating theories, to identification of the research question, to the definition of "what counts" as data, to the interpretation of that data as evidence, is infused with politics (Krieger, 1992, 1994). Ecosocial epidemiology "demands that epidemiologists consider how their social position affects the knowledge they desire and that which they produce" (Krieger, 1994, p. 898). At the same time, Krieger takes a strong realist stance toward the "recalcitrant" reality of biology; while social conditions may influence how biology is expressed, the biological is not "infinitely plastic" (Wylie, 1992b, p. 25) – our epidemiological understandings will always encounter its resistance, and our accounts must always acknowledge the particular conditions (*both* social and biological) that prevail at any moment of knowledge-production. Each "branch" in Krieger's fractal structure portrays one moment of epidemiological possibilities. Each branch is a representation of an epidemiological phenomenon – that is, it represents a situated and local knowledge that describes a particular "cut" between "health" or "disease" and the agencies of observation that measure it (see Barad, 1996). Krieger's fractal model does not prescribe a single answer for all disease, at all times and places (as miasma theory, or germ theory had done in the past). Nor does it avoid the question of cause altogether, by containing it in a "black box" or lodging it in a vacant web. Rather than closing off conversation about the cause of disease, Krieger's model asks a series of questions about social and cultural conditions, ecological environments, and even genetic variability that provide a point of entry for analysis of particular situations.

Yet Krieger's ecosocial epidemiology can still be refined. While Krieger gestures toward the social construction of scientific knowledge, her proposal expresses a problematic dichotomy between the biological and the social. She claims: "although the biologic may set the basis for the existence of humans and hence our social life, it is this social life that sets the path along which the biologic may flourish – or wilt" (Krieger, 1994, p. 899). Here, the biological (read "natural") world has a primary existence, and the secondary social acts upon it. This division implies that there is a truth of biology that is somehow more stable than any social knowledge. But if scientific knowledge is social knowledge (Longino, 1996, 1992), then biological knowledge does not have a primary stability, and despite a realist commitment, we can neither assume a truth of biology that is "covered over" by misdirected or inadequate investigation, nor that there is a significant distinction between biological and social facts. If ecosocial epidemiology is to be fully informed by feminist locational epistemologies, it must leave open the possibility that the "truth" of the biological world is just as elusive and fragile as that of the social.

NOTES

1. In 1855, editor of the *Journal of Public Health and Sanitary Review*, Dr. Benjamin Ward Richardson, acknowledged France's superiority in the field of public health:

> the French as a nation are some fifty or a hundred years ahead of us in the practical knowledge and application of the means of preserving health. In England, we have no standard literature on hygiene, no work on this subject showing the footprints either of genius or industry. In France, first class works of this kind are as common as biographies, histories, or elementary treatises on natural sciences. The French have their Dictionary of Hygiene; their records of sanitary improvements; and in a quarterly work, entitled Annales d'Hygiène Publique, the choicest epitome that can be imagined on all subjects relating to health and life (cited in Terris, 1987, p. 316)

Although the technology of vital statistics was more advanced elsewhere, France was unsurpassed in literary technologies of disseminating knowledge about public hygiene.

2. This attitude was consistent with that of subsequent "Baconian generalizers" in Britain; committed to discovering statistical laws of sickness (similar to laws of mortality), they believed that "the more numbers we have, the more inductions we shall be able to make. (. . .) Collect more numbers, and more regularities will appear" (Hacking, 1990, pp. 62–63).

3. The Poor Law of 1834 was based on three principles: (1) no relief except within a workhouse to the able-bodied; (2) such relief to be "less eligible" than the most unpleasant means of earning a living outside; and (3) separation of man and wife to prevent childbearing (Terris, 1985, p. 25).

4. "It is clear from its early history that statistical science was never a neutral enquiry; but was embedded in a broader metaphysic laden with value judgements about the rational rather than the mysterious mind of God and the natural order of human society" (Porter, 1999, p. 52).

5. This goal has been used in the present to justify the introduction of clinical epidemiology into medical practice (Gordon, 1988b).

6. The long-term advantage was the information gained, which made statistical mapping of disease movement possible, especially with regard to comparative analysis of districts (Porter, 1999, p. 135).

7. This "picture," standing in for the *population*, stands in turn for *any particular member* of that population. Here, the emphasis on the "average person" (usually characterized as male) is reminiscent of the early influences of statistics on epidemiology. The universalism of statistical epidemiological methods and their tendency to erase individual particularities, rendering populations homogeneous, has persisted to the present day.

8. Now, we are perhaps more captivated by "socially neutral" genes than by bacteria or viruses.

9. In Canada, for example, the federal department of health "created a division labelled 'Population Health,' claiming (. . .) that the new label denoted a significant shift in philosophical orientation away from the 'soft evidence of health promotion research' and

towards the 'hard, quantitative data' used by researchers in population health" (Kaufert, 1999, pp. 131–132).

10. Briefly, a political economy of health perspective focuses on social structural conditions that contribute to good health or illness and disease, with particular emphasis on economic and political determinants. This framework calls for " 'healthy public policies,' especially redistributive policies to reduce poverty and income inequality, if not for 'wider campaigns for sustainable development, political freedom, and economic and social justice' " (Krieger, 2001, p. 670).

11. GDP is the Gross Domestic Product; CPI is the Consumer Price Index.

12. In order for a variable to be considered statistically significant, it must be considered *theoretically* significant. In other words, it must appear on the conceptual "map" that guides data production. It is telling that even though gender is officially recognized as a determinant of health in Canada, there are few attempts in the production of population health data (e.g. the longitudinal National Population Health Survey) to model the complex relationship of gender to health status (Abdool & Vissandjée, 2001; Donner et al., 2001; Jackson, 2002).

13. According to several critics, Robert Evans (a health economist and key figure in CIAR population health) is inclined to recite the mantra "Data unites, theory divides," implying that scientific "truth" is ascertained from value-free data, while theory is inherently political (see Coburn et al., 1996; Poland et al., 1998; Robertson, 1998). While I don't dispute the latter conclusion, I join with others (for e.g. Code, 1995a, b; Haraway, 1997; Krieger, 1992; Longino, 1992, 1996; Wylie, 1992a, b) in contesting the former.

14. Focused on the guiding question *of "who and what drives current and changing patterns of social inequalities in health,"* the ecosocial approach (. . .) fully embraces a social production of disease perspective while aiming to bring in a comparably rich biological and ecological analysis (Krieger, 2001, p. 672).

ACKNOWLEDGMENTS

An early version of part of this paper was presented in May 2001 at the Annual Meeting of the Canadian Sociology and Anthropology Association, Congress of Learned Societies, Québec City. Many thanks to Lorna Weir, Pat Armstrong, and Lorraine Code for their insightful guidance and unfailing encouragement. Thanks to Rebecca Raby for patient reading of parts of this manuscript and for innumerable other supportive gestures. Thanks also to the editors of this volume for helpful comments on an earlier draft of this work.

REFERENCES

Abdool, S. N., & Vissandjée, B. (2001). NPHS: A gender perspective. A review and analysis of work to date. Report submitted to the Steering Committee on the Report Card on Canadian Women's Health, and to the Bureau of Respiratory Disease and Diabetes, Health Canada.
Anonymous (1994). Editorial: Population health looking upstream. *The Lancet, 343*(8895), 420–430.

Armstrong, P., Amaratunga, C., Bernier, J., Grant, K., Pederson, A., & Willson, K. (2001). *Exposing privatization: Women and health care reform in Canada.* Aurora, ON: Garamond Press.

Badgley, R. F. (1994). Health promotion and social change in the health of Canadians. In: A. Pederson, M. O'Neill & I. Rootman (Eds), *Health Promotion in Canada: Provincial, National & International Perspectives* (pp. 20–39). Toronto, Canada: W. B. Saunders.

Barad, K. (1996). Meeting the universe halfway: Realism and social constructivism without contradiction. In: L. H. Nelson & J. Nelson (Eds), *Feminism, Science, and the Philosophy of Science* (pp. 161–194). Great Britain: Kluwer Academic Publishers.

Bird, C., Conrad, P., & Fremont, A. M. (2000). Medical sociology at the millenium. In: C. Bird, P. Conrad & A. M. Fremont (Eds), *Handbook of Medical Sociology* (5th ed., pp. 1–10). Upper Saddle River, NJ: Prentice-Hall.

Bottomore, T. B. (1972). *Sociology: A guide to problems and literature* (Rev. ed.) (Second impression). London: George Allen & Unwin.

Buck, C. (1975). Popper's philosophy for epidemiologists. *International Journal of Epidemiology, 4*, 159–168.

Buck, C., Llopis, A., Najera, E., & Terris, M. (1988). *The challenge of epidemiology: Issues and selected readings.* Washington, DC: Pan American Health Association.

Coburn, D., Poland, B., and members of the Critical Social Science and Health Group (1996). The CIAR vision of the determinants of health. A critique. *Canadian Journal of Public Health, 87*(5), 308–310.

Code, L. (1995a). How do we know? Questions of method in feminist practice. In: S. Burt & L. Code (Eds), *Changing Methods: Feminists Transforming Practice* (pp. 13–44). Peterborough, Canada: Broadview Press.

Code, L. (1995b). *Rhetorical spaces: Essays on gendered locations.* New York: Routledge.

Dean, K., & Hunter, D. (1996). New directions for health: Towards a knowledge base for public health action. *Social Science and Medicine, 42*(5), 745–750.

Descartes, R. (1993). *Discourse on method and meditations on first philosophy* (3rd ed.) (Donald A. Cress, Trans.). Indianapolis: Hackett Publishing Company. (Original work published 1637, 1641.)

Dickens, C. (1998). *Hard times.* Oxford: Oxford University Press.

Donner, L., Horne, T., & Thurston, W. (2001). Population health data through a gender lens: A gender analysis of "Toward a healthy future: Second report on the health of Canadians" and selected other population health documents. Working document prepared for the Federal/Provincial/Territorial Status of Women Forum.

Epstein, S. (1996). *Impure science: AIDS, activism, and the politics of knowledge.* Berkeley: University of California Press.

Evans, R. G. (1994). Introduction. In: R. G. Evans, M. L. Barer & T. R. Marmor (Eds), *Why Are Some People Healthy and Others Not? The Determinants of Health of Populations* (pp. 3–26). New York: Aldine De Gruyter.

Evans, R. G., Barer, M. L., & Marmor, T. R. (1994). Preface. In: R. G. Evans, M. L. Barer & T. R. Marmor (Eds), *Why Are Some People Healthy and Others Not? The Determinants of Health of Populations* (pp. ix–xix). New York: Aldine De Gruyter.

Evans, R. G., & Stoddart, G. L. (1994). Producing health, consuming health care. In: R. G. Evans, M. L. Barer & T. R. Marmor (Eds), *Why Are Some People Healthy and Others Not? The Determinants of Health of Populations* (pp. 27–64). New York: Aldine De Gruyter.

Eyler, J. M. (1980). The conceptual origins of William Farr's epidemiology: Numerical methods and social thought in the 1830s. In: A. M. Lilienfeld (Ed.), *Times, Places and Persons* (pp. 1–21). Baltimore: Johns Hopkins University Press.

Foucault, M. (1980). The politics of health in the eighteenth century. In: C. Gordon (Ed.), *Power/Knowledge: Selected Interviews and Other Writings 1972–1977* (pp. 166–182). New York: Pantheon Books.

Foucault, M. (1990). *The history of sexuality, volume I: An introduction* (Robert Hurley, Trans.). New York: Vintage Books. (Original work published 1978.)

Gabe, J. (1995). Health, medicine and risk: The need for a sociological approach. In: J. Gabe (Ed.), *Medicine, Health and Risk: Sociological Approaches* (pp. 1–17). Oxford: Blackwell Publishers.

Gastaldo, D. (1997). Is health education good for you? Rethinking health education through the concept of bio-power. In: A. Peterson & R. Bunton (Eds), *Foucault, Health and Medicine* (pp. 113–133). London: Routledge.

Gordon, D. R. (1988a). Tenacious assumptions in western medicine. In: M. Lock & D. Gordon (Eds), *Biomedicine Examined* (pp. 19–56). Kluwer Academic Publishers.

Gordon, D. R. (1988b). Clinical science and clinical expertise: Changing boundaries between art and science in medicine. In: M. Lock & D. Gordon (Eds), *Biomedicine Examined* (pp. 19–56). Kluwer Academic Publishers.

Hacking, I. (1990). *The taming of chance*. Cambridge: Cambridge University Press.

Hannaway, C. (1980). Discussion. In: A. M. Lilienfeld (Ed.), *Times, Places and Persons* (pp. 39–42). Baltimore: Johns Hopkins University Press.

Haraway, D. J. (1991). Situated knowledges: The science question in feminism and the privilege of partial perspective. In: D. J. Haraway (Ed.), *Simians, Cyborgs and Women: The Reinvention of Nature* (pp. 183–201). New York: Routledge.

Haraway, D. (1997). *ModestWitness@Second@Millenium.FemaleMan©MeetsOncoMouse™*. New York: Routledge.

Hayes, M. V. (1994). Evidence, determinants of health and population epidemiology: Humming the tune, learning the lyrics. In: M. V. Hayes, L. T. Foster & H. D. Foster (Eds), *The Determinants of Population Health: A Critical Assessment* (pp. 121–133). Western Geographical Series, Volume 29. Victoria, BC: University of Victoria.

Hayes, M. V., & Dunn, J. R. (1998). Population health in Canada: A systematic review. CPRN Study No. H01. Ottawa: Canadian Policy Research Networks.

Hertzman, C., Frank, J., & Evans, R. G. (1994). Heterogeneities in health status and the determinants of population health. In: R. G. Evans, M. L. Barer & T. R. Marmor (Eds), *Why Are Some People Healthy and Others Not? The Determinants of Health of Populations* (pp. 67–92). New York: Aldine De Gruyter.

Jackson, B. E. (2002). A history of the NPHS: Measuring the health of the population. Report prepared for the Women's Health Bureau, Health Canada.

Kaufert, P. A. (1999). The vanishing woman: Gender and population health. In: T. M. Pollard & S. B. Hyatt (Eds), *Sex, Gender and Health* (pp. 118–136).

Krieger, N. (1992). The making of public health data: Paradigms, politics, and policy. *Journal of Public Health Policy* (Winter), 412–427.

Krieger, N. (1994). Epidemiology and the web of causation: Has anyone seen the spider? *Social Science and Medicine, 39*(7), 887–903.

Krieger, N. (1999). Questioning epidemiology: Objectivity, advocacy, and socially responsible science. *American Journal of Public Health, 89*(8), 1151–1152.

Krieger, N. (2001). Theories for social epidemiology in the 21st century: An ecosocial perspective. *International Journal of Epidemiology, 30*, 668–677.

Kronenfeld, J. J. (1979). Self care as a panacea for the ills of the health care system: An assessment. *Social Science and Medicine, 13A*, 263–267.

Labonté, R. (1994). Death of a program, birth of a metaphor: The development of health promotion in Canada. In: A. Pederson, M. O'Neill & I. Rootman (Eds), *Health Promotion in Canada: Provincial, National & International Perspectives* (pp. 72–90). Toronto, Canada: W. B. Saunders.

Labonté, R. (1995). Population health and health promotion: What do they have to say to each other? *Canadian Journal of Public Health, 86*(3), 165–168.

Lilienfeld, D. E., & Lilienfeld, A. M. (1980). The French influence on the development of epidemiology. In: A. M. Lilienfeld (Ed.), *Times, Places and Persons* (pp. 28–38). Baltimore: Johns Hopkins University Press.

Lilienfeld, D. E., & Stolley, P. D. (1994). *Foundations of epidemiology* (3rd ed., Rev.). New York: Oxford University Press. (Original edition by Abraham M. Lilienfeld.)

Lock, M. (1988). Introduction. In: M. Lock & D. Gordon (Eds), *Biomedicine Examined* (pp. 3–10). Kluwer Academic Publishers.

Longino, H. (1992). Essential tensions – Phase two: Feminist, philosophical, and social studies of science. In: E. McMullin (Ed.), *The Social Dimensions of Science* (pp. 198–216). Notre Dame, IN: University of Notre Dame Press.

Longino, H. (1996). Subjects, power, and knowledge: Description and prescription in feminist philosophies of science. In: E. F. Keller & H. Longino (Eds), *Feminism and Science* (pp. 264–279). Oxford: Oxford University Press.

McKinlay, J. B. (1997, 1974). A case for refocussing upstream: The political economy of illness. In: P. Conrad (Ed.), *The Sociology of Health and Illness: Critical Perspectives* (5th ed., pp. 519–533). New York: St. Martin's Press.

Mustard, J. F., & Frank, J. (1994). The determinants of health. In: M. V. Hayes, L. T. Foster & H. D. Foster (Eds), *The Determinants of Population Health: A Critical Assessment* (pp. 10–42). Western Geographical Series, Volume 29. Victoria, BC: University of Victoria.

Pearce, N. (1996). Traditional epidemiology, modern epidemiology, and public health. *American Journal of Public Health, 86*(5), 678–683.

Petersen, A., & Lupton, D. (1996). *The new public health*. London: Sage.

Poland, B., Coburn, D., Robertson, A., Eakin, J., and members of the Critical Social Science Group (1998). Wealth, equity and health care: A critique of a "Population Health" perspective on the determinants of health. *Social Science and Medicine, 46*(7), 785–798.

Popay, J., & Williams, G. (1996). Public health research and lay knowledge. *Social Science and Medicine, 42*(5), 759–768.

Porter, D. (1999). *Health, civilization and the state*. London: Routledge.

Raymond, J. S. (1989). Behavioural epidemiology: The science of health promotion. *Health Promotion, 4*(4), 281–286.

Robertson, A. (1998). Shifting discourses on health in Canada: From health promotion to population health. *Health Promotion International, 13*(2), 155–166.

Robertson, A., & Minkler, M. (1994). New health promotion movement: A critical examination. *Health Education Quarterly, 21*(3), 295–312.

Savitz, D. A., Poole, C., & Miller, W. C. (1999). Reassessing the role of epidemiology in public health. *American Journal of Public Health, 89*(8), 1158–1161.

Shields, J., & Evans, B. M. (1998). *Shrinking the state: Globalization and public administration "reform."* Halifax: Fernwood Publishing.

Stolley, P. D. (1985). Faith, evidence, and the epidemiologist. *Journal of Public Health Policy* (March), 37–42.

Susser, M. (1986). The logic of Sir Karl Popper and the practice of epidemiology. *American Journal of Epidemiology, 124*(5), 711–718.

Susser, M., & Susser, E. (1996a). Choosing a future for epidemiology: I. Eras and paradigms. *American Journal of Public Health, 86*(5), 668–673.

Susser, M., & Susser, E. (1996b). Choosing a future for epidemiology: II. From black box to Chinese boxes and eco-epidemiology. *American Journal of Public Health, 86*(5), 674–677.

Syme, S. L., & Yen, I. H. (2000). Social epidemiology and medical sociology: Different approaches to the same problem. In: C. E. Bird, P. Conrad & A. M. Fremont (Eds), *Handbook of Medical Sociology* (5th ed., pp. 365–376). Upper Saddle River, NJ: Prentice-Hall.

Tannahill, A. (1992). Epidemiology and health promotion: A common understanding. In: R. Bunton & G. Macdonald (Eds), *Health Promotion: Disciplines and Diversity* (pp. 86–107). London: Routledge.

Terris, M. (1985). The changing relationships of epidemiology and society: The Robert Cruikshank Lecture. *Journal of Public Health Policy* (March), 15–36.

Terris, M. (1987). Epidemiology and the public health movement. *Journal of Public Health Policy, 7*, 315–329.

Waring, M. (1988). *If women counted: A new feminist economics*. San Francisco: Harper and Row.

Waring, M. (1999). *Counting for nothing: What men value and what women are worth* (2nd ed.) Toronto: Toronto Press.

Wolfson, M. C. (1994). Social proprioception: Measurement, data, and information from a population health perspective. In: R. G. Evans, M. L. Barer & T. R. Marmor (Eds), *Why Are Some People Healthy and Others Not? The Determinants of Health of Populations* (pp. 287–316). New York: Aldine De Gruyter.

Wylie, A. (1991). Gender theory and the archeological record: Why is there no archeology of gender? In: J. M. Gero & M. W. Conkey (Eds), *Engendering Archeology: Women and Prehistory* (pp. 31–54). Oxford: Blackwell.

Wylie, A. (1992a). On 'Heavily decomposing red herrings': Scientific method in archeology and the ladening of evidence with theory. In: L. Embree (Ed.), *Metaarcheology: Reflections by Archeologists and Philosophers* (Vol. 147, pp. 269–288). Dordrecht: Kluwer Academic Publishers.

Wylie, A. (1992b). The interplay of evidential constraints and political interests: Recent archeological research on gender. *American Antiquity, 57*(1), 15–35.

Young, T. K. (1998). *Population health: Concepts and methods*. New York: Oxford University Press.

GENDERING THE MEDICALIZATION THESIS

Elianne Riska

INTRODUCTION

The medicalization thesis derives from a classic theme in the field of medical sociology. It addresses the broader issue of the power of medicine – as a culture and as a profession – to define and regulate social behavior. This issue was introduced into sociology 50 years ago by Talcott Parsons (1951) who suggested that medicine was a social institution that regulated the kind of deviance for which the individual was not held morally responsible and for which a medical diagnosis could be found. The agent of social control was the medical profession, an institutionalized structure in society that had been given the mandate to restore the health of the sick so that they could resume their expected role obligations. Inherent in this view of medicine was the functionalist perspective on the workings of society: the basic function of medicine was to maintain the established division of labor, a state that guaranteed the optimum working of society. For 20 years, the Parsonian interpretation of how medicine worked – including sick-role theory and the theory of the profession of medicine – dominated the bourgeoning field of medical sociology.

The principal challenge of the altruistic and consensus theory of the power of the medical profession was launched by Eliot Freidson (1970) in his incisive analysis of the medical profession and its desire to retain control over medical knowledge to maintain its autonomy. Freidson's monopolization thesis – the argument that the medical profession protects its own source of knowledge in order to retain its professional autonomy – sparked a debate and a started a new phase

Gender Perspectives on Health and Medicine: Key Themes
Advances in Gender Research, Volume 7, 59–87
Copyright © 2003 by Elsevier Ltd.
All rights of reproduction in any form reserved
ISSN: 1529-2126/doi:10.1016/S1529-2126(03)07003-6

in the sociology of professions in the early 1970s. Freidson's monopolization thesis more narrowly addressed the same issues of social control, norms, and deviance as the later medicalization thesis, but within the framework of the autonomy and internal division of labor of the medical profession. The defense of the profession's traditional autonomy and more lately the profession's internal division of labor – the emergence of a knowledge and administrative elite – were all mechanisms whereby the profession maintained its knowledge monopoly and thereby its professional power (Freidson, 1984, 1985). The latter argument – called the restratification-thesis – is that the medical profession has diversified in order to stay united and powerful vis-à-vis subordinate health professions and the patients. While intriguing and revitalizing the field of the sociology of professions for the next 20 years, Freidson's theses proved to be hard to operationalize and to use in empirical research. The application of the theses in comparative studies failed to point to a universal trend in how the power of the medical profession was developing (e.g. Hafferty & McKinlay, 1993; Johnson et al., 1995).

By contrast, the concept of medicalization proved to be fruitful in empirical research and in comparative studies. The medicalization thesis addressed the increased moral power of medicine, a trend perceived as universal in western, increasingly secularized societies. It also addressed the larger division of labor in health care, in which the patient/consumer was seen as a health worker with his or her own knowledge and competencies to integrate or resist the medical paradigm in his or her own medical thinking and health behavior.

When Irving Zola (1972) introduced the notion of medicine as an institution of social control, it was not therefore a totally new way of thinking. The medicalization thesis addresses the normative and control function of medicine, a notion central to Parsons's and Freidson's view of medicine. What was new was the challenge that medicine was delegated a task and power that extended its original mandate. Zola did not see this process as an imperialistic act of the medical profession alone but rather, as he phrased it, "an insidious and often undramatic phenomenon accomplished by 'medicalizing' much of daily living, by making medicine and the labels 'healthy' and 'ill' relevant to an ever increasing part of human existence" (Zola, 1972, p. 487). The reason for the so-called "medicalizing of society process" was, according to Zola (1972, pp. 487–496), the increasingly complex technological and bureaucratic system that fed a reliance on the expert. Even in this sense the involvement of medical expertise in the management of society was hardly novel, since public health, preventive medicine, and psychiatry had been given a built-in social emphasis and a task of regulating human behavior (Zola, 1972, p. 488).

The phrase "the medicalizing of society," used by Zola (1972), later became known as the medicalization thesis. The vulgar version of this thesis has tended to identify the medical profession as a promoter of medical imperialism and the patient as the victim of medicine's professional and economic desire to retain professional control over phenomena related to health. Unlike Freidson (1985), Zola does not speculate about any ongoing threats to the autonomy and unity of the medical profession. He takes for granted that the ideology or belief system of the medical profession is so strong that this fact alone will maintain the profession as united and powerful. For Zola, the medicalization process seemed more propelled by a cultural climate that looks for technical solutions to essentially social problems than merely the product of the desire of the medical profession to extend its professional domain. In Zola's analysis, medicalization is a tendency of society to reduce a social problem to an individual one and find a technical – in other words, a medical – solution at the individual level. Zola puts it: "By locating the source and the treatment of problems in an individual, other levels of intervention are effectively closed" (Zola, 1972, p. 500). For those familiar with C. Wright Mills's (1959) analysis of society, the process that Zola refers to is, in the words of Mills, the tendency to turn a public issue into a private problem.

The medicalization thesis was developed further by Zola's students, among whom Peter Conrad has been its most ardent examiner and interpreter. According to Conrad (1992, p. 209), medicalization denotes a process in which nonmedical problems come to be defined and treated as medical problems, usually as illnesses or disorders."Medicalization consists of defining a problem in medical terms, using medical language to describe a problem, adopting a medical framework to understand a problem, or using a medical intervention to 'treat it' " (Conrad, 1992, p. 211, 2000, p. 322).

The Inherent Paradox of the Medical Thinking Giving Rise to Medicalization

The medicalization thesis has highlighted two different ongoing shifts in medical thinking and treatment in biomedicine: a trend toward behavioral medicine and toward high-tech medicine. Behavioral medicine has focused on the behavioral components of illness and how cultural and psychological factors influence certain kinds of behavior detrimental or beneficial to a person's health. This field of medicine has its roots in the risk-factor approach, especially as related to coronary heart disease. As Aronowitz (1998, p. 122) has suggested, when mortality and morbidity from acute infectious diseases declined, the rates of chronic diseases began to increase. This "epidemiological transition" changed the medical thinking and prognosis about diseases and shifted the focus to specific and preventable individual risk factors. But as Aronowitz (1998, p. 138) indicates, other issues were tacitly involved:

> Risk factors thus gave scientfic backing for timeless and appealing notions that link individual choice and responsibility with health and disease.

Health psychology, stress research, health promotion have been new approaches to understand and influence individual behavior related to health. The behavioral and psychosocial factors became the new aspects of health and illness, aspects that had not previously been seen as part of the jurisdiction of medicine. As Zola (1972, p. 493) suggested in his pioneering essay, medicalization was been propelled by a change of the etiological thinking from a specific etiology to a multi-causal one, and one which suggests that it is necessary to intervene to change the habits of a patient's lifetime. Preventive medicine became an essential part of this new medical thinking. Conrad has called this aspect "healthicization," a trend characterized by the advancement of behavioral and social definitions for previously biomedically defined events – e.g. heart disease (Conrad, 1992, p. 223). While medicalization denotes a process whereby the moral turns into the medical, healthicization connotes a process whereby health turns into the moral – e.g. a healthy lifestyle. In his analysis of the rise of the risk-factor approach to chronic disease, Aronowitz (1998, p. 178) draws attention to the increasingly concealed moral content of this kind of epidemiological thinking.

> Increasingly, we believe or act as if any relationships between etiologic theories and the ideal moral order is merely coincidental fallout from truth-seeking medical research, rather than the congruence of similar belief systems.

Healthy lifestyle thinking has been represented by a larger cultural trend in society which Crawford (1980) has called "healthism." This concern with personal health and self-care endeavors is a lay effort to improve personal health. Crawford interprets such efforts within a larger sociopolitical system that does not initiate larger political changes that would influence health. In addition to this power perspective, there is the neoliberal interpretation promoted by those sociologists who perceive self-identity as tied to a "reflexive project of the self" and part of the emergence of a post-traditional social order (e.g. Giddens, 1991). Reflexive modernity provides the context for a lifestyle discourse of the self and self-help, and the culture of healthism becomes part of exploring and constructing the self.

High-tech medicine was previously connected with its technology, especially in the area of childbirth – e.g. fetal monitoring. Since the 1990s, genetic medicine and the genetic paradigm have represented high-tech medicine par excellance. The recent emphasis on genes as the primary explanation for major life-threatening diseases has also been called "genomania" (Hubbard, 1995), and is characterized by an overly optimistic belief in genes as the cause for illnesses and behaviors. Its vulgar form of medical thinking promotes genetic essentialism: illness and behaviors are assumed to be predetermined by the kind of genes a person is a carrier of (Rothman, 1998).

Conrad (1999) has argued that the genetic paradigm is not very different from the old germ-theory model because both rest on a reductionist medical thinking. The two paradigms are based on three interrelated assumptions: the doctrine of specific etiology, a focus on causes internal to the body rather than the external environment, and the metaphor of the body as a machine. What is new with the genetic paradigm is that it extends its gaze to behaviors previously considered to reside outside of the explanatory power of biomedicine. Such phenomena are behaviors that are expressed as alcoholism, obesity, mental illness, and homosexuality. As Conrad (1997, 2000) has shown, American and British media have touted that these behaviors reside in a certain identifiable gene. The explicit or tacit implication of defining these phenomena as genetically based is that medical research on these genes is called for, rather than social interventions.

The genetic discourse decontextualizes behavior from all institutionalized conditions influencing and constraining the behavior of individuals. In the genetic discourse, the social environment gets a secondary if not a totally irrelevant place in the explanation of individual behavior, including symptoms and illness. The genetic thinking, therefore, strengthens the societal trend focusing on the individual and placing the responsibility on the individual for his or her health and illness. This focus on the individual devalues the need for a social and health policy that would improve the material life circumstances of the individual and thereby his or her health. As several British studies have recently indicated, material conditions, far more than any other factors, determine the health status of an individual and thus constitute a major factor in explaining existing inequalities in the health of different population groups (Blaxter, 1990). In general, the preference for genetic explanation of behaviors, which sociologists have traditionally seen as residing in the social environment and in the structural inequality of society, has a certain cultural resonance today in most western societies. Policy makers are trying to grapple with increased public expenses because of the consequence of structural unemployment and of an aging population.

Perhaps the conflicting message of these two parallel developments in medical thinking – behavioral medicine and high-tech medicine – has all along been the underlying tension that has provided the momentum for the debate and interest in sorting out the implications for the individual. Both trends propose the expansion of medicine to explain certain behavior: one by introducing a multi-causal explanation, and the other by offering a mono-causal one. Paradoxically, both approaches are assumed to strengthen the discourse and power of medicine beyond its original mandate. The common denominator for the two trends is the risk-factor approach. There is an inherent paradox, as Aronowitz (1998, p. 112) has eminently shown, in the risk-factor approach in medicine. On the one hand, this approach is an attempt to shift the focus from a mono-causal and narrow explanation of diseases by adopting a multi-causal and interdisciplinary approach. On the other hand, risk factors, as the major explanatory model for chronic diseases, have been reified into specific mechanisms, quantifiable and measurable and also to be acted upon. This reification of risk factors, as a by product of the risk-factor approach, has resulted in a reductionist medical thinking.

In conclusion, the concept of medicalization has had a powerful populist appeal and become a useful concept in both public and sociological discourse. While the previously mentioned monopolization thesis, proposed by Freidson (1970), changed the research direction and revitalized the academic world of the sociology of professions, the medicalization thesis opened the academic world to the public. This thesis invited the public critically to analyze the path of medicine as a culture and profession and to evaluate whether in the end the trend implied good care. It is in this sense that this thesis has been connected to and been used as an analytical framework by a consumer movement in health care, a movement that also traces its roots to the early 1970s.

Over the past 30 years, the medicalization thesis has not only been a way of addressing the way that society interprets and reacts to social norms and deviance but also to the kind of power given certain social agents to maintain social order. At its inception, the medicalization thesis was launched as a gender-neutral analytical tool to analyze the character and power of modern medicine; but it soon was applied in a gendered way.

This chapter examines the medicalization thesis in terms of the different aspects of gender it has contained over the past 30 years. The chapter shows that, in terms of gender, the medicalization debate can be divided into three phases. In the first phase in the 1970s, the medicalization thesis was used in a gender-neutral way. In the second phase, feminists argued that existing medical knowledge and the male-dominated medical profession medicalized women's health. During this phase women were portrayed as the victims of medicine, a phase that in the 1990s evolved into a more active involvement of women in defining their own health, including their capacity to "medicalize" symptoms previously not recognized as medical – e.g. chronic fatigue syndrome. The third phase is characterized by a reductionist medical thinking spurred by the new genetic discourse, by means of which a number of "deviant" behaviors have come to be seen as genetically based and to be placed under the purview of the medical profession. This cultural climate has now also defined a number of aspects of men's health in the domain of medicalization. The chapter shows how in the 21st century the issues of men's reproductive health, have like women's earlier, been medicalized. The chapter concludes with the observation that the medicalization of men's health might finally unravel the gendered character of the medicalization debate. The concluding section of the chapter addresses the question of what the full gendering of medicalization implies for theorizing and action on gender and health.

THE FIRST PHASE: GENDER NEUTRALITY

The thesis about medicine's tendency to have a social and cultural power that extends its original medical mandate – a phenomenon called medicalization – was not merely an internal discussion among sociologists as the introduction of this chapter might suggest. Instead the concept captured the issues of a broader cultural and political debate about the character of twentieth-century biomedicine. This critique emerged in the early 1970s in an originally ideologically fragmented consumer movement with a populist core as a common denominator. One strand was a broad consumer movement in health care that, for example, criticized the pharmaceutical industry for its profits and the medical profession as its subservient ally (Seaman, 1969). Another was a radical and often marxist critique that pointed to the existence of a corporate layer of interest groups together forming the medical industrial complex (Navarro, 1976). A third cultural strand suggested that medicine was a cultural system actually more harmful than good for your health (Illich, 1976), and one serving mainly as a mechanism of social control (Ehrenreich, 1978; Zola, 1972). The social-control perspective eventually developed into the distinctly sociological argument of the medicalization thesis (Zola, 1972). Its theoretical predecessors in the 1950s and 1960s had been the anti-psychiatry movement and the labeling theory of deviance. Yet in the beginning, from its inception to its first empirical applications, the medicalization thesis was gender neutral. During the first phase, Illich's (1976) book *Medical Nemesis* was widely cited by sociologists and used to point to the harmful effect of medicine and to the health-care consumer's loss of autonomy. Nevertheless, the book did not contain a gender agenda. Similarly, a number of studies pointed to the medicalization of deviance: For example, Conrad (1975) studied the medicalization of hyperactive children, and Schneider (1978) examined the redefinition of alcoholism as a disease. Furthermore, Conrad and Schneider (1980) reviewed the topic of medicalization of deviance in a book – *Deviance and Medicalization: From Badness to Sickness* – which provided an analytical model for the process of medicalization. This five-stage sequential model came to have a significant impact on the research in the field.

THE SECOND PHASE: WOMEN AS VICTIMS AND ACTORS OF MEDICALIZATION

Feminists were the first to add a gender-sensitive component to the medicalization thesis, in the mid-1970s. Feminist scholars began to unravel the history of modern medicine and suggested that "professionalism in medicine is nothing more than the institutionalization of a male upper class monopoly" (e.g. Ehrenreich & English, 1973, p. 42). A number of studies suggested that the traditional role of women as lay healers was in the 19th century supplanted by a new scientific knowledge promoted by a cadre of male physicians, establishing themselves as the profession of scientific medicine (e.g. Ehrenreich & English, 1973; Walsh, 1977). The radical feminist critique of medicine described women as victims of this new scientific medicine (Ehrenreich & English, 1978). A typical example of this way of conceptualizing medicine was expressed in a review of the 1970s' literature on women and health: "Women, it would seem, have always been uninformed, misinformed, and therefore willing and docile guinea pigs for mass experimentation with a variety of chemical agents, contraceptives devices, and surgical and psychotherapeutic techniques" (Sandelowski, 1981, p. 139).

Scientific medicine was seen as abstract male knowledge, a biased and sexist knowledge perceived as having little in common with women's own and experiential knowledge of their bodies. In a review, Sandelowski (1981, p. 139) suggests: "Women have begun to publicly share their experiences as victims and unwitting accomplieces of a frequently hostile, paternalistic, and contemptuous male-defined medical system that purports to have the best interests of women in a priority position." Books like Gena Corea's (1977) *The Hidden Malpractice: How American Medicine Mistreats Women* provided ample, concrete examples on the anti-female bias of American medicine and its experimentation on women's reproductive health in the name of science: childbirth, birth control, mental health, breast cancer, hysterectomy. As the cover of the paperback version warns: "Any woman who assumes her doctor has her best interest at heart had better read this book." The victimization model was further popularized in Barbara Seaman's (1975) quest for an exclusion of male medical students from obstetrics and gynecology. As she stated: "Effective immediately, only women shall be admitted to obstetrics and gynecology residencies. Males who are currently in training may remain, as may those who are in practice" (Seaman, 1975, p. 45).

There was a common assumption shared by the various branches of the women's movement that women's health had been medicalized in the past, and that gender-biased medical knowledge and diagnoses and treatments decided by biased male physicians had resulted in the overtreatment of women documented in high surgery rates for hysterectomies and mastectomies, and overuse of drugs, especially psychotropics. A more optimistic view on women and medicine was voiced by liberal feminists. Liberal feminists demanded more women doctors and more medical information for women so that the previous gender-biased care and medical knowledge would be a matter of the past (e.g. Fee, 1977).

The view of the medicalization of women's health has been carried over to the ongoing debate since the 1990s on the merits and pitfalls of hormone replacement therapy in dealing with the medical risks of menopause, and similarly of mammography in the prevention of breast cancer. For example, the biomedical view of menopause tends to portray it as a hormone deficiency (disease) that is a significant risk factor for heart disease, osteoporosis, and Alzheimer's. This view of menopause has been criticized for not being medically valid and for not emphasizing that nonhormonal factors, like diet and exercise, have a far greater impact on women's health and longevity (Lorber, 1997; Meyer, 2001). On these issues feminists still seem to be divided: liberal feminists tend to view women's access to preventive services in the area of reproductive health as an equal-rights issue, while radical feminists tend to interpret preventive measures as a form of medical surveillance and part of a larger social control of women in a society guided by the interest of men and of the profit motive of corporate medicine.

A glance back at the women's health movement of the 1970s shows that it started by a cultural redefinition of women's health (Fee, 1977; Ruzek, 1978): women would emanicipate themselves from victimization by medicine and become actors who would promote their gender-specific health needs and health services. To advance this change, the cultural hegemony of male-dominated medicine had to be addressed in order to halt a further medicalization of women's health. First, with woman's body having been viewed as pathological and medicalized, feminists demanded a redefinition of it as *healthy*. Research began to document that woman's body had been pathologized because the male body was seen as the gender-neutral norm. This was the argument of feminist critics who looked at medical knowledge and medical textbooks: they suggested that the universal man was indeed a male. American feminist scholars showed, for example, that the information on female sexuality in standard medical textbooks from 1943 to 1972 reflected more values underlying traditional sex-role stereotypes than were informed by the findings of the studies on female and male sexuality conducted by Kinsey and Masters and Johnson (Scully & Bart, 1973). The argument the critics presented was that medical knowledge was gender biased and often took the male body or mind as the standard of "human health." Chesler (1972, pp. 67–69) noted in her pioneering book *Women and Madness*, which reviewed theories on mental health, that "only men can be mentally healthy" because "the ethic of mental health is masculine in our culture."

Out of this need to redefine woman's body emerged an academic interest in knowing more about women's health. Men's health as the norm was further confirmed by research using samples of men only, although the results were generalized to hold for both genders. This started the feminist empiricist approach to women's health in the 1980s.

An underlying assumption of the empiricist approach was that the new knowledge about women's health and illnesses would patch up the previous biased medical knowledge based on samples of men only. Many believed that if the new knowledge on women was added to the previous medical knowledge, medicine would be a more objective science. As Annandale and Hunt (2000) have shown, there have been several phases in this empirical research tradition in examining gender inequalities in health, and the American and British research have used different theoretical frameworks for approaching and examining the topic (Annandale & Hunt, 2000, p. 11). American research has been focused on "role occupancy" and "multiple role occupancy" (e.g. Waldron et al., 1998), especially in women-only studies, while European studies have focused on socio-economic factors and tried to find new indicators that would measure women's social position in the labor market better than would the indicators tailored for men (e.g. Arber, 1997; Roberts, 1991).

Second, the feminists pointed to the need to *demystify* women's bodies. Women had to learn about their own body and its normal functions so that they would know their health needs and be able to make rational decisions related to their health care. A concrete effort of the women's health advocates was the compilation of a woman-centered medical knowledge source entitled *Our Bodies, Ourselves* (Boston Women's Health Collective, 1973), which today is a classic in the self-help literature. The demand for medical information directed to women created women as health-care consumers who now could demand that there be available on the health care market a variety of services catering to women's specific needs. This endeavor had a distinctly middle-class character. Underlying the endeavor was a notion of a middle-class consumer with purchasing power and a belief that the market was the right location for offering the best service to women. Poor women without purchasing power got less attention and political support for the provision of family planning and health care services in the public sector. Rather than demedicalizing women's health needs, as the feminist health advocates originally had envisioned, the middle-class character of the movement resulted in a confirmation of the trend towards medicalization.

Riessman (1992, originally in 1983) was the first to point out the complexity of middle-class women's relation to medicine and to the medicalization of their health. She argues that women have simultaneously gained and lost with the medicalization of their life problems. Women were not always passive victims but, as Riessman (1992, p. 140) suggests, both physicians and women have contributed to the redefinitions of women's experience into medical categories. The common concern was based in specific class interests: medicalization rested in the mutual interest that physicians and women from the upper and middle classes have had in redefining certain human events and putting them into medical categories. The physicians' interest was material but also congruent with the world view of medicine. For women, medicine helped overcome their lack of control caused by a biological view of their body. Medicalization offered women an opportunity to gain more control over their body and to promote a view that resisted the assumption that biology – for example childbirth – was their destiny. Riessman (1992, p.129) points to the contradiction that this strategy has implied for women, because women have not generally been able to control the medical intervention. Hence, women continued to be subordinated by the medical profession although the new intervention or medical category was supposed to empower and provide them with a sense of personal control of their body.

Riessman uses historical material to prove her argument, but more recent claims by women point to the same strategy. Today a number of new symptoms have been raised by women's groups as medically valid. Women are now making claims for the "medicalization" of symptoms that medicine in the past has viewed as having a psychosocial etiology – for example, recognizing of the chronic fatigue syndrome as a physical and medically valid illness (Broom & Woodward, 1996; Richman & Jason, 2001). Similarly, Oinas (1998) has suggested that teenage girls prefer to turn to medical sources for information about sexuality and to get medical definitions of "normal" menstruation from a medical column in a youth magazine rather than turn to their mother or peers.The medicalized information was perceived by the young women as gender neutral, over against the perceived normative content of peer-group information.

The foregoing studies exemplify the empowering character of medicalization, suggested by Riessman, as opposed to repressive medicalization, which makes women the victims of medicine. The empowering aspects of medicalization have been further enhanced by access to a new technology: the Internet. Internet is a source of knowledge about health and it encourages an active and pluralistic approach to health (Hardey, 1999). The Internet has become a new forum for knowledge production and organization around women's health needs. Women are now actors in the search for medical knowledge about their bodies and treatments. They can scan the Internet for health information and establish chat groups to get and share information about their symptoms and illness. On the Internet, alternative medicine has the same status as scientific medicine in the "real" society. Information technology offers women a way of finding and sorting out medical knowledge, a process that can be characterized as "negotiating medical discourses"

(Pitts, 2002). Women can as "virtual selves" or "virtual communities" assemble their experiential knowledge and/or cyber medical knowledge in the form of a web page, easily accessible to other women. This strategy does not promote women as collective or political actors in traditional social-movement terms. Nevertheless, they can feel that they have power in their capacity as consumers. For example, a study of a Breast Cancer list showed that the on-line discussion group provided its members "cyber-support" and a sense of empowerment (Sharf, 1997).

It would therefore be wrong to draw the conclusion that the women's health movement is "dead" because women as a collective are not publicly criticizing organized medicine. The concealed character of the movement is illustrated by Ruzek and Becker's study of Internet sources. In their own surfing of U.S. websites, Ruzek and Becker (1999, p. 8) found 223 national women's health organizations serving as women's health advocates, a number incidentally almost the same as the one Ruzek (1978) found when examining the openly organized women's health groups at the peak of the women's health movement in 1975.

The recent strategies suggest that the issue of women's health has been transformed from a collective endeavor and collective identity into an individual strategy. While women's health was raised as a public issue by the women's health movement 30 years ago, it is currently perceived as a private issue. Women's self-help activism has been transformed to fit the age of information technology. The current web-page strategy is an accommodation to the valorization of self-reliance and technology in the 21st century. An individual strategy is more concealed, but it could also be argued that the individual strategy is more subversive since it is fragmented.

The empowering force of the "democratization" of access to medical knowledge was already envisioned in the mid-1970s by Marie Haug (1975, p. 211). She suggested that access to medical information through Medline and other new (pre-Internet age) computerized data sources would not only demystify medical knowledge previously monopolized by physicians but also serve as guides of action for women and the public for understanding their own health needs. Haug presumed that open access to medical knowledge would "deprofessionalize" the medical profession, because it could no longer maintain its knowledge monopoly. As she argued (Haug, 1975, p. 211):

> Professions are rapidly losing their control over their knowledge domain as a result of inroads from computerization, new occupations in the division of labor, and increasing public and client sophistication. As a result, their autonomy is challenged and demands for accountability and client rights are on the rise.

Internet access to medical knowledge has proved, however, that it is not medical knowledge per se, as assumed by Freidson (1970), that is the key to the medical profession's unique power. The power seems much more to reside in the monopoly that physicians still have to the "means of production" of medicine: entry to the hospital and access to prescribed drugs.

THE THIRD PHASE: A REVIVAL OF REDUCTIONISM

Medical knowledge pertinent to men's health has, at least implicitly, been assumed to be based on "objective" medical knowledge because the prototype for knowledge production about the human body has been man's body. Nevertheless, several scholars of gender have suggested that the notion of the universal man has tended to render the gendered man invisible (Hearn, 1998; Lunbeck, 1998; Potts, 2000) and resulted in the failure to problematize gender in the study of men's health (Annandale & Hunt, 2000, p. 4; Courtenay, 2000, p. 1387; Doyal, 2001, p. 1062; Sabo & Gordon, 1995). This lack of problematization of men's gender is also reflected in the first and second phase of the medicalization debate: there is almost no research on societal tendencies to medicalize men's health concerns. In the popular and scientific debate in the 1970s and 1980s, there was little concern over the commodification or ideologies revolving around men's health. Only by means of discursive reading of work published in the 1970s and 1980s can one identify the implicit male gendering of the medicalization thesis. For example, a large part of Conrad's (1975) early research deals with hyperactive children, a majority of whom are boys. Hyperactivity, likewise alcoholism and heart disease, are not gender-neutral symptoms – they have been related predominantly to persons of male gender.

Riessman (1992) raises an important point when she notes that women's life experiences have been medicalized more than men's. Medicalization has resulted, Riessman argues, in the construction of medical meanings of normal functions in women, while routine experiences uniquely male have not tended to be cast under the purview of medical science and treated by physicians as pathological. This point is given further evidence by scholars who have drawn attention to the medicalization of menopause. They argue that a medicalization of menopause has resulted in different and unequal approaches to disease prevention for men and women. Chronic diseases in women are attributed to "failed ovaries" and "hormone deficiency," which put women at risk, while lifestyle and physiological processes associated with aging are presented as the primary risks for men (Lorber, 1997; Meyer, 2001, p. 778).

Recently a need to look at men's coronary heart disease from a gender-sensitive perspective has been raised. Although most research on coronary heart disease (CHD) has been done on men, it has been argued that the approach has been gender neutral, resulting in knowledge that does not consider masculinity a risk factor in men's behavior, nor their lack of knowledge of important preventive factors related to CHD (White & Lockyer, 2001). Nevertheless, masculinity was raised as a risk factor in the early research on coronary heart disease.

Medicalizing Masculinity

In order to understand the early medical thinking about men's health, it is important to go back to the first challenge to the conceptualization of men's health in modern medicine: the factors that were viewed to cause coronary heart disease. The preventive approach of the 1950s, which addressed the risk factors for men's developing coronary heart disease, was an attempt within medicine itself to expand the medical framework in order to gain a broader understanding of men's health. If we look at medicine itself, this approach represented totally new medical thinking in the mid-1950s, when the etiology of men's major illness – coronary heart disease – was attributed to emotional factors (Friedman & Rosenman, 1974). The early risk factors were fat and smoking, but these were not seen as the real dangers by the American cardiologist pair Friedman and Rosenman (1959), who launched a theory about the impact of certain negative emotions on men's health. Men were then not to be viewed as merely biological beings, without taking notice of an important psychosocial component that explained their health.

There was little or no opposition among men to the new medical discourse on Type A or more precisely, Type A behavioral pattern (TABP), which valorized psychosocial factors as the major risk factors in the high prevalence of heart disease in men. The subsequent psychological discourse on the coronary-prone "Type A personality" became an important analytical framework as well as a diagnostic category for understanding American men's health in the era after World War II (Aronowitz, 1998; Riska, 2000). The relentless striving of the small entrepreneur became in the eyes of medicine a major risk factor for coronary heart disease. The "blind pursuit of a marketplace masculinity" (Kimmel, 1997, p. 266) was now cast as a major health hazard for middle-class men. Type A man – a hard-working male breadwinner – was constructed by the medicalization of the moral aspects of heterosexual masculinity. The psychosocial component of the Type A man – the Type A personality – can, however, be understood within the framework of the institutional dilemmas faced by middle-class, mostly white men in the prevailing economic and gender order. Instead of addressing those institutional dilemmas, the cultural component – men's masculinity – was medicalized. As Kimmel (1997, p. 265) has noted: "In the 1960s the relentless striving and competition that had defined the Self-Made Man and the fears and anxieties that accompanied him were cast as the problem, not the cure. Self-making was now characterized as a disease, the Type A personality."

By the mid-1980s, Type A personality had lost its relevance as a risk factor for CHD in medical discourse because in the late 1970s its empirical verification showed more negative than positive results. Nevertheless, the concept has had a deep resonance in cultural values and stereotypes in American society (Aronowitz, 1998, p. 149). The concept of Type A has continued to live in popular medical lore and public discourse in everyday language about the kind of aggressive and competitive behavior that is detrimental to your health. The notion of "Type A" has maintained its gendered content but it has been used in public discourse as a gender-neutral indicator of the kind of behavior that will result in burnout and stress, and in health problems in the long run.

Stress researchers embarked on a new research topic related to personality and health in the late 1970s, when the concept of hardiness was introduced (Kobasa, 1979). Hardiness was constructed by combining three personality features: commitment, challenge, and control. A hardy person was committed to his work, experienced change as a challenge rather than as a threat, and perceived himself to have control over his life. The studies done to test the hypotheses on how the hardy remained healthy despite stress were all done on male executives who in addition fullfilled the criteria of being Protestant, white, and married (e.g. Kobasa, 1979, p. 5). Hardiness was shown to be a personality predisposition to withstand stress and to maintain the traditional qualities associated with white middle-class masculinity. The concept of the hardy man demedicalized the traditional traits of masculinity: a hardy man could work hard and still be healthy. Here demedicalization refers to a behavioral aspect of health – traditional masculinity – that no longer retained its medical definition (Conrad, 1992, p. 224).

In conclusion, there is a genre of research within health psychology and behavioral medicine that has examined the relationship between personality types and health. In principle these personality theories have been launched as gender-neutral theories. Nevertheless, the empirical studies of the kind of personality assumed to be detrimental to health have been conducted on samples of men only, a circumstance that has gendered these theories. The researchers did not consciously intend to promote a gendered theory about men's health. The original theory on Type A personality pointed indirectly to traditional masculinity as a risk factor, but later theory on hardiness pointed to masculinity as a health-protective factor. While the theory on the Type A personality medicalized masculinity and made it a medical risk factor for developing coronary heart disease, hardiness was a quality among "hardy men," a personal competency that demedicalized the assumed impact of traditional masculinity on men's health (Riska, 2002).

Men as Victims

With the rise of the men's movement in the 1970s in the U.S. came also a general thinking about men as victims in the gender system.While the traditional white middle-class female sex-role characteristics and the imputed sick role became the target of the women's health movement in the early 1970s (Ruzek, 1978), the traditional white middle-class male sex-role characteristics were medicalized without any opposition from middle-class men in the 1980s. With the rise of men's studies, the lethal character of traditional masculinity was raised as a gender issue and the "health costs" of the traditional male sex role were pointed out (e.g. Courtenay, 2000; Harrison, 1978; Harrison et al., 1989; Helgeson, 1995; Messner, 1997; Sabo & Gordon, 1995; Waldron, 1995).The notion of the "health costs" of traditional masculinity has portrayed men as the victims of a gender system that assigns men the primary economic responsibility. This "burden" of the breadwinner male role and the notion of the "victimized male" (Nonn, 1995) are not viewed through the lens of the economic and social privileges that men have in the prevailing economic and gender system. Instead, this notion of the male victim has been the rallying cry for both a liberal and a rightist men's movement in the U.S. (Kimmel & Kaufman, 1995). The liberal strand has, as Messner (1998, p. 261) has shown, been based on a notion of a "sense of gender symmetry" – a belief that the traditional sex roles hurt both men and women equally: Women are "sex-objects" while men are "success objects" who are trapped in a male mystique. The other strand – the men's rights discourse – has portrayed men as the real victims of the current gender system that has enabled women's liberation. The rightist discourse has focused on the "victimized male" and privileged the resurrection of an essentialist masculine identity – a "deep, essential manhood" – which is seen as an equivalent to a healthy masculinity (Kimmel & Kaufman, 1995, p. 21; Messner, 1998, p. 266; Nonn, 1995, p. 174).

This view of men as victims has been carried over to recent epidemiological thinking. The "men-as-an-endangered-species" hypothesis tends to be a common concern among those public health advocates who have raised the issue of men's health (e.g. Meryn & Jadad, 2001). The "men's health discourse" rests on the assumption, as Schofield et al. (2000, p. 248) have suggested, that "men suffer a health disadvantage that is comparable to, if not greater than women's." Nevertheless, this notion of men as more seriously victimized than women renders invisible the health-promoting aspects of men's privileged position within existing race, class, and gendered hierachies and men's access to and control over valuable resources (Doyal, 2001, p. 1062; Messner, 1998; Schofield et al., 2000). The victimization argument suggests that the life-expectancy of men is influenced by the operative effects of the male mystique: men's own self-destructive and risky behavior to prove their heterosexual male identity. This so-called dark side of masculinity (Brooks, 2001, p. 287) is a leading cause of death among younger men (homicide, driving cars too fast, use of alcohol and drugs).

The victimization model as applied to health care for women and men tacitly or explicitly raises the issue of a gender symmetry. This kind of thinking has as its theoretical roots in sex-role theory and its broader notions of the functional and consensual character of the two sex categories and their institutionalized roles. The men's health crisis is, however, not generalizable to all men. Instead, it is a health disadvantage that is clustered among certain men – men of color, men of low income, rural and inner-city men (Courtenay & Keeling, 2000, p. 244; Schofield et al., 2000, p. 248). The health disadvantage is particularly evident among Afro-American males, whose health and life chances are shaped by current class, race, and gender relations (Schofield et al., 2000, p. 248; Staples, 1995, p. 122). There is still little exploration in the research literature on how social disadvantage and male gender influence men's health. More recently the notion of differences between men have resulted in a valorization of a new concept of gender for men – masculinities – to stress the heterogeneity among men (Connell, 1995). This new perspective, which follows the debate within feminist theory, will provide a fruitful starting point for future gender-informed research on men and health.

Medicalizing Men's Sexuality

Current medical approaches to men's health tend to eradicate the psychological component of men's health and to reintroduce a reductionistic biological thinking. In 21st century medicine, the psychological component of men's health introduced in the 1950s and revitalized in the early 1980s has been abandoned. Men's health is now equated with their sexual fitness, a view that reduces men's functions and health to their reproductive organs. The current medicalization of men's sexuality reduces men's health to a preventive regime of "penile fitness" by means of the new drug Viagra (Bordo, 2000; Marshall & Katz, 2001; Potts, 2000). This message is touted by advertising in newspapers and TV, which has generated a demand for the new product. The new syndrome "erectile dysfunction" suggests that male sexuality is not a matter of men's own will or control, but a "natural" and physical illness, requiring medical intervention. This thinking is characterized by a tendency to "naturalize" men's sexuality and their bodies. This naturalization of men's bodies stands in sharp contrast to the psychologization of men's health in the 1950s and 1960s. Men's bodies, especially men's sexual fitness, are – in as vulgar a way as women's were in the past – interpreted as machines that can be kept fit by means of medical and drug regimens. This is a *viagracization* of men's health: a tendency to reduce men's health to a capacity of their "natural" body. The sexual capacity of their "natural" body is perceived to have been lost or weakened, but it is assumed that this function can be restored by means of a drug regimen. This kind of medical diagnosis of men's ailing/failing bodies is not new – medical treatment of hair loss among men preceded the current drug intervention in men's perceived failing virility.

In short, men's bodies have been naturalized, commodified, and viagracized. The "viagracization" of men's health parallels the medicalization of women's menopause: both notions rest on a reductionist medical thinking that looks on the reproductive organs as the primary risk factor and cause for men's and women's physical and mental health.

Nevertheless, there seems to be little resistance to the medicalization and commodification of men's bodies among men themselves. In fact, in the 1990s and into the new century, the media seem even further to promote men's body image and sexuality. A whole industry has emerged that capitalizes on men's feelings of inadequacy and anxiety about their body image. Some researchers have called this distorted body image of men the "Adonis complex." This distorted image tends to have serious health consequences because men try to trim their bodies and muscles to fit the revered ideal of an overly muscular body. As Pope et al. (2000, pp. 40–45) shows, toy figures from Star Wars, the GI Joe toy, and various other action toys have over the past 20 years changed from slim males to steroid-pumped versions. Furthermore, this trend is reflected in the changes that have taken place in men's views of their own body: while 18% of American men surveyed in 1972 were dissatisfied with their chest and 48% with their weight, in 1997 the comparable figures were 38 and 51% respectively (Pope et al., 2000, p. 28). What the figures are telling is that men's views about their ideal weight have stayed almost the same while the norm of a muscular torso seems to haunt men twice as often today as it did 20 years ago. But why has there not emerged a men's health movement that would resist the seemingly stereotypical muscular image of the "normal" male body?

Is There a Men's Health Movement in Sight?

It has been suggested that it is hard to sell men the idea that they are endangered and victimized because few men are appealed to by a universalizing claim that men are frail and weak (Courtenay & Keeling, 2000, p. 243). This kind of appeal was more successful when directed to women in the 1970s. The women's health movement criticized the contemporary gender portrayal of women's being passive and weak as part of their "nature," although at issue was women's subordination to a male culture and male-dominated medical enterprise. In contrast to white middle-class women of the 1970s who resisted the medicalization of their health, on the surface it looks as if middle-class men still seem to have a deep faith in medical science. Or is this a too simplistic interpretation? Should men's reluctance to see a doctors for a check-up or to see a psychologist when experiencing psychiatric symptoms be interpreted as men's silent resistance to scientific medicine? Men's lower rate of using health services could be interpreted as men's tacit resistance of medicalization and reluctance to embrace the doctrines of scientific medicine about their health needs. Over the past 30 years, health researchers and health promoters in most western countries have documented that men use health services less than women do, and it has been argued that men *underutilize* such health services. In the 1970s, feminists criticized women's high use of health care and suggested that this was a sign of overutilization prompted by a male-dominated medical profession and the drug industry, which together constructed women's presumed need for services by medicalizing "normal" symptoms and life events. Meanwhile, women have been used by public health advocates as the statistical norm for a "proper" use of health services: men's "underutilization" has been constructed on the basis of women's health services, with their use serving as the norm.

If men's "underutilization" of primary and preventive health services is an indicator of men's silent resistance to biomedicine, what kind of measures would be needed to mobilize men to promote their "own" health needs more overtly? In the foregoing description of women's health movement of the 1970s, it was pointed out that this movement started with a cultural redefinition of women's health: women's health had to be redefined and demystified in order for women themselves to gain more control over their bodies and to be aware of their "own" health needs. If the two strategies of the women's health movement were to be used as strategies for starting a men's health movement, what would these two strategies entail?

First, the *redefinition* of men's health would imply that men's health would be removed from the domain of a "natural phenomenon" and placed in the domain of the social. The naturalization of men's health has made invisible the cultural and social component of men's health. The cultural component is the way that the masculine mystique shapes men's health and life chances, especially for some groups of men. While the early women's movement rested on a homogeneous notion of femininity and women's common interest, the 1990s witnessed the realization that there is diversity and femininities. Similarly, men's studies have emphasized the need to look for masculinities in order to make visible the hierarchies of super- and subordination by class and race among men (Connell, 1995; Kimmel, 2000). The emphasis on masculinities even further addresses the false notion of the universal man, a homogeneous representation that has made invisible the diversity among men. The notion of masculinites highlights the social component of men's health and deconstructs the notion of a universal man. The recognition of the social component prompts a need to locate men's health in a wider system of class, race, and gender relations and to look at how existing masculinities are shaped by these relations (see Schofield et al., 2000). A gender-informed approach is the focus of men's health studies. Sabo (2000) suggests that a distinction has to be made between men's health and men's health studies. The former he sees as focusing "almost totally on men's bodies, organismic functions, and physical vitality or susceptibility to illness." In contrast, the latter he defines as the "systematic analysis of men's health and illness that takes gender and gender health equity into theoretical account" (Sabo, 2000, p. 133).

Second, the *demystification* of men's health would imply that men recognize that their body responds with the same repertoire of symptoms that have been connected with the female body. Traditional masculinity has been perceived as a resource in fighting disease, as the war metaphor indicates. Stoicism, expressed as a notion that a "real man" is never ill or that he does not experience physical or emotional pain (e.g. Bendelow, 1993; Courtenay, 2000), has been shown to result in the denial of early symptoms of chronic illnesses that could be prevented if recognized. The male mystique serves as a cultural barrier and prevents many men from being receptive to gender-neutral health-promotion information, because such information is perceived as addressing the health needs of women and children. As Courtenay (2000, p. 1389) points out, men are in fact constructing gender by dismissing their health needs because masculinities are defined against positive health behaviors and beliefs. Health-defying behavior serves, as Courtenay (2000, p. 1390) suggests, both as a proof of men's superiority over women and as a proof of their ranking among "real" men. The valorization of independency of both the physical and mental self is linked to men's sense of power and control. As Charmaz (1995) has suggested, chronic illness can relegate a man to a position of "marginalization" and it also puts a man in a situation of being dependent upon others, usually a wife. The dependency relationship threatens traditional notions of masculinity and masculine identity.

For most men, health still means physical fitness – a muscular torso and sexual virility. The concern over men's health disadvantages have been more pushed by mainstream medicine and public health than by a men's grassroots health movement. In the the 21st century, men's health issues have began to be raised within academic medicine. A special issue of the *Journal of American College Health* on men's health calls for more research on men and health from an interdisciplinary perspective (Courtenay & Keeling, 2000). In the fall of 2001 a number of leading mainstream medical journals raised the issue of men's health and the need for a gender-sensitive approach. An editorial in *Lancet* noted that "the notion of there being an area of 'men's health' is less well defined than the female counterpart" (Lancet, 2001, p. 1831). A couple of months later, the *British Medical Journal* published a special issue on men's health. The leading article asks: "Are men the new women?" (Meryn & Jadad, 2001, p. 1013) and another article in the same issue suggests: "Until recently very little attention had been paid to the impact of gender on men's health" (Doyal, 2001, p. 1062).

The passage of the National Men's Health Week Act by the U.S. Congress in 1994 has been a concrete effort created from the top to set up a men's health agenda and to make both men and policy makers aware of men's gender-specific health needs. Nevertheless, mainstream men do not seem to be aware of or to organize around a gender-specific health agenda. By contrast, gay men have organized to promote their health needs both locally and nationally in the U.S. They have adopted the strategies of the women's health advocates and pursued a health agenda based on a civil-rights and policy-of-inclusion discourse. Similarly, the gay health advocacy endeavors have already resulted in a self-help manual entitled *Men like Us: The GMHC Complete Guide to Gay Men's Sexual, Physical, and Emotional Well-Being* (Wolfe, 2000). This manual captures the spirit and approach of the feminist self-help classic of the 1970s, *Our Bodies, Ourselves* (Boston Women's Health Collective, 1973). At the national level, the gay health concerns have been recognized in the process of planning the nation's health agenda for the coming decade.

CONCLUSION

This chapter has examined the medicalization thesis and the different gendered meanings it has contained during its existence over the past thirty years. It goes back to 1972, when Zola (1972) coined the phrase "the medicalizing of society." At this stage, the medicalization thesis was gender neutral and so were its first empirical applications. It could be argued that during the first phase of gender neutrality the medicalization thesis had a hidden gendered content, because the examples mentioned in the research literature were behaviors or symptoms experienced more frequently by one gender. For example, alcoholism and hyperactivity among children are behaviors expressed more often by males than females.

The second phase of the medicalization thesis dates from the mid-1970s, when feminists began to use the term medicalization to illustrate the excess power that medicine had in its definition of women's health and illness. This is the phase most closely connected with the term medicalization. It was mainly feminist health advocates who used the term to criticize the gender-biased treatment of women patients, generally implying an overtreatment or the overly technological approach to women's health. The message of the medicalization thesis appealed to a broader public, who as consumers of health care were confronted with the on-going structural changes in American medicine. These changes were defined later by Starr (1982) as the rise of "corporate medicine." The adverse effects of corporate medicine on costs and treatments began by the late 1980s to be regulated by means of managed-care plans. The larger issues related to the power of medical experts over consumers were pondered by using medicalization as an analytical tool.

A consumer approach has been most clearly represented by the liberal feminists. Liberal feminists identified gender-biased medical knowledge and treatments and demanded more women doctors and more objective information on women's health (Fee, 1977). It was assumed that if women were empowered as consumers, the resulting health care system would offer women more choices and provide less medicalized care.

In the 1990s, claims for a medical specialty in women's health were framed within medicine and a market-based organization of health care. A central claim has been that certain marginalized groups – poor, old, colored, and lesbian women – have not been provided the services that meet their needs in the health care market. The new type of physician – "the woman's health physician" – is envisioned, to "maintain a respectful, collaborative, and consumer-oriented approach, with women as their health care partners" (Johnson & Dawson, 1990, p. 223) and to encourage women patients to "maintain informed responsibility for their own health care choices" (Johnson & Hoffman, 1993, p. 117). The knowledge was to be holistic and interdisciplinary and, as one of the early promoters of a specialty in women's health (Johnson & Dawson, 1990, p. 224) phrased it, "Women's health is being defined as a specific body of knowledge and expertise that permits the comprehensive care of women." This approach is a contemporary version of the liberal feminist perspective on women's health needs, which are envisioned as met within a market-based system of health care and by means of a reform of medicine by forces within medicine.

Radical feminists have suggested that medicine's power over women was a tacit form of patriarchal control of women and that the medicalization of women's health and treatments had to be interpreted as a tool of male power (Ehrenreich & English, 1978). This framework has tended to portray women as victims of medicine.

Critics of the perspective, which interprets women as medicalized victims of the power of medicine, have suggested that it is an illusion that medical care could be totally demedicalized (Lupton, 1997; see also Riessman, 1992). It is argued that the existence of a "pure" nonmedicalized knowledge is hardly possible in western societies. This view has been proposed by representatives of a Foucauldian approach, who suggest that medicine is a disciplinary regime. It is in this sense that self-help, self-care, and psychological theories on self-advancement and increase of self-control in working and private life have been viewed as technologies of the self and perceived as part of a broader disciplinary regime (e.g. Foucault, 1988; Rose, 1999). This Foucauldian interpretation defines women as actors but also as individuals who have internalized the message of self-discipline and self-control inherent in the message of health promotion. It is in this sense that the current IT industry on health can be viewed as a technology of the self: the information is used as a guide for self-management and self-control in matters of health and health behavior. In the information-gathering process women negotiate between diverse medical discourses and construct and find legitimation for their own symptoms and illnesses. The knowledge-seeking process does not have the character of "demedicalization," but rather constitutes an alternative form of "medicalization" and medical control by women themselves. This view suggests that women are no longer victims, because information technology has transformed women to actors.

The third phase of the medicalization thesis and its gendered content began in the early 1990s, but its specific features have become more clearly visible in the 21st century. Genetic medicine reintroduced a reductionist medical thinking, which annexed a number of behaviors and declared them genetically based. The revival of reductionism in medical thinking has a certain cultural resonance in western economies, which are trying to grapple with rising health care costs. Research on genetic risk factors have been seen as a way of controling some chronic disases, like cancer and diabetes.

This cultural climate has influenced the thinking about men's health, which now is interpreted as an expression of their sexual fitness. As this chapter has indicated, during the heydays of the women's health movement, there was hardly any discussion about the commercial exploitation of men's bodies in the name of health. The male body, embodied as the incarnation of the universal man, has concealed the gendered character of men's health.

In the new century, the "naturalization" and commodification of men's bodies have become more overt. The new gender portrayal of men's bodies resembles the distorted image of women's bodies provided in the media and the medical literature in the early 1970s. During the 1980s, political activism among women's health advocates and feminist research on gender images resulted in the revelation of the sexist ideologies underlying the gender portrayal of women in drug advertising, medical textbooks, and the media (Hawkins & Aber, 1988; Prather & Fidell, 1975; Scully & Bart, 1973; Sullivan & O'Connor, 1988).

The current *viagracization* of men's health points to a medicalization of men's sexuality in the same way that women's sexuality and body have been subject of medicine in the past. In both versions, men's and women's reproductive organs are interpreted as constituting the major explanatory factor for their health. The *viagracization* of men's health introduces a reproductive theory of health similar to the *ovarian theory* that has been used to explain women's physical and mental health (e.g. Smith-Rosenberg, 1985, p. 186; Theriot, 1993, p. 24). Both versions of the reproductive health theory reduce the explanation for a person's health status to factors internal to the individual. These factors are biological and related to the individual's biological and reproductive function as a male or female. Health problems come to be interpreted as "hormone deficiency diseases" and treatable with an appropriate drug like Viagra or estrogen.

Nevertheless, it is important not to stretch the search for symmetry too far in mapping the medicalization of women's and men's health. While a victimization model generally is connected with medicalization, it has different implications for men and women. The victimization model generally has sex-role theory as its theoretical foundation. For women, the medicalization thesis has served as a heuristic device pointing to women's traditional role in society as passive and medicine as a cultural system tending to reinforce women's traditional sex role. Feminists pointed to the cultural hegemony of medicine, to the male-domination among physicians, and to the loss of power of women as consumers of health care. The view of medicine as a gendered organization and male-dominated culture has been powerful gender imagery for women, which has shown the institutionalized structure influencing the kind of health care all women tend to receive, especially in the areas of reproductive health and mental health.

The victimization model for men has also pointed to men's traditional sex role. Some have suggested that the traditional male role is a burden and takes its toll on men's health, while others have pointed in general to the "health costs" of traditional masculinity.

This chapter has shown how explanations of men's propensity for developing heart disease medicalized a number of values and behaviors which were crucial parts of middle-class white masculinity in the 1950s and 1960s. For example, "Type A personality" became a risk factor for coronary heart disease among men by constructing a certain kind of aggressive and competitive (male) conduct as a medical risk factor. Later, traditional risk factors for developing CHD – for example, high blood pressure and obesity – became themselves diseases to be treated. The risk-factor approach emerged from a new multi-causal medical thinking that strove to include psychosocial factors into the new epidemiological thinking. The risk-factor approach pointed to specific, quantifiable, and manageable mechanisms and resulted paradoxically in a reductionist medical thinking (Aronowitz, 1998).

The image of men as victims of traditional sex roles has not had as powerful an appeal in the area of men's health as it has had in women's. While the sex-role theory of women's health pointed to health disadvantages for *all* women, the metaphor of men as victims addresses the disadvantage of only certain categories of men. The victimization model tends in fact to conceal men's privileges in the gender hierarchy and the associated health benefits (Schofield et al., 2000, p. 249).

Gender and health is a theme by many still understood as shorthand for "women's health." The current third phase of the medicalization debate, which points to the medicalization of men's sexuality, might finally point to the underlying gendered character of the medicalization thesis during its 30 years' history. The recent medicalization of men's sexuality might be an issue that can result in a broader awareness of the gendered aspects of men's health. This view is becoming increasingly evident as men's health studies are gaining ground (Sabo, 2000), and also as sexual minorities are demanding recognition that their specific health needs and health risks are to be recognized in gender-relevant research (e.g. Wolfe, 2000).

The completed gendering of the medicalization thesis could increase awareness that the power and culture of medicine is not the issue for one gender only. Voices have therefore called for a new approach in research on gender and health: British researchers have called for a gender-comparative approach (Annandale & Hunt, 2000, p. 20), and American researchers a gender-relations approach (Schofield et al., 2000). Both emphasize the incorporation of the gender order and relations between the genders into the research on gender and health.

REFERENCES

Annandale, E., & Hunt, K. (2000). Gender inequalities in health: Research at the crossroads. In: E. Annandale & K. Hunt (Eds), *Gender Inequalities in Health* (pp. 1–35). Buckingham: Open University Press.

Arber, S. (1997). Comparing inequalities in women's and men's health: Britain in the 1990s. *Social Science and Medicine, 44*, 773–787.

Aronowitz, R. A. (1998). *Making sense of illness: Science, society, and disease.* Cambridge: Cambridge University Press.

Bendelow, G. (1993). Pain perceptions, emotions and gender. *Sociology of Health and Illness, 15*, 273–294.

Blaxter, M. (1990). *Health and lifestyles.* London: Routledge.

Bordo, S. (2000). *The male body: A new look at men in public and private.* New York: Farrar, Straus and Giroux.

Boston Women's Health Collective (1973). *Our bodies, ourselves: A book by and for women.* New York: Simon and Schuster.

Brooks, G. R. (2001). Masculinity and men's mental health. *Journal of American College Health, 49*, 285–297.

Broom, D. H., & Woodward, R. V. (1996). Medicalization considered: Toward a collaborative approach to care. *Sociology of Health and Illness, 18,* 357–378.

Charmaz, K. (1995). Identity dilemmas of chronically ill men. In: D. Sabo & D. F. Gordon (Eds), *Men's Health and Illness* (pp. 266–291). Thousand Oaks, CA: Sage.

Chesler, P. (1972). *Women and madness.* New York: Harcourt Brace Jovanovich.

Connell, R.W. (1995). *Masculinities.* Berkeley: University of California Press.

Conrad, P. (1975). The discovery of hyperkinesis: Notes on the medicalization of deviant behavior. *Social Problems, 23,* 12–21.

Conrad, P. (1992). Medicalization and social control. *Annual Review of Sociology, 18,* 209–232.

Conrad, P. (1997). Public eyes and private genes: Historical frames, news construction, and social problems. *Social Problems, 44,* 139–154.

Conrad, P. (1999). A mirage of genes. *Sociology of Health and Illness, 21,* 228–241.

Conrad, P. (2000). Medicalization, genetics, and human problems. In: C. E. Bird, P. Conrad & A. M. Fremont (Eds), *Handbook of Medical Sociology* (5th ed., pp. 322–333). Upper Saddle River, NJ: Prentice-Hall.

Conrad, P., & Schneider, J. W. (1980). *Deviance and medicalization: From badness to sickness.* St. Louis: C.V. Mosby Company.

Corea, G. (1977). *The hidden malpractice how American medicine treats women as patients and professionals.* New York: Morrow.

Courtenay, W. H. (2000). Constructions of masculinity and their influence on men's well-being: A theory of gender and health. *Social Science and Medicine, 50,* 1385–1401.

Courtenay, W. H., & Keeling, R. P. (2000). Men, gender, and health: Toward an interdisciplinary approach. *Journal of American College Health, 48,* 243–246.

Crawford, R. (1980). Healthism and the medicalization of everyday life. *International Journal of Health Services, 10,* 365–388.

Doyal, L. (2001). Sex, gender and health: The need for a new approach. *British Medical Journal, 323,* 1061–1063.

Ehrenreich, J. (Ed.) (1978). *The cultural crisis of modern medicine.* New York: Monthly Review Press.

Ehrenreich, B., & English, D. (1973). *Witches, midwives and nurses: A history of women healers.* Old Westbury: The Feminist Press.

Ehrenreich, B., & English, D. (1978). *For her own good: 150 years of the experts' advice to women.* Garden City, NY: Anchor Press.

Fee, E. (1977). Women and health care: A comparison of theories. In: V. Navarro (Ed.), *Health and Medical Care in the USA: A Critical Analysis* (pp. 115–132). Farmingdale, NY: Baywood Publishing.

Foucault, M. (1988). Technologies of the self. In: L. M. H. Martin, H. Gutman & P. H. Hutton (Eds), *Technologies of the Self* (pp. 16–49). Amherst: University of Massachusetts Press.

Freidson, E. (1970). *Profession of medicine.* New York: Mead and Company.

Freidson, E. (1984). The changing nature of professional control. *Annual Review of Sociology, 10,* 1–20.

Freidson, E. (1985). The reorganization of the medical profession. *Medical Care Review, 42,* 11–35.

Friedman, M., & Rosenman, R. H. (1959). Association of specific overt behavior pattern with blood and cardiovascular findings. *Journal of the American Medical Association, 169,* 1286–1296.

Friedman, M., & Rosenman, R. H. (1974). *Type A behavior and your heart.* New York: Alfred A. Knopf.

Giddens, A. (1991). *Modernity and self-identity: Self and society in the late modern age.* Cambridge: Polity Press.

Hafferty, F. W., & McKinlay, J. B. (1993). *The changing medical profession: An international perspective*. New York: Oxford University Press.

Hardey, M. (1999). Doctor in the house: The internet as a source of lay health knowledge and the challenge to expertise. *Sociology of Health and Illness, 21*, 820–835.

Harrison, J. (1978). Warning: The male sex role may be dangerous to your health. *Journal of Social Issues, 34*, 65–86.

Harrison, J., Chin, J., & Ficarrotto, T. (1989). Warning: Masculinity may be dangerous to your health. In: M. S. Kimmel & M. A. Messner (Eds), *Men's Lives* (pp. 246–309). New York: Macmillan Publishing.

Haug, M. (1975). The deprofessionalization of everyone? *Sociological Focus, 3*, 197–213.

Hawkins, J. W., & Aber, C. S. (1988). The content of advertisements in medical journals: Distorting the image of women. *Women and Health, 14*, 43–59.

Hearn, J. (1998). Theorizing men and men's theorizing: Varieties of discursive practices in men's theorizing of men. *Theory and Society, 27*, 781–816.

Helgeson, V. S. (1995). Masculinity, men's roles, and coronary heart disease. In: D. Sabo & D. F. Gordon (Eds), *Men's Health and Illness* (pp. 68–104). Thousand Oaks, CA: Sage.

Hubbard, R. (1995). Genomania and health. *American Scientist, 83*, 8–10.

Illich, I. (1976). *Medical nemesis: The expropriation of health*. New York: Pantheon Books.

Johnson, K., & Dawson, L. (1990). Women's health as a multidisciplinary specialty: An exploratory proposal. *Journal of the American Medical Women's Association, 45*, 222–224.

Johnson, K., & Hoffman, E. (1993). Women's health: Designing and implementing an interdisciplinary specialty. *Women's Health Issues, 3*, 115–119.

Johnson, T., Larkin, G., & Saks, M. (Eds) (1995). *Health professions and the state in Europe*. London: Routledge.

Kimmel, M. S. (1997). *Manhood in America: A cultural history*. New York: Free Press.

Kimmel, M. S. (2000). *Gendered society*. New York: Oxford University Press.

Kimmel, M. S., & Kaufman, M. (1995). Weekend warriors: The new men's movement. In: M. S. Kimmel (Ed.), *The Politics of Manhood* (pp. 15–43). Philadelphia: Temple University Press.

Kobasa, S. (1979). Stressful life events, personality, and health: An inquiry into hardiness. *Journal of Personality and Social Psychology, 37*, 1–11.

Lancet (2001). Editorial: Time for creative thinking about men's health. *Lancet, 357*, 1813.

Lorber, J. (1997). *Gender and the social construction of illness*. Thousand Oaks, CA: Sage.

Lunbeck, E. (1998). American psychiatrists and the modern man, 1900 to 1920. *Men and Masculinities, 1*, 58–86.

Lupton, D. (1997). Foucault and the medicalization critique. In: A. Petersen & R. Bunton (Eds), *Foucault: Health and Medicine* (pp. 94–110). London: Routledge.

Marshall, B. L., & Katz, K. (2001). Forever functional: Sexual fitness and the aging body. Paper presented at the 5th conference of the European Sociological Association, August 28th September 1st, 2001, Helsinki, Finland.

Meryn, S., & Jadad, A. R. (2001). The future of men and their health: Are men in danger of extinction? *British Medical Journal, 323*, 1013–1014.

Messner, M. A. (1997). *Politics of masculinities: Men in movements*. Thousand Oaks, CA: Sage.

Messner, M. A. (1998). The limits of "the male sex role": An analysis of the men's liberation and men's rights movements' discourse. *Gender and Society, 12*, 255–276.

Meyer, V. F. (2001). The medicalization of menopause: Critique and consequences. *International Journal of Health Services, 31*, 769–792.

Mills, C. W. (1959). *The sociological imagination*. New York: Oxford University Press.

Navarro, V. (1976). *Medicine under capitalism*. New York: Prodist.

Nonn, T. (1995). Renewal as retreat: The battle for men's souls. In: M. S. Kimmel (Ed.), *The Politics of Manhood* (pp. 173–185). Philadelphia: Temple University Press.

Oinas, E. (1998). Medicalization by whom: Accounts of menstruation conveyed by young women and medical experts in medical advisory columns. *Sociology of Health and Illness, 20*, 52–70.

Parsons, T. (1951). *The social system*. New York: Free Press.

Pitts, V. (2002). Technologies of the ill self: Fashion, biomedicine, and breast cancer. Paper presented at the 72nd annual meeting of the Eastern Sociological Society, March 7–10, 2002, in Boston.

Pope, H. G., Phillips, K. A., & Oliviardia, R. (2000). *The Adonis complex: The secret crisis of male body obsession*. New York: Free Press.

Potts, A. (2000). The essence of the hard on: Hegemonic masculinity and the cultural construction of erectile dysfunction. *Men and Masculinities, 3*, 85–103.

Prather, J. E., & Fidell, L. S. (1975). Sex differences in the content and style of medical advertisements. *Social Science and Medicine, 9*, 23–26.

Richman, J. A., & Jason, L. A. (2001). Gender biases underlying the social construction of illness states: The case of chronic fatigue syndrome. *Current Sociology, 49*, 15–29.

Riessman, C. K. (1992). Women and medicalization: A new perspective. In: G. Kirkup & L. S. Keller (Eds), *Inventing Women: Science, Technology and Gender* (pp. 123–144). Milton Keynes: Polity Press. (Originally in *Social Policy*, 1983, Summer, 3–19.)

Riska, E. (2000). The rise and fall of Type A man. *Social Science and Medicine, 51*, 1665–1674.

Riska, E. (2002). From Type A man to the hardy man: Masculinity and health. *Sociology of Health and Illness, 24*, 347–358.

Roberts, H. (1991). *Women's health counts*. London: Routledge.

Rose, N. (1999). *Governing the soul: The shaping of the private self* (2nd ed.). London: Free Association Books.

Rothman, B. K. (1998). *Genetic maps and human imaginations: The limits of science in understanding who we are*. New York: W. W. Norton & Company.

Ruzek, S. B. (1978). *The women's health movement: Feminist alternatives to medical control*. New York: Praeger.

Ruzek, S. B., & Becker, J. (1999). The women's health movement in the United States: From grassroots activism to professional agendas. *Journal of the American Medical Women's Association, 54*, 4–8.

Sabo, D. (2000). Men's health studies: Origins and trends. *Journal of American College Health, 49*, 133–142.

Sabo, D., & Gordon, D. F. (1995). Rethinking men's health and illness: The relevance of gender studies. In: D. Sabo & D. F. Gordon (Eds), *Men's Health and Illness* (pp. 1–21). Thousand Oaks, CA: Sage.

Sandelowski, M. (1981). *Women, health, and choice*. Englewood Cliffs, NJ: Prentice-Hall.

Schneider, J. W. (1978). Deviant drinking as a disease: Deviant drinking as a social accomplishment. *Social Problems, 25*, 361–372.

Schofield, T., Connell, R. W., Walker, L., Wood, J. F., & Butland, D. L. (2000). Understanding men's health and illness: A gender-relations approach to policy, research, and practice. *Journal of American College Health, 48*, 247–256.

Scully, D., & Bart, P. (1973). A funny thing happened on the way to the orifice: Women in gynecology textbooks. *American Journal of Sociology, 78*, 1045–1050.

Seaman, B. (1969). *Doctors' case against the pill*. New York: Peter H. Wyden Co.

Seaman, B. (1975). Pelvic autonomy: Four proposals. *Social Policy, 6*(September/October), 43–47.

Sharf, B. F. (1997). Communicating breast cancer on-line: Support and empowerment on.the internet. *Women and Health, 26*(1), 65–84.

Smith-Rosenberg, C. (1985). *Disorderly conduct: Visions of gender in Victorian America*. New York: Oxford University Press.

Staples, R. (1995). Health among Afro-American males. In: D. Sabo & D. F. Gordon (Eds), *Men's Health and Illness* (pp. 121–138). Thousand Oaks, CA: Sage.

Starr, P. (1982). *The Social transformation of American medicine*. New York: Basic Books.

Sullivan, G. L., & O'Connor, B. J. (1988). Women's role portrayals in magazine advertising: 1958–1983. *Sex Roles, 18*, 181–188.

Theriot, N. M. (1993). Women's voices in nineteenth century medical discourse: A step toward deconstructing science. *Signs, 19*, 1–31.

Waldron, I. (1995). Contributions of changing gender differences in behavior and social roles to changing gender differences in mortality. In: D. Sabo & D. F. Gordon (Eds), *Men's Health and Illness* (pp. 22–45). Thousand Oaks, CA: Sage.

Waldron, I., Weiss, C. C., & Hughes, M. E. (1998). Interacting effects of multiple roles on women's health. *Journal of Health and Social Behavior, 39*, 136–216.

Walsh, M. R. (1977). *Doctors wanted: No women need apply: Sexual barriers in the medical profession, 1835–1975*. New Haven: Yale University Press.

White, A., & Lockyer, L. (2001). Tackling coronary heart disease: A gender sensitive approach needed. *British Medical Journal, 323*, 1016–1017.

Wolfe, D. (2000). *Men like us: The GMHC complete guide to gay men's sexual, physical, and emotional well-being*. New York: Ballentine Books.

Zola, I. K. (1972). Medicine as an institution of social control. *Sociological Review, 20*, 487–503.

"BIG PHARMA" IN OUR BEDROOMS: AN ANALYSIS OF THE MEDICALIZATION OF WOMEN'S SEXUAL PROBLEMS

Heather Hartley

INTRODUCTION

We are in the midst of a broad societal change in which women's sexual problems are becoming increasingly medicalized, characterized as treatable medical conditions and defined and understood as a largely physiologically based disease, called "female sexual dysfunction" (FSD). When a condition is medicalized, a medical framework is used to understand it, and medical interventions are used to treat it. As part of this process, then, over the last several years, researchers and pharmaceutical companies have turned attention to developing medical treatments for FSD. As this medicalization continues to unfold with potentially important impacts, it is crucial that we understand the forces working to shape it.

Two events provide particularly essential background for beginning to understand this development, the first being the 1998 launch of Viagra as a treatment for erectile dysfunction (ED) in men, and the second being the 1999 publication of a heavily cited article on sexual problems in the *Journal of the American Medical Association* (*JAMA*). Both events had a dramatic influence on cultural perception of women's sexual problems. The market success of Viagra, which is dispensed at the rate of about 200,000 prescriptions each week (Cowley, 2000), is a story of triumph to a pharmaceutical industry that increasingly relies on "blockbuster

Gender Perspectives on Health and Medicine: Key Themes
Advances in Gender Research, Volume 7, 89–129
Copyright © 2003 by Elsevier Ltd.
All rights of reproduction in any form reserved
ISSN: 1529-2126/doi:10.1016/S1529-2126(03)07004-8

drugs" to bolster profits and market share (Angell, 2000a, b). Viagra's success not only prompted the pharmaceutical industry to develop other drugs for improving male sexual function but also created a context in which there are incentives for the industry to find a parallel product to treat FSD, as the market for such treatments is estimated to hit $1.7 billion by 2008 (Leland, 2000). The results of clinical trials of Viagra for women showed that it is no more effective than a placebo in treating sexual problems, but a variety of other pills, creams, patches, and devices to treat FSD are currently in development or clinical trials. In 2000, the U.S. Food and Drug Administration (FDA) approved the EROS-CTD for the treatment of FSD. This by-prescription-only mechanical device is used to stimulate the clitoris, and so far represents the only FDA-approved treatment for FSD. No drug therapies are currently approved to treat FSD.

The interest in FSD has also been roused by the publication of a study published in *JAMA* that concluded that more than four out of 10 women (43%) have sexual problems, a rate of sexual dysfunction reported to be higher than that of men (31%) (Laumann, Paik & Rosen, 1999, p. 537). This statistic, widely cited by both the media and professional literature, has been used to transmit the message that there is a virtual epidemic of sexual problems among women, even though the statistic itself is questionable (see Tiefer, 2000a for more detail on this point). The pharmaceutical industry has used this "inflated epidemiology" (Tiefer, 2002) in its efforts to expand a medicalized perspective on women's sexual problems. Additionally, the way in which this statistic has been conveyed has promoted a medicalized view of women's sexual problems. As argued by Hartley and Tiefer (2003),

> Although detailed data in the (*JAMA*) paper indicate that the prevalence of women's sexual problems varies by race, age, marital status, history of sexual abuse, economic location, and level of education, these socio-cultural predictors have been given little attention in popular or professional media as, again and again, the overall statistic has been used to emphasize the prevalence of physiological sexual problems and the urgent need for pharmaceutical companies to develop new treatments.

These two events provided infrastructure for the medicalization of women's sexual problems, which is a complicated process. Medicalization can occur at various levels: (1) the conceptual, in which medical language and models are used to understand a condition or process; (2) the interactional, in which, as part of doctor-patient interaction, the condition is diagnosed and understood as medical in nature; and (3) the institutional, in which the condition or process comes under the jurisdictional control of those with professional and economic interests in expanding medical domains, such as the medical profession or medical industries (Conrad, 1992; Zola, 1972). This paper will draw out and specify the complexities associated with this medicalization, which is progressing at conceptual, interactional, and institutional levels.

SCOPE OF PAPER

This research illustrates the ways in which women's sexual problems are becoming increasingly medicalized, at each of the three levels. After describing the methodology used for this research and briefly reviewing past research on the medicalization of women's bodies, the paper will show that women's sexual problems are medicalized at the *conceptual* level by reviewing the creation of and legitimacy accorded to diagnostic classification systems that both define such problems as "dysfunctions" and encourage attribution of these problems to biomedical causes. Specifically, I outline the definition of FSD as stated in the Diagnostic and Statistical Manual of Mental Disorders (DSM)'s classification system, and discuss two challenges to this system.

The argument then turns to a consideration of the drug development process and the conflicts of interest embedded within it. I begin with an overview of the changing trends associated with the performance of clinical drug trials, the dissemination of information on those drugs, and the increasing role of the pharmaceutical industry in sponsoring continuing medical education (CME) conferences. The overview is supplemented by specific information on *FSD treatments* currently in clinical trials and pharmaceutical industry sponsorship of conferences on FSD.

While this line of discussion highlights the changing nature of the *institutional* level of medicalization and the growing influence of the pharmaceutical industry, it also has relevance for a consideration of the *interactional* level of medicalization. Because medical treatments for FSD are only in the developmental stage, the interactional level of medicalization currently has an undeveloped form. In essence, the absence of drugs to prescribe for a condition limits the ability of health care providers to diagnose or treat a condition as medical in nature; however, the stage is set for a dramatic expansion of the interactional level of medicalization. As the discussion will show, increasing numbers of physicians and other health care providers are being exposed to CME conferences that espouse the medical model of sexual problems and the promise of forthcoming medical treatments for FSD, and even though only one product is FDA-approved for treating FSD, physicians do engage in the practice of giving "off-label" prescriptions of products approved to treat other conditions.

The paper next covers an active attempt to legitimate a new "syndrome," being called Female Androgen Deficiency Syndrome (FADS), which in effect represents an effort to expand the conceptual level of medicalization. To the extent that FADS gains legitimacy, it can be used as a justification for conceptualizing some of women's sexual problems as based in hormone "deficiencies" that can be treated with androgen replacement therapies. The overview of FADS also provides a specific example of the roles researchers, clinical trials, and CME conferences play in the legitimatization of a specific medicalized conceptualization of women's sexual problems.

While this first half of the paper describes the conceptual level of medicalization, suggests ways in which the interactional level is emerging, and provides critical background information about the institutional level, the second half of the paper examines the stories of prominent FSD researchers with the intent of expanding the conceptualization of the institutional level of medicalization, specifically in regards to the *significance of connections between researchers and industry*.

Such reconceptualization is needed in light of key changes impacting the health care arena. Sociologists considering the institutional level of medicalization have oftentimes focused on the role of the medical profession. However, in light of structural modifications and economic transformations brought by managed care, the decline of physician dominance, and the increasing role of industry in the funding of medical research and education (for background on each of these factors, see Abbott, 1988; Anderson, 1992; Bodenheimer, 2000; Freidson, 1970; Hafferty & Light, 1995; Hartley, 1999; Haug, 1973; Haug & Lavin, 1981; Kennedy, 1997; Larson, 1977; Light, 2000; McKinlay, 1988; McKinlay & Arches, 1985; Slaughter & Leslie, 1997; Starr, 1982; Tiefer, 2000a), it appears that sociological understanding of the institutional level of medicalization would be made more precise through an expanded account of the influence of industry. In essence, as physicians lose autonomy and power as a professional group, it is reasonable to expect that other players may assume larger and increasingly important roles in controlling the perceptions and treatments of particular conditions, and the pharmaceutical industry appears poised to assume an even a larger role in fostering the process of medicalization.

At this stage in the medicalization of women's sexual problems, one of the most significant aspects of the pharmaceutical industry's involvement in the medicalization of women's sexual problems is its *funding of biomedical research* on women's sexual problems. Through relating key components of the researchers' accounts, the second half of the paper will show that industry interest in funding biomedically-focused studies of women's sexual problems has had a demonstrable impact on the course of research in many instances. However, it will also be shown that researcher mobilization can also play a strong role in the medicalization of women's sexual problems.

DATA SOURCES AND METHODOLOGY

Data were collected through a combination of qualitative methods, including ethnographic work and participant-observation, key informant interviews, and analysis of written texts. The data were collected from 2000 to 2002 and derive from various sources:

- I consulted published documents, including scientific journal articles, summaries of scientific conference proceedings, newspaper articles, commentary and news pieces from on-line magazines, FDA reports and documents, material from the Pharmaceutical Research and Manufacturers of America (PhRMA) website, and editorials from prominent medical journals. I conducted a systematic search of the MEDLINE scientific information databases to identify and review pertinent research articles on the topic of FSD.
- I conducted participant-observation research at the 2000 and 2001 Female Sexual Function Forum (FSFF) conference. This four-day continuing medical education (CME) conference, taking place since 1999 and sponsored by the Boston University School of Medicine (Department of Urology), is the central international clearinghouse for research on FSD. My activities at both meetings included attending and taking fieldnotes on presentations, open business meetings, and social events (including the annual Saturday night clambake!). Both years, I engaged in numerous off-the-record conversations with both presenters and attendees.
- At the 2001 FSFF meetings, I conducted formal, tape-recorded interviews with research "insiders" from the following specialty fields: endocrinology, obstetrics/gynecology, urology, neuroradiology, neurology, epidemiology, psychology, psychiatry, physiology, and biochemistry. In all, I conducted 16 interviews, some taking place after the conference. The section on "researcher stories," where most of the interview data are discussed, provides more details about the methodology used for these interviews.
- I drew from experiences associated with my two-year involvement with the Working Group for a New View of Women's Sexual Problems ("New View" for short), a multidisciplinary group of clinicians and social scientists who came together in 2000 to develop and publicize an alternative (non-medicalized) view of women's sexual problems. My involvement with the New View included attending two planning meetings, participating in ongoing correspondence with those involved in the campaign, conducting research and writing on behalf of the New View campaign, presenting related research at several professional conferences, and participation in a press conference held in Boston in 2000.
- I conducted participant-observation at the conference entitled, "The New Female Sexual Dysfunction: Promises, Prescriptions and Profits," held in 2002 in San Francisco, California. The "New View" group organized this conference.

THE MEDICALIZATION OF WOMEN'S BODIES:
AN OVERVIEW

Feminist researchers have argued that women's bodies have been medicalized more than men's bodies (Findlay & Miller, 1994; Riessman, 1983). A substantial body of literature has documented the variety of conditions that primarily impact women that have come to be medicalized, including premenstrual syndrome (PMS), menopause, pregnancy and childbirth, appearance, abortion and contraception, fertility, and domestic violence (Bell, 1987, 1990; Coney, 1994; Donchlin, 1996; Figert, 1996; Leavitt, 1989; Marken, 1996; Oinas, 1998; Pugliesi, 1992; Riessman, 1983; Sullivan, 1993; Weitz, 1998). This literature identifies forces such as patriarchy, corporate profit motives, and the professionalization of medicine as contributing to the medicalization of women's bodies.

Over a 15-year period, starting in the 1980s, research on men's sexual problems became increasingly medical/physiological in nature, ultimately culminating in the development of a variety of medical treatments for these problems (Tiefer, 1994, 1996). The medicalization of sexuality shows a unique historical pattern in that the medicalization of *men's* sexual problems was accomplished prior to the medicalization of women's sexual problems. It can be argued that one of the implications of this exceptional case – in which men's sexual problems were medicalized prior to those of women – is that industry profit motives have became as important a force shaping medicalization as is patriarchy. In this case, because the conditions of the *majority* group (men) have been medicalized, it becomes all the more acceptable (and even gets labeled as a move for equality) to medicalize parallel conditions in the *minority* group (women).

Those familiar with the history of the medicalization of women's bodies might see historical ironies re-emerge in the current medicalization of women's sexual health. While medicalization has sometimes worked to legitimize women's bodily experiences, it has often ultimately disempowered women (Pugliesi, 1992; Riessman, 1983). For example, in the case of women's sexual functioning, women's health activists have long criticized the overwhelming lack of attention to female sexual anatomy and physiology in medical schools. While this new focus on FSD, then, may serve to enhance understanding of the characteristics of female sexual anatomy, a focus on finding medical and technological treatments may serve to benefit economic interests while obscuring important social factors associated with women's sexual health.[1] Feminists have argued that both male and female sexual problems have multiple underlying causes (i.e. can be partly psychological/emotional in origin, partly medical/physiological in origin, and partly cultural in origin), and when sexual problems are medicalized, the focus tends to center on biomedical factors to the exclusion of important socio-cultural and psychological factors (Tiefer, 1995).

CONCEPTUALIZING WOMEN'S SEXUAL PROBLEMS AS DYSFUNCTIONS

Classification of a condition as a "disease" is essential to the process of medicalization. The American Psychiatric Association's Diagnostic and Statistical Manual of Mental Disorders (DSM) is today's most widely used system for classifying women's sexual problems, recognizing four categories of sexual dysfunction (for both males and females): sexual desire disorders, sexual arousal disorders, orgasmic disorders, and sexual pain disorders (APA, 1994; see Tiefer, 2001 for discussion of the evolving nature of the DSM's classification of women's sexual problems since 1980). Feminists have criticized this classification system for being overly genital in focus, neglecting issues of relationship and social context, and for relying on outmoded work done by Masters and Johnson on the human sexual response cycle in the 1960s (Tiefer, 1995, 2001b). The Masters and Johnson research has been criticized on a variety of fronts, one charge being that their focus on a biologically-based human response cycle (with genital arousal and orgasm as the centerpiece) set a precedent for ignoring or downplaying the relational, cultural and individual factors impacting sexual experience (Tiefer, 1995). In 1998, the DSM's classification system was challenged by the first Consensus Development Panel of Female Sexual Dysfunction, convened by the Sexual Function Health Council of the American Foundation for Urologic Disease (see Basson et al., 2000; Tiefer, 2000b). The primary concern of this group, comprised of 19 sexuality researchers and clinicians, was that the DSM's focus on mental health issues was too narrow to use to classify, treat, and guide research in the arena of women's sexual problems. Tiefer (2000b) argues that those on the panel were most concerned that the existing classification system would not provide an appropriate platform for a biomedical approach to women's sexual problems. Noting that 18 of the 19 members of the panel indicated financial ties to the pharmaceutical industry and that the conference was funded through grants from a host of pharmaceutical companies, Tiefer (2000b) expresses concerns about conflicts of interest on the part of members the panel. The panel ultimately maintained the structure of the DSM classification system, making only a few changes. The two most significant changes included the addition of a "personal distress" criterion (meaning that the woman herself would have to be upset about her sexual functioning to be considered as having a dysfunction), and the creation of a new system for clinical diagnosis in which each diagnosis would be subtyped as to "etiologic origin (organic, psychogenic, mixed, unknown)," (Basson et al., 2000, p. 870). A main implication of this change is that the system has been expanded in such a manner as to better accommodate a *biomedical* perspective. As argued by Hartley and Tiefer (2003), "This subtyping sets the stage for doctors and new 'women's sexual health clinics' to inaugurate a battery of mandatory physical tests to make these etiological distinctions." Furthermore, because the specified etiologic categories do not include explicit consideration of relational or socio-cultural factors, it is likely that such factors may be increasingly downplayed. One result is that research and treatment protocols that flow from the classification of the nature of "the problem" will be inadequate in scope. Other factors that are far more common sources of women's sexual complaints – psychological and cultural conflicts, abuse history, or problems with a partner – will go unstudied and unaddressed.

The work of the Consensus Panel has been controversial, as evidenced by the dedication of an entire special issue of the *Journal of Sex and Marital Therapy* (Vol. 27, Issue 2, March 2001) to this topic. The issue contained 37 commentaries on the revised classification system, many of them highly critical of the Panel's work. This system, though, has attained a measure of institutional legitimacy, as shown by the FDA's reliance on it as a guide, a point discussed below.

In 2000, a multidisciplinary group of clinicians and social scientists developed an alternative classification system to both the DSM's model and the subsequent small modifications to that model put forth by the Consensus Panel. This system, called the "New View of Women's Sexual Problems," was built on a critique of medicalization that emphasized sociopolitical and relationship causes for women's sexual problems. The classification system, while not "officially sanctioned" like those discussed above, was published in several professional venues and was the centerpiece of a two-year long grassroots activist campaign (see Kaschak & Tiefer, 2001 for a complete documentation of the campaign). The system is based on the insights of feminist clinicians and scholars who locate women's sexual problems primarily in cultural and relational contexts and avoids specifying any one pattern of sexual experience as normal. The "New View" describes four categories of women's sexual problems: (1) those due to socio-cultural, political or economic factors; (2) those related to partner and relationship issues; (3) those due to individual psychology; and (4) those due to medical or physical factors (see Kaschak & Tiefer, 2001, for full document). This system of categorization eliminates the language of "dysfunction" as well as the biomedical, linear focus of Masters and Johnson's approach. While the authors acknowledge that medical or physical factors can contribute to *some* sexual problems in women, the system also builds in room for full consideration of the non-medical factors of significance. The intent of publicizing this "New View" was to provide an alternative to the increasingly medicalized conceptualizations of women's sexual problems.

THE MOST PROFITABLE INDUSTRY TODAY: CONTROVERSY AND CONFLICTS OF INTEREST

The pharmaceutical industry is the most profitable industry in the U.S. today, with a 1999 average rate of return on revenues of 18.6% (Angell, 2000b). Recent articles published in *The New England Journal of Medicine* (Angell, 2000a, b; Bodenheimer, 2000), argue that medical research, education, and treatment protocols are too strongly driven by the profit motives of this industry. Controversy and conflicts of interest exist at each stage of the drug development process, from testing the drugs in clinical trials through publication of results of those trials and dissemination of information on the drugs at CME conferences and other venues. In this section of the paper, I briefly review these controversies, focusing in particular on those topics most central to the emerging biomedical focus on FSD.

Clinical Trials and Drug Development

Overview
The first step in testing a pharmaceutical product is to subject the compound to *preclinical testing* in animals. These studies are intended to demonstrate the biological activity of the compound as well as its safety. After collecting these data, a pharmaceutical company can file an Investigational New Drug Application (IND) with the FDA to begin to test the drug in people. Explains Spilker (2002), "The IND shows results of previous experiments; how, where and by whom the new studies will be conducted; the chemical structure of the compound; how it is thought to work in the body; any toxic effects found in the animal studies; and how the compound is manufactured."

The next step of the drug development process is to begin clinical trials, which involve three phases. *Phase I* clinical trials are intended to evaluate the safety of the drug. These tests are conducted in small numbers (20–80) of normal, healthy volunteers. The tests study a drug's safety profile, including the safe dosage range. The studies also determine the duration of the drug's action as well as how it is absorbed, distributed, metabolized, and excreted. *Phase II* clinical trials focus on establishing the efficacy and safety of the drug in those who have the condition to be treated. A higher number of volunteers (100–300) are enrolled in this phase of study, which usually involves randomized trials. *Phase III* trials are larger still, involving 1,000–3,000 volunteers. The intent of this phase of study is to confirm efficacy and identify adverse events that may arise in diverse populations of those with the condition (e.g. in patients taking several drugs, in the elderly). Oftentimes these trials are multi-site studies, constructed this way in order to enroll adequate numbers of patients (Bodenheimer, 2000; Spilker, 2002).

Following the completion of all three phases of clinical trials and analyses, a company can file a New Drug Application (NDA) with the FDA. The NDA asks for approval to manufacture, distribute and market the drug in the U.S., based on the safety and efficacy data from the clinical trials. The NDA contains details of the trials and can typically run 100,000 pages or more. If the FDA approves the NDA, the new medicine becomes available for physicians to prescribe. Once on the market, the drug is taken by wider numbers of patients, which expands the quantity of safety information about the product. Due to the potential that new patterns of adverse reaction may emerge, the company is required to submit periodic reports to FDA on these events (Spilker, 2002).

Not surprisingly, clinical trials are heavily funded by industry, which provides 70% of the money for clinical drug trials in the U.S. (Bodenheimer, 2000). The National Institutes of Health (NIH) funds some clinical trials but is more likely to fund basic research that may later lead to drug development. Angell (2000b) argues that this NIH funding of basic research is a form of subsidy for the pharmaceutical industry, which usually does not get involved in funding until a potential clinical application has been identified. During the 1990s, the research networks associated with running clinical trials were dramatically transformed. Notes Bodenheimer (2000), "In 1990, 80% of industry money for clinical trials went to academic medical centers; by 1998, the figure had dropped precipitously to 40%." Industry's dependence on academia has lessened as new "commercial drug networks" have developed. Key players in this for-profit research marketplace include contract-research organizations (CROs) and site-management organizations (SMOs), which carry out tasks such as developing a network of researchers and research sites, implementing and overseeing trial protocols and data analysis. Dr. Sidney Wolfe of Public Citizen is critical of CROs, seeing them as "handmaidens of pharmaceutical companies" (Bodenheimer, 2000). Many of these organizations' Institutional Review Boards (IRBs), which are charged with insuring the safety of human subjects, operate on a for-profit basis, raising important questions about the adequacy of the safety precautions (Washburn, 2001).

One of the reasons that the pharmaceutical industry has shifted its research from the academic sector is industry perception that academic research takes too long and costs too much (Bodenheimer, 2000; Washburn, 2001). The required reviews by academic research offices and IRBs, combined with the multiple responsibilities of academic researchers, are increasingly perceived as slowing the course of research. An academic-based psychiatrist interviewed for this project strongly reinforced this point, saying that it is difficult for universities to "compete" with private research firms to attract pharmaceutical money:

> In a sense we almost can't compete with those groups. You know my human subjects committee takes *two months* and that's with us working flat out . . . The people in the private sector can use an IRB that get them through in *two weeks* . . . And many of them don't have any constraints about whether they want to publish the data or not.

Most universities and academic medical centers review contracts between their employees (though not necessarily researchers who have only clinical affiliations with the institutions) and industry and some require that academic investigators maintain the right to publish results from the research. Therefore, industry might be unable to exercise as much control over data analysis and authorship of publications when working with an academic partner. An academic-based ob-gyn interviewed for this research remarked,

> We're in the process of negotiating with Pfizer on some funding, and if they do not relinquish publication rights, then of course we won't participate in the funding . . . That's (the university's) rule, and I happen to think it's a good one . . . (The university) wants its investigators to retain full and complete ability to publish anything. Usually there's a 30 or 60-day sort of escrow period where the company gets to look at it before you publish it, but they can't prevent you from publishing it.

This researcher believes that these rules protect her freedom to publish. However, universities differ in their rules on this matter. A clinical psychologist interviewed for the project did not gain such protections for her work. She says, "It's in the contract that they (the company) own the data basically, and that, yes, you cannot publish it without their consent." Importantly, even though clinical research is increasingly moving out of the university setting, universities *heavily rely* on the industry research funds that they receive, a factor that can add potential conflicts of interest (Washburn, 2001). Academic publications, though not essential for drug approval, are a key element to achieving legitimacy and physician support (in the form of writing prescriptions) once the drug has been approved. For this reason, pharmaceutical companies have incentives to suppress the publication of negative results, and evidence suggests that the companies are having an impact on publications. As Altman (1997) and DeAngelis (2000) note, scientific investigators *with ties to drug companies* are more likely to report results *favorable* to the company's products than are investigators without these ties, and industry-funded research is demonstrated to be of lesser quality. Additionally, a variety of studies have documented the ways in which clinical trials are designed in a biased manner by pharmaceutical companies so as to increase the chances of getting a positive result (e.g. when comparing the drug to be tested with another drug already on the market, giving higher doses of the test drug) (Bodenheimer, 2002; DeAngelis, 2000). Even when industry shares control over data analysis and authorship of publications, as when they partner with an academic institution that insists on the right to publish, they sometimes utilize tactics to *delay* publication of unfavorable results, sometimes because they want to wait to publish the findings until they have done another study from a different angle (and that they hope will produce favorable results). Still, because pharmaceutical companies benefit from the prestige of having the stamp of academic medicine on its drug trials, many continue to seek out known academic investigators in the field to work on their clinical trials. However, some companies create arrangements explicitly intended to exploit the credentials of the academic "partner." An example is when a company has an in-house staff writer prepare ("ghost-write") a scientific journal article, though another individual, usually with an academic affiliation, is listed as the lead author (Bodenheimer, 2000).

FSD Treatments in Clinical Trials

The Pharmaceutical Research and Manufacturers of America (PhRMA), the main pharmaceutical company trade group, tracks drugs currently in the clinical trials stage of development. Table 1 lists the drugs intended to treat FSD that

Table 1. Clinical Trials of Drugs to Treat Female Sexual Dysfunction (FSD).

Drug	Company	Development Status – 2001	Development Status – 2002
Apomorphine HCL SL tablet	Pentech Pharmaceuticals (2001) and Nastech Pharmaceutical (2002)	Phase II	Phase II
Estra Test (esterified estrogens and methyltestosterone)	Solvay Pharmaceuticals	Phase III	Phase II
Testosterone patch	Procter & Gamble Pharmaceuticals	Phase II/III	Phase II/III
Vasofen (phentolamine mesylate)	Zonagen	Phase I	Phase II
Viagra	Pfizer	Phase II	
Femprox	NexMed		Phase II
Testosterone gel	Solvay Pharmaceuticals		Phase II
Tadalafil	ICOS		Phase II

Data from PhRMA website, consulted 3/8/01 and 1/18/02.

are currently in clinical trials, as reported on the PhRMA website in 2001 and 2002 (http://www.phrma.org/searchcures/newmeds/webdb/drugs.phtml). It is important to note that not all pharmaceutical companies necessarily list their clinical trials with PhRMA, so this list may be incomplete.

As Table 1 indicates, pharmaceutical companies are testing a variety of drug products to treat FSD. Still, due to the practice of "off-label" prescribing of FDA-approved drugs, some health care providers do currently prescribe products such as testosterone or Viagra to treat FSD (even though the current FDA information sheet on Viagra states that women should not take the product). Centerwatch, an organization that lists ongoing clinical trials, listed 30 active trials pertaining to female sexual dysfunction during my check of their website on March 13, 2002 (see http://www.centerwatch.com/patient/studies/cat333.html). Although Centerwatch does not identify the drugs that are being tested, it is evident that many of the trial sites are participating in larger multi-site trials of one or more products. Table 1 also shows the evolving nature of drug product testing. For example, while the initial testing of Viagra for FSD made a big media splash, PhRMA does not indicate that testing has continued past Phase II trials. Apomorphine, which is not a specific brand name, has been or is being tested by at least two companies.

In May 2000, the FDA released a draft guidance for industry entitled, "Female Sexual Dysfunction: Clinical Development of Drug Products for Treatment" (FDA, 2000). In guidance documents such as these, the FDA specifies its expectations regarding the clinical trial process, through, for example, defining its diagnostic categories and specifying qualifying endpoints. Interested parties (such as researchers) were able to submit comments and suggestions regarding the draft document for 60 days after its publication. At the time of writing, the guidance is still in this "draft" form.

At the 2000 FSFF meetings, Susan Allen, the FDA Division Director who authored the guidelines, gave a presentation in which she discussed this guidance and a selection of the comments and suggestions she received. The guidance identifies the same four components of FSD listed in the DSM and affirmed by the Consensus Conference discussed above. In her talk, Allen emphasized that in writing the guidance, she explicitly drew from that consensus document, thus highlighting important impacts of that document as well as the Consensus Panel's "ownership" over definitions of FSD (Tiefer, 2002). As in the guidance itself, Allen emphasized that it may be appropriate to exclude from clinical trials individuals with "complicating factors" (such as relationship difficulties that could affect sexual function). Critics argue that the generalizability of research findings coming out of these studies is severely impacted, and many non-medical sources of women's sexual problems are ignored (Tiefer, 2001). Allen noted that some of the comments she received on the guidance expressed concerns about the diagnostic definition of FSD and premature drug trials. Ironically, she said that premature drug trials were the pharmaceutical industry's problem, not her problem.

The CME Industry

Pharmaceutical companies routinely provide "unrestricted" educational grants to support the provision of continuing medical education (CME) programs. That "unrestricted" support often functions as a marketing tool. Relman (2001) has remarked, "CME is now so closely linked with the marketing of pharmaceuticals that its integrity and credibility are being questioned. The problem is not new, but it has recently grown to alarming proportions." In some cases, the involvement of the pharmaceutical industry in CME is so extreme that the companies help organize and advertise the events, prepare slides and other curricular materials, select and pay speakers, and subsidize the attendance of medical practitioners and residents. While the companies oftentimes call such involvement "educational" in intent, in most cases, this support comes from their marketing budgets, which belies the real intent (Relman, 2001). As with advertising, this strategy works – physicians attending such courses are more likely to prescribe featured products than other competing products (Wazana, 2000).

A new industry of for-profit "medical education businesses" is creating significant numbers of programs for CME and other educational venues (Relman, 2001). These Medical Education and Communication Companies (MECCs) are mainly funded by the pharmaceutical industry, and some have received accreditation by the medical profession's Accreditation Council on Continuing Medical Education (ACCME), leading Relman (2001) to remark, "Thus, the hired agents of pharmaceutical companies are given authority for the content of CME programs." ACCME has even directly accredited a pharmaceutical company to provide CME.

The pharmaceutical industry is currently involved in CME conferences on FSD. Because no drugs have yet received FDA approval for treatment of FSD (thus, "detailing" activities such as giving out free drug samples are not an option), the intent of the drug companies at this point can be understood as promoting the *idea* of the medical management of women's sexual problems, drawing on the widespread acceptance of drug treatments for men's sexual problems. Note Hartley and Tiefer (2003), "A singular accomplishment of the FSD conferences has been to promote the existence of the FSD condition through simple assertion." The CME objectives of the 2000 FSFF conference, for example, included teaching participants to "identify and recognize the prevalence, risk factors and mechanisms of female sexual dysfunction, diagnose and assess female sexual dysfunction,... make clinical decisions regarding selection of available treatment options" (Boston University School of Medicine, 2000, p. 16). In 2001 and 2002, a traveling CME conference subsidized by major pharmaceutical companies focused on "The pharmacologic management of male and female sexual dysfunction." The speakers have academic affiliations and are members of the drug company speakers' bureaus.

All but two of the pharmaceutical companies testing drug products to treat FSD (Table 1) have contributed monies to the FSFF conferences in the form of unrestricted educational grants (only Pentech Pharmaceuticals and Nastech Pharmaceuticals were not listed contributors to the conference either year).[2] In a related vein, although the Consensus Development Panel of Female Sexual Dysfunction discussed earlier was not a CME event, it was made possible through funding from all but two of the pharmaceutical companies listed in Table 1 (only Nastech Pharmaceuticals and MexMed were not funders of this event) (Basson et al., 2000).

The rules governing CME require that speakers disclose financial interests or other relationships with industry, though, as Relman (2001) argues, this practice does not necessarily protect against biased presentations. An examination of the program of the 2000 FSFF conference indicates that about half (53%) of those giving any presentation disclosed a research or consulting relationship with one or more pharmaceutical companies. However, 88% of those giving the higher profile "Grand Master" presentations disclosed such links, showing that those with *greater prominence* are more likely to be financially linked to industry. Additionally, the vast majority of these more prominent presentations represented a *biomedical* perspective (i.e. basic science, physiology, clinical trials of medical treatments). The 2001 FSFF program's disclosure list was far too incomplete for any analysis, if nothing else, throwing into relief the need for greater oversight as the CME disclosure rules were evidently not followed.

THE CONTESTED TERRAIN OF FEMALE ANDROGEN DEFICIENCY SYNDROME

Female androgen deficiency syndrome (FADS) is a "disease entity" in the process of being constructed. To the extent that FADS gains legitimacy, it can be used as a rationale for the further development and promotion of androgen replacement therapies – primarily testosterone and dehydroepiandrosterone (DHEA) treatments – for women. However, there is substantial controversy – *contested terrain* – about androgen replacement therapy for women, as well as the notion that this syndrome exists. This overview of the contested terrain surrounding FADS will provide a specific example of the roles researchers, clinical trials, industry, and CME conferences play in the legitimatization of a specific medicalized approach to women's sexual problems.

Treating a Syndrome Prior to its Legitimacy

As Table 1 indicates, both Proctor & Gamble and Solvay are testing testosterone products for the treatment of FSD. Additionally, another androgen, DHEA, is available over-the-counter as a "dietary supplement" (the Dietary Supplement Health and Education Act (DSHEA) of 1994 allowed this expanded availability). In spite of the paucity of studies on their efficacy and safety (and absence of FDA approval for testosterone treatments), both testosterone and DHEA are currently being *recommended* and/or *prescribed* by some physicians for treatment of FSD. The basis for these recommendations is that the treatments are intended to address hormone "deficiencies" that result in women's sexual problems.

While studies on the impact of androgens on female sexual functioning have been conducted since the 1940s, the concept of "female androgen deficiency syndrome" is just now gaining momentum (Basson et al., 2001). Research and clinical trials on medical treatments for this new "syndrome" became increasingly visible just as clinical trials of Viagra in women failed to demonstrate any widespread applicability in treating women's sexual problems. A collection of researchers actively advocates the position that women's sexuality can be adversely impacted by androgen deficiency. They specify the following factors as symptomatic of such deficiency: loss of sexual desire, low libido, decreased sensitivity to sexual stimulation in the nipples and clitoris, and decreased arousability and capacity for orgasm (e.g. Davis et al., 1995; Guay, 2001).

Critics argue that the research examining androgens in women is too limited to support such claims (Dennerstein, 2001; Randolph & Dennerstein, 2001). A key limitation, some argue, is that the radioimmunoassays used to measure total serum testosterone in women are designed to test for *excessive* rather than *insufficient* levels of the androgen (e.g. to uncover a reason for hirsuitism). Assays that are sensitive and accurate in the lower ranges are not yet available (Basson et al., 2001). "Normal" levels of testosterone in women are yet to be determined. As a result, there is no consensus on "appropriate" levels of testosterone for women and no agreed upon biochemical definition of the syndrome (Fourcroy, 2000). Additionally, it is not known which subfraction or metabolite of testosterone might be most associated with sexual function. Therefore, specific criteria for diagnosis – and *therapy* – are lacking (Randolph & Dennerstein, 2001). Argues

Basson et al. (2001), "We cannot speak of a deficiency state until we have accurate knowledge of the normal range of activity of the substance in question" (p. 45). Randolph and Dennerstein (2001) are skeptical of the concept of androgen deficiency syndrome in women:

> We are faced with a syndrome characterized by: (1) a variable cluster of symptoms, some non-specific and without validated measures; (2) a biochemical definition hampered by low assay sensitivity, a lack of defined population norms, and a lack of a clear correlation with specific measures of sexual dysfunction; and (3) and imprecise understanding of the relationship of androgens to sexual function in women, leading to uncertainty about what to measure.

According to Dennerstein (2001), many of the studies done on this purported syndrome have been small in scope and largely observational. Almost all of the double-blind, placebo-controlled, randomized clinical trials on the topic have focused on oophorectomized women (who no longer possess ovaries and thus do not receive the androgen contributions from the ovaries) and thus lack generalizability to most women. A widely-cited study by Shifren et al. (2000) indicates that the administration of high levels of testosterone to these women results in greater frequency of sexual activity, sexual fantasies, and orgasm. Fourcroy (2001) maintains that studies such as this one report an "enormous" placebo response that should make researchers skeptical of the results. Describing the lack of research in this area, Basson et al. (2001) note, "There are no scientific studies (placebo-controlled, using physiological replacement only) of ovarian-intact women with an established diagnosis of low sexual desire plus or minus inability to respond sexually" (p. 46). Yet, based on these limited data, the formation and utilization of treatments and treatment guidelines *are under way* (Arlt et al., 1999; Guay, 2001). Note Randolph and Dennerstein (2001), "Despite the lack of known correlation with specific measures of sexual function, it has been recommended that women with sexual dysfunction and a serum-free testosterone concentration in the lower third of the normal range be considered for androgen replacement therapy."

The Risks of Androgen Replacement Therapies

Both DHEA and testosterone are being used as androgen replacement therapies for women, even though they are associated with many known (and perhaps many as yet unknown) risks. The lack of long-term risk study on androgen therapy in women makes it impossible to be certain that all the risks of treatment are understood. One point of caution with DHEA in particular is that the quality of DHEA supplies is uncertain. Because it is considered a "food additive" and "dietary supplement," there is no standardization regarding the strength of DHEA products on the market, and there is no requirement that it be FDA-approved. On this point, Fourcroy (2001) notes: "The current unregulated androgenic dietary supplement

market has provided a huge unstudied and unsafe market for women and children."
The risks may be quite significant: because DHEA metabolizes into estrogens, it
might have implications for breast or ovarian cancer risk (Fourcroy, 2001).

Testosterone can have (sometimes permanent) masculinizing side effects in
women – such as increased hair growth, acne and deepening of the voice. Of a
potentially more serious nature are the increased risks of liver/heart disease and
high cholesterol, as well as masculinization of a female fetus if the androgens
are ingested in pregnancy (Fourcroy, 2001; Lobo, 2001). Due to concerns about
safety and efficacy, the American College of Obstetricians and Gynecologists
issued an opinion in October 2000 cautioning against using androgen therapy
(both testosterone and DHEA supplements) to treat FSD (Basson et al., 2001).

Dissemination of FADS

Androgen deficiency syndrome has been a hot topic at the 2000 and 2001
FSFF meetings, and in June 2001 (between the two FSFF meetings), Princeton
University sponsored a CME conference entitled, "Female Androgen Deficiency
Syndrome: Definition, Diagnosis, and Classification" (Dennerstein, 2001). Both
the 2000 and 2001 FSFF meetings had symposia dedicated to discussing research
on the possible existence of female androgen deficiency syndrome. In 2000,
the symposium was entitled, "Desire, Arousal, and Testosterone," while in
2001, it was called, "Androgen Deficiency Syndrome in Women: Implications,
Mechanisms, and Treatments." The title change is subtle but potentially speaks
volumes, with the title of the 2001 symposium in effect reinforcing the existence
of such a "syndrome." The 2000 panel consisted of three scientists who supported
the notion of such a syndrome and one who expressed a fair amount of caution.
The 2001 panel consisted of three scientists who defended the notion of such a
syndrome and one critic (Boston University School of Medicine, 2000, 2001).

The pharmaceutical industry has been involved in funding research on treatments for FADS, as well as in supporting these conferences. This involvement
causes some skeptics to link the growing industry interest in identifying androgen
deficiency in women directly to profit motives. Notes Fourcroy (2001), "Current
estimates suggest that between 20 and 30% of the female population are thought
to have low sexual desire. Therefore, it is no surprise that the pharmaceutical
industry recognizes this as a lucrative market. To make the advertising claim the
companies must still provide scientific evidence that physiological replacement
therapy improves this disease entity."

One conversation I had with a gynecologist at the 2001 FSFF illustrates
how these symposia can impact clinical practice and the interactional level of

medicalization. He said that one of the impacts of the 2000 FSFF conference was that he learned about prescribing testosterone to women, which propelled him to prescribe it to patients "off-label" in 2001. He explained that he is looking for a remedy for his female patients' sexual problems and that the pharmacological approach seems to provide some sort of an answer. He said he acknowledged risks such as potential masculinizing effects but was still willing to prescribe testosterone.

Once more medical treatments for FSD are on the market, it is likely that direct-to-consumer (DTC) advertising[3] of these products could promote the interactional level of medicalization by coaching the public to conceptualize sexual problems as medical in nature and prompting them to ask physicians for prescriptions to treat these conditions. Because studies have determined that half to three-quarters of consumers asking for a medication by name were given a prescription for that drug (Belkin, 2001; Kaiser Family Foundation, 2001; Wilkes et al., 2000), targeted advertising of medical treatments could both dramatically impact the numbers of prescriptions given to treat FSD and expand a medicalized view of women's sexual problems.

The message that taking testosterone can alleviate women's sexual complaints is already reaching a popular audience, thus potentially creating increased consumer demand for such treatments. For example, in their book called *For Women Only: A Revolutionary Guide to Overcoming Sexual Dysfunction and Reclaiming Your Sex Life* (Berman et al., 2001), intended for a such an audience, urologist Jennifer Berman and sex therapist Laura Berman continually reinforce the merits of testosterone (what they call "the hormone of desire") for many of their patients. As argued elsewhere (Hartley, 2002), while the Bermans mention that testosterone can have masculinizing side effects, their tone still remains uncritical. For example, they state,

> Unfortunately, many doctors still think that in any dose testosterone will cause women to grow a beard or become aggressive . . . To us, testosterone is so central to a woman's sexual function that no lover and no amount of sexual stimulation can make up for its absence.

They point out that there is no consensus on the "normal value" of testosterone in women, yet they do not explore these implications.

RESEARCH TRENDS: STORIES FROM THE FIELD

To better understand the extent to which and the ways in which industry research funds might shape the course of research on FSD, I conducted interviews with research "insiders." In this section, I describe the methodology used in this portion of my work and provide an analysis of the interviewees' stories, including discussion of what led these researchers to study FSD, the perspectives that guide their research, and, most significantly, the *impact of funding trends* on the shape of their work.

Interview Methodology

I interviewed 16 individuals from the following specialty fields: endocrinology, obstetrics/gynecology, urology, neuroradiology, neurology, epidemiology, psychology, psychiatry, physiology, and biochemistry. All but one of the individuals interviewed has either an academic appointment or clinical affiliation with a university. The interviewees were recruited from the list of the State of the Art speakers, Symposium speakers, and the Board of Directors for the 2001 Female Sexual Function Forum (FSFF) conference, which has been the central international clearinghouse for research on FSD since its inception in 1999.[4] Prior to the meeting, I emailed each of the individuals on this list[5] and asked to interview them either at the conference or later, over the phone. I interviewed about half of those on this list who attended the meeting. (Due to the timing of the October 2001 meeting – just over a month after the events of September 11 – several speakers and board members did not attend the meeting.) The other half were not interviewed either because they declined or because after listening to their presentation, I determined that their research focus fell outside the scope of my project (e.g. a symposium speaker who gave a talk on changing STD trends).

Nine of the interviews were conducted face-to-face, six were conducted over the phone, and one was conducted via e-mail.[6] Informed consent procedures were followed, and in the interest of respondent confidentiality, no specific names or institutional locations will be revealed. The face-to-face and phone interviews were tape-recorded and transcribed. The interviews were semi-structured, involving use of a set of standard questions while also allowing the respondent to craft open-ended answers.[7] The interviews ranged from 15 to 40 minutes in length. All interviews were conducted between October 2001 and December 2001. After the interviews were transcribed, I coded and analyzed them with an eye to identifying emerging themes and trends.

Why a Biomedical Perspective?

Those I interviewed in general had high levels of status at the 2001 FSFF meetings, as they were either State of the Art or Symposium speakers (these addresses are higher profile than are the general paper sessions) and/or members of the Board of

Directors. As was the case with the higher profile talks at the 2000 FSFF meetings, the vast majority of these forums represented a *biomedical* perspective (i.e. basic science, diagnostic studies, physiology, clinical trials of medical treatments, and the role of hormones). In general, psychological perspectives were more widely discussed than were the socio-cultural and political determinants of women's sexuality, but only *one* of the fourteen State of the Art addresses or Symposium sessions *focused specifically* on these non-biomedical perspectives.

Although *decades* of research in women's studies, sociology, psychology and related fields have outlined the ways in which relational, cultural, and psychological factors contribute to women's sexual problems (for example, Rich, 1980; Tiefer, 1995; Tolman & Higgins, 1996; Ussher & Baker, 1993; Vance, 1984), these perspectives appear to be downplayed and in short supply at the most prominent conference on FSD. As discussed earlier, the very conceptualization of "FSD" is one of a largely physiologically based disease. In essence, a distinction can be drawn, then, between the longstanding body of research on "women's sexual problems" and the newer work on "FSD" specifically. One of the intents behind these interviews, then, was to answer the question: How might the prominence of the biological perspective on FSD be related to research funding on the part of the pharmaceutical industry?

Pathways into Research on FSD

In untangling the points of significance in the researcher stories, the first step was to categorize the research trajectories of those interviewed. I grouped the researchers into four tracks: (1) the "continuity track," which includes five researchers studying FSD who continue a history of work on women's sexuality and/or sexual problems (of at least five years' in duration); (2) the "crossover track," comprised of four researchers who apply a history of studying male sexuality and/or sexual dysfunction to understanding female sexuality and/or sexual dysfunction; (3) the "expansion track," which consists of three researchers who have a history of studying female reproduction, disease epidemiology or anatomy and are expanding their research to include an explicit consideration of issues pertaining to sexual dysfunction; and (4) the "new applications" track, which involves two researchers who apply heretofore unrelated work to an understanding of FSD. See Table 2, which specifies the research tracks and disciplinary background of the researchers.

Through relating key components of the researchers' accounts, my analysis illustrates three important points: (1) in general, a post-Viagra influx of industry funds for biomedically-focused studies of women's sexual problems has impacted

Table 2.   Research on Female Sexual Problems: Four Tracks.

Tracks	Disciplines of Researchers
Continuity track	Clinical psychology
	Psychiatry
	Psychiatry
	Physiology
	Psychology
Crossover track	Endocrinology
	Endocrinology
	Biochemistry
	Urology
Expansion track	OB-GYN
	Epidemiology
	Neurology
New applications track	Neuroradiology
	Neurology

the course of research (though industry has been most interested in funding work investigating issues pertaining to sexual *desire* and *arousal* but not *pain*); (2) in particular, those with prior experience researching women's sexual problems from the perspective of clinical psychology or psychiatry found that after the success of Viagra for men, industry has asked them to work on drug clinical trials and has been interested in funding their *more physiologically-oriented work*; and (3) the intent of some researchers to press forward with their biomedical research on FSD, *in spite of* low levels of industry support for their line of work at this time, illustrates the joint importance of researcher mobilization and industry support in the medicalization of women's sexual problems.

At least one researcher in *each* of the four tracks has a story that provides evidence that industry has shaped the course of study of FSD by supporting research with a biomedical focus. However, prior to conducting the interviews, a main expectation was that those researchers who had a background in studying male sexual dysfunction (the "crossover track") would have attracted the most industry research support of all groups. The reasoning for this expectation was that because industry found success with biomedically-based sexual dysfunction treatments for men, they would turn to those with background in those lines of research (i.e. endocrinology, biochemistry, urology) to develop parallel treatments for women. While some of these researchers *have* attracted limited amounts of industry interest and support, it was surprising to find that, at least in the sample of researchers who were interviewed, it was those with prior experience researching *women's* sexual problems that seemed to have garnered more significant industry support. However, as the section on the "continuity track" shows, an important qualification is that this industry support came only after the approval of Viagra and has been directed toward only their more physiologically-oriented work.

Some of the stories indicate that such industry involvement does not entirely explain the new interest in studying FSD from a biomedical perspective. As the section on the "crossover track" in particular will indicate, where there is limited industry support, researcher mobilization can still play a significant role in the medicalization of women's sexual problems. Furthermore, as several of the stories indicate, industry is not equally interested in funding work on the variety of women's sexual "dysfunctions" listed in the DSM.

"Continuity Track": Industry Funds Biomedically-Oriented Research

Four of the five researchers in this category have a background in psychology: two are psychologists (one a clinical psychologist) and two identify primarily with psychiatry. The fifth is a physiologist. Each of these researchers has been studying or working in the field of women's sexuality for more than five years. Because their work centered on women's sexuality even before the approval of Viagra in 1998, their research on FSD cannot be considered to be a response to that particular shift. However, in at least four of the cases, the shape of their research enterprises has been *influenced* to some degree by the recent influx of industry funds for biomedically-oriented research this area.

The clinical psychologist has built a career based on studying the psychophysiology of women's sexual arousal and sexual response. She has published on topics ranging from the impact of neurotransmitters on women's sexual arousal (clearly physiological) to the impact of sexual abuse on sexual functioning (clearly psychosocial). Even before the approval of Viagra, some of her research assessed the influence of drug treatments on women's sexual response, but this work had not attracted substantial industry interest. After Viagra hit the market, however, things started to change. As she says, "And then I started to get quite a bit of funding from different pharmaceutical companies." Specifically, because of her reputation in the area, in the late 1990s this researcher was *approached by industry* to participate in multi-site clinical trials on products to treat low sexual arousal in women.

She believes she benefited in several ways from participating in industry-sponsored clinical trial research. This involvement enabled her to support graduate students, and she was able to conduct other research in the lab that was partially funded by industry. The monetary support also allowed her to meet certain expectations on the part of her university as well as learn new information:

I accepted the contract, honestly, for the money. We're expected as new faculty to bring in certain amounts of money, and you know, it's hard to get a big NIH grant . . . And it was also not just for the money. At this point I really wanted to learn what's the mechanism of nitric oxide systems in females. It's very much related to what I had done in the past and questions that I was interested in knowing for my own research.

Still, she identifies significant drawbacks to working on clinical trials: the work is time-intensive, uses her and her students' resources, and may not result in a publication or other type of credit for the work. She now has federal funding in the form of an NIH grant. The drawbacks of clinical trial work, she says, are significant enough to lead her to vow to *not participate* in this type of research again, though with some provisions: "I mean if it turns up my lab runs out of money and I can't get federal funding, of course I'll do anything to be able to continue my area of research. But you know, my least favorable option would be a multi-site big FDA clinical trial."

One of the psychiatrists is based in a university setting and has an academic appointment that is 50% research, 25% teaching, and 25% clinical. Her story contains several of the same themes as seen in that of the clinical psychologist; specifically, she began doing industry-funded work only in the last five years, these funds supported clinical trial work, and she has hesitancies about continuing to be involved in this work. Throughout her career studying women's sexuality, this psychiatrist has also sought to balance a focus on the physiological and the psychological, working to advance a psychophysiological model of sexual functioning. She has conducted research in this area since the 1970s, having published work on topics such as the role of physiology in women's sexuality as well as the influence of psychosocial factors such as ethnicity, body image, and culture. Since the approval of Viagra, she has become involved in studies funded by the pharmaceutical industry, including clinical trials. This research centers mainly on understanding the impact of various medications (and hormones that are not yet in the form of medication) on arousal. As with the clinical psychologist, her work on sexual arousal in women *intersects with industry interest* in developing products to "treat" low levels of arousal in women.

This psychiatrist identifies several constraints associated with industry-funded work, one being the secrecy associated with the research and a restricted flow of information (for example, due to confidentiality concerns, she could not provide me with specific information about these studies). As Tiefer (2000a) has discussed, industry often mandates a secrecy in the conduct of research and analysis of data that contrasts strongly to the openness expected in a scientific community. On this topic, the psychiatrist says,

What happens is that in the period of time that you are actually working on the study, you are under a confidentiality constraint about saying whether or not you're working on the study. And that's just the way it has to go . . . I'll tell you why that's a little bit of a problem. If you're used to being a scientist and not just working with industry, you're used to being open with colleagues, at least colleagues that you trust . . . think it interferes with sort of a natural flow of information.

She considers the chances of getting a publication out of the research to be uncertain, especially if the study has produced negative results. For these and other reasons, she says, industry-funded work may *seem* biased to others, which generally is not the case with research funded from other sources. All told, she is not sure if she will continue to participate in this type of industry-funded research. As her current industry-funded projects are completed, she will assess whether or not she will continue with such work. She notes that industry sources of funding are *increasingly important*, however: "That's where money is coming. There has not been good funding in sexual dysfunction. Not for 25 years, since I began in this field." An additional reason why industry funds are increasingly important is because federal funding agencies have "higher priorities" to fund right now (e.g. AIDS, bioterrorism). Therefore, even though she identifies a variety of constraints with industry funding, she may have fewer options in the future for alternative sources of funding, sources that would be more likely to support the more psychologically-oriented research she also conducts.

The other psychiatrist has found that non-industry sources of research support are quite limited and that industry tends to fund research that focuses on physiology. She has a clinical appointment (is a full-time clinician), and, in her own words, conducts research in her "spare time." She has specialized in the area of sexual medicine since the 1980s, though has conducted research only since 1993. A key interest of hers has been to reconceptualize models of women's sexual functioning to better account for the emergence of desire *during* (as opposed to prior to) the sexual experience. She notes, "As I listen to women recounting their sexual experiences, they clearly are not linear sequences of discreet events as in the traditional Masters and Johnson's 'mountain.' " In this work, which grew out of her clinical practice and has mainly been *unfunded*, she continually emphasizes that women's sexual arousal is far more than a physical genital event and that the field needs to adopt better models of women's sexual desire and response – models that more fully incorporate *psychological* factors – before progress can be made in regards to development of pharmacological treatments.

While this line of research involves explicit incorporation of non-biomedical factors, she has also been involved in research with a distinctly physiological focus. Specifically, in the last five years, this psychiatrist has worked with Pfizer to investigate the use of Viagra in women with low sexual desire and acquired loss of genital physiological congestion. Her perspective is that drugs aimed at increasing women's sexual desire *may have a role* in treatment of low desire, *if* psychological factors are addressed at the same time; however, she expressed some discontent that by the time she became involved in the Pfizer study, the protocol was already established, unfortunately relying on the traditional, biomedically-based view of women's sexual response that she critiques.

When asked to compare her experiences doing industry-funded research versus that funded through other sources, she said she really could not draw such comparisons because none of the funded research she has done has been supported through *non-industry* sources. Her comments parallel the other psychiatrist's observation about the prominent role of industry funding for FSD: "We have found funding to date in the area of sexual medicine *extremely limited* other than through pharmaceutical companies (emphasis mine)." She is concerned with this pattern of funding for research in the field in general, cautioning that researchers should take care to not "get caught up in a premature use of medications, especially that which has serious risk of a long-term untoward outcome."

The three stories above converge around a central theme: researchers who study both psychological and physiological influences on women's sexuality report that funding for their research has been limited until recently, that the pharmaceutical industry is an increasingly important source of research funding in this area, and that their research that has attracted industry support is biomedical in nature. A fourth researcher in the "continuity track" is a physiologist who has been studying the effects of sexual arousal on vaginal function since 1976. Although his work, unlike the three above, does not take into account psychosocial factors, his story parallels theirs in some key ways. Like them, he reports that at the early stages of his career, industry was not interested in funding his work. As he says, "There were no pharmaceutical companies in those days – and for many, many years after – that were the slightest bit interested in our work." Now, he claims, it is "much better," especially since the approval of Viagra.

Currently, he studies the physiology of sexual arousal in women, a research focus sustained by funding from "all over the place." Some of his current research is now funded by industry sources, Pfizer in particular. That particular line of study does not investigate a drug but represents an effort to develop a new technique for measuring vaginal blood flow.[8] In essence, the technique he is developing would derive "absolute values" that could indicate whether one woman actually has, for example, twice as much vaginal blood flow as compared to another woman. While he is not involved in clinical trials, such a technique, if successfully developed, could *apply* to clinical trials in that it could provide an "objective measure" of the impact of certain drugs on the vagina. Because of this potential application, he believes it is likely that he will get more industry funding in the future. He appears to have fewer reservations about industry money than the other three discussed, saying of the funding he has from Pfizer, "There's no strings attached to what we've got at the moment. It's basically, get on, do it, you are your own bosses, and if it works, it's terrific."

The fifth researcher on this track is also a psychologist, and he has studied sexuality in broad terms since the 1960s. Since 1990, he has conducted research on vulvar pain, taking the position that dyspareunia (which includes vulvar pain problems such as vestibulitis) is primarily a *pain syndrome* rather than a *sexual dysfunction*. His work is mainly federally funded (not in the U.S.), and unlike the other researchers in this category, *none* of his research has been funded by industry within the last five years. He has not sought out these funds, nor has he been approached by industry, perhaps because his research on vulvar pain by definition does not center around issues of *desire* or *arousal*, the two areas seeming to attract the most industry funds. He says that for his line of work "there really aren't many relevant drugs." He does note that he would seek industry money if he did not have federal money. While this psychologist argues that vulvar pain is not a sexual dysfunction, per se, he still presents his work on the topic at the conference on FSD, a choice he made mainly because he was asked to be a paid speaker at the conference several times. In fact, he was initially suspicious of the conference, concerned about a biomedical focus. It is important to note that these payments to speakers are made possible in part by industry support of the conference, showing at least the *indirect* influence of industry money on this researcher.

The stories of four of the researchers on the "continuity track" illustrate the importance industry accords to funding those with some track record in studying women's sexuality from a biomedical vantage point. With the exception of the psychologist who studies vulvar pain, these researchers have received industry support of and active interest in their line of research over the last five years. For the clinical psychologist and the academic-based psychiatrist in particular, the approval of Viagra explicitly precipitated increased industry interest in their more physiologically-oriented work and their subsequent decisions to work on clinical trials. That industry is selective in the types of research it funds raises questions about the extent to which these researchers who study both physiological and psychological factors will become increasingly *co-opted*, shifting their studies to the topics that might attract these funds. However, because both the clinical psychologist and the academic psychiatrist expressed strong reservations about continuing this type of involvement with industry, this outcome is uncertain. The clinically-based psychiatrist's research experience, however, illustrates this tension: While she is committed to promoting an alternative, *non-genitally focused view* of women's sexual desire and arousal, she finds that research support tends to be limited to industry sources, thus potentially limiting the range of any non-biomedical research she might undertake.

"Crossover Track": The Role of Researcher Mobilization

One of the themes that emerged from the review of the scientific literature on FSD to date, and that was echoed in many of the interviews with researchers, is that research done on male sexuality is now being applied to an understanding of female sexuality. However, as noted above, one of the striking conclusions to be drawn from the four stories of researchers from the "crossover track" is that industry money has played a surprisingly small role in this particular line of research thus far.

Taken together, the stories of these four researchers also illustrate the ongoing debate regarding the application of some of the research on men's sexuality (specifically, work on the role of androgens in sexual function) to understanding women's sexuality. All four of these researchers have worked with androgens, and the topic of FADS was a common theme among these interviews. The two endocrinologists are strong proponents of the existence of FADS, the biochemist is a bit more reserved about the possible existence of such a syndrome, and the urologist is a resolved critic of the concept of FADS.

The two endocrinologists both have a history of involvement in development and use of medical treatments for male sexual dysfunction. One has studied the impacts of male testosterone deficiency on sexual function, and the other has been involved in various clinical trials of medical treatments for men's sexual problems. In their presentations at the 2001 FSFF, they each asserted the existence of FADS, and each of them conducts research on the use of androgen replacement as a treatment for FADS.

One of the endocrinologists currently has "seed money" from industry sources for his research on this topic and is hoping to attract more funds, though he believes this process might be very difficult because work in this area is new. Companies have to be convinced, he says, "It's like bringing people kicking and screaming into an arena they don't want to be in." (Though, as discussed earlier, scores of clinical trials are currently being conducted on androgens.) He argues that research on androgens and women's sexuality can also be upsetting to some researchers, just as work on androgens and men's sexuality was several decades ago:

> In 1980, we published a paper in which we discovered that men who were impotent also had hormone problems. When we addressed their testosterone deficiency, their sexual function returned. Then, as now, there was a certain amount of resistance. I angered the psychiatrists and even colleagues in urology, as they had been dealing with this with implants. This is basically where we are right now with female sexuality . . . We are again looking at something that will anger some people as we trample on their territory.

The day of the interview, this endocrinologist had an appointment to meet with a pharmaceutical company about the possibility of testing one of their testosterone products. He also conducts research on use of DHEA in treating women's sexual problems. He notes that pharmaceutical companies have no interest in funding research on DHEA because, "It simply represents a threat to them." As discussed earlier, because DHEA is sold over-the-counter and is not patentable, pharmaceutical companies are not able to profit from it.

The second endocrinologist has attracted what he calls only *limited* amounts of industry funding for his research on women's sexual function, which has included studies on the use of hormones as well as products such as Viagra and prostaglandin cream for FSD. Currently, he is conducting privately-funded research (the money comes from an individual family) on the use of androgen replacement therapy as an FSD treatment. He believes that research like his will attract more industry funding in coming years due to the large market for FSD treatments (and in elaborating on this point, he quotes the *JAMA* study discussed above). Both endocrinologists expressed a strong desire to attract additional industry funding, and both downplayed any constraints associated with this funding mechanism.

The biochemist conducts basic science research, and his past research on the biology of penile smooth muscle had relevance to the development of medical treatments for male sexual dysfunction. He was approached in the late 1990s by other researchers who were interested in developing similar products for women, which led him to do related work on female biology. He notes that while his knowledge about men is not a direct crossover to women, it enables a useful initial focus. His specialty is cell biology, which is his entry into understanding the biochemistry of genital sexual arousal. He notes that this focus is new: "There was nothing to start with . . . no animal models, no cell culture models." He has *not* received industry funds for this work. In the late 1990s, with some other researchers, he received an NIH grant for one year of funding to study the biology of female sexual arousal in an animal model, focusing on the role of androgens, estrogens and neurotransmitters. Reinforcing arguments already covered in this paper, he notes that his research area is not attractive to industry funding sources at this point:

> There is no (industry) funding whatsoever . . . Industry is not stupid. They are not seeing there is something ready or taking shape or form. So there's no real funding, at least in our lab . . . This is basic science. This is animal study. No one really wants to fund something like this. . . . I don't have a drug to test today. . . . They play a very interesting game. They want to put the resources where they can maximize from it. They want to wait until someone brings something in science. And then they license it and spend money. They never want to come in way early in the process. Development is very expensive.

He maintains that even though he is conducting research on testosterone, because he's doing the research in animals, industry will not fund it. He has attracted some drug money funding, in the form of unrestricted educational grants (few "strings"), but not to study a particular substance or product.

While industry's lack of interest in the research of the biochemist and in research on DHEA are both understandable, given industry's general lack of involvement in basic research or with products that are not potentially profitable, the endocrinologists' difficulties in securing industry support for work on other hormonal treatments merits additional elaboration. Both of these researchers are actively seeking industry funding and have had success in securing what they consider to be small amounts of industry funds. Based on the potential market for hormone-based treatments, it is likely that both will attract more industry funds for this work in the future. One of the reasons for the delay may simply be the undeveloped nature of their research at this point in time. They will need to demonstrate to industry that their line of research has the potential to be profitable, and the limited funds they have received are, in essence, intended to assist them in that endeavor.

Just as *belief* in the existence of FADS can motivate researchers to pursue biomedically-oriented lines of research on women's sexual problems, *skepticism* about FADS can act as a force for another type of mobilization. The urologist, highly critical of the notion of FADS, has a research background that involves specialization in reproductive endocrinology and male reproductive drugs. She has worked as a medical officer at the FDA, and was responsible for all the approvals of androgen compounds. While she is not currently conducting research herself (thus, the issue of research funding is not pertinent to her situation), she often speaks to conferences about the topic of FADS. She has concerns that meetings such as the CME conference on androgen deficiency held at Princeton are "being pushed by pharmaceutical money, which doesn't make good scientific sense." She also has reservations about the science used to justify FADS, arguing that just because *high levels* of testosterone impact sexual desire does not mean that a "deficiency syndrome" exists:

> I'm perfectly sure that if you give pharmacological levels (high levels) of testosterone to any-body, you can make them horny. But that was not the purpose of giving testosterone. . . . I don't think anybody would argue that you can make people horny, if that's what you call desire, with large levels of testosterone.

Even one of the pro-FADS endocrinologists expresses reservations about the state of research on testosterone therapies for women:

> There was an excellent article by Jan Shifren in the *NEJM* on these (testosterone) patches for women with their ovaries removed who have sexual problems. Women were given two patches – a low dose and a high dose. The low dose brought these ladies' testosterone to a normal range but didn't do anything to improve sexual function. The high dose did, but the levels of testosterone were above normal range. So you get some side effects with it. People are trying . . . like Goldilocks . . . to find something 'just right'.

The urologist, not actively conducting research on female sexual function, has no industry funding or affiliation. Still, though, her professional work appears to have been impacted to some degree by the success of Viagra, if only to prompt her to publicly comment on the dangers of a pro-medicalization research climate, to engage in the contested terrain surrounding this topic. The research of the other three individuals in this track, though, has arguably been *directly impacted* by the Viagra sensation. None of these three were conducting research on female sexual function until after Viagra was approved. In the case of the biochemist, he was approached by and ultimately agreed to work with other researchers who were explicitly intent on finding a parallel treatment for women. The stories of the two endocrinologists attest to the impact of the medicalization of men's sexuality at the *conceptual* level. They appear to have internalized the medical model of men's sexual problems, using that framework in their approach to understanding the sexual problems of women. Their accounts attest to the importance of researcher mobilization and perspective in the medicalization of women's sexual problems.

"Expansion" and "New Applications Tracks": Selective Industry Involvement

The three researchers from the "expansion track" come from a range of professional backgrounds – ob-gyn, epidemiology, and neurology. All have a background of researching some aspect of women's health or anatomy, but their work began to shift to issues pertaining to sexuality only in the last five years (post-Viagra). The two researchers from the "new applications" track have backgrounds in neuroradiology and neurology. None of these five researchers studied women's sexuality prior to 1998, and with the exception of one of the neurologists (who has studied the sexual behavior of mice), none studied sexuality *at all* prior to that time. Two conclusions can be drawn from an examination of the accounts of these researchers: (1) the availability of industry funds can shape the course of research agendas in some cases; but (2) new research on "sexual pain disorders" is *not* an outgrowth of such industry interest.

Both the ob-gyn and the neuroradiologist moved into a new research area in part because of the availability of industry funds. The ob-gyn, who is based at a university and has a clinical practice, is conducting two lines of research on women's sexual function. This general area of research is fairly new for her, just a few years in development. One line of research examines the impact of a nutritional supplement called argenmax on women's sexual function, while the other utilizes brain imaging to discern elements of "normal sexual function" as a basis for defining "abnormal sexual function." She notes that her interest in researching women's sexual problems grew out of her clinical practice:

> A number of my patients were coming in and saying that they really had no libido, they really weren't interested in sex. They had had a nice normal sex life but now were no longer interested, and it was a problem. So, that's what got me interested . . . It was a patient issue.

However, when asked why she started this line of *research* when she did, she answers, "Oh, because somebody (the Daily Wellness Company, which makes argenmax) came to me and said, 'Are you interested in doing something?' and it resonated with what I was hearing from my patients, so I said sure. But I wasn't looking for it." While the Daily Wellness Company can best be categorized as a *nutriceutical* as opposed to a *pharmaceutical* company, still, a key element of her decision to start this new line of research involved being *actively approached by industry*. In the case of her diagnostic study, a colleague of hers approached Pfizer to fund the project, and the company agreed to do so. The ob-gyn's new research direction was influenced by industry's new interest in funding work on FSD (as well as her encounters with patients), and she appears interested in continuing to develop this new line of research.

The neuroradiologist is an academic researcher with a background in employing MRI for general diagnostic purposes. His movement into researching the application of functional MRI as a possible tool for assessing sexual arousal was explicitly a result of new patterns of funding. Specifically, he was asked to collaborate by colleagues who had industry funding to conduct research on a medical treatment. He accepted the offer of collaboration and has now been doing MRI research on sexual function for about three years. This work investigates the feasibility of using MRI to assess genital responsiveness to drug treatments. He describes the relevance of this technique: "There's a big interest in MR these days for use as a technique to validate drug response, in general, not just sexual response." He says that he "backed into" the research, but now feels "almost like I've started a new career here." Although the use of MRI as a technique to validate drug response is not itself novel, his research on the feasibility of using the technique to assess drugs to treat FSD seems to be a product, in large part, of industry support for this work. And now that he has moved into this line of research, his curiosity has been engaged, and he is interested in perhaps continuing with the work.

Both the epidemiologist and the neurologist began studying vulvar pain in the last several years. However, these shifts were *not* a result of an influx of industry funds, as neither has received industry funds to research vulvar pain. Nearly all of the epidemiologist's research is federally funded. He has a background in female reproductive disorders, cancers and depression, and in 2000, received NIH funds for a study to establish the *prevalence* of vulvar pain, as opposed to any implications it has for sexual functioning. He does not expect that pharmaceutical companies will fund his work, since they are more interested in testing the efficacy of treatments rather than the studies of etiology that he conducts.

The neurologist, who has a history of researching pain in general, has been studying vulvar pain for three to four years. Just as with the epidemiologist, while he is studying a condition with *implications* for female sexual function, the focus of his work is not on sexual function, per se. He *has* approached industry for support of his research, but has had little success. While his pelvic pain clinic has attracted some pharmaceutical industry financial support, his research on vulvar pain is "self-funded" through the clinical work in this unit. He laments the lack of drug company interest in this pain issue, and is frustrated that he has not been able to get any drug company interested in funding trials on their products. He believes that pharmaceutical companies will eventually "get on board" to fund this research area: "As more and more companies realize this is a huge problem (that vulvar pain is widespread), they will put more resources into it. They just don't know it yet." He imagines that the pharmaceutical company interest in FSD and the FSFF conferences might translate into a willingness to consider funding vulvar pain projects.

The motivations of the epidemiologist and the neurologist to begin work on vulvar pain over the last several years seem unrelated to industry funding patterns, appearing instead to reflect extensions of their past research on disease prevalence and pain, respectively. As was the case with the psychologist studying vulvar pain, the lack of industry interest in "sexual pain disorders" likely reflects industry perception that there is little potential for the development of drug treatments in this area.

The second neurologist's story differs from these others in that he only studies animals. Specifically, he has over 40 years of experience conducting basic research on animal sex response. One of the research subjects he currently studies is the hormonal and genetic influence on sexual arousal and motivation in female mice. Throughout his career, his research has been mainly funded through federal sources (NIH, NSF); because he is not working on humans, industry sources of funding are limited. To the extent that the intent of basic research has always been to apply it to humans, his work is not technically a "new application." However, his research *is* now applicable to this area of research on FSD in a way it *could not have been* in the pre-Viagra context, which likely accounts for his high-profile role at the FSFF meetings. Ultimately, as researchers and industry became increasingly interested in a biomedically-based account of female sexuality, his work on sexual motivation in female mice became even more strongly regarded as potentially applying to understanding the role of sexual motivation and desire *in women*.

CONCLUSION

This paper has outlined the processes through which women's sexual problems are becoming increasingly medicalized, highlighting the role of diagnostic systems, CME conferences, clinical trials, off-label prescribing practices, attempts to construct a new "syndrome" (FADS), and new biomedically-focused research. Throughout this examination, I have paid particular attention to the role of the pharmaceutical industry in promoting this medicalization, discussing its attempts to market itself and shape perceptions of health care providers; its fiscal sponsorship of the Consensus Panel, which ultimately produced a pro-medicalization classification system; and its efforts to generate a variety of products to treat FSD.

At this stage in the medicalization of women's sexual problems, one of the most significant aspects of the pharmaceutical industry's involvement in the medicalization of women's sexual problems is its funding of research. The analysis presented in this paper works to expand the understanding of the institutional level of medicalization by highlighting some of the complexities inherent in the connections forged between researchers and industry.

Institutional Level Medicalization: Industry and Researcher Roles

It is clear that an accounting of the institutional level of medicalization must consider the role of researchers, the medical profession, and the pharmaceutical industry. While it is unquestionable that the pharmaceutical industry is seeking to expand a medicalized conception of women's sexual problems, an examination of the researchers' stories provides additional documentation for that claim and shows that this endeavor contains a variety of nuances. The researchers' accounts show that industry interest in funding research on treatments for low sexual desire and arousal difficulties in women has impacted the course of research in many instances but that the motivations of some researchers themselves to develop such treatments, even with only seemingly minimal industry support, also work to advance a medicalized conceptualization of women's sexual problems.

Several researchers moved into research on women's sexual function only after the approval of Viagra: the biochemist, the two endocrinologists working on developing androgen therapies for women, the ob-gyn, and the neuroradiologist. The ob-gyn and the neuroradiologist moved into a new research area in part because of the availability of industry funds. While this was not the case for the biochemist or the endocrinologists, the medical *model* of male sexual problems (which arguably culminated in the approval and widespread acceptance of Viagra) still impacted the course of their research, showing that researchers themselves may also have a professional or economic interest in expanding medicalization.

While both the epidemiologist and the neurologist who study vulvar pain also moved into that research area since the approval of Viagra, their shifts do not appear to reflect either industry funding trends or an internalization of a medicalized model of sexual problems. Still, the accounts of those studying vulvar pain (these two researchers and the psychologist) – a condition which is classified as a sexual pain disorder – illustrate the priorities of pharmaceutical companies and the limits of their interest to work that has more clear commercial applications. For those studying women's sexuality since before the approval of Viagra, the impact of changed industry funding trends shows itself in a different manner. For all but the psychologist, that industry ultimately became interested in funding some aspects of their work shifted the course of their research to some degree, raising the possibility of co-optation.

The Bigger Picture

To conclude, I would like to emphasize that the medicalization of women's sexual problems is, of course, but one example of a larger phenomenon: the increasing power of "Big Pharma" (Horton, 2001). The immense profitability of the industry is one indication of that power. However, it is crucial to remember that such profitability is derived from a general expansion of medicalization. Each year, increasing numbers of "ailments" are treated by prescription drugs. People now are taking more prescription drugs than ever before, and per capita drug spending is at an all-time high (Wilkes et al., 2000). Notes the Kaiser Family Foundation (2001), "National spending on prescription drugs is the fastest growing segment of health care spending, accounting for 20% of the estimated increase in such spending between 1999 and 2000." The greatest cost increases, not surprisingly, are coming from those drugs most heavily advertised to consumers, thus highlighting the impact of the deregulation of prescription drug advertising (Belkin, 2001; Kaiser Family Foundation, 2001, Terzian, 1999).

That the pharmaceutical industry enjoys a climate of such deregulation is, in and of itself, also evidence of its growing power. Increasingly, the FDA is beholden to industry for the funds to operate the agency, and several cases of unethical behind-the-scenes relationships between the FDA and particular drug manufacturers have been brought to light (see Washburn, 2001). Such evolutions and diminishing FDA oversight powers threaten the health of the public. As Washburn (2001) describes, "With more than 100,000 Americans dying each year from adverse reactions to prescription drugs – drug reactions are the nation's fourth leading cause of death – the last thing we need is to dismantle the few regulatory checks and balances that remain."

Several practical recommendations flow from the analysis presented in this paper. For one, there is a need for greater government oversight over drug development and prescribing protocols. Specifically, there should be greater scrutiny given to the clinical trial and publication process, to guard against the types of bias discussed in this paper. That women are being given prescriptions for untested and unproven drugs also indicates that there should be greater oversight of "off label" prescribing practices. Additionally, the consumer public should be educated as to the growing power of the pharmaceutical industry in general, as well as its influence over approaches to solving women's sexual problems. The New View campaign is one example of an effort to educate the public about these matters, and it is important that this type of work be expanded. The medical profession, too, needs unbiased sources of education, and policies seeking to contain industry influence over CME would be an important step towards realizing such a goal.

With the medicalization of men's sexual problems and the success of Viagra, Big Pharma marched into our bedrooms. The medicalization of women's sexual problems kicks that march into higher gear, all the while promising to have liberating impacts but confronting us with a host of risks and potential pitfalls. While some of women's sexual problems are medical in nature and might be helped by some of the treatments currently in development, it is important to not overlook the dangers associated with this approach. Medicalization can lead to use of potentially ineffective treatment modalities and increased exposure to risks of side-effects and iatrogenesis, can raise false expectations, and can reinforce dependence on the medical establishment and the pharmaceutical industry (Tiefer, 2002). An important point of balance to what appears to be a pharmaceutical "take over bid" is to insist on incorporating the insights gleaned from the *many* decades of scholarship on the *many* sources of women's sexual problems in all approaches to solving these problems.

NOTES

1. Medical treatment for female sexual "problems" is not entirely novel. Maines (1999) has detailed the history of female "hysteria" – one of the most frequently diagnosed diseases in history – and the medical "treatments" for this condition. Physicians relieved the symptoms of hysteria, through the production of "hysterical paroxysms" (orgasms), which were regarded as the crisis of the illness. Vibrator technology, developed in the late 19th century, was widely used by physicians. Medical use of vibrators ceased once

the technology became popularized through the mainstream press and became available for home use, but it was not until 1952 that the American Psychiatric Association (APA) stopped classifying "hysteria" as a disease.

2. In both 2000 and 2001, Pfizer was a "platinum" level supporter of the conference. In 2001, that meant they donated $20,000–$30,000 (personal communication with Sue O'Sullivan, February 7th, 2002). Solvay Pharmaceuticals was a "silver" level contributor both years, donating $10,000 in 2001. NexMed was also a "silver" level contributor in 2001, up from their "bronze" level contribution in 2000. Proctor & Gamble and Lilly ICOS were "bronze" level contributors ($5,000) both years. Zonagan was a "bronze" level contributor in 2000, but did not contribute in 2001. Pentech Pharmaceuticals and Nastech Pharmaceuticals were not listed contributors to the conference either year. Urometrics, the company that makes the EROS-CTD, contributed to the FSFF both years and became a "platinum level" supporter in 2001.

3. Since 1997, as the result of FDA deregulation, the televised advertising of prescription drugs has expanded dramatically. In 1997, only 12 drugs were advertised on television, and by 2000, at least 50 were (Belkin, 2001; Terzian, 1999). Proponents of televised DTC advertising argue that the ads function as a useful form of education, with critics arguing that the ads promote demand for and use of unnecessary or inappropriate medication and contribute to rising health care costs (e.g., Hoen, 1998; Hoffman & Wilkes, 1999; Hollon, 1999; Holmer, 1999; Lipsky & Taylor, 1997).

4. At the business meeting of the 2001 FSFF meeting, it was decided to change the name of the organization to the International Society for the Study of Women's Sexual Health (ISSWSH).

5. I did not request an interview from one individual on this list because I work closely with her in the New View campaign. Through more informal conversations with her and through review of her published material, I came to understand her perspectives on and relationship to this field of study. Additionally, I was unable to get a valid email address for four of those on the list who lived in other countries.

6. I will not discuss two of the interviews in this paper. The tape recording of one was of poor quality, rendering the data unusable. The other interview is not included because the data were incomplete due to language difficulties.

7. Each respondent answered the following questions: What is your research background, and how long have you been studying FSD? What led you to become involved in studying FSD? In general, what research are you currently conducting, and how are your research projects currently funded? What is the nature of the your relationship (if any) to the pharmaceutical industry? (If have relationship) How did that/those relationship(s) develop? (If conducting research) Do you experience any different pressures/obligations when conducting pharmaceutical industry-funded research as opposed to (any of your) research funded from other sources? How are funding trends for the type of research you do changing/operating as compared to past? Have the types of studies you conduct changed over time in response to funding trends? If so, in what way?

8. According to this researcher, while clinical drug trials and other research often uses photoplesmography to assess vaginal changes (and thus arousal), this technique is riddled with many problems, a significant one being that it cannot function as an objective quantitative index to compare one woman with another woman, or vaginal conditions in one woman over two or more points in time. Over the last two years, he has been working on developing a technique that could be used as a valid index of comparison, both across different women and at different points in time in one woman.

ACKNOWLEDGMENTS

This research was funded through a Portland State University (PSU) Faculty Enhancement Award. In addition, the author would like to thank Kathy Muenzenberg for research assistance and Jeff Gersh for critical commentary.

REFERENCES

Abbott, A. (1988). *The system of professions*. Chicago: University of Chicago Press.
Altman, L. (1997). Experts see bias in drug data. *The New York Times*, p. C1, C8.
American Psychiatric Association (1994). *Diagnostic and statistical manual of mental disorders* (4th ed.). Washington, DC: APA.
Anderson, J. (1992). The deprofessionalization of American medicine. *Current Research on Occupations and Professions, 7*, 241–256.
Angell, M. (2000a). Is academic medicine for sale? *The New England Journal of Medicine, 342*(20), 1516–1518.
Angell, M. (2000b). The pharmaceutical industry: To whom is it accountable? *The New England Journal of Medicine, 342*(25), 1902–1904.
Arlt, W., Callies, F., Vlijmen, J. et al. (1999). Dehydroepiandrosterone replacement in women with adrenal insufficiency. *New England Journal of Medicine, 341*, 1013–1020.
Basson, R., Berman, J., Burnett, A., Derogatis, L., Ferguson, D., Fourcroy, J. et al. (2000). Report of the international consensus development conference on female sexual dysfunction: Definitions and classifications. *Journal of Urology, 163*, 888–892.
Basson, R., Bourgeois-Law, G., Fourcroy, J., Heiman, J., Priestman, A., Rowe, T., Stevenson, R., Thomson, S., & Tiefer, L. (2001). Androgen "deficiency" in women is problematic. *Medical Aspects of Human Sexuality*, 45–47. http://www.medicalsexuality.org
Belkin, L. (2001). Prime time pushers. *Mother Jones* (March/April), 31–37.
Bell, S. (1987). Changing ideas: The medicalization of menopause. *Social Science and Medicine, 24*(6), 535–542.
Bell, S. (1990). Sociological perspectives on the medicalization of menopause. *Annals New York Academy of Sciences, 592*, 173–178.
Berman, J., & Berman, L. (with Elisabeth Bumiller) (2001). *For women only: A revolutionary guide to overcoming sexual dysfunction and reclaiming your sex life*. New York: Henry Holt and Company.
Bodenheimer, T. (2000). Uneasy alliance: Clinical investigators and the pharmaceutical industry. *The New England Journal of Medicine, 342*(20), 1539–1544.
Bodenheimer, T. (2002). Research bias in clinical drug trials. The New female sexual dysfunction: Promises, prescriptions, and profits (conference). San Francisco, CA. March 9th, 2002.
Boston University School of Medicine, Female Sexual Function Forum: New Perspectives in the Management of Female Sexual Dysfunction. CME Conference proceedings, October 26th–29th, 2000.
Boston University School of Medicine, Female Sexual Function Forum: New Perspectives in the Management of Female Sexual Dysfunction. CME Conference proceedings, October 25th–28th, 2001.
Coney, S. (1994). *The menopause industry*. Alameda: Hunter House.

Conrad, P. (1992). Medicalization and social control. *Annual Review of Sociology, 18*, 209–232.

Cowley, G. (2000). Looking beyond viagra. *Newsweek*, April 24th.

Davis, D., McCloud, P., Straus, B., & Burger, H. (1995). Testosterone enhances estradiol's effects on postmenopausal bone density and sexuality. *Maturitas, 21*, 227–236.

DeAngelis, C. (2000). Conflict of interest and the public trust. *Journal of the American Medical Association, 284*(17), 2237–2238.

Dennerstein, L. (2001). Female androgen deficiency syndrome: Definition, diagnosis, and classification (on-line). Available: http://www.medscape.com/Medscare/CNO/2001/Androgen/pnt-Androgen.html

Donchlin, A. (1996). Feminist critiques of new fertility technologies: Implications for social policy. *The Journal of Medicine and Philosophy, 21*, 475–498.

Figert, A. (1996). *Women and the ownership of PMS*. Hawthorne: Aldine de Gruyter.

Findlay, D., & Miller, L. (1994). Through medical eyes: The medicalization of women's bodies and women's lives. In: B. S. Bolaria & H. Dickinson (Eds), *Health, Illness and Health Care in Canada* (2nd ed., pp. 276–305). Toronto: Harcourt Brace.

Food and Drug Administration (FDA) (2000). Guidance for industry. Female sexual dysfunction: Clinical development of drug products for treatment (on-line). Available: http://www.fda.gov/cder/guidance/index/htm

Fourcroy, J. (2000). Diagnostic challenges – Female androgen deficiency syndrome. Female Sexual Function Forum (FSFF). October 26th–29th, 2000. Boston, MA.

Fourcroy, J. (2001). Androgen deficiency syndrome in women: Implications, mechanisms and treatments. Female Sexual Function Forum (FSFF). October 25th–28th, 2001. Boston, MA.

Freidson, E. (1970). *Professional dominance: The social structure of medical care*. New York: Atherton Press.

Guay, A. (2001). Advances in the management of androgen deficiency in women (on-line). Available: http://www.medicalsexuality.org

Hafferty, F., & Light, D. (1995). Professional dynamics and the changing nature of medical work. *Journal of Health and Social Behavior* (Extra), 132–153.

Hartley, H. (1999). Influence of managed care on supply of certified nurse-midwives: An evaluation of the physician dominance thesis. *Journal of Health and Social Behavior, 40*, 87–101.

Hartley, H. (2002). Promising liberation but delivering business as usual? *Sexualities, 5*(1), 107–113.

Hartley, H., & Tiefer, L. (2003). Taking a biological turn: The push for a "female Viagra" and the medicalization of women's sexual problems. *Women's Studies Quarterly, 31*, 42–54.

Haug, M. (1973). Deprofessionalization: An alternative hypothesis for the future. *Sociological Review Monographs, 20*, 195–211.

Haug, M., & Lavin, B. (1981). Practitioner or patient – Who's in charge? *Journal of Health and Social Behavior, 22*, 212–229.

Hoen, E. (1998). Direct-to-consumer advertising: For better profits or better health? *American Journal of Health-System Pharmacy, 55*(6), 594–607.

Hoffman, J., & Wilkes, M. (1999). Direct to consumer advertising of prescription drugs: An idea whose time should not come. *British Medical Journal, 318*, 1301–1302.

Hollon, M. (1999). Direct-to-consumer marketing of prescription drugs: Creating consumer demand. *Journal of the American Medical Association, 281*(4), 382–384.

Holmer, A. (1999). Direct-to-consumer prescription drug advertising builds bridges between patients and physicians. *Journal of the American Medical Association, 281*(4), 380–382.

Horton, R. (2001). The tightening grip of big pharma. *Lancet, 357*, 1141.

Kaiser Family Foundation (2001). http://www.kff.org/content/2001/200111291/; consulted on 12/07/01.

Kaschak, E., & Tiefer, L. (Eds) (2001). *A new view of women's sexual problems*. New York: Haworth Press.

Kennedy, D. (1997). *Academic duty*. Cambridge: Harvard University Press.

Larson, M. (1977). *The rise of professionalism: A sociological analysis*. Berkeley: University of California Press.

Laumann, E., Paik, A., & Rosen, R. (1999). Sexual dysfunction in the United States: Prevalence and predictors. *Journal of the American Medical Association, 281*(6), 537–544.

Leavitt, J. (1989). The medicalization of childbirth in the twentieth century, Transactions. *Transactions & Studies of the College of Physicians of Philadelphia, 5*(11:4), 299–319.

Leland, J. (2000). The science of women and sex. *Newsweek*, May 29th.

Light, D. (2000). The medical profession and organizational change: From professional dominance to countervailing power. In: C. Bird, P. Conrad & A. Fremont (Eds), *Handbook of Medical Sociology* (5th ed., pp. 201–216). Prentice-Hall.

Lipsky, M., & Taylor, C. (1997). The opinions and experiences of family physicians regarding direct-to-consumer advertising. *The Journal of Family Practice, 45*(6), 495–499.

Lobo, R. (2001). Androgens in postmenopausal women: Production, possible role, and replacement options. *Obstetrical & Gynecological Survey, 56*, 361–376.

Maines, R. (1999). *The technology of orgasms: "Hysteria", the vibrator, and women's sexual satisfaction*. Baltimore and London: Johns Hopkins University Press.

Marken, S. (1996). The problematic of "experience": A political and cultural critique of PMS. *Gender and Society, 10*(1), 42–58.

McKinlay, J. (1988). The changing character of the medical profession: Introduction. *Milbank Quarterly, 66*(Suppl. 2), 1–9.

McKinlay, J., & Arches, J. (1985). Towards the proletarianization of physicians. *International Journal of Health Services, 15*, 161–195.

Oinas, E. (1998). Medicalization by whom? Accounts of menstruation conveyed by young women and medical experts in medical advisory columns. *Sociology of Health and Illness, 20*(1), 52–70.

Pugliesi, K. (1992). Premenstrual syndrome: The medicalization of emotion related to conflict and chronic role strain. *Humboldt Journal of Social Relations, 18*(2), 131–165.

Randolph, J., & Dennerstein, L. (2001). Female androgen deficiency syndrome: A hard look at a sexy issue. *Medscape Women's Health, 6*(2).

Relman, A. (2001). Separating continuing medical education from pharmaceutical marketing. *Journal of the American Medical Association, 285*(15), 2009–2111.

Rich, A. (1980). Compulsory heterosexuality and lesbian existence. *Signs, 5*, 647–650.

Riessman, C. (1983). Women and medicalization: A new perspective. *Social Policy, 14*, 3–18.

Shifren, J., Braunstein, G., Simon, J. et al. (2000). Transdermal testosterone treatment in women with impaired sexual function after oophorectomy. *New England Journal of Medicine, 343*, 682–688.

Slaughter, S., & Leslie, L. (1997). *Academic capitalism: Politics, policies, and the entrepreneurial university*. Baltimore: Johns Hopkins University Press.

Spilker, B. (2002). The drug development and approval process (on-line). Available: http://www.phrma.org/searchcures/newmeds/devapprovprocess.phtml

Sullivan, D. (1993). Cosmetic surgery: Market dynamics and medicalization. *Research in the Sociology of Health Care, 10*, 97–110.

Starr, P. (1982). *The social transformation of American medicine*. New York: Basic Books.

Terzian, T. (1999). Direct-to-consumer prescription drug advertising. *American Journal of Law and Medicine, 25,* 149–167.

Tiefer, L. (1994). The medicalization of impotence: Normalizing phallocentrism. *Gender and Society, 8*(3), 363–377.

Tiefer, L. (1995). *Sex is not a natural act, and other essays.* Boulder: Westview.

Tiefer, L. (1996). The medicalization of sexuality: Conceptual, normative, and professional issues. *Annual Journal of Sex Research, 7,* 252–282.

Tiefer, L. (2000a). Sexology and the pharmaceutical industry: The threat of co-optation. *The Journal of Sex Research, 37*(3), 273–283.

Tiefer, L. (2000b). The consensus conference on female sexual dysfunction: Conflicts of interest and hidden agendas. *Journal of Sex & Marital Therapy, 27*(2), 227–236.

Tiefer, L. (2001). Arriving at a new view of women's sexual problems: Background, theory, and activism. In: E. Kaschak & L. Tiefer (Eds), *A New View of Women's Sexual Problems* (pp. 63–98). New York: Haworth Press.

Tiefer, L. (2002). Female sexual dysfunction: Where'd it come from and where's it going? The new female sexual dysfunction: Promises, prescriptions, and profits (conference). San Francisco, CA, March 9th, 2002.

Tolman, D., & Higgins, T. (1996). How being a good girl can be bad for girls. In: A. Maglin & D. Perry (Eds), *Bad Girls, Good Girls: Women, Sex, and Power in the Nineties* (pp. 205–225). New Brunswick, NJ: Rutgers University Press.

Ussher, J., & Baker, C. (Eds) (1993). *Psychological perspectives on sexual problems: New directions in theory and practice.* New York: Routledge.

Vance, C. (Ed.) (1984). *Pleasure and danger: Exploring female sexuality.* Boston: Routledge and Kegan Paul.

Washburn, J. (2001). Undue influence: How the drug industry's power goes unchecked and why the problem is likely to get worse. *American Prospect* (August 13th), 16–22.

Wazana, A. (2000). Physicians and the pharmaceutical industry. *Journal of the American Medical Association, 283,* 373–380.

Weitz, R. (Ed.) (1998). *The politics of women's bodies: Sexuality, appearance and behavior.* New York: Oxford University Press.

Wilkes, M., Bell, R., & Kravitz, R. (2000). Drug research and development: Direct-to-consumer prescription drug advertising. *Health Affairs* (March/April), 110–128.

Zola, I. (1972). Medicine as an institution of social control. *Sociological Review, 20,* 487–504.

THE CONTINUUM: SOMATIC DISTRESS TO MEDICALIZATION IN WOMEN WITH BREAST CANCER: THEORETICAL AND EMPIRICAL ASSESSMENT

Erica S. Breslau

ABSTRACT

The sequence of stress, distress and somatization has occupied much of the late twentieth-century psychological research. The anatomy of stress can be viewed from interactional and hybrid theories that suggest that the individual relates with the surroundings by buffering the harmful effects of stressors. These acts or reactions are called coping strategies and are designed as protection from the stressors and adaptation to them. Failure to successfully adapt to stressors results in psychological distress. In some individuals, elevated levels of distress and failed coping are expressed in physical symptoms, rather than through feelings, words, or actions. Such "somatization" defends against the awareness of the psychological distress, as demonstrated in the psychosocial literature. The progression of behavior resulting from somatic distress moves from a private domain into the public arena, involving an elaborate medicalization process, is however less clear in sociological discourse. The invocation of a medical diagnosis

Gender Perspectives on Health and Medicine: Key Themes
Advances in Gender Research, Volume 7, 131–180
Copyright © 2003 by Elsevier Ltd.
All rights of reproduction in any form reserved
ISSN: 1529-2126/doi:10.1016/S1529-2126(03)07005-X

to communicate physical discomfort by way of repeated use of health care services poses a major medical, social and economic problem. The goal of this paper is to clarify this connection by investigating the relevant literature in the area of women with breast cancer. This manuscript focuses on the relationship of psychological stress, the stress response of distress, and the preoccupation with one's body, and proposes a new theoretical construct.

INTRODUCTION

Overview

Interest in the relationship between stress and stress responses has occupied much of the late 20th-century sociological and psychological literature. The literature demonstrates evidence of considerable variability in conceptual perspectives and diversity in methodological approaches to the study of stress and stress responses (Aneshensel, Rutter & Lachenbruch, 1991; Kaplan, 1996). Fundamental to the differences in perspectives and approaches is the distinction in the basic questions asked by respective disciplines. However, as noted by Kaplan (1996), all conceptual frameworks of social stress draw analytic distinction between certain separate components: life circumstances, subjective evaluation of life circumstances, adaptive-coping-defense responses, and stress consequences or outcomes (Kaplan, 1996; Kasl, 1984; Thoits, 1983).

As a means of integrating the current, somewhat fragmented knowledge of stress and its sequelae, it is suggested that progressive events occur in breast cancer patients, summarized as follows: psychological distress, preoccupation with one's body, physical symptoms, and the resultant search for medical care for explanations and relief of symptoms. The aim of this article is to understand the relationship between these constructs and integrate them into a perspective that describes the continuum from stress to medicalization. Specifically, the connections between a distress adjustment in breast cancer patients, the receptiveness of the medical system to the physical expression of distress, and the ultimate result in costly and generally unnecessary health care are explored, with the aim of treating psychosocial aspects of breast cancer patients more productively, efficiently and economically.

This article is divided into six sections. First, the overall relationships among conceptual domains of stress, distress, somatization, and medicalization are outlined in Fig. 1. The model guides the discussion of the interrelationships among psychological, social, political and economic forces and underscores the role each plays in breast cancer. Second, unique aspects of stress and distress

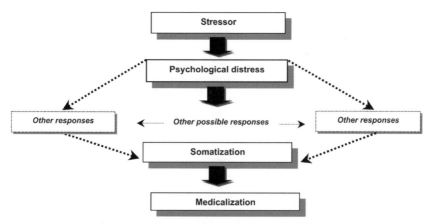

Fig. 1. Sequential Movement of the Somatic-Distress-Medicalization Continuum.

outcomes are described using theoretical frameworks and conceptualizations as they apply to breast cancer. Third, a discussion of the psychological distress reaction, somatization, is presented in the context of women with breast cancer. Fourth, the theoretical aspects of medicalization as a sociological construct are presented. Fifth, the progress of somatic behavior into the public arena is documented. A key feature in this evolutionary process is labeling somatic behavior a medical issue through common vernacular, institutions and communities alike. Application of a medical diagnosis is reinforced through technology use and consumption of health care resources. A formalized medicalized state transforms the character of somatic distress beyond a clinical problem to one involving many layers of society. Finally, concluding sections synthesize the discussion with a general critique of the literature and suggest how future research may reflect, in a unified way, the process of psychological distress that results in the phenomenon of medicalization.

SCOPE OF THE REVIEW

Entering the Health Care System

Breast cancer patients enter into the medical care system because of self- or physician-identification of a lump or an abnormal mammogram. The psychological impact of the breast cancer experience has been described as a continuum, which varies for patients throughout the course of illness. While the majority of women with cancer do not suffer short-term harm, there appears to be a small group of women who are adversely affected in the initial stages of diagnosis and treatment. A larger group of women is affected at some other distinct point during the course of illness, and others experience a delayed reaction six months or more after the end of treatment (Buick, 1997; Holland, 1997; Loscalozo & BritzenhofeSzoc, 1998; Meyerowitz, 1980; Rimer & Bluman, 1997). However, over the long haul, this crisis is weathered and most women have a favorable prognosis with the ultimate successful psychological management of distress (Loscalozo & BritzenhofeSzoc, 1998).

Psychological Responses and Adjustment to Cancer

Psychological responses to a precipitating stressor range from mild reactions of psychological distress, to psychological responses of vulnerability, sadness, or worry, and finally to discrete psychiatric disorders such as depression and anxiety disorders (Derogatis et al., 1983; Holland, 1997; Meyerowitz, 1980). The essential aspect of a response to illness is the perception that a serious threat (i.e. stressor) has occurred to an individual's physical and personal existence (Fig. 1). The intensity and duration of psychological symptoms produced by a diagnosis of breast cancer depend on a variety of factors connected with the individual, the illness, and the individual's social and interpersonal relationships with the medical team, family, and friends. Personal attitudes toward the illness reflect the values, attitudes and views of the culture, society, and social and familial groups, as well as the individual's less conscious and more symbolic meanings of symptoms, illness and cancer (Leventhal, 1986).

Cognitive responses and adjustment to breast cancer diagnosis and treatment involve a range of coping styles that reflect adaptation. The coping literature indicates that a small group of patients with elevated levels of distress expresses negative emotions through physical expressions of bodily symptoms, rather than through feelings, words, or other actions (Fig. 1). The process, known as *somatization*, is the expression of bodily symptoms, which defend against the awareness of psychological distress (Lipowski, 1987).

Patient Involvement

When a chronic illness, such as cancer intrudes, psychological stress may itself result in the perception of physical symptoms, and seeking of medical care to rule out pathological or organic causes. For some patients, the inclination is to focus on the somatic aspects of distress. This occurs particularly in the presence of a stressful life experience, concurrent stressors, a number of competing demands, or major emotional turmoil (Northhouse, Mood, Templin, Mellon & George, 2000). According to Barsky and Borus (1995), somatic expressions may be acute or chronic, coincidental with medical illness, or without a connection to medical illness. Patients who somatize stress may do so as a transient response to the cancer illness, or may have symptoms associated with persistent depression or anxiety (Lipowski, 1987). As explored in this article, when psychological morbidity, expressed as distress or somatization, poses a threat to distressed women, it affects quality of life, compromises life expectancy, impacts medical outcomes, and increases utilization of medical services (McKenna, Wellisch & Fawzy, 1995).

Physician Involvement

Once somatization is "named" by the physician via the application of a diagnosis and treatment, one may say medicalization occurs (Fig. 1). Medicalization occurs as patients rely on doctors as technical experts for an evaluation of their behavior, to define their illness and to treat their disease (Costa & McCrae, 1985). In the era of managed care, the economic, social and political climate has also encouraged medicalization by shifting psychological management of care to the primary care physician's domain and away from mental health specialists. In doing so, the emphasis has been shifted from interpersonal treatment to clinical treatment.

Medical System Involvement

From this perspective, the medical system's receptivity to a chronically ill person's physical complaints encourages the somatization of the ubiquitous distress that breast cancer patients experience, because of a vested interest in the illness condition. The proverbial outcome of medicalization is the identification of a diagnosis, which sanctions the use of broad-spectrum medical treatments, including elements of the growing technological apparatus (Costa & McCrae, 1985; Epstein, 1996). Understanding how these complex clinical and behavioral factors are influenced by technological, economic and political systems is a formidable task for those who wish to explain our system of oncological care.

CHARACTERISTICS OF STRESS AND DISTRESS

Psychological Stress

Theories of stress have focused on the relationships between disease and stress, and illness and stress. This is because it is useful to identify conditions as biological phenomenon or social phenomenon. The biomedical paradigm focuses on disease rather than illness since it is derived from a reductionist paradigm, which separates mind from body. It has, moreover, power to shape the world of disease in this image (Haug, Musil, Warner & Morris, 1998; Kanton, Kleinman & Rosen, 1982a; Kasl, 1984). In contrast, when considering theories of stress, the shift is to illness rather than disease, because illness can also be defined as a personal event or as a social phenomenon. Contrasted with disease, which evolved from the biomedical model (i.e. generally grounded in biology and specifically pathology), illness is an autonomous entity defined by standard and universal criteria, derived from the social sciences. As such, "disease" is a physician's evaluation and labeling of the bodily (somatic) change (Haug et al., 1998; Radley, 1994; Stahl & Feller, 1990). Accordingly, the biomedical model removes the social context of meaning (Mishler et al., 1981). "Illness," on the other hand, moves in sequence from private to public and only becomes a public and a social issue with the revelation and presentation of symptoms to medical providers or other authorities in a social context. However, as Haug and colleagues (1998) conclude, the vast majority of illness episodes remain private and are never brought to professional attention.

Many viewpoints of stress have been presented in the psychological and sociological literature, but psychosocial issues presented by interactional theories shed light on the connection of stress to characteristics of the individual and surrounding life context (Lazarus & Folkman, 1984). Interactional theories can be analyzed by studying three components: stressors that initiate the stress cycle; psychological filters that an individual uses to evaluate the stressor; and coping responses that are deployed to manage the processed stress (Jackson, 1999).

Conceptualization of Stress

As represented in Fig. 2, interactional theories emphasize an exchange between the cognitive processes of appraising and moderating the stressor and possible stress outcomes. This exchange psychologically buffers the harmful effects of stressors experienced by the individual (Derogatis & Coons, 1993; Pearlin, 1991; Spring & Coons, 1982). Exposure to stressful life events or *stressors*, the threatening

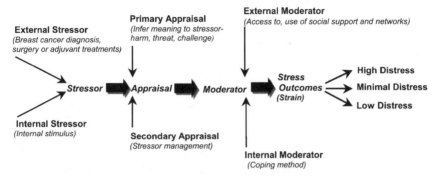

Adapted from Pearlin, 1991, and Permission to Reproduce from Plenum Press.

Fig. 2. Anatomy of the Stress-Distress Process.

conditions or demands on the individual are embedded in the social structure (Holmes & Rahe, 1967; Wheaton, 1996).

Appraisal
In the stress framework, when an individual confronts an external (i.e. breast cancer diagnosis, surgery, or treatment) or internal (i.e. personality structure) stressor distinct structural phases are traversed. Initially, one engages the process of *cognitive appraisal* to assess and interpret the encounter, thus giving the meaning to the stressor that something of importance is at stake. As Lazarus (1966), and Lazarus and Folkman (1984, 2000) propose, appraisal of the stressor event leads to an evaluation of the stressful experience with respect to subsequent physiological and behavioral responses. *Primary appraisal* involves estimating the degree of threat, harm, or challenge portrayed by the stressful event. *Secondary appraisal* involves managing the stressor, which is accomplished by utilizing personal resources to determine whether the effects of the stressor can be minimized or eliminated (Lazarus & Folkman, 1984; Park & Folkman, 1997; Taylor & Aspinwall, 1996). Assessment is a dynamic process and as new information is obtained, situations are constantly reappraised.

Moderators
Next, *moderators* explain the relationship between the stressor and a distress outcome (Breckler, 1995). A moderating process requires that an individual give meaning to a stressor event, and incorporate coping strategies to react or negate the stressor effects (Breckler, 1995; Eisdorfer, 1985). Both *external* (i.e. time, money or social support) and *internal* (i.e. personality traits and coping abilities)

factors are important to alleviate detrimental effects of the stressor one's quality of life and on the course of the cancer (Taylor & Aspinwall, 1996).

Coping
The subject of different coping styles has been identified and summarized in the psychosocial and the stress literature by Taylor and Aspinwall (1996). The five approaches to coping include: *avoidant* (minimizing); *active* ("fighting spirit"), *confrontive* (aggressive); *anxious* (worry), and *fatalistic* (helpless or hopeless).

Central to Lazarus' (1966) cognitive stress-appraisal model is the critical element in positive or negative coping, which emphasizes the contribution of the individual and their interaction with the environmental stressor. How patients perceive, appraise and manage their illness influences the resulting level of distress, coping approach, illness adjustment, and its sequelae (Buick, 1997; Lazarus, 1966; Lazarus & Folkman, 1984; Northhouse et al., 2000).

Psychosocial Reaction to Stress: Distress

There are many stress responses and consequences that bear on productivity, health and well being (Dougall & Baum, 2001). In addition to physiological changes, stress that affects mood, psychological distress can increase negative emotions such as depression, anxiety, anger, fear and overall symptom reporting (Fig. 2). These negative emotions occur when the perceived stressor exceeds personal resources, resulting in impaired functioning (Dougall & Baum, 2001; Kaplan, 1996; Lazarus, 1966; Lazarus & Folkman, 1984). In other words, it is the negative meaning uniformly attached to the extreme stressor (cancer diagnosis, treatment and the loss of personal control over one's health) that produces distress (Farmer & Ferraro, 1997).

DEFINITIONS OF PSYCHOSOCIAL DISTRESS IN CANCER

Distress, a multifaceted and complex concept, has been defined as "an unpleasant experience of a psychological, social, or spiritual nature that interferes with the ability to effectively solve problems associated with the cancer illness" (Derogatis, 1986, p. 634). In breast cancer, as in other cancer patients, psychosocial distress is the range of feelings and emotions expressed by individuals as they face personal and illness-related problems (Farber, Weinerman & Kuypers, 1984; Stefanek, Derogatis & Shaw, 1987). Distress may also be related to family problems or sever anxiety or depression (Holland & Gooen-Piels, 2000).

Some investigators have recognized that when a heightened psychological (cognitive, behavioral or emotional) response is clinically present in oncology patients it presents as a continuum of severity, which at maximum produces disabling symptoms (Holland & Gooen-Piels, 2000). For example, Holland (1997), notes that the distress spectrum varies from normal or mild feelings of vulnerability, sadness, and fears related to the illness, self, and family, to more severe reactions that constitute discrete psychiatric disorders such as depression and anxiety to psychoses. The constellation of signs and symptoms, may initially be elevated, or may begin as a crisis in response to the stressor. For the majority of patients (50%–75%), distress subsides after the critical cancer event is experienced (Baker et al., 1997; Passik, Kirsh, Rosenfeld, McDonald & Theobald, 2001). However, where distress remains clinically elevated, adjustment disorders are seen in about 30% and an additional 30% have exacerbated psychiatric syndromes, requiring psychological management (Passik et al., 2001).

Prevalence of Distress and Psychiatric Manifestations

Between 30% and 50% of patients diagnosed with breast cancer, develop significant distress-related problems adjusting to diagnosis and treatment (Breslau, Curbow, Zabora & Parmigiani, 2001; Massie & Holland, 1989; McKenna et al., 1995; Passik et al., 2001; Zabora, BritzenhofeSzoc, Curbow & Piantadosi, 2001). Recent research on many types of cancer suggests that one out of every three newly diagnosed cancer patients experiences higher levels of distress at diagnosis, than at any time in the course of their disease. This is because diagnosis of cancer provokes a questioning of the meaning of life, and a need to explore beliefs about life and death (Derogatis, Morrow & Fetting, 1983; Farber et al., 1984; Holland & Gooen-Piels, 2000; Zabora et al., 2001). Empirical breast cancer studies suggest that some experience higher levels of psychological distress early in the course of their disease, others later in treatment, remission, recurrence, progression, advancing, or terminal phases of the disease (Cassidy, 1986; Weisman, Worden & Sobel, 1980).

If distress symptoms are severe enough to constitute a recognizable psychiatric diagnosis, clinicians then regard distress symptoms as "subsyndromal" (Holland, 1997). Women reporting subsyndromal levels of psychological distress attribute the distress to an array of physical, social, sexual, employment, and insurance problems, rather than directly to the cancer. Among the subset where more severe distress symptoms are observed, psychiatric disturbances manifest as situational or reactive anxiety, or depressive symptoms requiring psychiatric treatment (Holland, 1997).

The frequency of psychiatric disorders has been studied in large populations of women with breast cancer and findings vary according to cancer site and diagnostic stage. Findings can be summarized as follows. Approximately 50% have no psychiatric disorder, 25%–30% have major depression or an adjustment disorder, and 20% will present with a more severe formal psychiatric diagnosis (Massie & Holland, 1989). According to Holland (1997), adjustment disorders are an intermediary psychological state flanked by psychiatric pathology and normal coping under stress. Among those with an adjustment reaction or a formal psychiatric diagnosis, depression, and to a lesser extent anxieties are most often seen (Derogatis et al., 1983; Massie & Holland, 1990). Less common are organic brain syndromes, no more common than in the general population (Barraclough, 1994). All however, affect everyday performance.

For a subset of women, the hallmark of a maladaptive response to breast cancer is extreme depression or anxiety. For these women, distress is frequently translated into psychopathology and expressed by a variety of physical symptoms that may or may not be related to active cancer treatment. Since maladaptation of physical and psychological symptoms remain until the stressor is removed or coping skills implemented, it follows then, that psychosocial screening for stress-related disorders early in the diagnostic process may facilitate identification of vulnerable breast cancer patients (Zabora, BritzenhofeSzoc, Curbow, Hooker & Piantadosi, 2001). This is an especially important goal in today's health care climate, since screening may prevent lengthy and more costly treatment of susceptible patients, predisposed to psychological distress.

Movement From Distress to Somatization

In general medicine, common expressions of psychological distress may be articulated as somatic illness, asthma, ulcers, chronic or psychogenic pain, hypochondriasis, or other diseases or syndromes (Holmes & Masuda, 1974; Kornblith, 1998). While some women with breast cancer can expect that they will suffer from the insidious and ambiguous effects of the disease and its treatment, the medical literature indicates a wide array of clinical expressions of somatic illnesses, suggestive of psychiatric and organic conditions among individuals with psychological distress (Passik et al., 2001).

As has been pointed out with chronic illnesses other than breast cancer, the experience of having symptoms forms the "illness identity" around which other illness beliefs develop. When individuals experience distress symptoms, it is natural that they will attempt to label them, apply meaning to them with resulting expectations. Alternatively, individuals who have an illness label will search for symptom information consistent with this label (Pennebaker, 1982). To explore these alternatives, in the following section, somatization is focused on as a particular and important outcome of psychological distress.

PSYCHOLOGICAL DISTRESS REACTION: SOMATIZATION

Theoretical Approaches

This section aims to frame the progress of distress resulting in physical symptoms within a theoretical framework. The psychosocial life-events approach proposed by Holmes and Rahe (1967) focuses on exogenous stressors as the stimuli that trigger a generalized vulnerability to illness. Conversely, the psychosomatic approach is interested in identifying individuals at risk for certain diseases because of their personality or responses to specific events (Zegans, 1982).

On a psychodynamic level, it has been postulated that physical complaining constitutes a discrete psychiatric diagnosis called "somatization disorder" (Gureje, Simon, Ustan & Goldberg, 1997; Kanton, Kleinman & Rosen, 1982a). Other literature suggests that articulation of somatization occurs as a defense against the awareness of psychological distress (Derogatis et al., 1983; Gureje et al., 1997; Kanton, Kleinman & Rosen, 1982b). The psychodynamic postulate suggests that the major life event stressor, including diagnosis, treatment and adjustment to breast cancer illness can result in psychological morbidity, which is then communicated by bodily symptoms, rather than through positive sequelae, expressed as coping through feelings, words, or actions (Andrykowski, Brady & Hunt, 1993; Chaturvedi & Maguire, 1998; Pennebaker, 1982).

Definition: Not a DSM-IV Diagnosis

As documented by medical historians, the clinician Wilhem Stekel introduced the term "somatization" early in the 20th century to refer to a hypothetical process whereby repressed neurosis was expressed as physical symptoms (Lipowski, 1986; Shorter, 1992; Waitzkin & Magana, 1997).

In the 1960s, Lipowski elaborated on somatization and defined *somatization* as a "tendency to experience and communicate psychological distress in the form of physical symptoms, and to seek medical help for them" (Lipowski, 1986, 1987). More recently, somatization has been described as both a syndrome and a figure of speech. The somatizing syndrome refers to a long history of multi-system complaints, medical investigations and clinical treatment, but with no physical cause being found for the symptoms. The somatic figure of speech describes the presentation of bodily symptoms instead of a direct verbal statement of disturbed emotions, with no demonstrable pathophysiological explanation present (Ben-Tovim & Esterman, 1998). What all somatizing patients have in common is that their bodily distress is related to underlying psychiatric or psychological morbidity, or social problems (Barsky & Borus, 1995; Ford, 1998; Kanton, Von Korff & Linn, 1990; Lipowski, 1988). According to Barsky and Borus (1995), somatization expressions may be acute or chronic, coincidental with medical illness, or a medical illness may not be present. Existing in all patients clinically is a common perspective: they fear having a serious physical disorder and seek medical treatment.

Conceptualization of Somatization

Studies encompassing the stress-illness and stress-symptom relationships have identified four broad components to explain the somatization process (Fig. 3). Two overarching phases entail progression from the individual's private experience with somatic distress to the public pursuit of health care for relief.

As depicted in Fig. 3, a theoretical model of somatization in breast cancer is organized around four phases – three private and one public. Private phases of somatization are: *individual* experience of distress and what is perceived in

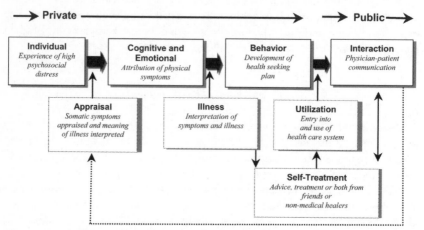

Fig. 3. Anatomy of the Distress-Somatization Process. Progression from a Private Experience of Distress to the Public Pursuit of Medical Health Care for Symptom Relief.

regard to bodily sensations; *cognitive and emotional* attribution of distress to physical illness, and the *behavioral* decision to seek health care. Within the private experience, individuals regulate their relationship to the distress event through four coping responses – appraisal, illness, self-treatment and utilization (Leventhal & Diefenbach, 1991; Schuman, 1965).

Two coping mechanisms – self-treatment and utilization bridge the junction between the private and the public experience. *Self-treatment* can include non-medical persons administering complementary treatments, and *utilization* involves a decision making process, resulting in a shift in the individual who recognizes that they need to seek professional care. Thus, begins the journey into the health care environment. Once within the health care system, the public phase is epitomized by *interaction* with health care professionals, physician-patient communication, and physicians reporting negative findings from presented symptoms (Lipowski, 1988; McWhinney, Epstein & Freeman, 1997).

Appraisal
The *individual phase*, discussed in the psychological distress section of this paper, does not need further elaboration. Appraisal, a coping mechanism as it is connected to psychosocial stress is different from the appraisal connection to somatization. Here, in the *appraisal phase*, frequently influenced by previous illness experience, individuals become aware of a bodily change and focus on somatic stimuli and sensations (i.e. changes produced by an illness or a disease). At this point, individuals construct a representation of an illness episode and create a coping plan, which may or may not result in formal medical treatment (Leventhal & Leventhal, 1993; Nerenz, Leventhal & Love, 1982). To process information about bodily sensations, basic subjective questions are asked, such as "is it illness?" and if so, "what illness is it?" Because of uncertainty associated with illness, these questions focus on ana-lyzing somatic changes, as well as serve to filter and interpret somatic information.

A common way to manage distress is to interject personal meaning into illness uncertainty (Mishel, 1993, 1996). To understand illness episodes, explanation of somatic modification may vary widely from obscure and diffuse to conscious self-awareness of bodily sensation (Gijsbers Van Wijk & Kolk, 1997; Leventhal & Diefenbach, 1991). As worried individuals decide if they are ill, symptoms are monitored, clustered according to abstract sensations (loss of appetite, nausea, or fatigue), and if illness is discerned, then symptom labeling (flu) begins a diagnostic process (Leventhal et al., 1983).

On the other hand, if symptoms are concrete and can be attributed to cancer, such as a lump in the breast, then a "wait and see" strategy may be adopted as an alternative to determine if symptoms are getting worse (Facione, 1993). Along these lines, appraisal delay – delay seeking medical treatment surrounding interpretation and meaning of complex and often protracted cancer symptoms accounted for 60% of the delay in women with breast symptoms compared to 80% of women with gynecologic cancer (Andersen, Golden-Kreutz & DiLillo, 2001).

Illness

In the *illness phase*, interpretation and meaning are attached to the symptoms, which are scaled according to hierarchical dimensions (acute-chronic, fatal-nonfatal, or normal) to assess their importance as an illness or non-illness (Leventhal et al., 1983). Generally, the illness episode is nested within a larger personal, social and cultural context that influences the reactions evoked and proce-dures to manage them (Leventhal, Leventhal & Cameron, 2001). For instance, 40% of women entering chemotherapy treatment for metastatic breast cancer believed their disease was equivalent to an acute, curable disease. These assumptions reflect how labels and meaning are attached to the somatic experience (Leventhal, 1986).

Help-Seeking Behavior

As the illness episode unfolds, a period of self-treatment is undertaken. However, if *self-treatment* is unsuccessful, too difficult or uncertain, initiation of information or *help-seeking behavior* occurs, resulting in a decision to consult a non-physician (i.e. non-medical healer, friends), physician or other medical services (Mishel, 1996; Morgan, Calnan & Manning, 1985). If uncertainty associated with symp-toms reaches a threshold and if illness-related information is not provided, it compromises psychosocial adjustment (Mishel, 1996).

An important step in health-seeking behavior reflects a change in the indi-vidual's views of their somatic and psychological system. When symptoms are regarded as serious, as in the case of breast cancer, very little time is spent before calling for expert advice, as compared to delayed time for symptoms that are mild. For symptoms judged possibly severe, the middle aged (i.e. age 45–55 years old) delayed calling for help-seeking behavior six times longer than the elderly (i.e. over age 65 years old), suggesting a fear of finding out about a life-threatening illness (Leventhal, Leventhal & Cameron, 2001).

Utilization

The *utilization phase* begins entry into the public arena with a decision to contact a traditional physician to alleviate symptoms (Kessler, Lloyd, Lewis & Gray, 1999). Utilization ends when medical contact and evaluation are made, resulting in physician interaction, adoption of a medical framework and medical intervention to treat the symptom (Caccioppo, Andersen, Turnquist & Petty, 1985; Leventhal & Diefenbach, 1991).

Self-Treatment
An alternate utilization pathway into the public arena involves unsuccessful *self-treatment* resulting in contact with a non-medical healer, as a complement or an alternative to established medical practices (Burnstein et al., 1999). Alternatively, non-traditional healers may be sought in response to particular changes in one's health status not warranting traditional medical intervention.

Burnstein and colleagues (1999) classified complementary medical therapies into two categories: healing therapies, which require physical action or exposure of the body (i.e. megavitamins, herbal remedies, diet, chiropractic, acupuncture, massage, energy healing, homeopathy, or folk remedies), and psychological therapies, involving primarily mental processes (i.e. relaxation, self-help groups, spiritual methods, imagery, biofeedback, or hypnosis). In dealing with the uncertainty of new diagnosis, early stage breast cancer women sought different forms of complementary medical therapies as an adjunct to conventional therapy. Three months after diagnosis, 28% (135 of 480) of new users of psychological and healing therapies used alternative medical treatments as a way to manage psychological distress (Burnstein et al., 1999; Holland, 1999). These mind-body techniques exemplify how uncertainty can be incorporated into daily routines to mobilize psychological well being.

Interaction – Communication Links the Private and Public Somatic Experience
The strategic element, the *interaction phase* is the cognitive decision to *communicate* facts about symptoms and in doing so actively seeking support from medical or non-medical professionals. The latter two phases, self-treatment and utilization initiate forward movement into the public domain.

The nature of the interaction between patient and doctor is determined in part by the way this experience is organized by the patient. For instance, two patient perspectives are identified. One, those patients who seek medical care as a problem-solving activity, and two, those who seek medical care purely for emotionally focused support (Leventhal et al., 1983). Another helpful perspective is the distinction between the patient's illness view and the patient's disease view. Furthermore, the attraction of the "sick role" may also determine the patient's choice of viewpoint (Parsons, 1951). On the other hand, the doctors' communication skills and attitudes also play a part in identifying distress-related somatic symptoms, however the outcome will be influenced by what the patient chooses to present (Fallowfield & Jenkins, 1999; Kessler et al., 1999). Alternatively, anxiety and fear inhibits some women from requesting a second opinion, or questioning doctors about pros and cons to pharmacological agents (Leventhal, Leventhal & Cameron, 2001).

Psychiatric Theories of Somatiztion

Theories of somatization with medically unexplained symptoms have been approached and analyzed in the psychiatric literature in three ways. *Functional somatization* refers to a count of the number of medically unexplained somatic symptoms occurring during a patient's lifetime. *Hypochondriacal somatization* refers to the worry or belief that one has, or is vulnerable to, a serious illness despite reassurances from physicians and the absence of demonstrable disease. *Presenting somatization* refers to the presentation of exclusively somatic symptoms to a physician, despite the presence of psychiatric illness (Robbins & Kirmayer, 1991). What all somatization syndromes have in common are person factors, the presence of symptoms which are contributing predictors for illness conditions, and the resulting use of medical care (Barsky, Wyshak & Klerman, 1986a, b).

Functional Somatization

Patients with *functional somatization syndromes*, present to specialty clinics with discrete forms of unexplained somatic distress. As the name implies, it is a disturbance of physiological function, rather than anatomical structure demon-strated by tissue abnormality. As Barsky and Borus (1999) observe "psychosocial factors and symptom amplifiers compound and perpetuate symptoms . . . making symptom relief difficult" (Barsky & Borus, 1999, p. 921; Kirmayer & Robbins, 1991).

The functional somatization diagnostic label has been applied to several syndromes, including chronic fatigue syndrome, multiple chemical sensitivity, fibromyalgia, sick building syndrome, chronic whiplash, Gulf War syndrome, as well as the side effects of silicone breast implants (Barsky & Borus, 1995). Common among all with this disorder are "the explicit and highly elaborated self-diagnoses, and symptoms that are often refractory to reassurance, explanation, and standard treatment. Patients share similar phenomenologies, high rates of co-occurrence and similar epidemiologic characteristics" (Barsky & Borus, 1999, p. 130).

Perhaps there are other yet unformulated explanations for these symptoms. De-bates in the scientific literature provide evidence for distinct physiologic symptoms or non-behavioral explanations for some of these syndromes (Antelman, 1988; Bennett, 1999; Haley, Hom, Roland, Bryan, Van Ness & Bronte, 1997). While the absence of a well-established medical cause does not mean that functional somatization does not exist, it has not been diagnosed using current techniques (Barsky & Borus, 1999). Furthermore, although these patients constitute a heterogeneous group, what individuals with these syndromes have in common are elevated rates of co-morbid psychiatric disorders (Barsky & Borus, 1999).

Hypochondriacal Somatization

Hypochondriacal somatization is distinct from functional somatization in that individuals are preoccupied with illness, not the symptom or disease experience (Barsky, Wyshak & Klerman, 1986a, b; Robbins & Kirmayer, 1991). The assumption about this syndrome is that it involves worry about the possibility that one has a serious illness, which begins with cognitive and perceptual deficits that cause an individual to experience normal bodily sensations as particularly noxious and intense. These individuals mistakenly attribute bodily sensations to serious disease and conclude that they are ill. To further explain this disorder, several authors suggest that hypochondriacal individuals may be more sensitive to sensory stimuli, have less tolerance for experimental pain, and exhibit lower pain thresholds than other individuals (Barsky & Wyshak, 1989; Barsky, Wyshak & Klerman, 1986a, b; Robbins & Kirmayer, 1991). As with functional somatization, co-morbid psychiatric disorders (i.e. major depression) are frequently seen with these individuals.

Presenting Somatization

Individuals with the third somatization disorder, *presenting somatization*, have complaints that predominantly involve only somatic symptoms. Clinically, the majority present with a diagnosable disorder, *not* psychiatric symptoms and clinicians report that most often major depression or anxiety may account for the symptoms (Robbins & Kirmayer, 1991). These patients are unwilling to admit that there is a psychosocial dimension to their distress, which frequently leads to psychiatric problems going unnoticed (Kanton, 1987; Robbins & Kirmayer, 1991). The literature, which deconstructs somatic types, provides a clear message that a concurrent psychiatric diagnosis of mood or anxiety disorder is most likely to be seen in presenting somatizers, but not in functional somatizers. Furthermore, along these lines, Robbins and Kirmayer (1991) point out that it is wrong to assume that all somatizers have an underlying major psychiatric disorder that accounts for their physical distress.

Transient and Persistent Somatization

Separate from the above literature, two behavioral characteristics of somatic behavior have been delineated, *transient* and *persistent*. According to Lipowski (1987), *transient* somatic behavior occurs as a relatively acute and self-limited response to a stressful life event or situation. This transient somatic behavior can take two courses. It either spontaneously goes, or goes once the physician reassures the individual that there is no physical illness.

On the other hand, *persistent* somatic behavior suggests a more chronic problem, which may persist a lifetime. These individuals are preoccupied with, or fear, having a physical illness and hunt for a medical diagnosis and treatment. This latter behavior is akin to hypochondriacal behavior described above. Persistent somatic behavior is a challenge to clinicians since these individuals insist they are physically ill when their only problem is a consequence of their somatic distress. Furthermore, persistent somatizers are patients who "doctor shop," and are eager to undergo medical diagnostic and therapeutic procedures (Lipowski, 1987).

A medical condition must be recurrent to support somatization over long periods, and while breast cancer sometimes involves a lengthy illness, it is largely a chronic illness manifesting in single episodes (i.e. initial breast cancer) or as a series of single episodes (i.e. breast cancer recurrence). Therefore, the disease does not provide a consistent context for a somatic explanation of the patient's psychological needs over time. That may explain why somatizers have been reported to cluster in general primary clinical or cardiac settings, but identified less often in oncology settings.

Conversion – Primary and Secondary Gain

Earlier theories of somatization connect the syndrome to the psychoanalytic concept of conversion (or hysterical neurosis), which can be described as the translation of a psychological conflict into bodily symptoms (McWhinney et al., 1997). Conversion is perceived as having two gains – primary and secondary.

The *primary gain* is obtained by avoiding internal conflict and the *secondary gain* by avoiding an unpleasant or harmful activity, with the resulting symptoms articulated as a form of communication about underlying distress (American Psychiatric Association, 1980).

Somatization in Breast Cancer Patients

In the oncology literature, three theories suggest a connection between somatization and breast cancer. In the first place, individuals who have a diagnosis of breast cancer may bring preexisting somatic concerns to the illness, which may mimic the cancer or the treatment. Alternatively, individuals with somatoform disorder may receive a breast cancer diagnosis. Finally, individuals with breast cancer may develop somatoform disorder as a coping method (emotion-focused strategy) and as an expression of distress (Ford, 1998). Additionally, the fact that psychological states can influence pain or somatic perception by intensifying the pain or somatic symptoms so that symptom-expression is exaggerated increased or persistent symptoms should not be overlooked (Agnew & Merskey, 1976; Chaturvedi, Hopwood & Maguire, 1993; Chaturvedi & Maguire, 1998).

Somatization Expressed as Anxiety and Depression

The nature and frequency of studies and reports of somatic complaints in both the general and breast oncology literature, is scant. In most cases, studies addressing various cancer populations frequently include anxiety and depression measures along with assessment of somatic complaints and psychiatric symptoms. Significant methodologic variability exists among studies examining symptoms, few are of a prospective follow-up or experimental design, and most have small sample sizes.

Clinicians acknowledge that it is difficult to identify the exact etiology of somatic symptoms in breast cancer patients since, in agreement with the above theories, several factors may be competing simultaneously: physical, psychological, or both (Chaturvedi & Maguire, 1998). Furthermore, other problems prevail including deciding which physical symptoms are due to the cancer, cytotoxic drugs, radiotherapy, psychiatric disorder or a combination (Chaturvedi & Maguire, 1998; Petty & Noyes, 1981).

Researchers agree that a diagnosis of breast cancer can elicit psychosocial distress, which can manifest as depression and anxiety. In fact, depression, followed by anxiety is the most prevalent psychological problem for cancer patients (Derogatis et al., 1983). Treatment expectations also are borne out through negative psychological responses. For example, patients expecting to suffer from pain commonly overestimate or underestimate treatment side effects. These expectations generate elevated psychological distress during specific adjuvant treatment phases, as well as throughout immediate months and years following treatment (Derogatis et al., 1983; Groenvold et al., 1999; Levy, Heberman, Lee, Lippman & d'Angelo, 1989; Meyerowitz, 1980; Morris, Greer & White, 1977; Passik et al., 2001; Schag, Ganz, Polinsky, Fred, Hirji & Petersen, 1993).

Studies that use the methodologies of patient self-report and observer ratings describe that the frequency of depression in newly diagnosed breast cancer patients varies widely from a low of 5% to a high of 53% (depending on tumor site and stage at diagnosis). Twenty to twenty-five percent of patients will manifest major depressive symptoms at some point in their illness, as compared to some 6%–7% of women in the general population who develop clinical depression (Derogatis et al., 1983; Massie & Holland, 1989, 1990; Meyerowitz, 1980; Pennebaker, 1982).

One study revealed that oncologists were able to perceive patients' physical symptoms correctly, but they underestimated levels of anxiety and depression (Holland & Gooen-Piels, 2000). Hospitalized patients have higher frequency of both psychosocial problems and psychiatric disorders due to level of active treatment illness. Ambulatory patients, screened for psychological distress in the waiting room, showed that a quarter to a third have significant distress (mixed anxiety and depressive symptoms) and should be referred for evaluation by a mental health professional (Holland & Gooen-Piels, 2000).

These findings suggest that the level of illness matters, and that a predisposition to depression depends on specific factors. Factors associated with a higher prevalence of depression among breast cancer patients include distinct risk markers. These are: family history of depression; previous episode of major depression; history of alcoholism; advanced stage of illness; poor prognosis; family history of breast cancer; level of social support and concurrent life stresses (Kash, Holland, Halper & Miller, 1992; Kash, Holland, Osborne & Miller, 1995; Massie & Holland, 1990; Massie, Spiegel, Lederberg & Holland, 1995).

Breast Surgery and Adjuvant Treatment

Breast surgery is another variable influencing depression outcomes in breast cancer patients. Undergoing surgery to remove the breast, although regarded as being more curative than other treatment modalities, is not desired by some patients because of physical and psychological disfigurement (McKenna et al., 1995; Psychological Aspects of Breast Cancer Study Group, 1987). Approximately one-third of women undergoing any type of breast surgery experience significant depression, and a similar proportion experience additional psychological distress in the year following surgical treatment (Morris et al., 1977; Sanger & Reznikoff, 1981).

Undergoing radiotherapy following surgery may be more psychologically disturbing than initially assumed (Rowland & Massie, 1998). Generally, patients are most anxious at the onset of treatment, uncertain during transitions, and more depressed at the end, apparently because of radiation side effects (Greenberg, 1998). In addition, since fatigue is a central symptom of depression and is frequently experienced with radiotherapy, radiation-fatigue may mask or increase depression (Massie & Holland, 1990; Rowland & Massie, 1998).

The picture is complicated for women who undergo adjuvant chemotherapy and/or hormonal treatment (or both). Depression that is experienced may be influenced by reduced levels of serotonin or by pharmacological drugs themselves (Maguire et al., 1980). Therefore, teasing out cause and effect with cytotoxic influence is recognizably complex.

In cancer patient research in general, and in breast cancer research specifically, a clear spectrum of depressive severity is recognized. Since some patients suffer from sub-clinical manifestations, physicians fail to recognize depression 50% of the time (Payne, Hoffman, Theodoulou, Dosik & Massie, 1999). As suggested, lack of recognition may also occur because many cancer patients are being treated with multiple cytotoxic medications, or have concurrent illnesses that produce depressive symptoms. Furthermore, many cancer patients are also polysympomatic (i.e. fatigue, appetite loss, weight loss, insomnia, and loss of energy), and many of these symptoms resemble the classic symptoms of depression (Passik, Dugan, McDonald, Rosenfeld, Theobald & Edgerton, 1998; Payne et al., 1999). In addition, depressed individuals may report more, as well as a greater variety of, more severe physical symptoms than in non-depressed patients, thus complicating the clinical picture further (Burnstein et al., 1999). Alternatively, some individuals may be reluctant or unwilling to disclose emotional responses, because they or clinical staff lacks the appropriate communication skills (Fallowfield & Jenkins, 1999). Thus, it is important for expected medication side effects to be explained, so the meaning of physical and psychological changes is comprehended.

Legitimizing Illness and Movement to Medicalization

In biomedicine, symptoms reported by patients are legitimate only if they have an organic basis and are caused by disease, can be diagnosed, treated with medication, and cured (Skelton, 1991). Symptoms associated with illness have broader psychological, behavioral and social consequences than disease, particularly because patients determine their degree of disability and compliance with treatment regimens based on illness, rather than disease (Lacrois, 1991).

Most important is the insight articulated by Parsons' (1951) theory of illness describing entry into a sick role and passage as a matter of personal gain through the medical system. When one becomes a patient, one is socially expected to seek medical help and to comply with recommended clinical treatment. The assumption is the sick role is relinquished once the illness disappears. The process of how a private behavioral episode or a behavioral condition becomes part of the public and social enterprise of medicine is not at once self-evident.

Understanding the anatomy of the stress-distress-somatization continuum, offers the possibility of influencing it to the benefit of medical care. Somatization can be seen as a visa, or entrance ticket, to the world of medical diagnosis and treatment. Implied in this perspective is that the patient and the doctor enter into a form of collusion which seems to further the patient's needs to receive and provide care but in fact does not do this effectively.

MEDICALIZATION: A SOCIAL CONSTRUCT

Medicalization is a social construct derived from an expansive sociological discourse. Theoretically, the concept is grounded in social construction and interaction paradigms. These models aim at explaining (from macro to micro phenomena) why somatic distress symptoms, initially a personal matter, emerge as popular discourse and become social and medical problems requiring the provision and management of health care.

Scholars of social construction submit that medical issues influenced initially by social and cultural forces, are molded further by those involved in the debate over the medical definition and management of a specific issue. Within the field of medical sociology, the theory of medicalization has had wide application. Diverse conditions have been medicalized, for example: mental health (Rosen, 1972); hyperkinesias (Conrad, 1975); childbirth and women's health in general (Barker, 2000; Oinas, 1998; Reissman, 1983); alcoholism and drug addiction (Appleton, 1995; Costa & McCrae, 1985); age and the aging process (Binney, Estes & Ingman, 1990), and chronic fatigue syndrome (Broom & Woodward, 1996). We propose that somatization; a deleterious outcome of psychological distress has also been medicalized.

In a landmark article, Ivan Illich (1982) contrived the expression "medicalization" as a description of various facets of medical life. He stated that *medicalization* occurs "whenever some aspect of ordinary, everyday life comes to be redefined so that it requires input from an institutionalized medical system" (Illich, 1982, p. 463). A decade later, the sociologist Peter Conrad (1992) stated that the approach to *medicalization* consists of "defining a problem in medical terms, using medical language to describe a problem, adopting a medical framework to understand a problem, or using a medical intervention to 'treat' it" (Conrad, 1992, p. 211). Conrad, elaborates by saying that:

> Medicalization occurs when a medical frame or definition has been applied to understand or manage a problem. . . . The interest in medicalization has predominantly focused on previously non-medical problems that have been medicalized . . . but actually, medicalization must include all problems that come to be defined in medical terms (Conrad, 1992, p. 211).

Finally, a third explanation of medicalization linked with somatization suggests that distress moves into the public domain when somatic sensations are translated into symptoms by breast cancer patients. Following Conrad's paradigm, a process of medicalization results from the doctor-patient exchange, whereby symptoms are communicated, medical labels, and diagnosis applied. Diagnosis involves technology, health care resources and a medical or pharmacological intervention to treat physical and or psychological somatic symptoms (Barsky & Borus, 1995).

From the medical sociological "gaze," Reissman (1983), recapitulates medicine's expanded influence over our lives with her analysis suggests that in fact, there are two interrelated medicalization processes. These processes bring about the objective validation of the condition under the rubric of allopathic medicine. Reissman states:

> First, certain behaviors or conditions are given medical meaning – that is, defined in terms of health and illness. Second, medical practice becomes a vehicle for eliminating or controlling problematic experiences that are defined as deviant, for the purpose of securing adherence to social norms (Reissman, 1983, p. 4).

Conceptualization of Medicalization

Medicalization occurs as a sequential redefinition of a personal state until sanctioned and defined as a "problem" by medical individuals who apply or do not apply a medical diagnosis (Fig. 4). The illness behavior of distress expressed as idiopathic symptoms is initially a private issue, unconnected to the medical system (Breslau, Curbow, Zabora & BritzenhofSzoc, 2001). When somatic distress experience by specific populations, such as breast cancer patients becomes a public problem, medicalization occurs at six levels of society, which Conrad and Schneider (1980), and more recently Conrad and Potter (2000) have eloquently summarized.

At the *conceptual level*, medical professionals use a medical vocabulary to define the problem at hand, although medical treatments are not necessarily applied.

At the *institutional level*, once the problem is understood and justified, organizations adopt a medical approach to treat a patient. Physicians function as gatekeepers and non-medical personnel accomplish everyday routine work related to the problem.

At the *interactional level* physician-patient communication occurs. Physicians define a problem as medical (i.e. gives a medical or psychological diagnosis),

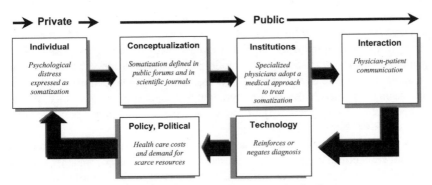

Fig. 4. Medicalization Validates the Somatization Process.

or treat "social" problems with a medical form of treatment (i.e. prescribing anti-depressant drugs).

At the *technology level*, the diagnoses is reinforced or refuted. If supported, technology, including biochemical and pharmacological methods are embraced since the perception is technology is cheaper, more efficient and evidence-based, rather than dependent on traditional, sustained psychological treatment. Independent of what technology determines on a scientific basis, within health care institutions, technology is frequently used to support economic and social decisions (Leventhal, Leventhal & Cameron, 2001).

The final public phase occurs at the *policy and political level* involves insurance companies, who have a stake in reducing clinical and medical costs. Evidenced by managed care guidelines, which direct chemical treatment for psychological disturbances and refuse to reimburse breast cancer patients who are not diagnosed as having a mood disorder. This brings about a managed care driven diagnosis (Rotwein, 1991; Sharfstein, 1998).

Conceptualization of the Medical Issue

Scientific ideology plays an important part in the conceptualization of medicalized issues. Reissman (1983) observed that the construction of scientific knowledge is a historically determined social activity, rather than the abstract, value-free quest of truth. Over time, particular scientific agendas are favored, certain issues embraced and are embedded within social and public agendas. Reissman (1983) and others, argue that the social medical agenda is rooted in the way biomedical professionals think about problems with patients (Dresser, 2001).

Emerging Scientific Knowledge

Medicalization in general, and construction of scientific knowledge specifically, evolved from the late 19th-century philosophical expansion to scientific medicine. The biomedical framework is firmly established within a cause-and-effect paradigm, unlike the social and emotional aspects of illness, which are unsuitable to a pathological disease process. The late 20th-century shift to an increasing commercialization of biomedicine, especially in oncology, further supports the technical authority of science and the cultural authority of medicine (Barker, 2000; Dresser, 2001).

A further argument advanced in support of how a condition, positioned in the social fabric can serve the interests of physicians, academicians, hospital administrators and political personnel is apparent with scientific discourse. As identified by Conrad and Schneider (1992), different institutions facilitate identification of a problem through scientific discourse, as follows. First, a concept or a condition (i.e. somatization) is codified as part of the "official medical and/or legal classification system" and a systematic description of the condition is published in professional diagnostic manuals (i.e. The Diagnostic and Statistical Manual of Mental Disorders-DSM) and disseminated to medical and scientific professionals. Second, over time, the condition becomes bureaucratized through normal and frequent use (i.e. with clinical oncology staff) and in the process is subsumed into large federal or national institutions (i.e. National Comprehensive Cancer Network) as scientific knowledge.

Professional Classification
One has only to look at how medical discourse labels specific psychosocial or behavioral phenomenon, then follow subsequent progress to observe its assimilation into public venues. Professional classification involves two steps. First, the purpose of disseminating findings from empirical studies is to elucidate, clarify and redefine concepts over time in order to advance scientific knowledge. However, publicizing study results may also confuse or change the original interpretation of the behavioral phenomenon, rather than refine it. As a result, public milieu, such as scientific meetings and conferences, designed to publicize discussions about particular academic and clinical viewpoints, provide open forums for clarification of ideas and presentation of theoretical research in general (Pilowsky, 1987). Scientific evidence from psychiatric, psychological and oncology studies upholds the premise that "illness behavior" leads to an increased attention of "somatic conditions" among certain groups of breast cancer patients (Derogatis et al., 1983; Lipowski, 1987). Over the past decade, scientists and clinicians took note of data discussed at academic and professional meetings and continued the discourse, which created a wider social appeal for concepts that originated in scholastic debates within narrow circles (Pilowsky, 1987).

Second, as the medical literature legitimized the descriptive label "somatization," professional organizations, such as the American Psychiatric Association convened expert committees to consider diverse viewpoints. Here, deliberations by "expert" clinicians and researchers symbolize the intellectual process of calling for a definition, diagnosis, clarifying etiology and proposing viable treatment for the condition, as well as providing terminology with which to discuss "somatization."

As Dresser (2001) notes, professional classification legitimizes descriptive labels that will affect different patient groups over time by integrating diagnosis and treatment into everyday clinical practice, so experts have an obligation to ponder the full impact of their decisions. As an example, it its ascent for validity, somatic illness has not been without controversy. An ardently debated issue within the psychiatric (but not in the oncology) community surrounded inclusion and exclusion of specific parameters categorized in the third and fourth edition of the DSM (Costa & McCrae, 1985; McWhinney, Epstein & Freeman, 1997).

For instance, the characterization of somatization in DSM-IV matured from a prior two-factor diagnosis in several ways. First, unexplained physical complaints must last at least six months, and physical complaints must cause significant distress. The diagnosis now comprises a larger number of criteria which, in addition to the above, include the following three components: the patient has undergone appropriate investigation with no resulting medical diagnosis; the symptoms are not intentionally feigned; the physical complaints or resulting occupational or social impairment are in excess of what would be expected (American Psychiatric Association, 1980).

Medical professionals and many practitioners alike, pay considerable attention to conditions included within the psychiatric manual, a guide which is used not only as a basic clinical reference book but as a means to achieve reimbursement for services based on diagnosis – a use for which DSM was never intended. Thus, the way in which patients' somatic symptoms are medicalized has far reaching economic consequences.

Public Endorsement – Electronic Dissemination
As a body of published research is first dispersed, two public responses have been recognized. First, either the public may be slow to accept professional concep-tualization, or alternatively the public may pressure institutions and professional organizations to accept the concept as professionals see it (Appleton, 1995; Dresser, 2001). In today's environment, two dissemination processes prevail simultane-ously making public dissemination of medical and scientific information almost instantaneous. Electronic broadcasting, via the Internet, television or the radio while providing immediate "sound bites" of information, distribution is reinforced through more traditional print media, which expands or clarifies technical jargon in common vernacular. Immediate electronic communication broadcast (i.e. e-mail, mailing lists, chat rooms, discussion or newsgroups and listservs on websites) to lay patient communities, special interest groups, educated individuals, and the pub-lic in general is intended to serve a variety of groups through quick dissemination. The portrayal in popular culture and films of psychologically distressed women with breast cancer experiencing somatic symptoms further coalesces information exchange, enabling cause-specific advocacy groups to circulate their experiences with others, continuing to shape public opinion (Breslau, 1999; Dresser, 2001).

Public Endorsement – Individual Dissemination
A second method of acceptance involves actions resulting from self-help and consumer advocacy groups. As Dresser (2001) observes, this occurs through

individual constituencies advocating a position, challenging opponents to create favorable public pressure, or disseminating public information. Since the 1980s, non-medical, lay organizations began to communicate with each other about specific chronic symptoms that did not resemble known illnesses (Dresser, 2001). Certain breast cancer groups began advocating for inclusion in chemoprevention trials that involved enrolling healthy "high-risk" individuals rather than cancer patients. Enrollment is complicated because of ethical concerns, not to mention temporary discomfort resulting from treatment side effects, as well as anxiety and depression symptoms resulting from somatic distress.

More recently, communication practices that use more savvy media techniques, such as individual testimonials and case histories are positioned as sympathetic news stories. A skill employed by breast cancer advocacy and consumer groups is to gauge public success by assessing the amount of medical, scientific and government attention attracted, measured incrementally over years. Examples of skilled constituencies include disparate groups who targeted public exposure for a collection of "specific" somatic symptoms, thought to be unrelated. For them, successful public awareness resulted with somatic evidence being unified, named and classified, as chronic fatigue syndrome (Fukuda et al., 1994). On the other hand, somatic distress in oncology has not yet found advocacy supporters, possibly because it is embedded within a constellation of psychosocial responses associated with the reality of the illness, treatment and palliative care. Although breast cancer treatment is episodic, those who do participate in clinical trials with toxic medications are likely to endure physiological disturbances in the hope of receiving curative therapy. Thus, problems arise when treatment-related symptoms are confused as distress-related symptoms, and are communicated publicly in a somatic form.

Institutional Classification
As Conrad and Schneider (1980, p. 270) point out once a syndrome becomes institutionalized, it "reaches a state of fixity and semi permanence." Within institutions, an intellectual convergence occurs and here, the individual and the medical viewpoints are legitimized. Governments, corporations and foundations enfold emerging medicalized concepts into their organization, particularly if "novel" ideas emphasize their purpose.

Today, many individuals and groups, besides institutions are interested in the outcome and direction of scientific decision making. As evidenced by a recent evolution in the review of scientific proposals, that involves the inclusion of members of the public, as advocates for a specific disease (i.e. breast cancer). These non-scientists sit on peer review panels with experts in relevant academic fields and together the two groups assess the biomedical science of breast cancer.

This transpired because previously, critics contended that funding decision making was not based on scientific merit or fair allocation, but was "closed" involving a predetermined priority setting (Dresser, 2001). This new trend, a patient-centered model opened a previously closed system, so that final decisions of what will be funded no longer remain inherently under an institutional and scientific influence.

Institutions Adopt a Medical Approach

Over the past century, two intellectual paradigms dominated the construction of social reality in biomedicine. These paradigms, influenced by inductive and deductive thinking, guided the interpretation of disease and illness, the training curriculum of basic and clinical scientists, and the philosophy of academic and medical institutions.

Inductive and Deductive Tension

Sanctioned by the medical community, a fundamental difference in interest and orientation exists between biomedical researchers, whose "primary commitment is to (pure) science, and practicing physicians, whose immediate commitment is to patients" (Epstein, 1996, p. 23). Consequently, basic researchers are "invested in the conception of biomedicine as science" from an inductive perspective, while clinical practitioners are "invested in the reductionist, exclusionary biomedical model" (Epstein, 1996, p. 24).

Unlike basic researchers, the cultural model for modern medicine and clinical sciences is shaped in reductionist empiricism, a paradigm that has been used to educate generations of physicians to base assumptions on scientific knowledge and to recognize a combination of signs and symptoms that locate the problem of disease within the individual body (Reissman, 1983). Intellectual and clinical information about illness and disease are processed in clinical settings where a history and physical examination occur first. This leads to a preliminary diagnosis by analogy, or in more difficult cases, identification is made through a pattern of recognition. Clinically, the deductive process is taught, learned, and then built on with years of clinical experience that reinforce it.

Therefore, attempting to understand scientific data from mind-body studies of somatic distress has only added to physician confusion, who until the mid-1980s were taught to apply diagnosis and treatment and not to consider the behavioral and social contributions to illness. Both of which may influence either diagnosis or treatment. We know now that distress is a normal part of the cancer adjustment process, but there are no definitive answers about the positive and negative influence of psychological states on cancer. This is especially so if somatization is expressed as a coping mechanism to adapt to "disease" or "illness" (Holland, 1997). Moreover, the mere presence of single or repeated symptoms can be stressful for a woman with cancer, and somatization expressions are frequently mistaken as treatment side effects, not psychological distress. Even so, elevated levels of symptom distress interfere with quality of life (Breslau, Curbow, Zabora & BritzenhofSzoc, 2001). While adhering to traditional medical principles, a recent phenomenon is the growing number of physicians who recognize the popularity of psychological therapy to alleviate somatic expressions of distress among cancer patients. Interestingly, patients themselves have high expectations of these therapies and persuade physicians to recommend them (Newell, Sanson-Fisher & Savolainen, 2002).

Institutional Influence
An important function of medical schools is to engage in training physicians in medical sciences and methods of comprehensive clinical care. In so doing, scientific ideology provides information, distinguishes medicine from other professions through its autonomy and control over training, resulting in an institutionalization not seen in other occupations. This is manifested in the medical profession's power to regulate itself by selecting individuals to perpetuate a unified thinking with future "expert" generations, committed to clinical science and to patients (Brown, 1979; Epstein, 1996). Medical education requires an academic concentration in a particular field of study with specialized knowledge beyond general medicine. Medical specialization trends began to be apparent by the mid-1930s with medicine's propensity to establish 12 sub-specialties. Psychiatry was established in 1934 and internal medicine in 1936, and psycho-oncology, a subspecialty of oncology in the mid-1980s (Holland, 1999; Rosen, 1983). These are important landmarks since the structural reorganization of medicine into sub-specialties provides a particular "expert" way of viewing illness and disease from a distinct clinical gaze. Specialization enabled medical experts to advance beyond the capabilities of general practitioners. A second landmark became apparent in the mid-1980s with the entrance of large numbers of female medical practitioners. Psychotherapists in particular began to advance scientific knowledge on gender differences in health and illness, and in female diseases in particular.

Emergence of Psychiatry and Psychosomatic Symptoms
After 1934, modern psychiatry already had a view of psychosomatic symptoms, having previously identified hysterical and hypochondriacal disorders, and historically gender biased against women (Shorter, 1992). The disorder of classic hysteria, with stigmatizing ideas about women's psychological illnesses originally under the umbrella of somatoform illness, had all but disappeared from psychiatric

colloquy after World War II. In the 1930s, with the growth of psychoanalysis in the U.S., the concept of somatoform illness ceased. As Edward Shorter writes, the idea of "psychosomatic had now been branded psychiatric instead of neurological" (Shorter, 1992, p. 261). What evolved between the 1960s and 1980s were the three theories of somatization, previously described. These theories coincided with a movement that included a social dimension to traditional medical practice, resulting in a psychosocial approach to oncological medical care.

Interestingly, while psychiatry solidified its own position, patients rejected the psychological interpretation of physical symptoms because they wanted medical treatment to relieve their bodily illness, not to improve their quality of life. It is apparent that somatic conditions are well integrated within the medical system because approximately 25% of primary care patients demonstrate some degree of somatization during their visit with the physician (Bridges & Goldberg, 1985). Shorter notices that today's patients have "acquired the unshakable belief that their symptoms represent a particular disease, a belief that remains unjarred by further medical consultation" (Shorter, 1992, p. 295). This implies that patients presenting with psychological disorders and common bodily symptoms tend to "think of themselves as physically ill," not mentally ill (Kessler, Lloyd, Lewis & Gray, 1999, p. 436).

Psychosomatic Distress an Institutional Issue
The question is why is somatic distress such a problem? Although most con-sultations are initiated by the patient, the outcome will be influenced by what the patient chooses to present and how he or she chooses to present it (Kessler et al., 1999). The physician, on the other hand, will tell the patient what procedures are needed.

Somatizing patients in general and female breast cancer patients in particular at times present to physicians with perplexing complaints and confusion about their medical condition. It takes clinical skills in medical diagnostic methodology of careful history taking, physical examination, laboratory testing, and other diagnostic technology to safely identify underlying physical illness (Leventhal, Leventhal & Cameron, 2001). Moreover with breast cancer patients whose primary disease and physical complications are ever present, the issue is less distinguishing between physical and psychological illness, rather understanding the blend and interaction between the two. Since the 1990s, oncologists have observed that elevated numbers of well educated female breast cancer patients at various disease stages and without traceable illnesses present with somatic illnesses. Whether it is a social or cultural trend or a transition in medical care, many women are requesting non-traditional psychological therapies (i.e. relaxation, mediation, visual imagery, and hypnotherapy). Somatically distressed patients have high expectations that these interventions will improve not only their emotional adjustment, quality of life, coping skills, but also improve their physical health and functional adjustment to the cancer as well (Newell, Sanson-Fisher & Savolainen, 2002).

Physician-Patient Communication

The doctor-patient relationship, as Mechanic (1992) points out, is often the context in which negotiations about illness and disability take place, and approaches to these negotiations have an important role in the future trajectory of the patient's illness.

The most basic element of the connection is the rapport between clinician and patient. Accumulating evidence places importance on effective communication during a consultation to determine the accuracy and completeness of information gathered, the range and number of symptoms elicited, and sharing of emotional well being (Fallowfield & Jenkins, 1999). A recent study by Robinson and Roter (1999), identified when psychological information is conveyed by patients. The study suggests that less than 35% (6 out of 17) of patients presented psychosocial concerns during the opening segment of a communication with physicians. Another 59% (62 out of 105) disclosed concerns after the opening segment of their communication when physicians were taking histories or discussing treatment recommendations for somatic problems. Medical dialogue is essential to determine why patients seek help. Unless bi-directional communication occurs during the clinical encounter patients may not identify and physicians may treat the wrong problem (Silberman, 1992).

Communication Styles
The literature on interpersonal communication styles between doctors and patients describes three communication approaches. First, the traditional *paternalistic* interaction method occurs between an "inexpert" patient and "expert" physician. Second, the *mutual communication* style is one in which patient and physician are seen as partners or equals in the decision making and each benefits from the relationship. The third type of interaction, *consumerism*, involves the patients as the consumer ("buyer") who seeks a service from the physician ("seller") (Roter & Hall, 1993; Salmon, 2000).

Any interpersonal dialogue between physicians and patients can have mixed results. The various outcomes depend on the type of alliance, the intent of the health-seeking behavior, the type of communication approaches, the extent of medical or cultural vocabularies used, the interest and ability to listen, and the stage of the breast cancer. Patient communication styles about ailments may be poorly defined, vague, mislabeled, or presented in arcane language (Fallowfield & Jenkins, 1999; Haug, Musil, Warner & Morris, 1998). Disclosure driven by a poor communication or a unidirectional flow of information from patient to physician (or vice versa) leads to an ineffective and incomplete exchange of facts (Roter & Hall, 1993).

Patients who are able to "tell their story" in an open manner, augment physician understanding (Roter & Hall, 1993). Research suggests that patients presenting with functional somatic complaints are common in general medical practices, while patients who seek medical attention to convey unexplained symptoms in response to psychological stress, depression, or anxiety are less so (Barsky & Borus, 1999). In the later, physician interpretation is less obvious. The rationale for the type of information patients deliver can vary according to illness and practice type. In oncology, distressed or anxious breast cancer patients who understand the specific or diffuse nature of symptoms, may have a need to have their "bodily complaints" validated, thus achieving secondary gain. This pattern of patient care-seeking behavior, pursuing a secondary gain evokes "favorable" responses from others, and is executed in order to obtain comfort and a sense of security (Peters, Stanley, Rose & Salmon, 1997; Stuart & Noyes, 1999). As the goal shifts from a curative approach to a palliative one, two-thirds of patients have a high period of distress as they adapt to care-seeking behavior. Here, assurances of the physician's commitment to continued care, and symptom and pain control become an important objective in managing advanced cancer, in addition to managing psychological and spiritual needs (Holland & Gooen-Piels, 2000).

Technology Reinforces or Does Not Reinforce a Somatization Diagnosis

Health care technology is perceived as a craft, an engineering discipline, and an applied science that has transformed oncological clinical practice specifically, and the public's expectations of medical care generally. However, for biological or chemical agents, medical devices or clinical procedures to be of value they need to be both sensitive and specific to reinforce or refute diagnosis (Keller, 1992; Reiser, 1978). Rapid advances in *medical technology*, broadly defined as encompassing "medical devices, instrumentation, pharmaceuticals, biologics, diagnostic and therapeutic procedures" are integrated into systems of health care delivery (Laubach, Wennberg & Gelijns, 1992). Medicine's dependence on technology has raised complex economic and social issues, which are discussed below.

Economic Issues – Supply and Demand
Because demand for health care exceeds supply of resources allotted to finance it, setting priorities is a problem for health care systems worldwide (Singer, Martin, Giacomini & Purdy, 2000). Two key issues are at the heart of setting priorities – competition and safety.

Intense price competition to develop and adopt new medical technologies characterizes today's health care market. Led by corporate for-profit medicine, one of the fastest growing economic sectors is the development of new cost-effective technological products and medical devices, intended for existing and emerging health care markets (Government Accounting Office, 1997). In recent decades, prodigious technological growth proved too costly for individual physicians' offices, which resulted in sophisticated technologies being housed increasingly in hospitals and academic institutions (Hillman, 1992).

Because of the Federal Drug Administration (FDA) involvement in pre-marketing approval of medical devices, technological innovation has emphasized biomedicine's mission to develop safer, less invasive and refined diagnostic proce-dures that improve quality of life (Government Accounting Office, 1997). Although essential, federal oversight of manufactured devices, particularly those involved in life-support or life sustaining have contributed to the increase in health care costs at the expense of traditional therapeutic methods. For instance, important advances within molecular biology and genetic engineering have produced startling findings linking types of depression to genetic origins, resulting in an increased use of pharmaceuticals to target biological mechanisms. While technological progress is vital, the public debate, of course, centers on cost and who bears it.

The price for high-technology devices, including the development of magnetic resonance imaging (MRI), positive emission tomography (PET) and single positive emission computerized technology (SPECT) although expensive, are good examples of new technological ways to improve care and the quality of life (Hillman, 1992). Provider and patient enthusiasm for each of these technologies is tempered by those at all cancer stages. This is particularly so for those at terminal stages who require sophisticated diagnostic methods to detect, diagnose and stage breast tumors or other concomitant diseases, particularly somatic diseases that manifest in diffuse body parts. However, medical imaging, while both exceedingly expensive and overused, is favored as outpatient administration and receives insurance reimbursement (Hillman, 1992; King, 1997; Singer et al., 2000).

Social Influence – Accountability
Competitive market pressure from hospital administrators has led to monitoring technology, pharmaceutical and biologic consumption and variation between diagnoses, physicians, specialties, institutions, as well as between regions of

the country. Resulting from escalating costs, public and third-party payers have questioned the value of medical care for which they pay, use, overuse or inappropriately use. Ironically, although controlling costs is far reaching, to consumers who frequently do not pay medical bills directly, medical resources appear to be free or almost free (King, 1997; Silberman, 1992).

Another aspect of accountability now includes patients, vigorously insisting on shared decision making relating to their care. On the face of it, this new account-ability involves both an ethical and scientific imperative. Clearly, more concerned breast cancer patients, and especially somatically distressed patients may request specific diagnostic tests. It is ethical, as Silberman (1992) points out, because most medical procedures have multiple, contradictory, as well as uncertain outcomes and patients differ in the values they attach to various outcomes, especially if emotions are attached to a potentially life-threatening disease such as breast cancer. It is scientific because physicians use medical technology as a way of "reducing anxiety generated by uncertainty under which they often have to act," and this is more revealing (Reiser, 1978, p. 104). Physicians make medical judgments that patients are ill equipped to make on their own. Yet, physician use of excessive laboratory tests or medical equipment is a medicalized psychological treatment, necessitated by the physician's uncertainty. Use of diagnostic investigations and reliance on technology, although excessive provides professional comfort in a medically litigious society (King, 1997). The problems of this type of "defensive medicine" are apparent, and ultimately we as a society pay heavy economic and social prices.

Policy: Managed Care Influence

Although the influence of managed care is substantial; this section will deal with only one policy aspect – the effect of corporate-based managed care organizations. Many policy arguments familiar with health care debates in the mid-1990s raised of the influence of for-profit industries and overlapping interests among diverse for-profit groups. Three recurrent themes are central to policy debates – resolving health care discrepancies, establishing national guidelines and balancing the social public agenda.

Resolving Health Care Discrepancies

Large gaps between the quality of health care that people should and do receive exist. Discrepancies are seen across different types of health conditions, health care facilities, health insurance groups, geographical locations, gender, race and ethnically diverse cultural groups, age and socio-economic groups

(The President's Advisory Commission on Consumer Protection and Quality in the Health Care Industry, 1998).

At the heart of these discrepancies are immense variations in health care practices: (1) rationing of health care through a set number of clinic visits per illness episode (i.e. physicians follow a template known as clinical practice guidelines); (2) cost of medicalizing illness (i.e. demand for scarce resources for breast cancer as opposed to an "orphan" cancer); (3) access to health care in general and to specialists in particular (i.e. variation in gate-keeping methods by providers); (4) debates about insurance and government coverage for experimental treatments (i.e. coverage of experimental chemotherapy trials once a woman is identified as having breast cancer); (5) overuse of health care (i.e. patient or physician instance on conducting a specific test to rule-out or confirm a possible cause of illess is wasteful); (6) differences in standards of care between and across medical specialties (i.e. generalists versus board certified specialists); and (7) escalating cost of health care (The President's Advisory Commission on Consumer Protection and Quality in the Health Care Industry, 1998). The personal, social, economic and ethical consequences of these discrepancies are widespread and worthy of attention, not here, but elsewhere.

The issue of discrepancies across standards of care was addressed in 1997 by the Agency for Health Care Policy and Research (AHCPR, now known as the Agency for Healthcare Research and Quality, or AHQR) with the implementation of an Evidence-Based Practice Center program (Eisenberg, 1997). Evidenced-based programs aim to "improve the quality, effectiveness and appropriateness of clinical practice and interventions, and technologies" (Eisenberg, 1997). Across disease spectrums, acceptance has been widespread because evidence is based on standardized, cost-effective protocols affecting detection, diagnosis and treatment.

Establishment of National Guidelines
Unlike clinical counterparts, evidence-based measures are not pervasive among diagnosis and treatment of all behavioral or mental illnesses. In addition, corporate health plans reluctantly address psychosocial needs resulting from the impact of major illnesses in policy documents because of society-derived factors that continue to stigmatize distress-related symptoms associated with cancer. When addressed, standards of care vary between health care providers and plans. Consequently, a lack of clarity concerning appropriate delivery systems have not been established and psychosocial practitioners continue the debate about who should deliver support (Hurowitz, 1993).

To clarify contradictory recommendations and barriers contributing to under-recognition of psychosocial distress and its sequelae, national policy makers, mental health care providers and cancer researchers at major cancer centers developed psycho-oncology treatment guidelines to manage psychosocial distress at every stage of cancer treatment (Holland, 1997; Holland, Foley, Handzo, Levy & Loscalzo, 1999; Holland & Gooen-Piels, 2000). In addition to developing national guidelines, the National Comprehensive Cancer Network (NCCN) offers a general framework for providing clear and relevant information concerning psychosocial issues in oncology to bridge the gap between theoretical research and implementation for clinical practice. These quality of life practice guidelines remain to be evaluated in order to address whether patient's needs are fully integrated into health plans.

Similar standards of care addressing treatment needs of somatically distressed patients has not yet risen to corporate or to policy levels, nor to a national agenda because the issue remains fragmented, especially with cancer patients within different clinical and academic medicine specialties. Until a unified liaison between the patient, the clinician and the health care system occurs, policy thinking will not synthesize this medicalized problem as an important issue.

That is because the medical care system functions as a funnel and individual illnesses, such as diverse somatic illness in breast cancer result in the medical care system responding to patients in a piecemeal, inconsistent, expensive, and often-inadequate way. Theoretically, the medical system acknowledges there is disjunction and recognizes that prevention and psychosocial well being would be a less expensive way to deal with ongoing somatic use of oncological resources as a way of reducing psychosocial distress and resulting somatization (Hurowitz, 1993). The health care system is struggling to successfully make the organizational transition away from a primary focus on the treatment of illness to one of prevention. This has not yet been done.

Making a Mark on the Social and Public Agenda

Until policy arguments address the financial burden and dramatic overuse of medical services by those with somatic illness, the health care system itself will continue to unintentionally encourage the behavior and continue to medicalize the distress of women with breast cancer. As the issue of medicalizing somatic distress becomes more conspicuous on the political landscape, the health care system will eventually develop a policy for less reliance on clinical oncology services. This will occur only when as organizational and financial structures, and physician incentives become aligned with patient health needs (Hurowitz, 1993).

Viewed in this context, the breakdown in responsibility for medicalization of somatic distress will continue. For example, major issues on the public social agenda are disagreement in who is accountable and how to address medical overuse by somatically distressed patients. Also, the unfulfilled realization that a "social model of health, based on the premise that improvement in the health status of the population is a primary goal" of managed care organizations, has not happened (Hurowitz, 1993). Only when tensions between the universal concept of equitable distribution of scarce health care resources and corporate economic needs are reinforced by societal interests will the values of consumers of medical services be balanced.

Political Influence on Medicalization

There is no question that health and health care are political issues. Thus far, the implication of medicalization has been discussed from a micro sense, describing the human factors that enter the decision to medicalize an issue. Moving to a macro perspective, political alliances from all sectors of society are at the core of medical priorities influencing what is medicalized. This section describes the political movement to a formal medicalized state, the players' voices, including those who have completed active treatment (i.e. survivors of breast cancer) and patient advocacy (i.e. The National Coalition of Cancer Survivorship).

Movement to a Formalized Medicalized State
Beginning with appeals from special interest groups, the medical industry and regulatory agencies responded to issues as a way to shape health and research priorities through political channels (Morgan, 1998). These relationships however, do not occur in a void. Clearly, many social forces affect alliances as each social element attempts to sway the health care system to its own end.

It is clear that once an illness progresses into a formal medicalized state, a "complex social and political dynamic set of institutions" reinforces or undermines it through a "preeminent status of medical experts and medical knowledge" (Morgan, 1998, p. 105). Similar attention with appeals to congress, formalizes the progress of medicalization at the national level.

Players and Voices – Industry, Special Interest Groups and the Public
With the current system of health delivery in flux and financial shifts at global levels affecting national medical and health-related businesses, tension is felt at many levels. Since the later 1980s, expansion became the norm, particularly with biotechnology, pharmaceutical, health insurance and hospital conglomerates.

At the core of the vast wealth and growth lies a large and powerful support industry of politically well-connected special interest groups and lobbyists. Lobbying groups attempt to influence legislation either directly, by providing policy-relevant information to legislators to stimulate market competition, or indirectly, by mobilizing the public on behalf of or against an issue (King, 1997).

For a specific health issue to rise above legislative "clutter" depends on public interest. Several factors affect the political response to an illness. Political movements successfully mobilize in several ways on behalf of or against a cause, and today's savvy breast cancer advocates have learned well from past political movements. Successful lobbying about a specific disease or specific illness is based on knowledge, presenting facts about a cure, a vaccine or a drug. Other essential strategies include promoting a unified awareness campaign and educating lobbyists to specific issues (Rotwein, 1991). One of the most successful groups have been breast cancer survivors, women who rose from a grassroots constituency level to offer political support to legislators, and in the process gained respect and legitimacy for their cause.

Women and Disease-Specific Patient Advocacy
The political consequence of medicalization on health in general, and on women in particular, has a rich history surrounding somatic illness. For instance, in medicine some "excitable" patients (mainly women) were considered far from ideal, and the "hysteric and hypochondriac affections" illness they experienced, as stated by physicians was "in their mind," suggesting a stereotyped socially-imposed gender role (Morgan, 1998; Shorter, 1992). These women lived with the social consequences accompanying a diagnosis or non-diagnosis label and were unable to do much about it. Although somatic symptoms today are not very different from those one hundred years ago, the same type of prolific pigeonholing of a "diffuse" diagnosis is less likely to occur. Nonetheless, current medicine has "borderline personality," which is the contemporary "hysteria" (Shorter, 1992).

Breast cancer survivors, like other disease survivors have tackled many issues politically, especially if psychosocial concerns surround fear of recurrence, worry about delayed physical effects and symptoms, risk of second cancer and sterility (Holland & Gooen-Piels, 2000). While most female cancer survivors emerge from treatment psychologically healthy, 15% show significant problems, up to 11 years post-treatment. These women can be profiled as having fewer social supports, have symptoms of post traumatic stress syndrome, have recurrent fears about death, frequent physician visits for minor physical symptoms, and are obviously less politically active.

Thus, the work of dedicated women involved in the politics of breast cancer patient advocacy has left a sizable mark on broadening our understanding of the psychosocial, economic and political aspects of medicalization in many ways. Activities of these advocates were most notable for the following innovative interventions: (1) since the 1950s, female patients have used the courts to challenge medical paternalism, resulting in laws that provide patients' informed consent for experimental medical treatments such as, treatment after a positive mammogram reading (Faden & Beauchamp, 1986); (2) as women consumers became part of the health care system, they also became a political voice and began to tell personal stories in public forums as a way to draw attention to overlooked issues (Epstein, 1996; Rodwin, 1994); (3) beginning with the HIV/AIDS movement, the current political movement in breast as in other cancers, is towards sharing anecdotes at non-professional and professional meetings, on television, radio and newspaper, on the Internet, to Congress and to Federal Agencies (Epstein, 1996); (4) across the country, a widespread and growing public trend is to change technology and technical procedures, and to exercise choices that are more therapeutic over illnesses and health (Morgan, 1998; Rodwin, 1994); (5) fueled by insistent consumers, who demanded changes in the practice of health care, advocates prodded the social and political debates to reshape the face of corporate-run health care so that it benefits patients (Morgan, 1998; Schauffler & Wilkerson, 1997); and (6) informed and knowledgeable breast cancer consumer advocates are challenging a multi-layered health system's medicalization model of "medical experts as universally committed to impartial benevolence" (Morgan, 1998, p. 110); (7) initially breast cancer (and now other cancer) survivors as patient advocates are members of policy, cooperative groups and peer review committees at the National Cancer Institute and the Department of Defense (Andejeski et al., 2002; Rich et al., 1998).

DISCUSSION AND SUGGESTIONS FOR FUTURE RESEARCH

The purpose of this paper was to examine the connection between psychosocial somatic distress and its interaction with the complex process of medicalization. A review of the literature indicates that these concepts have not been synthesized into an integrated and unifying model, although such an effort would be rewarding. It is conceded however, that our medical system is an evolving, forever-moving target. A common practice is to follow a defined paradigm specific to a particular scientific perspective, and although this may serve the needs of a single discipline, it does not further creative thinking across borders.

Given the influence of cultural, social, economic, and political factors in our daily lives and in biomedicine specifically, a preferable way to view somatic distress's impact on breast cancer patients is from an integrated scientific paradigm. Initial discussion cited the mind-body dichotomy as the problem and the way it compartmentalizes personal, psychological, physical and social issues away from disease issues. It provides a contextual framework for understanding stress responses of somatic distress, which separates cause and effect in such a way as to reduce treatment possibilities. Future research needs to confirm this process, to further understand the personal influence of cognitive and emotional attributes of physical symptoms and one's appraisal of the stress-illness and stress-symptom relationship that results in distress, especially in breast cancer. The cultural and social influences that surround an individual's regulation of a single acute distress response or a series of chronic distress event(s) that lead to a list of physical, psychological, social or spiritual problems presented as illness to those in the medical community.

As a public event, utilizing health care resources, somatically distressed breast cancer patients will vary widely in how they adapt to the cancer illness over time. Distress responses that predict adaptation depend on society-derived factors (i.e. social attitudes and beliefs about cancer); patient-derived factors (i.e. personal attributes the individual brings to illness); and cancer-driven factors (i.e. clinical reality of the illness to which the individual must adapt) (Holland & Gooen-Piels, 2000).

Within the clinical arena, a somatically distress breast cancer patient becomes enmeshed within a system governed by biological medicine, a clinical system that wishes to identify and manage somatic distress symptoms. As somatic distress is defined as a problem and a medical diagnosis is applied, here, we can take into consideration how somatic distress impacts on the universe of interacters including the matrix of the biotechnology, the clinical, the medical, the social, the political and the economic players. With this in mind, a conceptual framework is proposed that links the disparate thoughts into a unified model. The name of this new conceptual model is the *Continuum of Somatic Distress to Medicalization*.

The goal of this paper has been to draw a map describing various pathways somatization takes once it moves from a private experience and becomes part of a public discourse. The model presented evolved from psychological and sociological dialogue. Consequently, the scientific ideology of the medical system classified the concept of somatization via professional medical vernacular and integrated it into its institutions. The impact of managed care on methods of approaching somatic distress within the oncology arena was examined. Although some pathways are clear, the map remains overly complex and not fully documented. It does indicate, however, the likely outcomes in management and treatment of those patients whose psychosocial concerns of distress are voiced as bodily concerns. Specifically, the effect of corporate based managed care organizations was discussed. The ideal goal identified was the improvement in the health status of the population. This is directed towards individual breast cancer patients on the one hand and all patients on the other. In contrast to this lofty goal, managed care may be largely or completely economic. That means that managed care's response to somatic concerns is likely to be based on what is least expensive.

Effective patient-physician communication was cited as a major determinant of completeness of information. The success of communication determines how well the doctor understands and manages the patient's complaints. Use of technology and laboratory methods were discussed, especially in terms of their suitability as a means to explore the breast cancer patient's concerns. It was noted that the physician might use these laboratory tests secondarily as a means of supporting the breast cancer patient's psychosocial concerns – a costly and somewhat irrational method. Corporate-based organizations, on the other hand, developed concerns when laboratory testing and other procedures appear excessive or inappropriate.

The final element in the medicalization process is the political impact. Through the work of particular stakeholders, women active in policy debates, the political momentum to slow or to contain costs in medicine has been realized somewhat with recent shifts in the implementation of managed care restraints. Rising momentum, on the other hand, attempts to restore to the breast cancer patient's power lost in the first round of managed care negotiations.

Because of the vagueness and lack of congruity between participants, further study about the management of somatization in breast cancer is of crucial importance at this time. Empirical studies that consider different patient economic circumstances (i.e. access to care and compliance with medical recommendations); medical personnel attitudes towards somatic distress (i.e. treatment protocols and technological interventions); and current social, political and economic environments (i.e. patient bill of rights) will be most valuable. The true challenge will emerge with interdisciplinary studies designed to assess social antecedents and social consequences. Although difficult methodologically, they present unique information about breast cancer patients and illness and how each interacts with the health system and will yield the most useful information.

CONCLUSION

In summary, it is clear that a strong conceptual relationship exists between somatic distress and medicalization. It appears that some individuals who experience psychosocial distress in breast cancer are more prone to experience symptoms associated with their illness or treatment than those with no distress. In addition, it is apparent that medicalization reinforces somatic illness in distinct ways. By conceiving of the influence of distress on medicalization and vice versa in the comprehensive way presented, the literature has been reviewed and synthesized from an interdisciplinary perspective. The main challenge for future social scientist researchers will be to test these conceptual relationships in the clinical setting from a unified discipline that considers the individual interacting within the clinical, the social, the economic and the political environments.

ACKNOWLEDGMENTS

Erica S. Breslau, Ph.D., M.P.H. is now at the National Cancer Institute. At the time this work was conducted, Dr. Breslau was at the Johns Hopkins Bloomberg School of Public Health.

This study was supported by a grant from the Susan G. Komen Breast Cancer Foundation DRA99-003018. The author thanks Barbara A. Curbow, Ph.D., James R. Zabora, Sc.D., Kathy Helzlsouer, M.D., and Donald Steinwachs, Ph.D. for reviewing earlier drafts of the manuscript.

REFERENCES

Agnew, D. L., & Merskey, H. (1976). Words of chronic pain. *Pain, 2,* 73–81.
American Psychiatric Association (1980). *Somatoform disorders.* Washington, DC: American Psychiatric Association.
Andejeski, Y., Breslau, E. S., Hart, E., Lythcott, N., Alexander, L., Rich, I., Bisceglio, I., Smith, H. S., & Visco, F. M. (2002). Benefits and drawbacks of including consumer reviewers in the scientific merit review of breast cancer research. *Journal of Women's Health and Gender-Based Medicine, 11*(2), 119–136.
Andersen, B. L., Golden-Kreutz, D. M., & DiLillo, V. (2001). Cancer. In: A. Baum, T. A. Revenson & J. E. Singer (Eds), *Handbook of Health Psychology* (pp. 709–725). Mahwah, NJ: Lawrence Erlabum Associates.
Andrykowski, M. A., Brady, M. J., & Hung, J. W. (1993). Positive psychosocial adjustment in potential bone marrow transplant recipients: Cancer as a psychosocial transition. *Psycho-Oncology, 2,* 261–276.
Aneshensel, C. S., Rutter, C. M., & Lachenbruch, P. A. (1991). Social structure, stress, and mental health: Competing conceptual and analytic models. *American Sociological Review, 56*(2), 166–178.
Antelman, S. M. (1988). Time-dependent sensation as the cornerstone for a new approach to pharmacotherapy: Drugs as foreign/stressful stimuli. *Drug Development Research, 14,* 1–30.
Appleton, L. M. (1995). Rethinking medicalization: Alcoholism and anomalies. In: J. Best (Ed.), *Images of Issues: Typifying Contemporary Social Problems* (pp. 59–80). New York, NY: Aldine de Gruyter
Baker, R., Marcellus, D., Zabora, J., Polland, A., & Jodrey, D. (1997). Psychological distress among adult patients being evaluated for bone marrow transplantation. *Psychosomatics, 38*(1), 10–19.
Barker, K. K. (2000). A ship upon a stormy sea: The medicalization of pregnancy. *Social Science and Medicine, 47*(8), 1067–1976.
Barraclough, J. (1994). *Cancer and emotion.* New York, NY: Wiley.
Barsky, A. J., & Borus, J. F. (1995). Somatization and medicalization in the era of managed care. *Journal of the American Medical Association, 274,* 1931–1934.

Barsky, A. J., & Borus, J. F. (1999). Functional somatic syndromes. *Annals of Internal Medicine, 130*, 910–921.

Barsky, A. J., & Wyshak, G. (1989). Hypochondriasis and related health attitudes. *Psychosomatics, 30*, 412–420.

Barsky, A. J., Wyshak, G., & Klerman, G. L. (1986a). Medical and psychiatric determinants of outpatient medical utilization. *Medical Care, 24*, 548–560.

Barsky, A. J., Wyshak, G., & Klerman, G. L. (1986b). Medical and psychiatric determinants of outpatient medical utilization. *Medical Care, 25*, 548–560.

Bennett, R. M. (1999). Emerging concepts in the neurobiology of chronic pain: Evidence of abnormal sensory processing in fibromyalgia. *Mayo Clinic Proceedings, 74*, 385–398.

Ben-Tovim, D. I., & Esterman, A. (1998). Zero progress with hypochondriasis. *The Lancet, 352*, 1798–1799.

Binney, E. A., Estes, C. L., & Ingman, S. R. (1990). Medicalization, public policy and the elderly: Social services in jeopardy? *Social Science and Medicine, 30*(7), 761–771.

Breckler, S. J. (1995). Psychosocial resource variables in cancer research: Statistical and analytical considerations. *Journal of Psychosocial Oncology, 13*(1/2), 161–170.

Breslau, E. S. (1999). Computer-mediated communication with breast cancer patients. *American Public Health Association*, 126th Annual Meeting and Exposition, November 15th–18th, Washington, DC, p. 115.

Breslau, E. S., Curbow, B. A., Zabora, J. R., & BritzenhofSzoc, K. (2001). Psychological distress in post-surgical women with breast cancer. *37th American Society of Clinical Oncology Meeting*, May 12th–15th, San Francisco, CA, Vol. 20, p. 125.

Bridges, K. W., & Goldberg, D. P. (1985). Somatic presentation of DSM-III disorders in primary care. *Journal of Psychosomatic Research, 29*, 563–569.

Broom, D. H., & Woodward, R. V. (1996). Medicalization reconsidered: Toward a collaborative approach to care. *Sociology of Health and Illness, 18*(3), 357–378.

Buick, D. L. (1997). Illness representations and breast cancer: Coping with radiation and chemotherapy. In: K. J. Petrie & J. A. Weinman (Eds), *Perceptions of Health and Illness: Current Research and Applications* (pp. 379–409). Amsterdam, The Netherlands: Harwood Academic Publishers.

Burnstein, H. J., Gelber, M. S., Guadagnoli, E., & Weeks, J. (1999). Use of alternative medicine by women with early-stage breast cancer. *The New England Journal of Medicine, 340*(22), 1733–1739.

Caccioppo, J. T., Anderson, B. L., Turnquist, D. C., & Petty, R. E. (1985). Psychophysiological comparison processes: Interpreting cancer symptoms. In: B. L. Anderson (Ed.), *Women with Cancer: Psychological Perspectives* (pp. 141–171). New York, NY: Springer-Verlag.

Cassidy, S. (1986). Emotional distress in terminal care: Discussion paper. *Journal of the Royal Society of Medicine, 79*, 117–120.

Chaturvedi, S. K., Hopwood, P., & Maguire, P. (1993). Non-organic somatic symptoms in cancer. *European Journal of Cancer, 29A*, 1006–1008.

Chaturvedi, S. K., & Maguire, P. G. (1998). Persistent somatization in cancer: A controlled follow-up study. *Journal of Psychosomatic Research, 45*(3), 249–256.

Conrad, P. (1975). The discovery of hyperkinesias: Notes on the medicalization of deviant behavior. *Social Problems, 23*(1), 12–21.

Conrad, P. (1992). Medicalization and social control. *Annual Review of Sociology, 18*, 209–232.

Conrad, P., & Potter, D. (2000). From hyperactive children to ADHD adults: Some observations on the expansion of medical categories. Paper delivered at Society for the Study of Social Problems.

Conrad, P., & Schneider, J. W. (1980). Looking at levels of medicalization: A comment on Strong's critique of the thesis of medical imperialism. *Social Science and Medicine, 14A*, 75–79.

Conrad, P., & Schneider, J. W. (1992). *Deviance and medicalization.* Philadelphia, PA: Temple University Press.

Costa, P. T., & McCrae, M. (1985). Hypochondriasis, neuroticism, and aging. When are somatic complaints unfounded? *American Psychologist, 40*(1), 19–28.

Derogatis, L. R. (1986). Psychology in cancer medicine: A perspective and overview. *Journal of Consulting and Clinical Psychology, 54*(5), 632–638.

Derogatis, L. R., & Coons, H. L. (1993). Self-reported measures of stress. In: L. Goldberger & S. Breznitz (Eds), *Handbook of Stress: Theoretical and Clinical Aspects* (pp. 200–233). New York, NY: Free Press.

Derogatis, L. R., Morrow, G. R., Fetting, J., Penman, D., Piastesky, S., Schmale, A. M., Henrichs, M., & Carnicke, C. L. M. (1983). The prevalence of psychiatric disorders among cancer patients. *Journal of the American Medical Association, 249,* 751–757.

Dougall & Baum (2001) In: A. Baum, T. A. Revenson & J. E. Singer (Eds), *Handbook of Health Psychology* (pp. 709–725). Mahwah, NJ: Lawrence Erlabum Associates.

Dresser, R. (2001). When Science Offers Salvation. *Patient advocacy and research ethics.* New York, NY: Oxford University Press.

Eisdorfer, C. (1985). The conceptualization of stress and a model for further study. In: M. R. Zales (Ed.), *Stress in Health and Disease* (pp. 5–23). New York, NY: Brunner/Mazel Publishers.

Eisenberg, J. M. (1997). Testimony on Medicare Coverage Decisions. Report given to the House Ways and Means Subcommittee on Health, April 17th (Electronic Citation: http://www. ahcpr.gov/news/testi417.htm).

Epstein, S. (1996). *Impure science. AIDS, activism, and the politics of knowledge.* Berkley, CA: University of California Press.

Facione, N. C. (1993). Delay versus help seeking for breast cancer symptoms: A critical review of the literature on patient and provider delay. *Social Science & Medicine, 376,* 1521–1534.

Faden, R., & Beauchamp, T. L. (1986). The development of consent requirements in research ethics. *A History and Theory of Informed Consent* (pp. 37–65). New York, NY: Oxford University Press.

Fallowfield, L., & Jenkins, V. (1999). Effective communication skills are the key to good cancer care. *European Journal of Cancer, 35*(11), 1592–1597.

Farber, J. M., Weinerman, B. H., & Kuypers, J. A. (1984). Psychosocial distress in oncology outpatients. *Journal of Psychosocial Oncology, 2*(3–4), 109–118.

Farmer, M. A., & Ferraro, K. F. (1997). Distress and perceived health: Mechanisms of health decline. *Journal of Health and Social Behavior, 39,* 298–311.

Ford, C. V. (1998). Somatoform and factitious disorders and cancer. In: J. C. Holland (Ed.), *Psycho-Oncology* (pp. 608–613). New York, NY: Oxford University Press.

Fukuda, K., Straus, S. E., Hickie, I., Sharpe, M. C., Dobbins, J. G., & Komaroff, A. (1994). The chronic fatigue syndrome: A comprehensive approach to its definition and study. International Chronic Fatigue Syndrome Study Group. *Annals of Internal Medicine, 121,* 953–959.

Gijsbers Van Wijk, C. M. T., & Kolk, A. M. (1997). Sex differences in physical symptoms: The contribution of symptom perception theory. *Social Science and Medicine, 45*(2), 231–246.

Government Accounting Office (1997). Medical Device Reporting. Improvements Needed in FDA's System for Monitoring Problems with Approved Devices. Washington, DC: Government Accounting Office. GAO/HEHS-97-21.

Greenberg, D. B. (1998). Radiotherapy. In: J. C. Holland (Ed.), *Psycho-Oncology* (pp. 269–276). New York, NY: Oxford University Press.

Groenvold, M., Fayers, P. M., Sprangers, M. A. G., Bjorner, J. B., Klee, M. C., Aeronson, N. K., Bech, P., & Mouridsen, H. T. (1999). Anxiety and depression in breast cancer. Patients at low risk of recurrence compared with the general population. *Journal of Clinical Epidemiology, 52*(6), 523–530.

Gureje, O., Simon, G. E., Ustun, T. B., & Goldberg, D. P. (1997). Somatization a cross-cultural perspective: A World Health Organization study in primary care. *American Journal of Psychiatry, 16*(3), 1022–1029.

Haley, R. W., Hom, J., Roland, P. S., Bryan, W. W., Van Ness, P. C., & Bronte, F. J. (1997). Evaluation of neurologic function in Gulf War veterans: A blinded case-control study. *Journal of the American Medical Association, 277*, 223–230.

Haug, M. R., Musil, C. M., Warner, C. D., & Marteau, T. M. (1998). Interpreting bodily changes as illness: A longitudinal study of older adults. *Social Science and Medicine, 46*(12), 1553–1567.

Hillman, B. J. (1992). Physicians' acquisition and use of new technology in an era of economic constraints. In: A. J. Gelinjs (Ed.), *Technology and Health Care in an Era of Limits* (pp. 133–149). Washington, DC: National Academy Press, Institute of Medicine.

Holland, J. C. (1997). Preliminary guidelines for the treatment of distress. *Oncology, 11*, 11A.

Holland, J. C. (1999). Use of alternative medicine – A marker for distress? *The New England Journal of Medicine, 340*(22), 1731–1732.

Holland, J. C., Foley, G. V., Handzo, G. F., Levy, M. H., & Loscalzo, M. J. (1999). *Update: NCCN distress management guidelines.* Bethesda, MD: National Comprehensive Cancer Network, Version 1.

Holland, J. C., & Gooen-Piels, J. (2000). Principles of psycho-oncology. In: J. Holland & J. Frei (Eds), *Cancer Medicine.* Hamilton, Ont.: B.C. Decker.

Holmes, T. H., & Masuda, M. (1974). Life changes and illness susceptibility. In: B. S. Dohrenwend & B. P. Dohrenwend (Eds), *Stressful Life Events: Their Nature and Effects.* New York, NY: Wiley.

Holmes, T. H., & Rahe, R. H. (1967). The social readjustment rating scale. *Journal of Psychosomatic Medicine, 11*, 213–218.

Hurowitz, J. C. (1993). Toward a social policy for health. *New England Journal of Medicine, 329*(2), 130–133.

Illich, I. (1982). Medicalization and primary care. *Journal of the Royal College of General Practitioners, 32*, 463–470.

Jackson, S. H. (1999). The role of stress in anesthetists' health and well-being. *Acta Anaesthesiologica Scandinavia, 43*, 583–601.

Kanton, W. (1987). The epidemiology of depression in medical care. *International Journal of Psychiatry and Medicine, 17*, 93–112.

Kanton, W., Kleinman, A., & Rosen, G. (1982a). Depression and somatization: A review. Part I. *The American Journal of Medicine, 72*, 127–135.

Kanton, W., Kleinman, A., & Rosen, G. (1982b). Depression and somatization: A review. Part II. *The American Journal of Medicine, 72*, 241–247.

Kanton, W., Von Korff, M., & Lin, E. (1990). Distressed high utilizers of medical care: DSM-III-R diagnoses and treatment needs. *General Hospital Psychiatry, 12*, 355–362.

Kaplan, H. B. (1996). Perspectives on Psychosocial Stress. In: H. B. Kaplan (Ed.), *Psychosocial Stress: Perspectives on Structure, Theory, Life-Course, and Methods* (pp. 3–28). San Diego, CA: Academic Press, A Division of Harcourt Brace & Company.

Kash, K. M., Holland, J. C., Halper, M. S., & Miller, D. G. (1992). Psychological distress and surveillance behavior of women with a family history of breast cancer. *Journal of the National Cancer Institute, 84*, 24–30.

Kash, K. M., Holland, J. C., Osborne, M. P., & Miller, D. G. (1995). Psychological counseling strategies for women at risk of breast cancer. *Journal of the National Cancer Institute Monographs, 17,* 73–79.

Kasl, S. V. (1984). Stress and health. *Annual Review of Public Health, 5,* 319–341.

Keller, L. S. (1992). Discovering and doing: Science and technology, an introduction. In: G. Kirkup & L. S. Keller (Eds), *Inventing Women. Science, Technology and Gender* (pp. 12–33). Cambridge, MA: Blackwell Publishers Ltd.

Kessler, D., Lloyd, K., Lewis, G., & Gray, D. P. (1999). Cross sectional study of symptom attribution and recognition of depression and anxiety in primary care. *British Medical Journal, 318,* 436–440.

King, W. J. (1997). Medicalization in the U.S.: Past, present, and future prospects (Unpublished manuscript).

Kirmayer, L. J., & Robbins, J. M. (1991). Three forms of somatization in primary care – prevalence, cooccurrence, and sociodemographic characteristics. *Journal of Nervous and Mental Diseases, 179*(11), 647–655.

Kornblith, A. B. (1998). Psychosocial adaptation in cancer survivors. In: J. C. Holland (Ed.), *Psycho-Oncology* (pp. 223–256). New York, NY: Oxford University Press.

Lacrois, J. M. (1991). Assessing illness schemata in patient populations. In: J. A. Skelton & R. T. Coyle (Eds), *Mental Representation in Health and Illness* (pp. 193–219). New York, NY: Springer-Verlag.

Laubach, G. D., Wennberg, J. E., & Gelinjs, A. C. (1992). Setting the stage. In: A. C. Gelinjs (Ed.), *Technology and Health Care in An Era of Limits* (pp. 3–8). Washington, DC: National Academy Press, Institute of Medicine.

Lazarus, R. S. (1966). *Psychological stress and the coping process.* New York, NY: McGraw-Hill Publishing Company.

Lazarus, R. S., & Folkman, S. (1984). *Stress, appraisal, and coping.* New York, NY: Springer-Verlag.

Lazarus, R. S., & Folkman, S. (2000). Coping and adaptation. In: W. D. Gentry (Ed.), *The Handbook of Behavioral Medicine.* New York, NY: Guilford.

Leventhal, H. (1986). Symptom reporting: A focus on process. In: S. McHugh & T. M. Vallis (Eds), *Illness Behavior: A Multidisciplinary Model* (pp. 219–237). New York, NY: Plenum.

Leventhal, H., & Diefenbach, M. (1991). The active side of illness cognition. In: J. A. Skelton & R. T. Coyle (Eds), *Mental Representations in Health and Illness* (pp. 247–272). New York, NY: Springer-Verlag.

Leventhal, H., & Leventhal, E. A. (1993). Affect, cognition and symptom reporting. In: C. R. Chapman & K. M. Foley (Eds), *Current and Emerging Issues in Cancer Pain: Research and Practice* (pp. 153–173). New York, NY: Raven.

Leventhal, H., Leventhal, E. A., & Cameron, L. (2001). Representations, procedures, and affect in illness self-regulation: A perceptual-cognitive model. In: A. Baum, T. A. Revenson & J. E. Singer (Eds), *Handbook of Health Psychology* (pp. 19–48). Mahwah, NJ: Lawrence Erlabum Associates.

Leventhal, H., Safer, M. A., & Panagis, D. M. (1983). The impact of communications on the self-regulation of health beliefs, decisions, and behavior. *Health Education Quarterly, 10*(1), 3–29.

Levy, S. M., Herberman, R. B., Lee, J. K., Lippman, M. E., & d'Angelo, T. (1989). Breast conservation versus mastectomy: Distress sequelae as a function of choice. *Journal of Clinical Oncology, 7,* 367–375.

Lipowski, Z. J. (1986). Somatization: A borderland between medicine and psychiatry. *Canadian Medical Association Journal, 135*, 609–614.

Lipowski, Z. J. (1987). Somatization: The experience and communication of psychological distress as somatic symptoms. *Psychotherapy Psychosomatic, 47*, 160–167.

Lipowski, Z. J. (1988). Somatization: The concept and its clinical application. *American Journal of Psychiatry, 145*, 1358–1368.

Loscalozo, M. J., & BritzenhofeSzoc, K. (1998). Brief Crisis Counseling. In: J. C. Holland (Ed.), *Psycho-Oncology* (pp. 662–675). New York, NY: Oxford University Press.

Maguire, G. P., Tait, A., Brooke, M., Thomas, C., Howat, J. M. T., Sellwood, R. A., & Bush, H. (1980). Psychiatric morbidity and physical toxicity associated with adjuvant chemotherapy after mastectomy. *British Medical Journal, 281*, 1179.

Massie, M. J., & Holland, J. C. (1989). Overview of normal reactions and prevalence of psychiatric disorders. In: J. C. Holland & J. H. Rowland (Eds), *Handbook of Psychooncology*. New York, NY: Oxford University Press.

Massie, M. J., & Holland, J. C. (1990). Depression and the cancer patient. *Journal of Clinical Psychiatry, 51*(Suppl.), 12–17.

Massie, M. J., Spiegel, L., Lederberg, M. S., & Holland, J. C. (1995). Psychiatric complications in cancer patients. In: G. P. Murphy & W. R. E. L. Lawrence (Eds), *American Cancer Society Textbook of Clinical Oncology* (pp. 685–698). Atlanta, GA: American Cancer Society.

McKenna, R. J., Wellisch, D. K., & Fawzy F. I. (1995). Rehabilitation and supportive care of the cancer patient. In: G. P. Murphy, W. Lawrence & R. E. Lenhard (Eds), *American Cancer Society Textbook of Clinical Oncology* (pp. 635–654). Atlanta, GA: American Cancer Society.

McWhinney, I. R., Epstein, R. M., & Freeman, T. R. (1997). Lingua Medica: Rethinking somatization. *Annals of Internal Medicine, 126*(9), 747–750.

Mechanic, D. (1992). Health and illness behavior and patient-practitioner relationships. *Social Science and Medicine, 34*(12), 1345–1350.

Meyerowitz, B. E. (1980). Psychosocial correlates of breast cancer and its treatment. *Psychological Bulletin, 87*, 108.

Mishel, M. H. (1993). Living with chronic illness: Living with uncertainty. In: S. G. Funk, E. M. Tornquist, M. A. T. Champagne & R. A. Wiese (Eds), *Key Aspects of Caring for the Chronically Ill* (pp. 46–58). New York, NY: Springer.

Mishel, M. H. (1996). Commentary to: Uncertainty and coping in fathers of children with cancer. *Journal of Pediatric Nurses, 13*(2), 89–90.

Mishler, E. G., Amarasingham, L., Hauser, S., Osherson, S., Waxler, N., & Liem, R. (1981). *Social contexts of health, illness and patient care*. Cambridge, UK: Cambridge University Press.

Morgan, K. P. (1998). Contested bodies, contested knowledge's: Women, health, and the politics of medicalization. In: S. Sherwin (Ed.), *The Politics of Women's Health. Exploring Agency and Autonomy* (pp. 83–121). Philadelphia, PA: Temple University Press.

Morgan, M., Calnan, M., & Manning, N. (1985). Lay interpretations and responses to illness. In: *Sociological Approaches to Health and Medicine* (pp. 76–105). Sydney, NSW: Croom Helm Australia Pty Ltd.

Morris, T., Greer, H. S., & White, P. (1977). Psychological and social adjustment to mastectomy. A two-year follow-up study. *Cancer, 40*, 2381–2387.

Nerenz, D. R., Levelthal, H., & Love, R. R. (1982). Factors contributing to emotional distress during cancer chemotherapy. *Cancer, 50*(5), 1020–1027.

Newell, S. A., Sanson-Fisher, R. W., & Savolainen, N. J. (2002). Systematic review of psychological therapies for cancer patients: Overview and recommendations for future research. *Journal of the National Cancer Institute*, 94(8), 558–584.

Northhouse, L. L., Mood, D., Templin, T., Mellon, S., & George, T. (2000). Couples' pattern of adjustment to colon cancer. *Social Science and Medicine*, 50, 271–284.

Oinas, E. (1998). Medicalization by whom? Accounts of menstruation conveyed by young women and medical experts in medical advisory columns. *Sociology of Health and Illness*, 20(1), 52–70.

Park, C. L., & Folkman, S. (1997). Meaning in the context of stress and coping. *Review of General Psychology*, 1(2), 115–144.

Parsons, T. (1951). *The social system*. New York, NY: Free Press.

Passik, S. D., Dugan, W., McDonald, M. V., Rosenfeld, B., Theobald, D. E., & Edgerton, S. (1998). Oncologists' recognition of depression in their patients with cancer. *Journal of Clinical Oncology*, 16(4), 1594–1600.

Passik, S., Kirsh, K. L., Rosenfeld, B., McDonald, M. V., & Theobald, D. E. (2001). The changeable nature of patients' fears regarding chemotherapy: Implications for palliative care. *Journal of Pain and Symptom Management*, 21(2), 113–120.

Payne, D. K., Hoffman, R. G., Theodoulou, M., Dosik, M., & Massie, M. J. (1999). Screening for anxiety and depression in women with breast cancer. Psychiatry and medical oncology gear up for managed care. *Psychosomatics*, 40(1), 64–69.

Pearlin, L. I. (1991). The study of coping: An overview of problems and directions. In: J. Eckenrode (Ed.), *The Social Context of Coping* (pp. 261–276). New York, NY: Plenum.

Pennebaker, J. W. (1982). *The psychology of physical symptoms*. New York, NY: Springer-Verlag.

Peters, S., Stanley, I., Rose, M., & Salmon, P. (1997). Patients' accounts of medically unexplained symptoms: Sources of patients' authority and implications for demands on medical care. *Social Science and Medicine*, 46(559), 565.

Petty, F., & Noyes, R. (1981). Depression secondary to cancer. *Biological Psychiatry*, 16, 1203–1220.

Pilowsky, I. (1987). Psychiatric medicine. In: R. C. W. Hall (Ed.), *Illness Behavior* (pp. 1–3). Longwood, FL: Barry Blackwell.

Psychological Aspects of Breast Cancer Study Group (1987). Psychological response to mastectomy: A prospective comparison study. *Cancer*, 59(189).

Radley, A. (1994). *Making sense of illness: The social psychology of health and disease*. London, UK: Sage Publications.

Reiser, S. J. (1978). *Medicine and the reign of technology*. Cambridge, UK: Cambridge University Press.

Reissman, C. K. (1983). Women and medicalization: A new perspective. *Social Policy* (Summer), 3–18.

Rich, I. M., Andejeski, Y., Alciati, M. H., Bisceglio, I., Breslau, E. S., McCall, L., & Valadez, A. (1998). Consumer participation in breast cancer research. *Breast Disease*, 10(56), 33–45.

Rimer, B. K., & Bluman, L. G. (1997). The psychosocial consequences of mammography. *Monograph National Cancer Institute*, 22, 131–138.

Robbins, J. M., & Kirmayer, L. J. (1991). Cognitive and social factors in somatization. In: L. J. Kirmayer & J. M. Robbins (Eds), *Current Concepts of Somatization: Research and Clinical Perspectives* (pp. 107–142). Washington, DC: American Psychiatric Press.

Robinson, J. W., & Roter, D. L. (1999). Psychosocial problem disclosure by primary care patients. *Social Science and Medicine*, 48, 1353–1362.

Rodwin, M. A. (1994). Patient accountability and quality of care: Lessons from medical consumerism and the patients' rights, women's heath and disability rights movements. *American Journal of Law and Medicine*, 20(1–2), 147–167.

Rosen, G. (1972). The evolution of social medicine. In: H. E. Freeman, S. Levine & L. Reeder (Eds), *Handbook of Medical Sociology*. Englewood Cliffs, NJ: Prentice-Hall.

Rosen, G. (1983). *The structure of American medical practice: 1875–1941*. Philadelphia, PA: University of Pennsylvania Press.

Roter, D. L., & Hall, J. A. (1993). *Doctors talking with patients/patients talking with doctors: Improving communication in medical visits*. Westport, CT: Auburn House.

Rotwein, S. (1991). The Medicalization of Alzheimer's Disease: Process and Consequences for Public Policy (unpublished manuscript).

Rowland, J. H., & Massie, M. J. (1998). Breast cancer. In: J. C. Holland (Ed.), *Psycho-Oncology* (pp. 380–401). New York, NY: Oxford University Press.

Salmon, P. (2000). Patients who present physical symptoms in the absence of physical pathology: A challenge to existing models of doctor-patient interaction. *Patient Education and Counseling, 39*(1), 105–113.

Sanger, C. K., & Reznikoff, M. A. (1981). A comparison of the psychological effects of breast-saving procedures with the modified mastectomy. *Cancer, 48*, 2341.

Schag, C. A. C., Ganz, P. A., Polinsky, M. L., Fred, C., Hirji, K., & Petersen, L. (1993). Characteristics of women at risk for psychosocial distress in the year after breast cancer. *Journal of Clinical Oncology, 11*, 783–793.

Schauffler, H. H., & Wilkerson, J. (1997). National health care reform and the 103rd Congress: The activities and influence of public health advocates. *American Journal of Public Health, 87*(7), 1107–1112.

Schuman, E. A. (1965). Stages of illness and medical care. *Journal of Health Social Behavior, 6*, 114.

Sharfstein, S. S. (1998). The high cost of spending less on care. *Psychiatric Services, 49*, 1523–1529.

Shorter, E. (1992). *From paralysis to fatigue: A history of psychosomatic illness in the modern era*. New York, NY: Free Press.

Silberman, C. E. (1992). What is it like to be a patient in the 1990s? In: A. C. Gelijns (Ed.), *Medical Innovation at the Crossroads. Technology and Health Care in An Era of Limits* (Vol. III, pp. 165–119). Washington, DC: National Academy Press.

Singer, P. A., Martin, D. K., Giacomini, M., & Purdy, L. (2000). Priority setting for new technologies in medicine: Qualitative case study. *British Medical Journal, 321*, 1316–1318.

Skelton, J. A. (1991). Laypersons' judgments of patient credibility and the study of illness representations. In: J. A. Skelton & R. T. Coyle (Eds), *Mental Representation in Health and Illness* (pp. 108–131). New York, NY: Springer-Verlag.

Spring, B., & Coons, H. (1982). Stress as a precursor to schizophrenia. In: W. J. Neufeld (Ed.), *Psychological Stress and Psychopathology* (pp. 13–54). New York, NY: McGraw-Hill Book Company.

Stahl, S. M., & Feller, J. R. (1990). Old equals sick: An ontogenic fallacy. In: S. M. Stahl (Ed.), *The Legacy of Longevity, Health and Health Care in Later Life* (pp. 21–34). New York, NY: Sage Publications.

Stefanek, M., Derogatis, L., & Shaw, A. (1987). Psychological distress among oncology outpatients. *Psychosomatics, 28*, 530.

Stuart, S., & Noyes, R. (1999). Attachment and interpersonal communication in somatization. *Psychosomatics, 40*(1), 34–43.

Taylor, S. E., & Aspinwall, L. G. (1996). Mediating and moderating processes in psychosocial stress. Appraisal, coping resistance, and vulnerability. In: H. B. Kaplan (Ed.), *Psychosocial Stress. Perspectives on Structure, Theory, Life-Course, and Methods* (pp. 71–110). San Diego, CA: Academic Press.

The President's Advisory Commission on Consumer Protection and Quality in the Health Care Industry (1998). *Quality First: Better Health Care for All Americans*. Washington, DC: U.S. Government Printing Office.

Thoits, P. A. (1983). Dimensions of life events that influence psychological distress: An evaluation and synthesis of the literature. In: H. B. Kaplan (Ed.), *Psychological Stress: Trends in Theory and Research* (pp. 33–87). Orlando, FL: Academic Press.

Waitzkin, H., & Magana, H. (1997). The black box in somatization: Unexplained physical symptoms, culture, and narratives of trauma. *Social Science and Medicine, 45*(6), 811–825.

Weisman, A. D., Worden, J. W., & Sobel, H. J. (1980). *Psychosocial screening and intervention with cancer patients: Research report*. Boston, MA: Harvard Medical School and Massachusetts General Hospital.

Wheaton, B. (1996). The domains and boundaries of stress concepts. In: H. B. Kaplan (Ed.), *Psychosocial Stress: Perspectives on Structure, Theory, Life-Course, and Methods* (pp. 29–70). San Diego, CA: Academic Press.

Zabora, J., BritzenhofeSzoc, K., Curbow, B., Hooker, C., & Piantadosi, S. (2001). The prevalence of psychological distress by cancer site. *Psycho-Oncology* (in press).

Zegans, L. A. (1982). Stress and the development of somatic disorders. In: L. Goldberger & S. Breznitz (Eds), *Handbook of Stress. Theoretical and Clinical Aspects* (pp. 134–151). New York, NY: Collier Macmillian Publishers.

INTERSECTIONALITY AND WOMEN'S HEALTH: CHARTING A PATH TO ELIMINATING HEALTH DISPARITIES

Lynn Weber and Deborah Parra-Medina

INTRODUCTION

The stubborn persistence of gross health disparities – differences in the incidence, prevalence, mortality, and burden of diseases and other adverse health conditions that exist among specific population groups in the U.S. – has become a cause for concern among the privileged and powerful as well as among the racial ethnic communities who live with and die from their consequences. In his radio address on February 21st, 1998, President Clinton committed the nation to an ambitious goal by the year 2010: eliminating disparities in six areas of health status experienced by racial and ethnic minority populations while continuing the progress made in improving the overall health of the American people. Infant mortality, cancer screening and management, cardiovascular disease, diabetes, HIV/AIDS and immunizations were selected for emphasis because they reflect areas of disparity that are known to affect multiple racial and ethnic minority groups at all life stages. Elimination of persistent health disparities has become a major priority for national health agencies, politicians, health advocates, and researchers:

- In July 2002, over 2,000 people attended the first "National Leadership Summit on Eliminating Racial and Ethnic Disparities in Health," sponsored by the Office of Minority Health, U.S. Dept. of Health and Human Services.

Gender Perspectives on Health and Medicine: Key Themes
Advances in Gender Research, Volume 7, 181–230
© 2003 Published by Elsevier Ltd.
ISSN: 1529-2126/doi:10.1016/S1529-2126(03)07006-1

- *Healthy People 2010* has as one of its top two priorities eliminating racial and ethnic health disparities.
- The National Institutes of Health developed a strategic plan to reduce and eliminate health disparities by 2006 and established a National Center on Minority Health and Health Disparities.

Out of survival needs, concern for their youth and their futures, and a sense of social justice racial and ethnic communities have, of course, mobilized to eliminate health disparities. But it is clear that for many reasons the powerful and privileged have also come to view health disparities as a problem. The rapid growth in racial ethnic populations means that maintaining a healthy workforce necessitates addressing health disparities. In the political arena, people of color represent increasingly significant constituencies whose support can be crucial to election outcomes and other loci of political power. And in the global arena, where health is viewed less as a commodity and more as a human right, the persistence of health disparities weakens the United States' claims to leadership over other less wealthy nations who nonetheless have healthier populations and more widely beneficial social, political and economic arrangements.

Scholars and activists working both within and outside the massive health-related machinery of government and the private sector and within and outside communities of color address the same fundamental questions: Why do health disparities exist? Why have they persisted over such a long time? What can be done to significantly reduce or eliminate them?

This paper examines two different research paradigms that have attempted to answer these questions – traditional psychosocial/biobehavioral/biomedical research centered in the social sciences, epidemiology and public health[1] and feminist scholarship on the intersections of multiple inequalities of race, class, gender, and sexuality centered primarily in the humanities and social sciences. With the massive national investment in biomedical research and related medical interventions and treatments, it is almost unnecessary to note that applications of the biomedical model have improved the health of the population and many individuals. Likewise, psychosocial and biobehavioral research that extends that model to incorporate more psychological and social traits, such as health-related behaviors (e.g. smoking, exercise, diet) and psychological and social characteristics and processes among individuals and/or as manifest in individuals (e.g. social supports, locus of control, faulty logic, self-esteem, stress of discrimination, perceptions of mastery and control), has also increased our knowledge of the disease process and supported behavioral interventions that work for individuals (House, 2002; House & Williams, 2000; Lantz et al., 1998; Smedley & Syme, 2000).

But there is also a growing recognition – certainly in feminist, racial/ethnic and other critical scholarly traditions but even in more traditional ones – that health disparities centered in social group inequalities have only nominally been affected by the research and applications of the biomedically-driven health model in the U.S. and the psychosocial and biobehavioral elaborations of that model. Many different explanations for this failure have been offered – some more critical than others (Adler & Newman, 2002; Clarke & Olesen, 1999; Krieger & Fee, 1994a, b; NIH, 2000, 2001; Rosser, 1994; Ruzek et al., 1997a, b; Smedley et al., 2002; Smedley & Syme, 2000).

The biomedical and intersectional traditions have developed in relative isolation from one another. While the former overwhelmingly dominates not only health research and practice but also public conceptions and experiences of health and illness, we contend that the latter has great potential to provide new knowledge that can more effectively guide actions toward eliminating health disparities across race and ethnicity but also across gender, sexual orientation, social class and socioeconomic status, and other critical dimensions of social inequality.

Psychosocial/Biobehavioral/Biomedical Models

Operating from a positivist paradigm, traditional biomedically-driven research on health disparities typically employs a multifactorial model to identify the many environmental, social, psychological, behavioral, and biological processes and traits that determine health outcomes and that can be conceptualized as "risk factors" (e.g. poverty, depression, smoking, lack of exercise, genetics) to guide health practices, education, and policies (Shim, 2002). Scholarship in this tradition now widely acknowledges that:

- significant health disparities exist across multiple indicators of morbidity and mortality;
- these disparities have persisted throughout this century despite efforts to eliminate them and despite significant progress in increasing overall life expectancy and eliminating and/or significantly reducing some major threats to health;
- new approaches are needed to address the problem (cf. House, 2002; House & Williams, 2000; Krieger, 1999; Link & Phelan, 2000; National Institutes of Health (NIH) 2000, 2001; Robert & House 2000a, b; Smedley et al., 2002).

One major direction that the search for new approaches has taken in this tradition is toward addressing the connections between racial and ethnic health disparities and socioeconomic status and gender disparities. To date, the dominant construction of health disparities among government agencies, researchers, politicians and activists has been and continues to be on racial and ethnic minority populations: African-Americans, Asians, Pacific Islanders, Hispanics and Latinos, Native Americans, and Native Alaskans. While that focus persists, some researchers are now exploring the interrelationships of race and ethnicity with indicators of socioeconomic status – most commonly income, but also with education and occupation. Strains of this scholarship now contend that:

- unravelling race and ethnic disparities will certainly also require addressing the ways that they often appear in research as proxies for unexamined socioeconomic disparities;
- socioeconomic disparities themselves need to be eliminated (for reviews, see Adler & Newman, 2002; Krieger et al., 1997; Navarro, 1990; Smedley & Syme, 2000; Williams, 1996);
- gender significantly shapes racial and ethnic and/or socioeconomic disparities (Breen, 2001; Krieger, 1999; Williams, 2002);
- community-based, ecological models of research and action are necessary to address all types of disparities (cf. Fetterman, 1996, 2001; Goodman, 1996; Goodman et al., 1993; Krieger, 1999).

Intersectional Women's Health Models

A second strand of research by feminist health scholars and activists has developed largely outside traditional biomedical and epidemiological scholarship and as a part of an interdisciplinary agenda (women's studies, ethnic studies, labor studies) to explicate the socially constructed and intricately intertwined nature of race, class, gender, and sexuality systems of social inequality. The need to understand this "intersectionality" is today a primary concern of feminist scholars across disciplinary, thematic, and scholar-activist boundaries.[2] Three broad questions drive examinations of the intersections of race, gender, ethnicity and other dimensions of inequality:

- What is the meaning of race, ethnicity, class, gender, sexuality, and other systems of inequality across the ideological, political, and economic domains of society in institutional structures and in individual lives?
- How are these co-constructed systems of inequality simultaneously produced, reinforced, resisted, and transformed – over time, in different social locations, and in different institutional domains (e.g. health, education, economy, religion, polity, family)?
- How can our understanding of the intersecting dynamics of these systems guide us in the pursuit of social justice?

And although there is no unified theory of "intersectionality," several features, when taken together, distinguish this scholarship:

- It examines the ways these dimensions are simultaneously socially constructed in specific times and places, creating distinct social formations.
- It explores these systems as macro institutional and micro interpersonal power relations that create and sustain social hierarchies – not merely as differences in the distribution of resources that exist and take meaning independent of social relationships of power and control.
- It is centered in the perspectives and experiences of multiply oppressed groups – most commonly, women of color.
- It is driven by the pursuit of social justice.
- It is interdisciplinary (cf. Zinn & Dill, 1996; Collins, 1998, 2000; Weber, 2001; Zambrana, 1987, 2001).

By placing primary attention on the construction of multiple social inequalities as they are simultaneously produced, this research is particularly well-suited to addressing the question of disparities in our social worlds in the economy and labor, education, family and other institutional arenas but also, as feminist women's health research has aptly demonstrated, in health, especially reproductive health. Feminist intersectional scholarship has problematized and sought to revision women's health in a more complex and inclusive way by taking seriously the intersectional processes that co-construct inequality and women's health.[3] (e.g. Clarke & Olesen, 1999; Krieger et al., 1993; Ruzek et al., 1997b; Shim, 2002; Zambrana, 2001). Among other themes, this scholarship:

- argues for an expanded conception of health that incorporates a broad framework of social relations and institutions, not just diseases and disorders, and situates health in communities and families, not simply in individual bodies;
- emphasizes power relationships, not just distributional differences in resources, as central to social inequality and health disparities;
- calls for health research that simultaneously addresses the intersections of race and ethnicity with gender, class, socioeconomic status, sexuality, age, rural-urban residence, region and other markers of social difference;
- centers that work in the lives and perspectives of multiply oppressed groups, particularly women of color;
- sees activism for social justice in health for all people as an integral part of the knowledge acquisition process (cf. Clarke & Olesen, 1999; Krieger et al., 1993; Morgen, 2002; Ruzek et al., 1997b; Zambrana, 2001, 2002).

Many of these same features are increasingly being called for and emphasized in mainstream biomedical, biobehavioral, and psychosocial health disparities research, research agendas, and intervention strategies (cf. National Institutes of Health, 2000, 2001; Robert & House, 2000b; Smedley & Syme, 2000). Yet because those models are not primarily designed to explicate and challenge the social systemic processes that constitute social inequality and because they typically do not emerge from the perspective and experiences of multiply oppressed communities – for example, poor elderly women of color (Rosser, 1994) – we believe that merely modifying these models is unlikely to *significantly* change our understanding of *health disparities*.

By focusing on the social construction of inequality and centering research in the perspectives of multiply oppressed groups, intersectional scholars provide situated knowledge that raises new questions and presents new opportunities for understanding health disparities. But as Brace and O'Connell Davidson (2000, p. 1048) caution, the promise of intersectional scholarship will not be realized until ". . . there is greater dialogue and critical exchange between general theorists and those whose research and theorizing is focused on substantive issues."

The purpose of this paper is to facilitate that dialogue between traditional health disparities scholarship emerging from a biomedical paradigm and intersectional women's health scholarship. We plan to do so by clarifying the taken-for-granted assumptions and common practices of the former through comparing it with related themes in intersectional scholarship which emerges from a different historical, political, scientific location and yet has similar goals: addressing the core questions about the existence, persistence and processes for change in health disparities. In so doing, we hope to illustrate the potential of intersectional women's health scholarship for providing new avenues for addressing health disparities – not just across race and ethnicity but also across gender, class, sexuality and other dimensions of social inequality.

This intersectional approach to health emerges from approximately twenty years of feminist scholarship seeking to understand the intersecting dynamics of race, class, gender, sexuality and other dimensions of inequality (Zinn & Dill, 1996; Weber, 2001). The themes in that scholarship identify fundamental characteristics of these intersecting systems of social inequality and address: (1) the fundamental processes involved in the social construction of inequality; (2) the methodologies employed to understand these processes; and (3) the process of change to achieve social justice.

Contrasting Themes in Biomedical and Intersectional Models of Health Disparities

Several core thematic foci distinguish the biomedical paradigm and its closely allied biobehavioral and psychosocial offshoots from intersectional models of health disparities. We briefly summarize them here and then take them up in more detail in the following section. Since our purpose is to highlight the unique contributions of intersectional research, we present the core themes that maximally distinguish between the two paradigms. It should be noted, however, that these oppositions do not capture the nuance and considerable overlapping that exists in theory, method, practice, and constructions of health. Nor do they capture the significant variations within the biomedical and intersectional paradigms we present here:

- *Individual as Unit Obscuring Social Structures.* Focus on the individual body vs. the social structural context as the locus of a population's health. The biomedical paradigm fails to fully consider the social forces and contexts that shape women's health and women's lives – the situatedness of social inequality in history and place, and its operation at the macro social structural as well as micro individual level. In research, individuals are the units of analysis not social groups. Psychosocial and biobehavioral elaborations of the biomedical paradigm seek to "decompose" the effects of social inequality variables on health and illness outcomes by looking for mediating factors – pathways or proximate causes – to explain the effects of social inequality on a particular health outcome. In contrast, intersectional approaches problematize the processes generating and maintaining the macro social structures of race, class, gender, and sexuality and seek to identify their relationships to individual and collective identities, behaviors, and health statuses.
- *Distributional or Relational Constructions of Social Inequality: Having More or Having Power Over?* Conceptualization and measurement of social inequalities as distributional – representing differences in valued resources vs. social relationships of power and control, dominance and subordination. The former asks the question "Who has more (education, wealth, income, cultural capital, prestige, etc.)?" The latter asks the question "Who has power and control over whom?" Distributional models employ rankings, linear, incremental measurements of inequalities; relational models examine categorical groupings in relations of dominance and subordination with one another (e.g. owners, managers, workers; whites and other racial groups; men and women).
- *Dominant Culture-Centered or Oppressed Group-Centered?* The biomedical paradigm emerges from and represents a dominant culture world view; intersectional models represent the world views of multiply oppressed groups – most commonly poor and working class women of color. Biomedical research emanates from dominant culture perspectives and concerns, relies on clinical and population studies (primarily cross-sectional surveys) obtained from large random samples of individuals, and employs quantifiable measures that support statistical generalizations about correlations among variables. Health disparities

research in this tradition tends to employ Whites as a reference group and describe other groups' health as it differs from Whites. Intersectional research emerges from the perspectives of multiply oppressed groups, especially women of color, so that women of color serve as the reference point, and their health is examined in its own context, not as it deviates from White norms. This research relies more heavily on historical and interpretive, qualitative methods while using multiple methods in the same study, multiple data sources, and multidisciplinary approaches – incorporating humanistic as well as social science theoretical insights and analytic techniques.

- *Independent, Single Inequalities or Intersecting, Multiple Inequalities?* Conceptualization and measurement of inequalities as discrete dimensions, independently assessed vs. multiple systems, intricately intertwined, co-constructed and inseparable. The psychosocial and biobehavioral models of health disparities typically address one or two dimensions of systemic inequality, such as race/ethnicity, socioeconomic status, and/or gender but rarely more than two in the same study. This practice derives from theoretical conceptualizations of the dimensions as separate and distinct, a balkanization of research traditions studying these dimensions as isolated entities, and the methodological requirements of survey research for very large (expensive) samples to enable statistical assessments of the "interactions" of these factors with one another. Intersectional scholarship, which views these systems as simultaneously co-constructed at both the macro level of social institutions and the micro level of individual lives, has employed a diversity of methods for simultaneously considering multiple dimensions of inequality at macro and micro levels even when some dimensions seem absent in a particular context (e.g. analysis of gender dynamics in studies with only women). This kind of analysis is made possible because of the view of race, class, gender, and sexuality as social constructions, not as individual (biological) attributes, and a belief in the situated (in time and place) nature of social life and our understanding of it.
- *Value Freedom, Researcher Objectivity or Knowledge from Active Researcher Engagement?* The biomedical paradigm claims its research process as value-free, while valuing a presumably attainable objective distance between researcher and researched. Knowledge acquisition and social activism are seen as antithetical to one another – activism is believed to taint the researcher's ability to obtain accurate, objective, reliable, and reproducible results. Intersectional models assume a connection between oppression and resistance, between gaining knowledge of oppressive systems and engagement in social activism to challenge them. Far from tainting the process of knowledge acquisition, activism enhances it (Collins, 1998, 2000; DeVault, 1999; Mies, 1991; Rosser, 1994; Ruzek, 1999).

From an intersectional perspective, adherence to these core themes of traditional biomedical approaches to the exclusion of other perspectives has impeded biomedical science and its psychosocial and biobehavioral elaborations in the development of effective models and interventions to reduce racial, ethnic, and other socially structured disparities in health, including gender and women's health. These themes are elaborated below.

CONTRASTING THEMES: A CLOSER LOOK

Individual as Unit Obscuring Social Structures

In biomedical, biobehavioral, and psychosocial models of health the individual – specifically the individual body with its diseases and disorders, most typically presented in clinical settings – is the focus of attention. The individual is the starting point of theory, the unit of analysis in research, and the target for intervention. By focusing on the individual and structuring research and interventions accordingly, however, we cannot adequately address the fundamental character of race, social class, gender, and sexuality – that they are constructed and take meaning in social groups. Blanchard and Crosby's (1989) research, for example, has demonstrated that systemic processes of discrimination against women and people of color in work settings are not observable except through group level data. When for purposes of research we designate an *individual* as of a particular race, gender, etc., we have merely given ourselves a static marker of *the place to go* if we actually want to observe and to understand how those systemic group processes producing social inequality are shaping health outcomes. We have not yet gone there.

As Ruzek et al. (1997b, p. 12) state ". . . dominant biomedical conceptualizations of health, with their narrow disease focus, inadequately represent health because they leave out, or only nominally consider, the social forces and contexts that shape women's health and women's lives." They also point out that even though biomedicine has responded to feminist insights about how gender affects the etiology, natural history, and treatment of disease by initiating changes in policy such as mandated inclusion of women in clinical trials, the clinical practice framework remains. That framework also permeates research designed to broaden the biomedical model by examining psychosocial factors in the etiology of disease and gender-related health practices in the use of medical services. But these models do not adequately represent health because "the underlying social dynamics of what actually *produces* (sic) health for different groups of women are not integral to biomedical models" (Ruzek et al., 1997b, p. 13).

Mediational Models The Search for Pathways
In most health research, dimensions of social inequality such as race, ethnicity, social class, and gender, if included at all, are treated as control variables that go unproblematized and unanalyzed in quantitative analyses of population data. However, many psychosocial and biobehavioral elaborations of the biomedical paradigm seek to identify the "pathways" between race/ethnicity, gender, social class, socioeconomic status and disease where these social systems of inequality are taken as essentially "unknowable and unalterable," and the mediators – individual level attributes and behaviors, seen as both "knowable and alterable" – are taken to represent the "true" proximate causes of disease (e.g. behaviors such as smoking, diet, exercise; psychosocial variables such as social supports, psychological dispositions, social roles). For example, some common intervening factors in mental health research on depression in women have been sense of control, resilience, stress, role overload, and social supports (Bird, 1999; Bullers, 1994; Matthews et al., 1998; Pavalko & Woodbury, 2000; Swanson et al., 1997; Waldron et al., 1998). But even when these factors reduce or explain variance in particular depression indicators that are attributed to race, gender, class, socioeconomic status or other dimensions of inequality, fundamental questions about how these systems are generated and maintained go unanswered, and the dimensions are simply taken as "givens" in the research. First, the methodological "gold standard" for this kind of health disparities research – survey data obtained from large random samples with quantifiable measures that support statistical generalizations about correlations among variables in the population – has limitations. While such studies can identify factors that are correlated with depression, they cannot explicate how these factors are experienced in individual lives. Consequently, we remain unclear about how they shape mental health and what can be done to improve health outcomes. Furthermore, since they are based on individual level data, they do not capture the group processes that define systems of social inequality. By ignoring the social processes that generate and sustain race, class, gender, and other dimensions of inequality they cannot see beyond the "proximate causes" to challenge the "fundamental causes" of health disparities (Link & Phelan, 2000). Interventions generated out of this line of psychosocial research are also unlikely to have a significant impact on *health disparities* because discoveries about intervening pathways or proximate causes of disease and illness get introduced into a social order hierarchically organized by race, ethnicity, class, socioeconomic status, and gender (Link & Phelan, 1995, 1996, 2000; Ruzek, 1999). As Williams (1997, p. 327) states of social inequality, "As long as the basic causal forces are in operation, the alteration of surface causes will give rise to new intervening mechanisms to maintain the same outcome."

For several reasons, privileged groups benefit and oppressed racial and ethnic and social class groups lose when new knowledge and interventions are introduced into the population. As Link and Phelan (2000) note, coronary artery disease was seen as a "disease of affluence" until the last fifty years when it has become more common among the poor and working classes. Breast cancer mortality, once more common among women of high socioeconomic status, is now no more so, at least among White women. And AIDS while not associated with socioeconomic status early in the epidemic has become so. In each of these cases, the most likely explanation for the change in relationship is the ability of dominant groups to take advantage of new developments and knowledge in the etiology of diseases and treatments for them. Link and Phelan (2000, p. 39) summarize some of the reasons that the relationship between socioeconomic status and disease persists is that socioeconomic status ". . . embodies resources like knowledge, money, power, and prestige that can be used in different ways in different situations to avoid risks for disease and death" (Link & Phelan, 1995, 1996). When interventions are developed to address health disparities, new intervening pathways spring up to replace the ones that may have been reduced or eliminated.

Beyond Pathways: The Need to Look Further "Upstream"
Recognizing the limits of existing models, Smedley and Syme (2000, p. 3) argue that ". . . intervention efforts should address not only 'downstream' individual-level phenomena (e.g. physiologic pathways to disease, individual and life-style factors) and 'mainstream' factors (e.g. population-based interventions) but also 'upstream,' societal-level phenomena (e.g. public policies)." They suggest that the need to move upstream exists for several reasons.

- Many risks for disease and poor health are shared by large numbers of people.
- Many population groups have characteristic patterns of disease and injury over time even though individuals move in and out of the groups.
- Many improvements in health over the last century can be attributed not to medical interventions but to factors such as hygiene, rising standards of living, and nutrition.
- Many narrow, individually-focused models of behavior change have proven insufficient to help people change high-risk behavior (Smedley & Syme, 2000, p. 3–4).

Arguments to move "upstream" have included calls for multilevel (household, neighborhood and community) as well as individual-level data and multidisciplinary research and new, consistent measures of social inequality variables. (Breen, 2001; Krieger, 1999; Krieger et al., 1993, 1997; NIH, 2001; Robert & House, 2000b; Smedley & Syme, 2000). But from a feminist intersectional perspective, even those measures may not be enough. For example, Ruzek et al. (1997b, p. 22) state, "Grafting psychosocial factors onto biomedical models may lead to incremental improvements in primary prevention, screening, and treatment, but these are not adequate substitutes for providing the prerequisites for health. Nor does such grafting even begin to address women's differences and the complexities of meeting their health needs."

Distributional and Relational Constructions of Social Inequality: Having More or Having Power Over?

The biomedical, biobehavioral, and psychosocial models of health disparites almost universally conceptualize race, class, gender, and sexuality as representing systems of social ranking that merely reflect differences in:

- resources (e.g. income, wealth, educational degrees, health insurance);
- lifestyle preferences;
- social roles;
- prestige;
- cultural beliefs, values, and practices.

Race, class, gender, and sexuality groups' resources, behavioral, and cultural patterns are also most commonly described and understood as they deviate from dominant culture White, patriarchal, upper- and middle-class, heterosexual norms. So, for example, the very notion of health disparities is predicated on the measurement of deviations of "minority" groups' health statuses from White norms, and the charge to eliminate the disparities is predicated on the assumption that there should be little or no morbidity and mortality differences between Whites (and in some versions middle classes, males, and heterosexuals) and people of color (and working classes/poor, women, gays and lesbians). In short, this approach asks questions such as the following.

- Who has more valued resources (education, wealth, cultural capital, prestige)?
- How do roles, beliefs, values, and practices vary from dominant culture norms?
- How does having more and valuing, thinking, and acting in particular socially desirable ways translate into lower mortality and morbidity?

It does not ask questions about the *relationships* of dominant and subordinate groups to each other and how those *relationships* might determine the resources as well as values, beliefs, etc., of *both*. Instead, distributional approaches conceive of race, class, gender, and sexuality as differences that are primarily centered in women's and men's bodies, their social roles, their material resources, and in cultural variations in traditions such as food, clothing, rituals, speech patterns, leisure activities, child-rearing practices, and sexual practices – in the things that a people are, have, believe, and do – not in their relationships to oppositional groups. For example, distributional approaches to class characterized as "gradational" perspectives represent class inequality as socioeconomic status (SES) – most commonly measured as relative rankings along a continuous scale of prestige, income, and/ or education (a ladder image) (reviewed in Krieger et al., 1997; Lucal, 1994; Vannerman & Weber Cannon, 1987; Wright, 1995). "Ethnicity approaches" conceive of race as ethnic groups whose different cultural practices, beliefs, and preferences have no intrinsically different value yet bring different consequences (reviewed in Omi & Winant, 1994). "Sex roles" approaches most frequently conceive of gender as a set of expectations for behaviors, beliefs, and values that are deemed more or less constraining, functional, or effective (reviewed in Fenstermaker & West, 2002). And moral or biological perspectives on sexuality construct it as variations in sexual practices and orientations (reviewed in D'Emilio & Freedman, 1988).

In each case, the focus of attention is typically on how the values, practices, roles, or even resources of subordinate groups deviate from those of dominant groups. And dominant groups become the unquestioned norm – so much so that the concepts of race, class, gender, and sexuality are themselves typically seen as markers for people of color, the working classes and poor, women, and homosexuals while Whites, the middle and upper classes, men, and heterosexuals are seen as having no race, class, gender, or sexuality (Herek, 1997; Lucal, 1994, 1996). And these processes of ranking, comparing, and treating dominant groups as the unmarked norm hide the privileged status of Whites, men, heterosexuals, and the upper and middle classes. They obscure the nature of race, class, gender, and sexuality as social relationships between dominant and subordinate groups – hiding the role of power in producing and sustaining social inequalities.

Perhaps because race, class, gender, and sexuality studies primarily emerged from the experiences and analyses of groups who face multiple dimensions of oppression and perhaps because power relationships are simply much more apparent when more than one dimension of inequality is addressed, distributional – "cultural difference," "gender roles," "gradational," or "ranking" – approaches are almost nonexistent in intersectional scholarship. Instead, the almost universal theme in that scholarship is that race, class, gender, and sexuality are systems of power relationships among groups, where one group or groups hold power over others and uses that power to secure material resources – such as wealth, income, or access to health care and to education. Socially valued resources such as money and prestige both accrue to those in power and, once procured, serve as tools for maintaining and extending that power into future social relations. Relationships between dominant and subordinate groups are between opposing groups, not between positions on a scale of prestige, money, or cultural preferences. The gender roles that restrict women's lives exist in relation to the roles that give men power, devalued races and sexualities give Whiteness and heterosexuality value, and workers produce the goods and services that enable owners and managers to exist. Because one group cannot exist without the other, analyses of race, class, gender, and sexuality incorporate an understanding of the ways that the privilege of dominant groups is tied to the oppression of subordinate groups. Therefore, the scholarship in this field explores the social construction of Whiteness (cf. Frankenberg, 1993; McIntosh, 1995; Roediger, 1991), of masculinity (cf. Brod & Kaufman, 1994; Connell, 1995; Messner, 1992), and of heterosexual privilege (Giuffre & Williams, 1994; Rich, 1980). Critical questions from an intersectional approach ask not "Who has more?" but rather "Who has control over whom?" "What advantages does power bring?" and "How do subordinate groups resist control?" (Baca Zinn & Dill, 1996; Connell, 1987, 1995; Glenn, 1992; Griscom, 1992; Guinier & Torres, 2002; Lucal, 1994, 1996; Vannerman & Weber Cannon, 1987; Weber, 1995, 2001; Weber et al., 1997; Wyche & Graves, 1992; Yoder & Kahn, 1992).

Rather than pictured as a ladder representing a hierarchy of resources, these systems are sometimes described as interlocking dimensions in a matrix of domination where race, class, gender, and sexuality represent axes. Individuals and groups can be identified by their location in a position of dominance (power) or subordination (lacking power) along each dimension (cf. Zinn & Dill, 1994, 1996; Collins, 1998, 2000; Weber, 1998, 2001). However pictured, thinking of race, class, gender, and sexuality as power relationships encourages us to consider the nature of their relation to each other as well. They are not independent but rather interdependent, mutually reinforcing systems.

One can also think of power-based conceptions of these inequalities as logically and temporally prior to distributional conceptions in the following sense. It is the procurement of power over others that enables the accumulation of material resources and control over the institutions (e.g. media, education) through which particular dominant culture values, beliefs, and behaviors become defined as ideal and enforced in everyday life. Once this definitional process has taken place, for example, the enactment of these values, beliefs, and behaviors by dominant groups serves to further reinforce their power. Likewise, race, gender, and sexuality privilege and power are at least partially maintained by White male heterosexuals because they also hold power in the social class system and can restrict access to valued economic resources (e.g. income, education, occupational prestige – socioeconomic status) among women, people of color, and gays, bisexuals and lesbians. And research has consistently associated socioeconomic status with morbidity (low birthweight, cardiovascular disease, hypertension, arthritis, diabetes, and cancer) and mortality and has documented that socioeconomic status is at least partially responsible for observable race, ethnic, and gender differences in health and well-being (Adler & Newman, 2002; House, 2002; Krieger et al., 1993, 1997; Link & Phelan, 1995, 1996; Robert & House, 2000b; Williams, 1990, 1996).

Few health disparities researchers have addressed the conceptual distinction between distributional and relational conceptions of social inequalities or the measurement issues that accompany them (for recent reviews ignoring these dimensions see House, 2002; Robert & House, 2000b). An exception is Krieger et al. (1997) who address both conceptual and methodological issues in a review of social class research in public health. Krieger et al. (1997) describe the conceptual distinction between group – and conflict-based relational constructions of class and traditional constructions of socioeconomic position – arguing for the place of relational class measures as logically prior to distributional measures such as socioeconomic status. In research assessing the relationship of socioeconomic conditions and health outcomes, they issue a call for researchers to begin to employ relational and group-level measures of social class. Krieger et al. (1997) remain among the few who have issued such a call, however, and they could cite only two studies one of which was not in the U.S. – that employed a "dominance" model. That research, by Krieger (1991) found that household and block level measures of social class were more significant than individual level measures and than education in predicting reproductive outcomes. Finally, there is little significant evidence that other U.S. researchers have since taken up the call (Duncan et al., 2002), and while calls for employing group-level data have become more common (cf. Smedley & Syme, 2000), conceiving of the groups as in conflict with one another and of dominant groups' actions and control over resources and social, political, and economic life as responsible for subordinate group's lack of well-being has not become so.

For example, one trend in health disparities research focuses on the health consequences of discrimination, most commonly against racial ethnic minorities. While this research and the calls for it are clearly predicated on the notion that there is a relationship of dominance and subordination underlying the practice of discrimination, the relationship is not typically addressed directly and the focus of attention in the research remains on the psychosocial effects of experiencing discrimination on the health of individual minority group members. (Krieger, 1990, 1999; Williams & Neighbors, 2001). And even though some scholars call for the use of population as well as individual measures of determinants of health, these approaches leave the actions of dominant groups in the production of the negative health outcomes out of the research and therefore out of the picture when interventions are designed.

Dominant Culture-Centered or Oppressed Group-Centered?

The critical role of power relationships in understanding inequality and health disparities emerges from an intersectional world view that is centered in the perspectives and experiences of multiply oppressed groups, most commonly poor and working class women of color. From this starting point, intersectional scholarship demonstrates that although the experience of privilege is associated with a failure to understand the connection between privilege and oppression, the experience of exploitation gives a unique angle of vision on the nature of oppression (Collins, 2000; Guinier & Torres, 2002). As Albert Hourani, an Arab philosopher, described it:

> To be in someone else's power...induces doubts about the ordering of the universe, while those who have power can assume it is part of the natural order of things and invent or adopt ideas which justify their possession of it (quoted in Terkel, 1992).

Biomedical and related psychosocial and biobehavioral models – even most of those investigating health disparities – in contrast, emerge from and assume a dominant culture world-view as exemplified in the common practice of employing Whites as a reference group and assessing the health of minorities in relation to Whites. The dominant perspective is evidenced in the motivations for research, theoretical models, research methodologies, and intervention strategies.

Outsiders-Within: The Perspectives of Subordinates on Oppression

Intersectional scholars argue that the social location of groups situated at the intersections of multiple systems of inequality provides not only a unique but also a privileged position from which to understand systems of oppression (Collins, 1998, 2000; DeVault, 1999; Fonow & Cook, 1991; Guinier & Torres, 2002). This argument both emanates from and provides confirming evidence for the structuring of research so that it examines the perspectives of the oppressed on their own terms. In so doing, it makes visible the oppressive relationships that are rendered invisible by the very processes that produce privileged social locations – most significantly, the denial of discriminatory social structures.

Women of color and other groups that experience oppression, such as gay men and lesbians, the disabled, and working class White women, often occupy social locations or "border spaces" that provide them with some access to power. Patricia Hill Collins (1986, 1991, 1998, 2000) labeled people in these locations "outsiders-within." Outsiders-within occupy a contradictory "border space" wherein they have knowledge of dominant groups but at the same time lack the full privileges afforded true insiders. Collins first made the argument regarding African-American women who have historically occupied particular social locations such as domestic worker that allowed them intimate knowledge of White upper-class worlds without granting them the power to share in the advantages that the White upper class has.

In particular, Collins contends that because of their experience of multiple oppressions, Black women have a clearer view of oppressive systems even than Black men or White women because they can neither use an appeal to manhood to negate racial oppression nor to Whiteness to negate gender oppression. From their outsider within location, Black women can more readlily observe the contadictions in the operations of power. For example, Black domestic workers can be uniquely situated to see that the wives of wealthy White men, who may experience much material comfort and may come to think that they are "running their own lives," are subject to patriarchal authority and power in the household. As Nancy White, a Black inner city domestic, stated, "If he (husband) tells them that they ain't seeing what they know they *are* seeing, then they have to go on like it wasn't there!" (Gwaltney, 1980, p. 148) (cited in Collins, 2000, p. 11). Collins (1986) further contends that outsiders-within intellectual communities, such as Black women scholars, have unique advantages when they choose to use their location to investigate social life:

- A kind of "objectivity" that is a peculiar combination of nearness and remoteness, concern and indifference.
- A tendency for people to confide in a stranger in ways they would not with each other.
- The ability of a stranger to see patterns those immersed can't see.
- The creativity that is spurred by marginality.

Far from valuing the perspectives of subordinate groups, or of outsiders within, traditional health disparities scholarship exists solidly within a positivist paradigm that:

- asserts the value neutrality of scientists and emotional distance between researcher and researched;
- seeks control of behavior by modeling its study after procedures used by scientists studying the physical universe;
- values quantification of observable behaviors, codification of data, enumeration, correlation, verification, and prediction;
- seeks universal laws governing human behavior in all settings (LeCompte & Schensul, 1999).

Rosser (1994, p. 5) also notes that the very choice of problems for study in medical research is substantially determined by a

> ... national agenda that defines what is worthy of study, i.e. funding. As Marxist (Zimmerman et al., 1980), African-American (McLeod, 1987) and feminist (Hubbard, 1990) critics of scientific research have pointed out, the research that is undertaken reflects the societal bias toward the powerful, who are overwhelmingly white, middle- to upper-class, and male in the United

States. Obviously, the majority of members of Congress, who appropriate the funds for NIH
and other federal agencies, fit this description; they are more likely to vote funds for health
research which they view as beneficial as defined from their perspective.

In contrast, intersectional scholarship by privileging the perspectives of, for
example, women of color and women of color intellectuals, asserts the subjective,
political, and situationally specific nature of research and knowledge about
all of social life but especially about oppression. Specific methodologies for
studying oppression (e.g. research design, data gathering and analysis methods)
are not completely unique from methodologies employed in mainstream research
– many methods used are in fact the same. Most feminist researchers now
contend that the use of multiple methods makes for the best research, that no
particular methodology is either uniquely feminist or not feminist, and decry the
binary oppositional construct of qualitative vs. quantitative research (Spraque
& Zimmerman, 1993). Yet in practice, research methods are labeled feminist
more often by researchers "working in interpretive traditions," and there is little
writing about quantitative methods as explicitly feminist (DeVault, 1999; Fonow
& Cook, 1991; Weber Cannon et al., 1988). Even still, different approaches to,
questions about, and interpretations of quantitative methods are common among
scholars who place the experiences of multiply oppressed groups at the center
of their work.

For example, traditional health disparities research most commonly relies on
clinical and population studies (typically cross-sectional or more highly valued
longitudinal designs) employing large samples to maximize representativeness
and enable statistical generalization. Since none of the racial and ethnic groups
that constitute the primary focus of health disparities are larger than African-
Americans, who make up 12.9% of the population, and most are quite small (e.g.
Puerto Ricans (1.2%), Mexican-Americans (7.3%), Asian-Americans (4.2%),
American Indian/Alaska Native (1.5%) (U.S. Bureau of the Census, 2001a, b,
c, d), most national surveys do not contain enough cases in any group to allow
for estimation of models for these individual races and ethnicities. Some surveys
address this problem by "oversampling" specific minority groups, but that practice
is not routine. And because the groups that are oversampled vary from survey to
survey, possibilities for comparisons across these more respected data bases are
limited. Furthermore, as Wornie Reed noted in his testimony before the American
Academy of Sciences hearing on racial and ethnic designators at the "National
Leadership Summit on Eliminating Racial and Ethnic Disparities in Health," the
practice of "oversampling" – as well as the very word itself – reveals the dominant
culture values and priorities that undergird this most common and respected sampling method. Speaking from the perspective of a Black "outsider-within" scholar,
he asked:

- Why do we call it *over*sampling when this is the process necessary to obtain representative samples of the major racial and ethnic groups in the country?
- Why do we allow the samples obtained using traditional methods to be called representative?

He argued for establishing a standard of "appropriate sampling" where government agencies, funders, and researchers would require that studies obtain samples of sizes appropriate to enable model estimates at least for the five major racial and ethnic groups designated by the OMB and that funding be provided to do so. The lack of funding to mandate "appropriate sampling" in research reveals the low priority placed in dominant culture institutions on the generation of knowledge by and about racial and ethnic groups. When we further suggest that researchers routinely investigate the intersections of race and ethnicity with other dimensions of social inequality such as gender, sexuality, social class, and socioeconomic status, few studies of the general population can support such comparisons.

Independent, Single Inequalities or Intersecting, Multiple Inequalities?

When viewed through the lenses of multiply oppressed groups, the complexities and interconnected nature of social hierarchies and social life are revealed. Intersectional scholarship thus contends that race, class, gender, and sexuality are interrelated systems at the macro institutional level – they are created, maintained, and transformed simultaneously and in relationship to one another and cannot be understood independently of one another. At the micro level of the individual, scholars focus on the ways these systems are experienced in our lives simultaneously, each contributing to our identities and our views of the world (Zinn & Dill, 1996; Collins, 2000; Weber, 2001). The significance of complex intersections of multiple inequalities was forcefully asserted by women of color and working class women involved in early feminist movements who refused to subscribe to a "global sisterhood" in support of a strategic goal of unity that in fact reflected White middle class women's specific gender concerns. Ruzek et al. (1999, p. 54) give an example of the kind of challenge posed by conflicting interests across race and class in the early days of the women's health movement:

> ...although some affluent white women struggled for the right to give birth at home with attendants of their own choosing, many low-income women desperately sought access to hospitals, doctors, and the technologies and interventions that their more affluent sisters struggled to avoid. Why? The "home births" that educated women could have were worlds apart from the "out-of-hospital births" poor women found themselves having not out of choice but out of necessity.

In a similar vein, the Black power movement of the 1960s was undermined and lost women's participation in part because of its patriarchal demands that racism, not sexism, was the primary oppressor and that Black women should play traditional women's roles in the organization. As former Black panther Elaine Brown said, the party was "a very misogynistic organization" (Jackson, 1998, p. 45). Out of their experience of these contradictions, feminist scholars of color have pioneered intersectional scholarship and broadened the lens through which feminists now commonly view gender. For example, the pressure to separate one's self into different (and competing) parts was eloquently resisted in one of the first anthologies about Black women's studies: *All the Women were White, All the Blacks were Men, But Some of Us Are Brave: Black Women's Studies* (Hull et al., 1982).

Balkanized Research

Although intersectional scholarship highlights the complexities and contradictions experienced especially by groups situated at the intersections of oppressive forces, traditional health disparities scholarship has emerged from scholarly traditions that treat race, class, socioeconomic status, gender, ethnicity, and sexuality separately. Conceptualizations of the processes producing differential health outcomes across these dimensions of social inequality are thus unique for each dimension. In her 2002 presidential address to the American Sociological Association, Barbara Reskin lamented this balkanization of research on social inequality, arguing that it has precluded integrated knowledge across systems of oppression. Further, in her own research area on workplace discrimination, this balkanization has fostered contradictory workplace discrimination policies where women and people of color now have different options for redress in the face of sex or race discrimination, where women of color have to choose which one of their statuses they will argue was the source of discrimination against them if they contest employers' unfair actions, and where the outcome will likely differ depending on their choice.

Reskin argues that this balkanization of scholarship, especially in combination with the individual focus of most research, is responsible for the failure to identify the mechanisms of discrimination. For the different theories generated about different sources of oppression (e.g. race or social class or gender) employ different sets of intervening mechanisms and stories to explain the relationship between a particular macro structural system of oppression and its life consequences for oppressed individuals and groups. For example, in most health disparities scholarship, discrimination is a concept primarily reserved for mistreatment on the basis of race and ethnicity. When Robert and House (2000a, p. 84) reviewed literature on race, socioeconomic position and health, they noted that socioeconomic inequalities do not fully explain the race-health relationship and suggest that when seeking to identify factors other than socioeonomic status which might "explain" the relationship between race and health "... other experiences associated with race in our society, *such as discrimination* (sic) ... may also account for some race effects on health." Yet when they identified research challenges for the study of gender, socioeconomic status, and health, "discrimination" was not mentioned. Nonetheless, some scholars apply the concept to the analysis of gender inequality and even to sexuality, but never to socioeconomic status or social class (Breen, 2001; Krieger, 1990).

The dominant culture stories or "master narratives" we tell about the different oppressions posit different mechanisms producing health, and the master narrative about race, gender, and at least one of the narratives about sexuality – that it is biologically/genetically determined – contends that these are "ascribed characteristics of individuals" over which the individual has no choice and no control. Consequently, a basic sense of democratic fairness implies that opportunities and options should not be ascribed on the basis of these, nor should we tolerate health differences because of social location along any or all of these dimensions. Discrimination is an unfair process of treatment that is deemed to interfere with the otherwise fair system of allocation. Socioeconomic status and social class, on the other hand, are constructed both in research and in the master narrative as "achieved characteristics" of individuals – statuses we are supposed to have in our own control. This belief is powerfully represented in the American dream ideology – that America is an open society with equal opportunities for success defined primarily in economic terms (Hochschild, 1995). There is a fundamental belief in the fairness of socioeconomic status and social class inequalities and in the responsibility of everyone for his or her own place in the system. These beliefs are powerfully reproduced in our health disparities research – discrimination comes to be a concept that is employed about race and occasionally about gender, but never about socioeconomic status and social class. When women of color are the center of analyses, this kind of balkanization of the notions of unfair, discriminatory treatment appears ludicrous.

For example, in their review of the literature on socioeconomic status and health, Robert and House (2000a, b) did not identify discrimination as a research need in the area of gender and socioeconomic status. But they did call for research to understand the reasons that the relationship between socioeconomic status and health is weaker among women than among men. And they suggest that researchers should examine the connection of community socioeconomic characteristics and health, "... especially for women who *do not work* and may spend a substantial amount of time in their community environment [emphasis added]" (Robert & House, 2000a, p. 84). The clear implication in this statement is that women not in the paid labor force (and therefore not captured in traditional measurements of work) are *not working* and are *at home* in their communities – reifying the largely White and middle class view of women as either in the paid labor force (and therefore working *outside* their communities) or housewives (and therefore not working, but living *inside* their communities).

But intersectional scholarship, centering its perspective in the everyday lives of groups situated at the intersections of multiple inequalities, has revealed the limits of traditional constructions of work, unmasking its hidden assumptions: that it is productive, for pay, and conducted outside the home. It has also demonstrated the inadequacy of this notion of work for explaining much of what most women in the world do and its relationship to their health (Daniels, 1987). In fact, intersectional scholarship reveals that women's work occurs in many sites (both inside and out-side the home) and takes on many forms as yet unrecognized by traditional health research including domestic work, cottage industries, underground economy work, unpaid work in the home, and "health work" – the work of caring for and managing their family's and community's health (Messias et al., 1997). For example, research on women of color and immigrant domestic workers has problematized the notion of work "outside the home" since these women in fact work for pay "inside the homes" of largely White employers (Dill, 1994; Glenn, 1986; Hondagnu-Sotelo, 1997; Kaplan, 1987; Palmer, 1989; Rollins, 1985; Romero, 1992; Salzinger, 1991). In this case, the middle-class employer's community environment is the workplace for her domestic and other workers – e.g. yard workers. Furthermore, domestics who work in multiple homes have no clearly defined workplace. Or when low-income women work for pay in their own homes by providing, for example, day care for neighborhood children, the division between market/productive work and home/reproductive work is shattered – a division that is also shattered in the work worlds of middle-class women and men through such practices as telecommuting and job sharing. So even though it emerges from analysis of the lives of marginal-ized people, the knowledge gained in intersectional scholarship sheds new light on and raises new questions about the ways we conceive of and investigate the lives of others even in more privileged social locations.

Multiple Inequalities and Methodology
As mentioned above, one of the limitations of the quantitative analysis of clinical and population surveys is that national surveys rarely obtain samples large enough to investigate multiple racial ethnic groups and almost never have samples large enough to examine the interactions of race/ethnicity with socioeconomic status, social class, gender, age, and other key dimensions of inequality. Consequently, the lives that form the starting point for intersectional scholars – for example, poor and working class women of color – are either absent altogether or are not examined in any depth in most health disparities research.

Because feminist intersectional scholarship conceives of race, class, gender, sexuality and other dimensions of difference not as individual attributes, but rather as social constructions that are generated, challenged, and maintained in group processes, the place to observe and thus to understand inequality is in dynamic interactions among groups, particularly among those that involve groups experiencing multiple oppressions. Likewise, although positivist research goals include generalizing results from one place and time to subsequent similar phenomena and identifying universal laws of human behavior, intersectional scholars are more concerned with the development of shared understandings that operate in particular locales and times with specific groups. Consequently, in intersectional approaches, it is possible to study the processes of oppression even when all possible combinations of groups are not present in the research setting – since comparison with the dominant group on gradational resource measures is not the goal of the research.

From the perspective of traditional health disparities scholarship, the many small group observations, historical macro analyses, and in-depth interview studies of various multiply oppressed groups that characterize intersectional scholarship are inadequate. In fact, Krieger et al. (1993, p. 99), in arguing from the point of view of the biomedical/psychosocial model but for more attention to work on race, class, gender, and sexuality said, "... research regarding racism, sexism, social class, and health remains rudimentary and fragmented, a reflection of its position on the outskirts of mainstream epidemiology and the contingent deficit of wide-reaching and active debate within the discipline on the causes of social inequalities in health." But not being engaged in debate with mainstream scholarship does not mean that the work is "rudimentary and fragmented." Instead, it just appears to be rudimentary and fragmented from the positivist perspective, which searches for universal laws through the methodological strategies of quantification, prediction, and generalization.

Additivity, Ranking, and Binaries
One further consequence of balkanization of research on oppressions and the positivist goal of representativeness (and large samples) is that research considering more than one dimension, for example, race and socioeconomic status, typically assumes that these dimensions of inequality have additive effects on all outcomes. For example, it implies that the consequences of racial minority status on health can simply be added to the effect of being a woman and further to the effects of education and income to predict one's health status. Yet intersectional scholarship and some traditional health disparities scholarship has consistently argued that additivity does not hold. For example, Krieger et al. (1993, p. 99) state "Many studies, however, inappropriately assume that the effects of racism, sexism, and social class are simply additive. Instead, their specific combinations reflect unique historical experience

forged by the social realities of life in the United States and should be studied accordingly."

Furthermore, the position of multiply oppressed groups belies the notion that oppressions can be ranked – identifying which status is worse, who are the greatest victims (Collins, 2000; DeVault, 1999; Weber, 2001). How can a poor Latina be expected to identify the sole – or even primary – source of her oppression? How can scholars with no real connection to her life do so? Likewise, recognizing multiple oppressions also forces us to consider that most individuals occupy both dominant and subordinate positions at the same time (e.g. middle-class, Black women), so that there are no pure oppressors or oppressed in our society.

The direct exploration of the lives of many different groups situated at multiple intersections of social inequalities (poor Latinas; middle-class gay and lesbian Whites; working-class, Asian American women) has also revealed the limits of dominant constructions of these inequalities as binaries (Black and White; men and women; heterosexual and homosexual). Scholars have noted that these binary oppositions serve to obscure the complexities of oppression by denying the experience of groups situated in other locations and further serve to increase the power of dominant groups by enhancing their position as the model against which others are clearly and simply contrasted and ranked (Collins, 2000; Weber, 2001).

Intersectional scholarship highlights in many different ways that race, class, gender, and sexuality are not simple binaries, separate and additive dimensions of inequality, or reducible to immutable personality traits or seemingly permanent individual characteristics. They are social constructions that often give us power and options in some arenas while restricting our power and options in others. This recognition – that we each simultaneously experience all of these dimensions – can help us to see the often obscured ways in which we benefit from existing race, class, gender, and sexuality social arrangements as well as the ways in which we are disadvantaged. Such an awareness can be key in working together across different groups to achieve a more equitable distribution of society's valued resources.

Value Freedom, Researcher Objectivity or Knowledge from
Active Researcher Engagement?

Feminist scholars document the White androcentric bias and absence of "value neutrality" in biomedical science (Krieger & Fee, 1996; Longino, 1990; Rose, 1994; Rosser, 1997). For example, Krieger and Fee (1996) argue that race and sex were constructed as key biomedical categories out of social struggles over inequality beginning in the 19th century. At that time, women's pain in childbirth was deemed proof of God's displeasure with Eve and all women. Likewise, during the slavery period beliefs about Black inferiority were rationalized in part by the work of physicians, "scientists" who sought to detail every possible "racial" difference – from texture of hair to length of bones and even the color of internal organs. Throughout the 20th century, physicians have continued to fuel political conflicts between races, classes, and genders by "seeing" differences in the bodies of presumably inferior groups. These presumed differences were used until recently as rationales to exclude oppressed groups from epidemiologic research – for example, women were excluded for most of the 20th century from clinical trials because of presumed "hormonal interference" induced by menstrual cycles. That exclusion, no longer accepted practice, was reversed not by science contradicting the theory of hormonal interference but by political action from feminists pressuring Congress to mandate the inclusion of women in clinical trials (Fee & Krieger, 1994; Morgen, 2002; Rosser, 1997; Ruzek et al., 1997b). As a consequence of scholarship that deconstructs these presumed gender oppositions (e.g. that women's hormones are unstable, men's are constant), the ways that men routinely experience hormonal cycles have only recently become known.

Feminist intersectional scholarship assert that values, subjectivity, and researcher involvement are present in all aspects of research. As Cook and Fonow (1991, p. 5) said, "This action orientation is reflected in the statement of purpose, topic selection, theoretical orientation, choice of method, view of human nature, and definitions of the researcher's roles." Indeed, what makes scholarship feminist is its primary goal of improving the life circumstances of women by:

- Developing new methods to study women's strengths, not simply their victimization.
- Seeing women as actors not as objects of study.
- Engaging in research for the purpose of empowering women to oppose oppression.
- Seeking to understand the causes of oppression.
- Valuing experiential knowledge, honoring women's intelligence (Reinharz & Davidman, 1992).

Value is also placed on collaborative, interdisciplinary work that reflexively explores the nature of the research process as well as the knowledge to be gained through it (Cook & Fonow, 1991). These scholars and others (cf. Collins, 1998, 2000; DeVault, 1999; Mies, 1983, 1991) also note the integral connection between the production of knowledge about oppression and both an explicit goal of social change for liberation and, in such methods as participatory action research, actions seeking to facilitate that liberation. In advocating participatory action research, Maria Mies wrote (1983, p. 125): "Social change is the starting point of science, and in order to understand the content, form, and consequences of patriarchy, the researcher must be actively involved in the fight against it; one has to change something before it can be understood." And while this notion of changing something to learn about it is the foundation of the laboratory experimental research design, the most highly regarded of standard positivist scientific methods, the same practice when pursued outside of the laboratory is viewed as dangerously subjective – eliminating the necessary distance between observer and observed and the control of the researcher over the research process and the researched. This contrast reflects key oppositions in intersectional feminist and traditional biomedical and social scientific views of:

- the goals and purposes of research;
- the role of the researcher;
- theoretical orientations;
- views of human nature;
- methodologies.

But even though feminist scholars explicitly call for an activist research, that goal is easier stated than achieved. Although most feminist research calls for social change, few write about the more difficult task of assessing whether change has occurred. In reviewing feminist methodology, DeVault (1999, p. 32) concludes: "Too often, I believe, the call for change functions as a slogan in writing on feminist methodology, and authors make assumptions about change without sufficient examination of their own implicit theories of social change."

And intersectional scholars, aware of the conflicting interests of various feminist groups are overtly critical of scholarship and an activism that benefits and reflects the interests of White, middle-class women and ignores less advantaged groups of women. For example, Ruzek (1999, p. 304) challenges feminists to reformulate feminist ideas and ideologies about "individual choice," which she argues are incompatible with achieving universal access to medical care, or to ". . . abandon empty rhetoric about feminism's relevance to women who are less privileged in American society."

THE CASE OF HEALTH DISPARITIES IN PHYSICAL ACTIVITY AND CARDIOVASCULAR DISEASE

We contend that critical intersectional scholarship holds great promise for developing new models that significantly expand, complicate, and deepen our knowledge of health disparities and our approaches to redressing them. By employing selective examples from each tradition to illustrate the themes, our argument to this point has been made by identifying themes which differ in intersectional and biomedically-derived health disparities scholarship. In this section, we hope to further develop our argument and to explore the prevalence and validity of our claims about traditional health disparities scholarship by exploring how the themes are played out in a single, coherent research program organized around specific questions and concerns. We examine racial and ethnic disparities among women in physical inactivity, a leading "proximate" cause of Cardiovascular disease (CVD).

Cardiovascular disease is a significant public health problem and is a leading cause of death and disease for American women (American Heart Association (AHA), 2000; United States Department of Health and Human Services (USDHHS), 2002). National prevalence studies have repeatedly demonstrated that racial and ethnic minorities and low-income populations experience a disproportionate burden from this condition and as a result CVD is one of six conditions targeted in the national agenda to eliminate health disparities (AHA, 2000; Casper, Barnett, Halverson et al., 1999; Sorlie, Johnson & Backlund, 1995; USDHHS, 2002). Several risk factors for CVD including physical inactivity as well as adverse dietary patterns, smoking and obesity are well recognized (Johnson & Sempos, 1995). Population-wide surveillance data indicate that inactivity rates are particularly prevalent among women, older adults, adults with lower educational achievement and racial/ethnic minorities. Physical inactivity is a primary target for research and intervention to eliminate disparities in CVD because unlike race, gender or social class, physical inactivity is believed to be modifiable, a "true" proximal cause of disease and to hold great potential for reducing or preventing CVD and other chronic conditions (Johnson & Sempos, 1995).

Although it would be impossible to review the entire history and expanse of health disparities scholarship on physical inactivity and CVD here, we chose to approach the review by setting some parameters and examining all the studies that we could identify within those parameters. We hoped that this approach would at least make clear the limitations of the review and eliminate the degree of selectivity bias that we would introduce in a less systematic approach. To enable examination of the treatment of multiple intersections of social inequalities, we limited the search to studies of U.S. women and physical activity which included race and at least one measure of social class or socioeconomic status. Because intervention studies tend to focus on tests of program effectiveness and not on the factors presumed to be causes of health outcomes such as race, social class, and gender, we also excluded those studies. Finally, to capture the most recent trends in the work, we limited the search to studies published since 1990. Within these parameters, we searched the Eric, Psych Info, Sociological Abstracts and Ovid Medline databases using – alone or in combination – the following keywords: women, physical activity, exercise, women's health, obesity. This approach yielded 12 quantitative and two qualitative studies, which are presented in Table 1.

Table 1. Summary of Survey Examining the Relationship Between Race, Social Class and Physical Activity in U.S. Women, 1990–2000.

No.	Study	Research Design	Race**	Education#	Income
1	Johnson et al. (1990). Perceived barriers to exercise and weight control practices in community women. *Women and Health, 16,* 177–191.	Community-based sample – mall recruitment: $n^* = 226$; 100% women	48% Black (Black working class area); 52% White (White middle class area)		
2	Ainsworth et al. (1991). Physical activity and hypertension in black adults: The Pitt County study. *American Journal of Public Health, 81,* 1477–1479.	Community-based sample – Pitt County: $n = 1096$; 63% women	100% Black	Less than 12 years, Greater than 12 years	
3	Folsom et al. (1991). Differences in leisure-time physical activity levels between blacks and whites in population-based samples: The Minnesota Heart Survey. *Journal of Behavioral Medicine, 14,* 1–9.	Population-based sample – Minnesota: $n = 635$; 53% women	$n = 227$ Black; $n = 408$ White	≤HS; Some college; college graduate	
4	Jeffery et al. (1991). Socioeconomic status differences in health behaviors related to obesity: The Healthy Worker Project. *International Journal of Obesity, 15,* 689–696.	Worksite based sample – Minneapolis, St. Paul $n = 2539$; 55% women	95% White; 100% employed		
5	Yeager et al. (1993). Socioeconomic influences on leisure-time sedentary behavior among women. *Health Values, 17,* 50–54.	Population-based sample – national sample: $n = 32852$; 100% women	$n = 2902$ Black; $n = 27339$ White; $n = 1415$ Hispanic; $n = 1178$ other	<HS; HS grad; some coll; college graduate	Annual income cat. <10 K; 10–20 K; 20–25 K; 35–50 K; 50+ K
6	Arihihenbuwa et al. (1995). Perceptions and beliefs about exercise, rest, and health among African Americans. *American Journal of Health Promotion, 9*(6), 426–429.	Qualitative study community-based sample – South Central Pennsylvania $n = 32$; 60% women	$n = 32$ African-American		Low income area residents & middle to high income professionals

Occupation	PA**** Behaviors	Hypothesis/Purpose	Results	Conclusions
3 Categories: prof, mgr/clerical, service/housewife, student unemployed	(%) participate in regular exercise program	To examine prevalence of exercise and diet habits and perceived barriers to these behaviors	No b/w; young/old; work/no-work diff. in (%) PA so women combined for analyses of perceived barriers to PA and weight loss; PA barrier lack of time	Results suggest program strategies (time management, social support and involve employers and worksites)
Employed vs. unemployed	Active-engaging in work or exercise enough to sweat for at least 20 min; Sedentary-exercising or laboring less often	Describe the level of PA in a community based sample of black adults	Hypertension associated with sedentary behavior among women; unemployment and being a high school graduate associated with sedentary behavior	Work may be a source of PA for those with less education or work provides financial means for engaging in LT activity
	Total LTPA*** performed over last month	Investigate racial differences in PA and adjust for counfounding due to age and education	LTPA declined with age and increased with level of formal education in both groups. LTPA differences between blacks and whites largest among those with ≤HS education. LPTA higher in B vs. W independent of age and education. Black women report more occupational PA compared to white counterparts	Given observable differences in LTPA by race and education, may want to target strategies to high risk groups (less educated minorities)
Index (educ. & occup.) – low/med/high	Total LTPA performed over a week period	Social class differences in health behaviors hypothesized to mediate an SES-obesity relationship	Higher SES respondents report more exercise; SES remained as a sig. Predictor of obesity after controlling for health behaviors (lo fat diet; exercise, dieting)	Behavior measures used may not accurately capture relevant SES differences or obesity may influence occupational class by affecting opportunities for upward mobility
	LTPA performed over past month	Because SES disparity between white and non-white groups exists the role of SES in accounting for sedentary behavior is explored among women	30% of white and 45% black women were sedentary; overall sedentary beh. increased with less educ., lower income, age and formerly married; sedentary behavior decreased for both groups as SES increased; greatest diff. between blacks and whites observed at lowest level of education and income and no sig. diff. at the highest levels; adjustment for education narrows but does not eliminate racial gap	Questions the concept of leisure time as conventionally defined, relevance of the PA measure for women; may need to capture purposeful activity (emp., child care, housework)
	Importance of exercise and rest; meaning of exercise; influences on attitudes about exercise; perception of relationship b/w exercise and health	To explore culture specific values and beliefs about exercise among African-American men and women	African-Americans perceived themselves as a group that currently and historically has limited economic resources. Self-perception as physical laborers at work and at home, emphasize the need to rest to maintain good health, the concept of leisure time did not fit in their world view	Findings suggest that lower LTPA among African-Americans may be influenced by specific attitudes that limit adoption in addition to practical and logistical barriers

Table 1.   (Continued)

No.	Study	Research Design	Race**	Education[#]	Income
7	Jeffery and French (1996). Socioeconomic status and weight control practices among 20 to 45 year old women. *American Journal of Public Health, 86,* 1005–1010.	Community-based sample – Minneapolis, St. Paul: $n = 998$; 100% women	$n = 599$ White; $n = 399$ other	HS or less, vocational training, college education w/o degree, college degree, more than college degree	Annual income cat. <10 K; 10–20 K; 20–30 K; 30–40 K; 40+ K
8	Eyler et al. (1998). Physical activity and minority women: A qualitative study. *Health Education & Behavior,* 25(5), 640–652.	Qualitative study/community-based sample – California, Missouri $n = 100$; 100% women	$n = 20$ Filipino American; $n = 30$ Chinese American; $n = 20$ American Indian; $n = 20$ Black; $n = 10$ Hispanic		
9	Harrell and Gore (1998). Cardiovascular risk factors and socioeconomic status in African American and Caucasian Women. *Research in Nursing and Health, 21,* 285–295.	Population-based sample – North Carolina $n = 1945$; 100% women	$n = 389$ Black; $n = 1556$ White	Less than HS, HS, some college, college graduate, post graduate degree	Total family income cat: <$20 K/$20+ K; SES index (income & educ.) low/med/high
10	Sternfeld, Ainsworth and Quesenberry (1999). Physical activity patterns in a diverse population of women. *Preventive Medicine, 28,* 313–323.	Clinical-based sample – national health maintenance organization $n = 2636$; 100% women	$n = 185$ African-American; $n = 382$ Asian; $n = 237$ Hispanic; $n = 105$ other; $n = 1727$ White	≤HS; some college; ≥college	

Occupation	PA**** Behaviors	Hypothesis/Purpose	Results	Conclusions
Employed vs. unemployed	PA over previous year	Examine the relationship between SES and weight control practices in women; to uncover the mechansims responsible for behavioral differences by SES; Ho: discrimination; resource dist.; cultural norms	Higher SES respondents report more exercise; SES remained as a sig. predictor of obesity after controlling for health behaviors; behavior measures used may not accurately capture relevant SES differences	Data provide some support for resource distribution and discrimination of obese people hypotheses, may not be capturing cultural values or other social and economic barriers
	Amount of PA and exercise	To explore patterns of physical activity among minority women	While participants did not recognize themselves as exercisers, they indicated that they got a lot of PA from caregiving, housekeeping, and workday activities. Common environmental barriers include safety, availability and cost. Personal barriers include lack of time, health concerns and lack of motivation	Results point to the importance of terminology and assessment in PA research in women of color, in addition many of the barriers reported are changeable with policies and interventions
	LTPA performed over past six months	Identify differences between black and white women for CVD risk factors and determine if they vary by SES; examine within race group differences by SES; Ho: there is no difference in self-reported risk factors by race when controlling for income and education	39% of black women were obese and 52% were inactive; compared to 20 and 31% for whites, respectively; Education, Income and SES differed by race; low and middle SES black women much more likely to be obese and inactive than high SES blacks; Among whites the lowest SES groups were more likely to be obese and inactive than med and high SES whites. After controlling for income and education black women twice as likely to be obese and inactive	Potential explanation for obesity: low PA in blacks or genetic weight patterns (muscle mass); potential explanation for LTPA: access to safe places, ability to pay for facilities, attitudes towards PA, type of occupation or "even" racism
Employed vs. unemployed	Activity indices for sport/exercise; active living; house-hold/caregiving; occupational; total	To assess level of PA in various domains incl. household and occup., in a large randomly selected sample of women	Women with highest participation in sport/ex and active living were more likely younger, white, college educated, without children at home and leaner; women with the highest household activity were more likely older, Hispanic, married/young children, unemployed; women with highest level of occupational activity have no more than a HS education and more likely to be smokers	Results suggest a particular social cultural environment that promotes and reinforces (necessitates) women's participation in domain specific activity; one fourth of sample not employed so no occ activity

Table 1. (Continued)

No.	Study	Research Design	Race**	Education[#]	Income
11	Scharff et al. (1999). Factors associated with physical activity in women across the life span: Implications for program development. *Women and Health, 29,* 115–134.	Clinical-based sample– Community family medicine clinics, SE Missouri n = 653; 100% women	No race data	≤12 years; >12 years	
12	Crespo et al. (2000). Race/ethnicity, social class, and their relation to physical inactivity during leisure time: Results from the third national health and nutrition examination survey, 1988–1994. *American Journal of Preventive Medicine, 18,* 46–53.	National-based sample – health and nutrition examination survey n = 9609; 53%women	n = 4412 Caucasian; n = 2771 African-American; n = 2426 Mexican-American	<12 yrs; 12 yrs; 13–15 yrs; 16+ yrs	Annual household income cat. <10 K; 10–19 K; 20–34 K; 35–49 K; 50+ K/below poverty; at or above poverty
13	King et al. (2000). Personal and environmental factors associated with physical inactivity among different racial/ethnic groups of U.S. middle-aged and older-aged women. *Health Psychology, 19,* 354–364.	National-based sample – U.S. women's determinants study n = 2912; 100% women	n = 757 White; n = 757 Black; n = 728 American Indian; n = 670 Hispanic	<HS; HS grad; some coll; college graduate	Annual household income cat. <10 K; 10–19 K; 20–34 K; 35–49K; 50+ K/below poverty; at or above poverty
14	Wilcox et al. (2000). Determinants of leisure time physical activity in rural compared with urban older and ethnically diverse women in the United States. *Journal of Epidemiology and Community Health, 54,* 667–672.	National-based sample – U.S. women's determinants study n = 1096 urban, n = 1242 rural; 100% women	n = 757 White; n = 757 Black; n = 728 American Indian; n = 670 Hispanic	≤HS; >HS	

*N = Total number of women in study.
**Race categories based on author terminology.
***LTPA = Leisure time physical activity.
****PA = Physical activity.
[#]Education – some studies use number of years, others use completed degrees.

Occupation	PA**** Behaviors	Hypothesis/Purpose	Results	Conclusions
	LTPA performed per week	To determine characteristics and patterns associated with various types of PA in women of different ages; provide practical implications for developing PA programs for women	Women with more than 12 years of education were more likely than less educated women to perform LTPA; majority of the women (57%) did not meet surgeon general recommendations; younger women perform more PA than older women	Incorporate occupational activity in addition to home work/activity; rule out cohort effect
6 Categories: white collar prof./white collar other/blue collar/retired/ homemaker/other; employment status: emp/not emp/not in labor force	LTPA performed during previous month	To examine the prevalence of LTPA in a national representative sample of White, Black and Mexican-Americans men and women and to compare LTPA in these groups across SES	Black and Mexican-American women had higher LT inactivity compared to whites across individual SES indicators (education, occupation, employment) and family SES indicators (family income, poverty and marital status); blue collar workers and homemakers more inactive in leisure time	Current individual indicators of social class (education, occupation, employment) do not explain higher prevalence of inactivity during leisure time among blacks and Mexican Americans; i.e. occup does not provide info on the "nature" of the work
Employed full-time/other	LTPA or household activity performed over previous two weeks	Explore personal and environmental barriers to PA in a population derived sample of women 40 years and older as a whole and for targeted ethnic subgroups	Factors associated with inactivity include American Indian ethnicity, older age, less education; lack of energy, lack of hills in neighborhood; scenery; lack role models; caregiving duties prevalent barrier; Ethnic group specific profiles provided in paper vary	Used education rather than income because of higher corr.; reliability and less missing data; whites (-age educ, hills); blacks (dogs, seeing others, caregiving duties); Hispanic (education, hills, others discourage, -tired); American Indians (educ, self-conscious, -not good health)
	LTPA performed over previous two weeks	Examine rural/ urban differences in LTPA by sociodemographic factors/ determinants of LTPA	Ethnicity, age and education associated with LTPA, rural women especially southern and less educated were more sedentary than urban women; care giving duties a top barrier; rural/urban women face different barriers to PA	Sociodemographics an immutable but we can target these "underserved" groups in innovative ways. Tells us where to go and who is in need.

Individual as Unit Obscuring Social Structures

Although all were squarely situated in a biomedical paradigm, conceptual approaches, questions, measurements, and analyses of these fourteen studies shifted focus as they moved from the oldest to the most recent. In particular they began as individual-focused prevalence studies and developed into studies with more social structural and situational concerns – although never shifting to the primary emphasis on these factors common in intersectional approaches. The earliest studies included in our review (Numbers 1–3) were primarily descriptive and included relatively small cross-sectional community-based samples (e.g. *N*'s of 226, 674 and 337 women, respectively). They each treat race, class, and gender as discrete independent variables representing individual characteristics in bivariate analyses with physical activity, also treated as an individual level trait. These correlational studies identify recurring patterns in the relationships between race, socioeconomic status, and physical activity among women:

- People of color were less active than Whites (Folsom et al., 1991; Harrell & Gore, 1998; Yeager et al., 1993).
- Women with lower education, lower income, unemployed or working in blue-collar occupations were less active during leisure time (Ainsworth et al., 1991; Harrell & Gore, 1998; Jeffery et al., 1991).
- All of these groups were more likely to be obese and to have CVD (Ainsworth et al., 1991; Folsom et al., 1991; Harrell & Gore, 1998; Jeffery & French, 1996).

The studies following this initial set (Numbers 3–5, 7–9) are also cross-sectional quantitative surveys but include substantially larger community-based and population-based samples. In these studies researchers move beyond describing associations and attempt to explain the effect of social inequality on behavior. Building on the previous findings, they hypothesize that

- The higher prevalence of a sedentary lifestyle during leisure time observed among women and minorities would be explained by differences in socioeconomic status (Folsom et al., 1991; Harrell & Gore, 1998; Yeager et al., 1993) – that is, the relationship between race and physical activity would be mediated by socioeconomic status.
- The relationship between socioeconomic status and disease would be mediated by physical activity (Jeffery et al., 1991; Jeffery & French, 1996).

In these studies observed racial differences in physical activity were not entirely explained by differences in socioeconomic status such as income, education or occupation (Folsom et al., 1991; Harrell & Gore, 1998; Yeager et al., 1993) and the relationship between socioeconomic status and disease was not fully mediated by physical activity.

This body of research, like others in the biomedical, psychosocial and biobehavioral traditions, explored racial/ethnic health disparities by looking for intervening/mediating individual level risk factors (behaviors, cognitions, values) such as physical activity that may "explain" the relationship between race/ethnicity and disease, especially CVD. Although focused on eliminating the disproportionate burden of disease in minorities and the poor, these studies use "downstream" approaches – attempting to decompose the effects of inequality on CVD by looking for mediating factors, pathways or more proximate causes. Assuming that social location in race/ethnicity, gender and other hierarchies is immutable, scholars focus on identifying presumably proximate and mutable behaviors, mental and emotional states that might impede individuals from engaging in physical activity and target those factors for intervention (Folsom et al., 1991; Johnson et al., 1990; Wilcox et al., 2000). For example, in their study of the determinants of physical activity in an ethnically diverse sample of rural and urban women, Wilcox et al. (2000) note the consistency of their findings with previously published reports on the relation between ethnicity, age, education and leisure time physical activity. They conclude that observed differences in these "immutable factors" draws attention to specific groups that need to be reached in innovative ways, to the probable influence of cultural norms on physical activity and the need to better understand lifestyle, social and cultural factors.

By not directly addressing the social processes that generate and sustain inequalities, researchers are unable to see beyond the proximate causes (e.g. physical activity) to challenge fundamental causes of CVD that may reside in systemic political, economic, and social inequalities. There is evidence, however, that scholars are beginning to recognize the limitations of this approach. Movement to more "upstream" approaches, although modest, is apparent in the most recent studies we reviewed. For example in an effort to move beyond the individual level, Crespo et al. (2000) includes family level indicators of socioeconomic status and King et al. (2000) include both personal and environmental determinants of physical activity.

Distributional and Relational Constructions of Social Inequality: Having More or Having Power Over?

Rather than focusing on social inequalities as relational constructs, all of the studies treat them as gradational indicators of resources, values, and roles that have White middle-class men and women as a standard. For example, the primary aim of most of the studies was to understand why women of color do not participate in regular leisure time physical activity – a behavior that would clearly improve their health outcomes – at the same rates as White women. Some researchers hypothesize that women of color do not exercise because current physical activity programs and strategies – designed for the White middle class – do not meet the unique needs of poor women of color who have different cultural values and beliefs, access to financial resources, and social roles. King et al. (2000) report that among women, caregiving duties were a prevalent barrier to physical activity and point to the need to "identify the types of physical activity regimens that are most appropriate to the caregiving situation" (King et al., 2000, p. 361). They do not attempt to understand

- what factors in women's social environment promotes or necessitates their role as caregiver;
- who benefits from this unrecognized work that restricts women's autonomy and opportunities for a healthy lifestyle;
- what would be required to significantly change health outcomes for these women (Sternfeld et al., 1999).

Other researchers (Eyler et al., 1998; Folsom et al., 1991; Yeager et al., 1993) focus on methodological issues emphasizing that current assessments of physical activity may not be valid for the groups under study. A standard practice in biomedical research is to use measures of physical activity that are deemed valid and reliable – measuring the concept of physical activity in ways that can be counted on for use in different settings and times and with different groups. However, many of the assessments used in early studies of physical activity in women were developed and validated on White middle-class male populations (Jeffery et al., 1991; Johnson et al., 1990). Researchers began to assert that there may be racial or gender differences in the preferred types of physical activities and in the domains of life in which they are performed (Ainsworth et al., 1991; Scharff et al., 1999; Sternfeld et al., 1999). Examples include the appropriateness of measures that do not capture, count, or recognize purposeful activity involved in the physically demanding jobs of blue-collar workers or homemakers (Ainsworth et al., 1991; Sternfeld et al., 1999; Yeager et al., 1993). Further, surveys measuring "leisure time" physical activity may be misinterpreted by women, especially minority women, who have no "leisure time" as it is conventionally defined (Arihihenbuwa et al., 1995; Eyler et al., 1998). Yet others emphasize that the physical activity measures do not adequately capture relevant socioeconomic status differences such as access to safe places to exercise, ability to pay for facilities, attitudes towards physical activity and type of occupation (Harrell & Gore, 1998; Jeffery et al., 1991; Jeffery & French, 1996). All of these examples are based on conceptualizations of race, class and gender as representing systems of social ranking that are understood as they deviate from dominant norms – not as social relations of dominance and control where one group is seen as restricting access to physical activity or a healthy life and engaging in purposeful actions designed to reinforce the group's power over subordinates.

In these studies, socioeconomic status, race, class, and gender are treated as individual attributes and individual level measures of education, income and occupation are used as indicators of socioeoconomic status while relational constructions of these inequalities are not employed. The question they addressed was "How does having higher status (e.g. income, education, prestige) affect an individual's physical activity?" In contrast, a relational approach might ask "What group(s) control the conditions that support greater physical activity among some groups and less among others?" Although interval level measures of inequalities (e.g. personal income measured in dollars) in no way represent a relational, group or conflict-based conception of inequality, categorical measures (e.g. college education or business ownership) may or may not do so depending upon whether the categories are conceived in that way and examined as power relationships rather than as rankings on a scale of resources. Yet in these studies, a theoretical rationale for the use of a particular measure is rarely provided beyond the relative ease of obtaining the measure and its reliability – factors most commonly employed to justify using education as a measure of socioeconomic position. And although categorical measures of education, occupation, household income, and employment status were common, they were not employed to operationalize a theoretical construct of groups in a relation of opposition to one another. Instead, indicators of socioeconomic position were theorized as representing an individual's access to social and economic resources – not as markers of control over others and over the resources affecting others' lives.

The implications of these conceptualizations are critical particularly when we consider how to reduce health inequality. When race and ethnicity, class, gender, and sexuality are treated as resource deficits, for example, programs to increase access to resources or to change the values, behaviors, and cognitions of subordinate groups to the presumably more healthy styles common among dominant groups are the logical outgrowth. Typical programs might be designed to increase physical activity among care-giving, poor women of color. If social inequalities are viewed as relationships of dominance and subordination, however, the ways in which dominant groups benefit from denying others adequate child-care, medical access, etc., become the focus of attention. In this case, changes that might alter the balance of power such as a living wage; universal, affordable, quality child care; accessible public transportation; equal access to quality education; and universal prevention-focused health care become the preferred interventions. While the former may change the lives of those involved in targeted programs, the latter is more likely to effect change that would significantly reduce health *disparities* between, for example, poor women of color and White middle class women and men.

Dominant Culture-Centered or Oppressed Group-Centered?

Most of the studies identified and included in this review were large cross-sectional surveys that used community, clinic – or population-based samples. The studies were centered in dominant culture perspectives where White women were routinely used as the reference group whose lives were compared with Black women's lives – either alone or in combination with all "other" racial ethnic minorities (Folsom et al., 1991; Harrell & Gore, 1998; Sternfeld et al., 1999; Yeager et al., 1993). Non-white women were typically grouped into a single category because there were not enough women in any specific racial ethnic group to conduct race specific analyses (Jeffery & French, 1996; Johnson, 1990). Only the three most recent studies included nationally representative samples of sufficient size to allow for analyses of racial groups other than Black or White women (Crespo et al., 2000; King et al., 2000; Wilcox et al., 2000). Crespo et al. (2000) used the Third National Health and Nutrition Examination Survey, a nationally representative cross-sectional survey where Mexican-Americans and African-Americans were "over-sampled." Both the King et al. (2000) and the Wilcox et al. (2000) studies relied on data from the U.S. Women's Determinants Study that "over-sampled" African-Americans, Hispanics and Native Americans. Data sources such as these that appropriately sample and allow generalizability to the major U.S. racial ethnic groups are rare because the White, dominant culture is the perspective from which research parameters are funded, conducted, and interpreted. From the dominant culture perspective, studies that obtain appropriate samples of multiple racial ethnic groups are too expensive and complex to merit establishing as a national standard.

While the quantitative studies examined above identified differences and similarities in physical activity patterns between women of different racial ethnic groups, they could not tell us about the women's lived experiences, the meanings of physical activity in their lives, and thus why women may choose not to engage in physical activity. Qualitative studies, in contrast, at least hold the potential for addressing these questions because they are intended to promote inductive explorations of everyday lived experiences. Nevertheless, the two qualitative studies in this review (Arihihenbuwa et al., 1995; Eyler et al., 1998), while being more closely centered in the lives of women of color, were driven by the same dominant culture assumptions about the nature of the social inequality-disease relationship as the quantitative studies. In both cases, the fundamental research question was: Why do women and people of color have lower than average levels of physical activity?

The study by Arihihenbuwa et al. (1995) explores perceptions and beliefs about physical activity among African-Americans in an attempt to revise current interventions that do not appear to be effective in African-American populations. Eyler et al. (1998) ask whether the assessments used to measure physical activity levels are flawed or biased towards capturing the activities of men rather than women.

Health disparities scholarship has begun to acknowledge that no one method or data type can effectively address such complex questions as the relationship between social inequalities and health behavior, and increasingly they call for the use of multiple methods (Smedley & Syme, 2002; NIH, 2000, 2001). Yet this new call for a more expansive and multifaceted approach to research is not easily incorporated into the research strategies of health disparities scholars, most of whom have been schooled in a biomedical paradigm. Consequently, even these qualitative studies more clearly reflect the values and methods of a positivist rather than an interpretivist paradigm. For example, Eyler et al. (1998) developed their focus group questions and protocol using theoretical constructs found to be important in previous studies that did not "oversample" minorities and were most representative of White middle-class lives. And even though the research is purportedly to address racial and ethnic experiences, to researchers schooled in the biomedical paradigm, structuring the discussion with racial and ethnic minorities based on knowledge gained from research on the dominant group is both more comfortable and more highly valued than entering a discussion with an open agenda and risking the work being dismissed as "atheoretical." Incorporating grounded theory, phenomenology, and other interpretive frameworks designed to allow for inductively identifying new concepts and ideas might have proved to be more fruitful in this research. Yet to do so would require expertise that traditionally trained health disparities scholars do not typically possess – a testimony to the value of employing multidisciplinary research teams.

The positivist influence in these two qualitative studies is also illustrated by the fact that rarely do stories describing the meanings that women attach to the social processes they experience appear in official reports of the research – most typically journal articles. Further, the researchers do not situate themselves in the research process, providing no information about how their values and beliefs inform their science and failing to articulate their relationship to the women they study.

Independent, Single Inequalities or Intersecting, Multiple Inequalities?

Most studies examined only one or two indicators of socioeconomic position (e.g. income, education or occupation) and they were usually analyzed separately from race and gender. None examined sexual orientation an omission pervasive in health disparities scholarship. These measures were usually operationalized at the level of the individual at a single point in time, an approach that does not consider the cumulative and dynamic nature of socio-economic structures and experiences (Duncan et al., 2002). Statistical interactions that could allow for the possibility of uncovering different and non-additive relationships between the several dimensions of inequality and physical activity – for example, the effects of unique combinations of race, gender and social class positions, such as poor Latinas – require large samples and were employed in only two studies. Both Crespo et al. (2000) and King et al. (2000) examine variation across two dimensions of inequality simultaneously by estimating the relationship between a single measure of social inequality (e.g. education, occupation, marital status) and physical activity among women separately for each of the racial ethnic groups. In this way they could identify the level of physical activity among a variety of different groups (for example, Black women with less than a high school education or Hispanic women who are unemployed) but could not look at more than two dimensions simultaneously (e.g. unemployed Latinas who are college educated and/or lesbian and/or married and/or mothers, etc.)

That systems of inequality can be ranked is another assumption of these studies. A common practice is to rank the importance of different social inequalities to physical activity by comparing the size and significance of the beta coefficients and odds ratios. For example, by stating that the strongest predictor of physical inactivity is low education or unemployment, researchers are suggesting that those are the most important and meaningful forms of inequality. Furthermore, since most researchers are not examining the interactions of multiple dimensions of inequality, they are unable to address the fact that social class, race, or gender may have different meanings and effects for different groups. A well-known example is the non-equivalence of social class measures across race or gender – that minorities and women do not gain the same economic returns for receiving a college education (Williams, 2002).

Value Freedom, Researcher Objectivity or Knowledge from Active Researcher Engagement?

Virtually all of the research reviewed here emerged from a positivist biomedical paradigm that:

- values researcher objectivity and distance between the researcher and researched;
- separates research from the process of change;
- conceptualizes change from a dominant culture perspective – as researchers "intervening" in the lives of subordinate groups to effect changes in their lives that will improve their health status;

- treats the macro social inequalities of race, class, gender, and social class as underlying causes, not subject to researcher intervention.

Still, some shifts of emphasis toward changes in social inequality are also apparent in these works. For example, Harrell and Gore (1998) call for the institution of policies to increase the socioeconomic conditions of women, particularly their income, as a way of improving their position vis a vis more proximal risk factors. Yet most scholarship reflects a more traditional positivist approach that sees individual and societal transformations as a result of interventions that emerge from and follow basic research designed to uncover the proximate causes of physical activity and CVD. In this vein, these studies and the researchers who conduct them operate from a position of distance in relation to the subjects of study and fail to see the research process itself as a setting for and agent of change.

There is, however, growing evidence that public health researchers are beginning to look for points of leverage on societal factors that may be driving health disparities and are calling for and engaging in more community-based interventions that involve researcher-community partnerships to develop strong infrastructures for change (cf. Fetterman, 1996, 2001; Goodman, 1996; Goodman et al., 1993; Krieger, 1999). For example, the Robert Wood Johnson Foundation recently issued a call for proposals on "Active Living Policy and Environmental Studies" to stimulate and support research to identify environmental factors and public and private policies that influence activity within communities and populations (The Robert Woods Johnson Foundation, 2002). Efforts such as these are looking at environmental issues such as land use and zoning, safe communities, parks and green space, lighting and sidewalks, and even policies regarding physical activity in schools, worksites and health systems. Efforts to target these environmental determinants will require ecological intervention approaches where the researcher and the researched work in partnership to empower communities to change their environments through engagement in political processes. It will also require examining the ways that these environments shape and are shaped by inequalities of race, class, gender, sexuality and other dimensions of difference.

CONCLUSIONS

We contend that intersectional scholarship on race, class, gender, sexuality and other dimensions of difference provides promising avenues for expanding our knowledge of health disparities and of identifying new ways of going about eliminating the persistent and pervasive social inequalities of race, class, gender, and sexuality as well as the health disparities that accompany them. By focusing attention on the:

- group level social processes that produce and sustain social inequality;
- power relationships that are at their core;
- perspectives of oppressed groups;
- areas of intersection among multiple oppressions;
- active engagement of outsider-within scholars in an activist agenda for change.

We can move beyond some of the limitations of traditional health disparities scholarship. Intersectional approaches to the social inequalities of race, class, gender, and sexuality have exposed their nature as socially constructed, historically and geographically specific, power relationships that are simultaneously expressed in macro institutions and individual lives. Understanding health disparities requires that we examine the broader social, cultural, economic and political processes of social inequality that control or influence the nature and extent of disparities. Many of the actions necessary to eliminate health disparities will require strategies that involve changing social structures in sectors other than health. A lack of research to clarify underlying causes and routes of effective prevention at the macro level of institutions as well as the micro level of the individual is certain to allow their persistence and perhaps even contribute to increasing the disparities and the disease burden on oppressed groups. Employing theoretical approaches and methodological strategies that attend to these themes will push scholars, policy makers, and health activists to think differently about the nature of social inequality, its role in shaping the health not only of individuals but of families, communities, and nations. On the one hand, intersectional approaches complicate the traditional models of health and illness by incorporating more dimensions, situationally specific interpretations, group dynamics and an explicit emphasis on social change. On the other hand, they provide a powerful alternative way of addressing questions about health disparities that traditional approaches have been unsuccessful in answering.

Some of the implications of taking an intersectional perspective include reframing what we mean by the very concept of health and beginning to think about health as located in families and communities not simply in individual bodies. Such a reframing allows us to engage difficult questions about the connections between the individual choices available to the privileged and the consequences of those choices for the public good – a discussion which Ruzek (1999) and others have argued is necessary if we hope to make any serious progress against persistent health disparities. For example, she contends that to make headway on health disparities, we will need to temper entitlements, reduce personal choices, and shift national expenditures away from highly profitable capital-intensive investments in medical technologies and toward primary and preventive, labor intensive care for the common good. She (1999, p. 304) cautions

> ... feminist commitments to widening access and increasing quality are not achieveable until recognition of the urgency of cost containment, some degree of rationing, and some restriction of individual choice is integrated into feminists' agendas for health reform.

To achieve such goals we will need to improve the dialogue between those who theorize intersections, the women's health research community, and health disparities scholars in the biomedical tradition. Interdisciplinarity, an increasingly common stated goal in each of these traditions, will need to become an increasingly common practice. We will need to broaden the definition of interdisciplinarity – which in current health disparities scholarship most typically means collaborations among scientists from different disciplines (e.g. biology, chemistry, epidemiology) but who all operate from a biomedical framework – to include the humanities and a range of social scientists operating from more "interpretive" traditions. To do so will require funding for research and practice into how to conduct interdisciplinary work that truly achieves an integration of ideas, a "trans-formation," and to look to women's studies and other interdisciplinary and activist fields in the social arena as leaders in that effort.

To truly achieve a "trans-formation" of ideas about, approaches to, and the operation of systems of social inequality, we will need to privilege the perspectives of oppressed and marginalized groups – to learn from the "outsiders within" – both within our research communities and the communities whose lives we aim to understand and to improve. Collaborations will need to involve not only scholars but also communities, and scholars will need to be actively engaged in the research process as observers and as partners with communities in defining problems and identifying solutions.

NOTES

1. Most scholarship on health disparities that is considered "mainstream" in public health, the social sciences, and the sciences and that receives the lion's share of research funding emerges from a biomedical, positivist paradigm and its psychosocial and biobehavioral offshoots. This paper will contrast this vast and complex literature with intersectional feminist scholarship. Throughout the paper the former will variously be referred to as traditional health disparities scholarship, psychosocial, biobehavioral, and biomedical, and mainstream health disparities scholarship.

2. For example, in a special issue entitled, "Feminisms at the Millennium," of one of the leading journals in women's studies, *Signs: A Journal of Women in Culture and Society*, 25(4), 2000, asked 55 former editors, U.S. and international advisory board members, senior and junior scholars spanning the sciences, social sciences and humanities

to reflect on anything they wanted to emphasize at the millennium. In those 55 essays, the significance of and need for addressing theoretical, empirical, and activist questions regarding "intersectionality," or stated otherwise as inequality, difference, or diversity was present in virtually every essay. Further, addressing the intersections of race, class, gender, and sexuality was also identified as a current "best practice" in feminist scholarship.

3. For overviews see Clarke and Olesen (1999). Krieger, Rowley, Herman, Avery and Phillips (1993), Ruzek, Olesen and Clarke (1997b).

REFERENCES

Adler, N. E., & Newman, K. (2002). Socioeconomic disparities in health: Pathways and policies. *Health Affairs, 21*(2), 60–76.

Ainsworth, B. E., Keenan, N. L., Strogatz, D. S., Garrett, J. M., & James, S. A. (1991). Physical activity and hypertension in black adults: The Pitt County study. *American Journal of Public Health, 81*(11), 1477–1479.

American Heart Association (2000). *Heart and stroke statistical update: 1999.* Dallas, TX: Author.

Arihihenbuwa, C. O., Kumanyika, S. K., Agurs, T. D., & Lowe, A. (1995). Perceptions and beliefs about exercise, rest, and health among African-Americans. *American Journal of Health Promotion, 9*(6), 426–429.

Bird, C. (1999). Gender, household labor, and psychological distress: The impact of the amount and division of housework. *Journal of Health and Social Behavior, 40,* 32–45.

Blanchard, F. A., & Crosby, F. A. (1989). *Affirmative action in perspective.* New York: Springer-Verlag.

Brace, L., & Davidson, J. (2000). Minding the gap: General and substantive theorizing on power and exploration. *Signs: A Journal of Women in Culture and Society, 25*(4), 1045–1050.

Breen, N. (2001). Social discrimination and health: Understanding gender and its interaction with other social determinants. Retrieved October 30, 2001 from http://www.hsph.harvard.edu/Organizations/healthnet/Hupapers/gender/breen.html

Brod, H., & Kaufman, M. (1994). *Theorizing masculinities.* Thousand Oakes, CA: Sage.

Bullers, S. (1994). Women's roles and health: The mediating effect of perceived control. *Women and Health, 22*(2), 11–30.

Casper, M. L., Barnett, E., Halverson, J. A., Elmes, G. A., Braham, V. E., Majeed, Z. A. et al. (1999). *Women and heart disease: An atlas of racial and ethnic disparities in mortality* (2nd ed.). Morgantown, WV: Office for Social Environment and Health Research, West Virginia University.

Clarke, A., & Olesen, V. (Eds) (1999). *Revisioning women, health, and healing: Feminist, cultural, and technoscience perspectives.* New York: Routledge.

Collins, P. H. (1986). Learning from the outsider within: The sociological significance of Black feminist thought. *Social Problems, 33*(6), 14–32.

Collins, P. H. (1991). Learning from the outsider within: The sociological significance of Black feminist thought. In: M. M. Fonow & J. A. Cook (Eds), *Beyond Methodology: Feminist Scholarship as Lived Research* (pp. 35–39). Bloomington, IN: Indiana University Press.

Collins, P. H. (1998). *Fighting words: Black women and the search for justice.* Minneapolis, MN: University of Minnesota Press.

Collins, P. H. (2000). *Black feminist thought.* New York: Routledge.

Connell, R. W. (1987). *Gender and power: Society, the person, and sexual politics.* Stanford, CA: Stanford University Press.

Connell, R. W. (1995). *Masculinities*. Berkeley, CA: University of California Press.

Crespo, C. J., Smit, E., Anderson, R. E., Carter-Pokras, O., & Ainsworth, B. E. (2000). Race/ethnicity, social class, and their relation to physical inactivity during leisure time: Results from the Third National Health and Nutrition Examination Survey, 1988–1994. *American Journal of Preventive Medicine*, *18*(1), 46–53.

Daniels, A. (1987). Invisible work. *Social Problems*, *34*, 403–415.

D'Emilio, J., & Freedman, E. (1988). *Intimate matters: A history of sexuality in America*. New York: Harper and Row.

DeVault, M. L. (1999). *Liberating method: Feminism and social research*. Philadelphia, PA: Temple University Press.

Dill, B. (1994). *Across the boundaries of race and class*. New York: Garland.

Duncan, G. J., Daly, M. C., McDonough, P., & Williams, D. R. (2002). Optimal indicators of socioeconomic status for health research. *American Journal of Public Health*, *92*(7), 1151–1157.

Eyler, A. A., Baker, E., Cromer, L., King, A. C., Brownson, R. C., & Donatelle, R. J. (1998). Physcial activity and minority women: A qualitative study. *Health Education and Behavior*, *25*(5), 640–652.

Fee, E., & Krieger, N. (Eds) (1994). *Women's health, politics, and power: Essays on sex/gender, medicine, and public health*. Amityville, NY: Baywood.

Feminisms at the millennium [Special Issue] (2000). *Signs: A Journal of Women in Culture and Society*, *25*(4).

Fenstermaker, S., & West, C. (Eds) (2002). *Doing gender, doing difference: Social inequality, power, and resistance*. New York: Routledge.

Fetterman, D. M. (1996). Empowerment evaluation: An introduction to theory and practice. In: D. M. Fetterman, S. J. Kaftarian & A. Wandersman (Eds), *Empowerment Evaluation: Knowledge and Tools for Self-assessment & Accountability* (pp. 3–46). Thousand Oaks, CA: Sage.

Fetterman, D. M. (2001). *Foundations of empowerment evaluation*. Thousand Oaks, CA: Sage.

Folsom, A. R., Cook, T. J., Sprafka, J. M., Burke, G. L., Norsted, S. W., & Jacobs, D. R. (1991). Differences in leisure-time physical activity levels between blacks and whites in population-based samples: The Minnesota Heart Survey. *Journal of Behavioral Medicine*, *14*, 1–9.

Fonow, M. M., & Cook, J. A. (Eds) (1991). *Beyond methodology: Feminist scholarship as lived research*. Bloomington, IN: Indiana University Press.

Frankenberg, R. (1993). *The social construction of whiteness: White women, race matters*. Minneapolis, MN: University of Minnesota Press.

Giuffre, P. A., & Williams, C. L. (1994). Boundary lines: Labeling sexual harassment in restaurants. *Gender & Society*, *8*(4), 378–401.

Glenn, E. N. (1986). *Issei, nisei, war bride: Three generations of Japanese American women in domestic service*. Philadelphia, PA: Temple University Press.

Glenn, E. N. (1992). From servitude to service work: Historical continuities in the racial division of paid reproductive labor. *Signs*, *18*(Autumn), 1–43.

Goodman, R. M. (1996). An ecological assessment of community coalitions: Approaches to measuring community-based interventions for prevention and health promotion. *American Journal of Community Psychology*, *24*, 3–61.

Goodman, R. M., Steckler, A., Hoover, S., & Schwartz, R. (1993). A critique of contemporary health promotion approaches: Based on a qualitative review of six programs in Maine. *American Journal of Health Promotion*, *7*, 208–220.

Griscom, J. L. (1992). Women and power: Definition, dualism, and difference. *Psychology of Women Quarterly*, *16*(4), 389–414.

Guinier, L., & Torres, G. (2002). *The miner's canary: Enlisting race, resisting power, transforming democracy.* Cambridge, MA: Harvard University Press.

Gwaltney, J. L. (1980). *Drylongso: A self-portrait of Black America.* New York: Vintage.

Harrell, J. S., & Gore, S. V. (1998). Cardiovascular risk factors and socioeconomic status in African American and Caucasian Women. *Research in Nursing and Health, 21,* 285–295.

Herek, G. (1997). On heterosexual masculinity. In: M. Kimmel (Ed.), *Changing Men: New Directions in Research on Men and Masculinity.* Newbury Park, CA: Sage.

Hochschild, J. (1995). *Facing up to the American dream: Race, class, and the soul of the nation.* Princeton, NJ: Princeton University Press.

Hondagnu-Sotelo, P. (1997). Working "without papers" in the United States: Toward the integration of legal status in frameworks of race, class, and gender. In: E. Higginbotham & M. Romero (Eds), *Women and Work: Exploring Race, Ethnicity, and Class* (pp. 101–126). Thousand Oaks, CA: Sage.

House, J. S. (2002). Understanding social factors and inequalities in health: 20th century progress and 21st century prospects. *Journal of Health and Social Behavior, 43*(2), 125–142.

House, J. S., & Williams, D. R. (2000). Understanding and reducing socioeconomic and racial/ethnic disparities in health. In: B. D. Smedley & S. L. Syme (Eds), *Promoting Health: Interventions Strategies from Social and Behavioral Research* (pp. 81–124). Washington, DC: 284 National Academy Press.

Hubbard, R. (1990). *The politics of women's biology.* New Brunswick, NJ: Rutgers University Press.

Hull, G., Scott, P. B., & Smith, B. (Eds) (1982). *All the women are white, all the Blacks are men, but some of us are brave: Black women's studies.* Old Westbury, NY: Feminist Press.

Jackson, S. (1998). Something about the word: African American women and feminism. In: K. Blee (Ed.), *No Middle Ground: Women and Radical Protest.* New York: New York University Press.

Jeffery, R. W., & French, S. A. (1996). Socioeconomic status and weight control practices among 20 to 45 year old women. *American Journal of Public Health, 86*(7), 1005–1010.

Jeffery, R. W., French, S. A., Forster, J. L., & Spry, V. M. (1991). Socioeconomic status differences in health behaviors related to obesity: The Healthy Worker Project. *International Journal of Obesity, 15,* 689–696.

Johnson, C. A., Corrigan, S. A., Dubbert, P. M., & Gramling, S. E. (1990). Perceived barriers to exercise and weight control practices in community women. *Women and Health, 16*(3/4), 177–191.

Johnson, C. L., & Sempos, C. T. (1995). Socioeconomic status and biomedical, lifestyle, and psychosocial risk factors for CVD: Selected US national data and trends. Report of the Conference on Socioeconomic Status and CVD Health and Disease. USDHHS-PHS-NIH-NHLBI (November 6–7).

Kaplan, E. B. (1987). "I don't do no windows": Competition between domestic worker and housewife. In: V. Miner & H. Longino (Eds), *Competition: A Feminist Taboo?* (pp. 92–105). New York: Feminist Press.

King, A. C., Castro, C., Wilcox, S., Eyler, A. A., Brownson, R. C., & Sallis, J. F. (2000). Personal and environmental factors associated with physical inactivity among different racial/ethnic groups of US middle-aged and older-aged women. *Health Psychology, 19*(4), 354–364.

Krieger, N. (1990). Racial and gender discrimination: Risk factors for high blood pressure? *Social Science and Medicine, 30*(12), 1273–1281.

Krieger, N. (1991). Women and social class: A methodological study comparing individual, household, and census measures as predictors of black/white differences in reproductive history. *Journal of Epidemiology and Community Health, 45,* 35–42.

Krieger, N. (1999). Embodying inequality: A review of concepts, measures, and methods for studying health consequences of discrimination. *International Journal of Health Services, 29*(2), 295–353.

Krieger, N., & Fee, E. (1994a). Man-made medicine and women's health: The biopolitics of sex/gender and race/ethnicity. *International Journal of Health Services, 24*(1), 265–283.

Krieger, N., & Fee, E. (1994b). Social class: The missing link in US health data. *International Journal of Health Services, 24*(1), 25–44.

Krieger, N., & Fee, E. (1996). Measuring social inequalities in health in the United States: A historical review, 1900–1950. *International Journal of Health Services, 26*, 391–418.

Krieger, N., Rowley, D., Herman, A., Avery, B., & Phillips, M. (1993). Racism, sexism, and social class: Implications for studies of health, disease, and well-being. *American Journal of Preventive Medicine, 9*(Suppl. 6), 82–122.

Krieger, N., Williams, D. R., & Moss, N. E. (1997). Measuring social class in US public health research: Concepts, methodologies, and guidelines. *Annual Review of Public Health, 18*, 341–378.

Lantz, P. M., House, J. S., Lepkowski, J. M., Williams, D. R., Mero, R. P., & Chen, J. (1998). Socioeconomic factors, health behaviors, and mortality. *Journal of the American Medical Association, 279*, 1703–1708.

LeCompte, M. D., & Schensul, J. J. (1999). *Designing and conducting ethnographic research.* Walnut Creek, CA: Alta Mira Press.

Link, B. G., & Phelan, J. C. (1995). Social conditions as fundamental causes of disease. *Journal of Health and Social Behavior* (extra issue), 80–94.

Link, B. G., & Phelan, J. C. (1996). Understanding sociodemographic differences in health: The role of fundamental causes. *American Journal of Public Health, 86*, 471–473.

Link, B. G., & Phelan, J. C. (2000). Evaluating the fundamental cause explanation for social disparities in health. In: C. Bird, P. Conrad & A. M. Fremont (Eds), *Handbook of Medical Sociology* (5th ed., pp. 33–46). Upper Saddle River, NJ: Prentice-Hall.

Longino, H. (1990). *Science as knowledge: Values and objectivity in scientific inquiry.* Princeton, NJ: Princeton University Press.

Lucal, B. (1994). Class stratification in introductory textbooks: Relational or distributional models? *Teaching Sociology, 22*, 139–150.

Lucal, B. (1996). Oppression and privilege: Toward a relational conceptualization of race. *Teaching Sociology, 24*, 245–255.

Matthews, S., Hertzman, C., Ostry, A., & Power, C. (1998). Gender, work roles, and psychosocial work characteristics as determinants of health. *Social Science and Medicine, 46*(11), 1417–1424.

McIntosh, P. (1995). White privilege and male privilege: A personal account of coming to see correspondences through work in women's studies. In: M. Andersen & P. H. Collins (Eds), *Race, Class, Gender: An Anthology* (pp. 76–86). Belmont, CA: Wadsworth.

McLeod, S. (1987). *Scientific colonialism: A cross-cultural comparison.* Washington, DC: Smithsonian Institution Press.

Messias, D. K., Eun-Ok, I., Page, A., Regev, H., Spiers, J., Yoder, L., & Meleis, A. I. (1997). Defining and redefining work: Implications for women's health. *Gender & Society, 11*(3), 296–323.

Messner, M. (1992). *Power at play: Sports and the problem of masculinity.* Boston, MA: Beacon.

Mies, M. (1983). Towards a methodology for feminist research. In: G. Bowles & R. D. Klein (Eds), *Theories of Women's Studies* (pp. 117–139). London: Routledge and Kegan Paul.

Mies, M. (1991). Women's research or feminist research? The debate surrounding feminist science and methodology. In: J. Cook & M. M. Fonow (Eds), *Beyond Methodology: Feminist Scholarship as Lived Research* (pp. 60–84). Bloomington, IN: Indiana University Press.

Morgen, S. (2002). Into our own hands: The women's health movement in the United States 1969–1990.

National Institutes of Health (2000). *A strategic research plan to reduce and ultimately eliminate health disparities: Strategic plan 2002–2006* (Draft, October 6, 2000). Washington, DC: Author.

National Institutes of Health/Office of Behavioral and Social Science Report (2001). Towards higher levels of analysis: Progress and promise in research on social and cultural dimensions of health: Executive summary. NIH Publication No. 21-5020, September.

Navarro, V. (1990). Race or class versus race and class: Mortality differentials in the United States. *The Lancet, 342,* 1238–1240.

Omi, M., & Winant, H. (1994). *Racial formation in the United States from the 1960's to the 1990's.* New York: Routledge.

Palmer, P. (1989). *Domesticity and dirt: Housewives and domestic servants in the United States, 1920–1945.* Philadelphia, PA: Temple University Press.

Pavalko, E. K., & Woodbury, S. (2000). Social roles as process: Caregiving careers and women's health. *Journal of Health and Social Behavior, 41,* 91–105.

Reinharz, S., & Davidman, L. (1992). *Feminist methods in social research.* New York: Oxford University Press.

Reskin, B. (2002). How did the poison get in Mr. Bartlett's Stomach? Motives and mechanisms in modeling inequality. Presidential Address, Annual Meeting American Sociological Association, Chicago, August.

Rich, A. (1980). Compulsory heterosexuality and lesbian existence. *Signs: Journal of Women in Culture and Society, 5*(4), 631–660.

Robert, S. A., & House, J. S. (2000a). Socioeconomic inequalities in health: An enduring sociological problem. In: C. E. Bird, P. Conrad & A. M. Fremont (Eds), *Handbook of Medical Sociology* (pp. 79–97). Upper Saddle River, NJ: Prentice-Hall.

Robert, S. A. & House, J. S. (2000b). Socioeconomic inequalities in health: Integrating individual-, community-, and societal-level theory and research. In: G. L. Albrecht, R. Fitzpatrick & S. C. Scrimshaw (Eds), *Handbook of Social Studies in Health and Medicine* (pp. 115–135). Thousand Oaks, CA: Sage.

Robert Woods Johnson Foundation (2002). Active living policy and environmental studies program. Retrieved on September, 12, 2002 from http://www.rwjf.org/applyForGrant/closedAbstract.jsp

Roediger, D. (1991). *The wages of whiteness: Race and the making of the American working class.* London: Verso.

Rollins, J. (1985). *Between women: Domestics and their employers.* Philadelphia, PA: Temple University Press.

Romero, M. (1992). *Maid in the USA.* New York: Routledge.

Rose, H. (1994). *Love, power, and knowledge: Toward a feminist transformation of the sciences.* Bloomington, IN: Indiana University Press.

Rosser, S. (1994). *Women's health: Missing from US medicine.* Bloomington, IN: Indiana University Press.

Rosser, S. (1997). *Re-engineering female friendly science.* New York: Teachers College Press.

Ruzek, S. (1999). Rethinking feminist ideologies and actions: Thoughts on past and future of health reform. In: A. Clarke & V. Olesen (Eds), *Revisioning Women, Health, and Healing: Feminist, Cultural, and Technoscience Perspectives* (pp. 303–323). New York: Routledge.

Ruzek, S., Olesen, V., & Clarke, A. (1997a). What are the dynamics of difference? In: S. Ruzek, V. Olesen & A. Clarke (Eds), *Women's Health: Complexities and Differences* (pp. 51–95). Columbus, OH: Ohio State University Press.

Ruzek, S., Olesen, V., & Clarke, A. (Eds) (1997b). *Women's health: Complexities and differences.* Columbus, OH: Ohio State University Press.

Salzinger, L. (1991). A maid by any other name: The transformation of "dirty work" by Central American immigrants. In: *Ethnography Unbound: Power and Resistance in the Modern Metropolis* (pp. 139–160). Berkeley, CA: University of California Press.

Scharff, D. P., Homan, S., Kreuter, M., & Brennan, L. (1999). Factors associated with physical activity in women across the life span: Implications for program development. *Women and Health, 29*(2), 115–134.

Shim, J. K. (2002). Understanding the routinised inclusion of race, socioeconomic status and sex in epidemiology: The utility of concepts from technoscience studies. *Sociology of Health & Illness, 29*(2), 129–150.

Smedley, B. D., Stith, A. Y., & Nelson, A. R. (Eds) (2002). *Institute of Medicine Report. Unequal treatment: Confronting racial and ethnic disparities in health care.* Washington, DC: National Academy Press.

Smedley, B. D., & Syme, S. L. (Eds) (2000). *Institute of Medicine Report. Promoting health: Intervention strategies from social and behavioral research.* Washington, DC: National Academy Press.

Sorlie, P. D., Johnson, N. J., & Backlund, E. (1995). Socioeconomic status and cardiovascular disease mortality: National longitudinal mortality study. In: *Report of the Conference on Socioeconomic Status and Cardiovascular Health and Disease* (pp. 23–26). USDHHS-PHS-NIH-NHLBI (November 6–7).

Spraque, J., & Zimmerman, M. (1993). Overcoming dualisms: A feminist agenda for sociological methodology. In: P. England (Ed.), *Theory on Gender/Feminism on Theory* (pp. 255–280). New York: Aldine.

Sternfeld, B., Ainsworth, B. E., & Quesenberry, C. P. (1999). Physical activity patterns in a diverse population of women. *Preventive Medicine, 28,* 313–323.

Swanson, N. G., Piotrkowski, C. S., Keita, G. P., & Becker, A. B. (1997). Occupational stress and women's health. In: S. J. Gallant, G. P. Keita & R. Royak-Schaler (Eds), *Health Care for Women: Psychological, Social, and Behavioral Influences* (pp. 147–159).

Terkel, S. (1992). *Race: How Blacks and Whites think and feel about the American obsession.* New York: New Press.

U.S. Bureau of the Census (2001a). Census Brief 2000: The American Indian and Alaska Native Population 2000. Retrieved on July 15, 2002 from http://www.census.gov/prod/2002pubs/c2kbr01-15.pdf

U.S. Bureau of the Census (2001b). Census Brief 2000: The Asian population 2000. Retrieved on July 15, 2002 from http://www.census.gov/prod/2002pubs/c2kbr01-16.pdf

U. S. Bureau of the Census (2001c). Census Brief 2000: The Black population 2000. Retrieved on July 15, 2002 from http://www.census.gov/prod/2002pubs/c2kbr01-5.pdf

U.S. Bureau of the Census (2001d). Census Brief 2000: The Hispanic population 2000. Retrieved on July 15, 2002 from http://www.census.gov/prod/2002pubs/c2kbr01-3.pdf

USDHHS (2002). Morbidity and Mortality: 2002 Chartbook on Cardiovascular, Lung, and Blood Diseases. USDHHS-PHS-NIH-NHLBI (pp. 5–14) (May).

Vannerman, R., & Weber Cannon, L. (1987). *The American perception of class.* Philadelphia, PA: Temple University Press.

Waldron, I., Weiss, C. C., & Hughes, M. E. (1998). Interacting effects of multiple roles on women's health. *Journal of Health and Social Behavior, 39,* 216–236.

Weber, L. (1995). Comment on "Doing difference". *Gender & Society, 9*(1), 8–37.

Weber, L. (1998). A conceptual framework for understanding race, class, gender, and sexuality. *Psychology of Women Quarterly, 22*, 13–32.

Weber, L. (2001). *Understanding race, class, gender, and sexuality: A conceptual framework.* New York: McGraw-Hill.

Weber, L., Hancock, T., & Higginbotham, E. (1997). Women, power, and mental health. In: S. Ruzek, V. Olesen & A. Clarke (Eds), *Women's Health: Complexities and Differences* (pp. 380–396). Columbus, OH: Ohio State University Press.

Weber Cannon, L., Higginbotham, E., & Leung, M. L. A. (1988). Race and class bias in qualitative research on women. *Gender & Society, 2*(Winter), 449–462.

Wilcox, S., Castro, C., King, A. C., Housemann, R., & Brownson, R. C. (2000). Determinants of leisure time physical activity in rural compared with urban older and ethnically diverse women in the United States. *Journal of Epidemiology and Community Health, 54*, 667–672.

Williams, D. R. (1990). Socioeconomic differentials in health: A review and redirection. *Social Psychology Quarterly, 53*, 31–99.

Williams, D. R. (1996). Race/ethnicity and socioeconomic status: Measurement and methodological issues. *International Journal of Health Services, 26*, 483–505.

Williams, D. R. (1997). Race and health: Basic questions, emerging directions. *Annals of Epidemiology, 7*(5), 322–333.

Williams, D. R. (2002). Racial/Ethnic variations in women's health: The social imbeddedness of health. *American Journal of Public Health, 92*(4), 588–597.

Williams, D. R., & Neighbors, H. (2001). Racism, discrimination, and hypertension: Evidence and needed research. *Ethnicity and Disease, 11*(Suppl.), 800–816.

Wright, E. O. (1995). The class analysis of poverty. *International Journal of Health Services, 25*, 85–100.

Wyche, K. F., & Graves, S. B. (1992). Minority women in academia: Access and barriers to professional participation. *Psychology of Women Quarterly, 16*(4), 429–438.

Yeager, K. K., Macera, C. A., & Merritt, R. K. (1993). Socioeconomic influences on leisure-time sedentary behavior among women. *Health Values, 17*(6), 50–54.

Yoder, J. D., & Kahn, A. S. (1992). Toward a feminist understanding of women and power. *Psychology of Women Quarterly, 16*(4), 381–388.

Zambrana, R. E. (1987). A research agenda on issues affecting poor and minority women: A model for understanding their health needs. *Women and Health* (Winter), 137–160.

Zambrana, R. E. (2001). Improving access and quality for ethnic minority women: Panel discussion. *Women's Health Issues, 11*(4), 354–359.

Zambrana, R. E. (2002, August). Profiling in Health. Paper presented at the Annual Meeting of the American Sociological Association, Chicago, IL.

Zimmerman, B. et al. (1980). People's science. In: R. Arditti, P. Brennan & S. Cavrak (Eds), *Science and Liberation* (pp. 299–319). Boston: South End Press.

Zinn, M. B., & Dill, B. T. (1994). Difference and domination. In: M. B. Zinn & B. T. Dill (Eds), *Women of Color in U.S. Society* (pp. 3–12). Philadelphia, PA: Temple University Press.

Zinn, M. B., & Dill, B. T. (1996). Theorizing difference from multiracial feminism. *Feminist Studies, 22*(2), 321–333.

"WE'RE NOT A PART OF SOCIETY, WE DON'T HAVE A SAY": EXCLUSION AS A DETERMINANT OF POOR WOMEN'S HEALTH

Colleen Reid

INTRODUCTION

The association between income distribution and measures of health has been well established such that societies with smaller income differences between rich and poor people have increased longevity (Wilkinson, 1996). While more egalitarian societies tend to have better health, in most developed societies people lower down the social scale have death rates two to four times higher than those nearer the top. Inequities in income distribution and the consequent disparities in health status are particularly problematic for many women, including single mothers, older women, and women of colour. The feminization of poverty is the rapidly increasing proportion of women in the adult poverty population (Doyal, 1995; Fraser, 1987).

In addition to having a smaller burden of relative deprivation pressing down on health standards, more egalitarian societies also seem to be more socially cohesive (Wilkinson, 2000). Yet in many societies poor women are systematically excluded from resources and opportunities (Raphael, 2001a). Exclusionary processes preserve relative and absolute disparities between the rich and the poor, confine women's material lives, perpetuate harmful stereotypes and discriminatory practices, and limit the opportunities women have to pursue their health. In this chapter I explore how a group of women on low income understood and

Gender Perspectives on Health and Medicine: Key Themes
Advances in Gender Research, Volume 7, 231–279
© 2003 Published by Elsevier Ltd.
ISSN: 1529-2126/doi:10.1016/S1529-2126(03)07007-3

experienced poverty and health, in particular the experiences of exclusion, stereo-typing, and invisibility. The feminization of poverty, reduced social cohesion, and the exclusion of the poor indicate that better understanding the experiences of living in poverty and women's health is relevant and timely. The relationship between social inequity and women's health is indeed too significant to be ignored.

In this chapter I begin with an overview of societal trends that have increasingly excluded poor and unhealthy women and forward a theory of cultural, institutional, and material exclusion. I then provide an overview of the research context – the collective organization "Women Organizing Activities for Women" – and the research methods. This section is followed by an analysis of the ways that the women were culturally, institutionally, and materially excluded, and how their experiences of exclusion influenced their health in terms of inaccessibility of services, stigmatization and shame, material deprivation, stress and depression, and unhealthy behaviors.

UNDERSTANDING POVERTY, EXCLUSION, AND WOMEN'S HEALTH

The Social Trend of Exclusion

In the last 60 years major transformations in economic, social, and political systems have occurred. Arguments for social progress and increased economic efficiency have rationalized the deregulation of global markets, the development of supra-national institutions, and the decreasing role of government. These globalization[1] trends support a reduced role of government because of the purportedly "self-regulating" nature of global economies and the threat of government intervention to economic processes. Governments increasingly support corporate interests and sanction industry relocations to places where labor costs are lower, unions are non-existent, and state regulations are less expensive (Colantonio, 1988). In the early 1980s the welfare state entered a fiscal crisis and lost legitimacy as a consequence of political and economic trends that favor corporate interests. The principle of universality in government services was blamed for excessive spending, inordinate bureaucratization, and halted economic progress (Harvey, 2001). The diminution of manufacturing-based employment, twinned with the shredding of the public safety net, produced conditions that exacerbated the growing inequality between the rich and the poor (Fine & Weis, 1998). Indeed, "the legacy of the 20th century is the cynical defeat by capital and the state of social equality" (Fine & Weis, 1998, p. 258).

An important aspect of the legacy of the 20th century are societal institutions that promote individuation as opposed to collectivity or community, or, in other words, the spilling over of the self-interested individualism of the marketplace into other areas of social life (Wilkinson, 1996). At the centre of the concept of individuation is the separation of each person's interests and identity from those of others. With the loss of community and rising individuation, people tend to assume that their position in society is a reflection of their innate worth and that the poor are the principal authors of their own fate (Harvey, 2001).

The individualism that is engendered with globalization impedes some people's rights and their ability to fully function in society. Those who conform to the market-driven ideals of individualism are included and can participate in society, while those who fall outside of the criteria for inclusion and participation, because they are single mothers, sick, disabled, or poor – because they are dependent – are excluded (Reason, 1998). Exclusion involves disintegration from common cultural processes, lack of participation in societal activities, alienation from decision-making and civic participation, and barriers to employment and material resources (Raphael, 2001a). The individualistic values that drive the economy and human interaction legitimize the withholding or denial of an individual's right and need to participate equitably in society.

Poverty and Women's Health

One of the most pervasive and enduring observations in public health is the "gradient of health." This gradient can be pictured as a line on a graph that remains consistent across sex, age groups, cultural groups, countries, and diseases. The gradient of health shows that people who have the lowest socioeconomic status $(SES)^2$ experience the highest rates of mortality and morbidity. As people move up the socioeconomic gradient, their health improves relative to the gradient (Deaton, 2002; Reid, 2002).[3] The research suggests that more egalitarian societies, that is societies with smaller differences in income between rich and poor, tend to have better health (Wilkinson, 1996). The social and economic structure of society, especially low income, income inequality, discrimination, and social exclusion, are seen as the ultimate determinants, the "causes of the causes," of disease and death (Deaton, 2002). Indeed, the human experiences of birth, death, illness, and disability are embedded in social contexts.

Although poverty and exclusion can be seen as the ultimate causes of ill-health and disease, in any gender-dichotomized society, the fact that we are born biologically female or male means that our environments will be different, we will live different lives (Lorber, 1997), and we will have different experiences of health. Women's health is a continuum that extends throughout the lifecycle and is intimately related to the conditions under which women live. Women's health researchers suggest that it is important to focus not only on diseases that are more common, prevalent, and serious among women, but also on priority health issues identified by women themselves, women's diversity, the determinants of health, and the impact of gender on health (Cohen, 1998, p. 187; Ruzek, Clarke & Olesen, 1997).

Women are extremely and increasingly vulnerable to poverty for reasons often beyond their control. The main causes for women's poverty are labor market inequities, marriage breakdown, and motherhood (National Council of Welfare, 2000). As a consequence poor women have more illnesses and die in greater numbers and earlier than people with more income and education (Salk et al., 1992; cited in Sargent & Brettell, 1996). Given the increasing rates and severity of women's poverty, it is imperative to better understand the social, economic, cultural, and political practices and institutions that create and perpetuate it (Razavi, 1998), and to examine the complex ways that these societal forces affect women's opportunities for health and experiences of health and well-being (Ruzek & Hill, 1986).[4]

Poor Women as Other: A Theory of Exclusion

Poor and unhealthy[5] women are stigmatized and find little place in the dominant social fabric. According to Iris Young (1990), cultural imperialism is the construction of dominant societal meanings that render the perspectives of marginalized groups invisible while simultaneously stereotyping marginalized groups and marking them as "Other."[6] In so doing, the dominant group's experience and culture are universalized and established as the norm. "Other" groups are brought under the measure of dominant norms and are constructed as non-adherent, deviant, and inferior. Since only the dominant group's cultural expressions receive wide dissemination, they become the normal, the universal, and thereby the unremarkable. "Others" are thus on the margins or excluded altogether from the social fabric, and are forced outside the definition of full humanity and citizenship (Young, 1990). This process of othering a person and labeling them as deviant depersonalizes that individual, who is then treated as a mere instance of a discreditable category, rather than as a full human being. The imposition of a stigma then provides a basis for collective discrimination against them (Schur, 1980).

The selective stigmatization of Others is rationalized through the dominant means of interpretation and communication in society (Fraser, 1987). Typically, societal means of interpretation and communication are expressed through hegemonic discourses that fuel self-evident descriptions of social reality that normally go without saying and escape critical scrutiny (Fraser & Gordon, 1997). Particular interpretations of social life are enshrined as authoritative while others are de-legitimized and obscured, to the advantage of dominant groups in society and to the disadvantage of subordinate ones (Fraser & Gordon, 1997).

Exclusion processes preserve poor women's multidimensional disadvantage and constructions as Other. Poor women are *culturally excluded* as a consequence of being stigmatized, stereotyped, and invisible.[7] Wendell (1996) asserts that we project rejected aspects of ourselves onto groups of people who are designated the Other. "We see "the Other" primarily as symbolic of something else – usually something we reject and fear and project onto them" (Wendell, 1996, p. 60). Dominant cultural[8] understandings portray women on welfare as draining resources and undermining social coherence. Women on welfare create division and difference – they are "others" haunting the "norm" (Batsleer & Humphries, 2000), and are viewed as non-adherents of the individualized ideals of independence and self-control. They are culturally branded with having insufficient resolve, knowledge, and willpower to conform. In contrast, the powerful mainstream is portrayed as possessing the willpower and resolve to be independent, healthy, and working for pay.

Cultural exclusion processes portray poor and unhealthy women in particular ways – as either in control of or at the mercy of poverty and ill-health, or, in other words, in control of or at the mercy of their "free will." The notion of free will questions the origins and conditions of responsible behavior, whether humans are free in what they do, or whether they are determined by external events beyond their control (Audi, 1995). Thus, poor and unhealthy women are othered because they have insufficiently exercised their free will. Dominant discourses rarely examine social, political, or economic factors; rather, the poor and unhealthy should harness their free will, take control of their situations, and make better choices and decisions. The processes of cultural exclusion do not realistically portray poor women's experiences – rather such processes are generally controlled by "right-thinkers" for whom being indigent or placing demands on the state to take care of the body are signs of moral weakness (Ingham, 1985). Consequently, only partial accounts of the world that are constructed from within particular historical contexts and that serve particular economic, political, and social interests are presented (Kelly, 1996).

Institutional exclusion is fueled by the deeply held assumption that moral agency and full citizenship require that a person be autonomous and independent. Poor women on government assistance depend on bureaucratic institutions for support and services. Being a dependent in our society implies being legitimately subjected to the often arbitrary and invasive authority of social service providers and other public and private administrators, who enforce rules with which dependents must comply. Consequently poor women are subjected to patronizing, punitive, and arbitrary treatment by the policies and people associated with welfare bureaucracies. Paternalistic authorities construct the needs of people in their service, claiming to know what is good for them.[9] Dependency in our society implies, as it has in all liberal societies, a sufficient warrant to suspend basic rights to privacy, respect, and individual choice (Young, 1990).

While those who are more socially included have greater access to economic, educational, and social resources and support (Shaw, Dorling & Smith, 2000), cultural and institutional exclusion processes rationalize poor women's *material exclusion*. Exclusionary processes confine poor women's material lives, including the resources they have access to and the opportunities they have or do not have to develop and exercise their capacities (Young, 1990). Poor women are economically excluded since they are expelled or retreat from useful participation in social life (Young, 1990).

Metaphorically, exclusion "trickles down" to profoundly affect poor women's health. It trickles from cultural assumptions and stereotypes, fuels punitive institutional policies and practices, and legitimizes material deprivation. Exclusion as a "trickle down" means that linear measures and conceptualizations of health and poverty are not enough. What matters are women's multi-faceted experiences living in poverty, how these experiences are socially isolating, and the consequential effects on health. Cultural exclusion processes, such as stereotyping, surveillance, and threatening, shame poor women. Institutional exclusion trickles from cultural exclusion and denies people the opportunity to participate in and contribute to society and to enjoy an acceptable supply of goods and services. It functions through discriminatory practices that create barriers to accessing services and resources. Meanwhile, poor women's material exclusion and scarcity is legitimized. Cultural, institutional, and material exclusion lead to human misery, loss of potential, and poor health (Shaw, Dorling & Smith, 2000; Raphael, 2001b).

Unpacking The Other: Provisional Identities and Women's Diversity

In a culture that systematically excludes and devalues poor and unhealthy women, only partial and distorted understandings of ourselves and the world around us can be produced (Harding, 1987). According to Fraser (1997), people's social identities are complexes of meanings and networks of interpretation. To have a social identity is to live under a set of descriptions that is drawn from the fund of interpretive possibilities available to individuals in specific societies. Since everyone acts in multiple social contexts, the different descriptions comprising any individual's social identity fade in and out of focus. People's social identities are fashioned and altered over time (Fraser, 1997).

In many instances the weight of ideology has systematically distorted people's views of their world and their own capabilities (Rahman, 1983) and the result can be shame, passivity, and a resignation to the status quo as an unchangeable and natural experience (Comstock & Fox, 1993). Some theorists believe that shame is the key to social conformity, forcing the shamed to avoid embarrassment and being thought different, inadequate, or stupid (Wilkinson, 2000). "Unacknowledged shame plays a central role in causing subjects to yield to group influence, even when it contradicts their own direct perceptions" (Scheff, Retzinger & Ryan, 1989, p. 184).

Although stereotyped and inferiorized images may be internalized by group members, "deviants" must also make various efforts to avoid or counteract the social and psychological impact of the stigma (Goffman, 1963). Despite the power of dominant exclusion processes, under conditions of inequality social groups are formed and at times work towards emancipatory social change (Fraser, 1997). Indeed, oppressed people often refuse to adhere to the dominant group's devaluing, objectifying, stereotyping visions. "Individuals make use of the discursive resources available to them while at the same time positioning themselves in ways that represent the least risk in terms of challenges to existing systems of knowledge and belief" (Croghan & Miell, 1998, p. 449). Although stereotypes and shame can produce passivity, they can also facilitate a kind of agency to re-create identity (Sedgewick, 1993). According to Hooks (1990), shame and marginalization can give birth to a process of politicization, become a place of action, and enable a reclamation and reinterpretation of socially derided identities (Hooks, 1990).

Identity is saturated with the voices of others and needs to be understood not as a unified and static entity but as constructed in order to achieve specific strategic and presentational ends (Croghan & Miell, 1998). People come into interactions by assuming situational identities that enhance their own self-conceptions or serve their own needs, which my be context specific rather than socially or culturally normative (Angrosino & Mays de Perez, 2000). What people say in interviews, in writing, or in their everyday interactions can differ from what they really think, and attitudes and behavior may not always match each other. Language is by nature metaphorical, figurative, and context-dependent and not very successful at mirroring complex circumstances (Alvesson & Skoldberg, 2000). Language can also be used to construct individual subjectivity in ways that are historically and locally specific. Reality is continually constructed and reconstructed moment by moment through linguistic and social practices and self-conscious reflection. This multiple and changing world includes multiple and changing selves. Persons are understood to not possess a single, stable, internal identity but to have many selves which are constructed and then reconstructed depending on the context (Drew & Dobson, 1999).

In my efforts to study a group of poor women's health, it was important to understand the cultural, institutional, and material dimensions of exclusion while also recognizing that the women did not solely define themselves as "poor" but had complex lives and experiences. As Wendell (1996) wrote, "I do not imagine that my own worldview is complete or even very accurate" (p. 104). My analysis is indeed only a partial picture of the women's lives that is conveyed through the lenses of my research questions, personal experiences, and worldview.

RESEARCH CONTEXT AND METHODS

For two years I worked with a collective organization named "Women Organizing Activities for Women" (WOAW) as a project manager and doctoral researcher. WOAW was a partnership between university-based researchers, community service providers, and women on low income that aimed to examine and address poor women's health concerns and access to community services. The five academic researchers formed a group called the "U.B.C. Working Group" that met regularly and was comprised of Principal Investigator (Dr. Wendy Frisby), research collaborators, and graduate students. Eleven community service providers worked with WOAW – seven were from the local parks and recreation departments and the four others worked in family services, community schools, and a local women's center. Over 60 women on low income were involved in WOAW. They were diverse in terms of age range (24–70), educational background, and previous work experience. All of the women identified themselves as being "poor" and most of them subsisted on B.C. Benefits.[10] The women used the terms "poor women," "low-income women," "women on low income," "women with limited resources," "women facing barriers," and "isolated women" alternatively. There was tension and disagreement around the use of terms such as "poor" and "low income." Given that there was no consensus among the women, both "women on low income" and "poor women" are used throughout this chapter. Although the above descriptors are useful for distinguishing the different partners involved in WOAW, naming them falsely categorizes and falsely differentiates those involved. For instance, before their involvement in WOAW, two of the women on low income were social workers, a researcher was previously a woman on low income, and a service provider had a graduate degree. These categories roughly describe WOAW members at the time of their involvement in WOAW and should not be seen as fixed or static.

WOAW's complex structure and diverse members enabled different kinds of participation. Most of the women on low income participated in WOAW's activities, including community recreation, workshops, and social activities. WOAW members were also involved in WOAW's organizing, such as attending meetings, planning workshops, and coordinating activities. Involvement in a research project was the third form of involvement in WOAW. The Social Sciences and Humanities Research Council of Canada (SSHRC) provided three years of funding to investigate women on low income's key health constraints and alternative forms of community organizing. All of the researchers were guided by the principles of feminist action research, including collaboration and participation in all phases of the research design, valuing the experiential knowledge of the research participants, and developing action plans towards personal and social transformation (Maguire, 2001; Reid, 2000). At all research and planning meetings, recreational activities, and educational workshops, WOAW aimed to foster inclusion, enable all voices to be heard, and ensure equitable participation in decision-making.

For a year and a half a group of 20 women on low income and I worked together as the Research Team. It was with the members of the Research Team that I conducted the research for my dissertation – 32 one-on-one interviews, 15 group meetings, and ongoing participant observations and reflective journaling. In the interviews, I asked the women about their health concerns and their experiences living in poverty. In the Research Team meetings, the women repeatedly identified social isolation as one of their main health concerns and discussed how they were stigmatized, excluded, and felt invisible. An average of eleven women attended the Research Team meetings. My data set included 71 primary documents. I sorted, coded, and analyzed my data set with the qualitative data analysis program Atlas.ti 4.1.

EXPERIENCES LIVING IN POVERTY: CULTURAL, INSTITUTIONAL, AND MATERIAL EXCLUSION

In this section the women's experiences of exclusion are explored. Although they are described as distinct experiences, cultural, institutional, and material exclusion support and perpetuate each other. Willow explained the "trickle-down" of cultural, institutional, and material exclusion in this way: "it all drains into the whole pool of being in poverty. And that's where all the tributaries run" (Willow's interview, March 2000).

Cultural Exclusion: They Label You, They Typecast You[11]

The women spoke passionately about being stereotyped "You're poor or you're a welfare case. You hear those things coming from people's mouths. I guess on buses and in the malls. You hear people talking" (Virginia Dawn's interview, June 6th, 2000), and suggested that the stereotype was rooted in the misperception that welfare recipients choose to be on welfare. It's the biggest stereotype in the world is to be a single mother on welfare... So I'm a welfare bum who could get out if she wanted to. But she chooses to be there" (Willow's interview, September 20th, 2000). Maey spoke of the stereotype in these terms: "that they're (welfare recipients) lazy. They want everything just handed to them. They don't have to work. And you know live off the system" (Maey's interview, June 9th, 2000). The stereotype of the welfare recipient is predicated upon the notion that recipients do not have a valid reason for being on social assistance, and that they choose to rely on the government for their financial support though they could easily find work and be financially self-reliant. "Like you're just laying back and enjoying a free ride" (Elizabeth's interview, March 20th, 2000).

The women felt that they were treated with distrust as liars and criminals "even if you are honest it makes you feel that you're not" (Rene, group meeting, May 16th, 2000). Perceiving welfare recipients as liars and thieves rationalized institutional surveillance and monitoring. Katharine relayed her experience of being stereotyped and treated as a criminal: "It's totally misunderstood, they think you're there because you want to be there, and you're killing inside. You're just as bad as a crook" (Katharine, group meeting, May 16th, 2000). The women acknowledged that they were stereotyped as choosing to live on welfare, stealing from society, abusing tax-payers' money, lazy, and illegitimately disabled or sick.

Stereotyping: Welfare Single Mothers

The younger women suggested that they were stereotyped as "welfare single mothers." Inherent in the stereotype of the welfare single mother was the judgment that they were bad mothers and did not know or care to do what was right for their children. Virginia Dawn commented that because of her young appearance she felt she had been stereotyped as a bad mother:

> You could just feel it, they (people on the bus) would be groaning because they'd hear her crying. They thought I was a bad mother. They thought I was just this young stupid teenager. I wasn't even a teenager when I had her. But because I look younger they did stereotype me that way (Virginia Dawn's interview, June 6th, 2000).

In Canada, 15% of all families are lone-parent, and more that five-sixths of them are headed by women (Health Canada, 1999). Although increasingly fewer families conform to the pattern of a husband as the head of the household and an at-home wife who cares for the children, this standard continues to be held as the norm, and families headed by women are viewed as "failed families" and the women as "bad mothers" (Schroeder & Ward, 1998). According to Ballantyne (1999), attitudes towards mothers on assistance are one of hatred and are propagated by those who know little about it.

Not only do many single mothers bear the stigma of "bad mother," but single motherhood is also held responsible for the persistence of social problems from one generation to the next. Lone-mother families are demonized in government rhetoric, policies and popular media, leading to a moral panic over lone motherhood with lone mothers portrayed as a "social threat" or "social problem" (Standing, 1998). Some of the research participants remarked that the same stereotype was not cast on single fathers "I'm sure there are some single fathers out there, but it's always just the single mothers that I think are stereotyped and more judged" (Elizabeth's interview, June 12th, 2000). Mothers have been singled out while the role of fathers and of wider social conditions are ignored, thus leading to a highly distorted view of social problems and punitive institutional practices and policies (Abramovitz, 1995).

Consequently, single mothers' lives are under constant supervision from school, health, welfare, and benefit agencies (Standing, 1998). The lives of women on government assistance are scrutinized on a daily basis social service workers and agencies. A woman can have as many as four social workers in her life at one time, each of them mandated by the social service system to monitor a specific aspect of her life, including parenting, house keeping skills, and how she uses her leisure time (Wall, 1993). The young mothers reported that they were surveyed and threatened with the apprehension of their children. They acknowledged that raising a child in material scarcity with little emotional and financial support was difficult, but they did not risk telling their workers for fear of being penalized with the apprehension of their children.

> She reached out for help, she was just going bonkers with her kid, she wasn't taking care of herself, she was getting worse and worse and worse, she went to social services, and the first thing they said "well, if you can't take care of your children we'll put them in foster care." And that's the threat that is constantly handed out to single parent families on social assistance (Susan, group meeting, April 26th, 2000).

Willow suggested that workers rationalized investigating bad mothering when recipients struggled on their meager budgets. "She threatened me because I applied for the crisis grant, 'we're going to have to look into your childrearing capabilities if you can't manage your money properly' " (Willow, group meeting, May 16th, 2000). As a consequence of being stereotyped, threatened, and surveyed, the women learned to never divulge their personal struggles and attempted to conceal their impoverished subsistence.

Invisibility: Women as the "Unseen Poor"

According to Young (1990), poor women are culturally excluded when dominant groups fail to recognize the perspective embodied in their cultural expressions (Young, 1990). Many of the women spoke of being the "unseen poor" because they were women, middle-aged, single, and poor. Trina spoke of herself as "lost," raising children in poverty, and not having the resources or support from the community or the government.

> My generation is kind of lost... We worked, us single mothers have worked really hard with very little help from the government or our husbands or ex-husbands and we survived. We didn't have the good things for the kids. You know, we had the community centers and cubs and scouts, but we didn't have anything extra for the children. And they're losing, plus we've lost because we didn't get the education, we don't have the pensions, we don't have a house and we don't have the cars. We're just surviving (Trina's interview, March 21st, 2000).

Rene explained that women, as the unseen poor, were socialized to be silent and to adopt roles unquestioningly. "Women are the unseen poor. We're taught to hide it instead of standing up and saying (slammed fist on table)" (Rene, Beth's fieldnotes, group meeting, March 7th, 2000). In her second interview Rene suggested that women are shamed into concealing their impoverished situations and are thus invisible.

> That people are ashamed to say they're on welfare. Or to ask for help. Or to say, you know, what can I do, where can I go? This isolates them a big deal. And they talk about women between 45 and is it 60 or 65, as being the unseen poor. Because they will keep up appearances because we've been taught to. But they may go without food or whatever you know to keep those appearances up (Rene's interview, June 5th, 2000).

Some women, particularly those middle-aged and older, saw their experiences through the oppression of women in society. In her first interview Katharine emphatically recounted:

> (We are) looked down, discriminated, many times I feel that poor women once they've past the age of having kids, they're just the rots of society. They're the sewers of society because many men don't see us anymore; they don't want to see you (Katharine's interview, March 14th, 2000).

As a singe middle-aged woman Katharine felt that she had become invisible. Later in her interview Katharine spoke of poor women "they're silent, they're invisible" (Katharine's interview, March 14th, 2000). Wanda said that the stereotyping and mistreatment of welfare workers forced some women to isolate and be invisible. "I've seen Rene go through some dandies (with welfare). And somebody less strong just wouldn't have managed. They would have gone home and shut the door. And I'm sure that's what happens to a lot of people" (Wanda's interview, June 5th, 2000).

The women's isolation and sense of being invisible also arose from living in a "couples' society." Wanda said "this world seems to be dominated by couples, when you become a widow you learn that real quick" (Wanda, group meeting, April 4th, 2000). Christine commented "a woman is not a real woman unless she has a man" (Christine, WOAW retreat, October 20th, 2001). Susan went further in explaining her isolation in relation to her domestic status "you're more important as a couple, because you have a man in your life . . . you isolate into the male" (Susan, group meeting, April 4th, 2000). Susan, a single woman with no children stated that for her isolation occurred because she did not have children to introduce her to social circles: "I not only find it a couples society, I don't have children. So, it's hard for me to find somebody that is single, and doesn't have kids, to talk to. So, there's another isolation" (Susan, group meeting, April 4th, 2000). The women's domestic status and poverty excluded them from society. As poor single women reliant on government assistance they did not conform to dominant social expectations. Many felt that they were the "unseen poor" and were generally unwanted in society. As a consequence they were excluded and felt invisible.

Simultaneous Stereotyping and Invisibility

As WOAW became a recognized organization in the community it gained the attention of some local newspapers. Two women who acted as WOAW representatives to the local media were culturally excluded – they were simultaneously stereotyped and rendered invisible. In one instance, Elizabeth felt pressured to answer leading questions in a way that would increase the newsworthiness of the story about WOAW while perpetuating the stereotype of a poor single mother. When being asked by a reporter about the lack of funding for a community kitchens project, she commented "I was supposed to look into the bowls longingly as if I was wishing they were full" (Elizabeth, group meeting, May 15, 2000). Later she reflected on her experience:

> (A WOAW community service provider) said I did a really good job of not answering what I didn't want to answer, and in turn, he (reporter) just made assumptions . . . but excuse me buddy, I didn't tell you that for one reason, I didn't want the world to know I'm a poor struggling single mother, you don't need to flaunt it to the world (Elizabeth, group meeting, June 29th, 2000).

Katharine felt that she had been betrayed by her involvement with the local media, and as a result did not trust reporters.

> That journalist guy, he ticked me off. I told him not to use "poor," and many things that I said, I gave him a sheet, the night before, I typed a whole page (on WOAW) . . . So I'm going to write a letter to that paper. Because he really tricked me, he said the article was going to be about WOAW, and yet it's all about me, and it's all wrong. This guy doesn't listen at all. He's just a male chauvinist pig (Katharine, group meeting, June 29th, 2000).

Elizabeth and Katharine shared their negative experiences with the local media and warned other women about falling prey to the media's stereotyping of poor women. From these experiences there was a ongoing wariness and skepticism towards the media.

One can be excluded from social production through not being able to be an active contributor to society because of being labelled as undesirable, unacceptable, or in need of control (White, 1998). The women's experiences with the local media provided an example of how the women's daily interactions and involvements heightened their awareness of the stereotype. Through their interactions with the media and the way their stories were convoluted to fit existing stereotypes, Elizabeth and Katharine were openly stigmatized in a public forum. Their real challenges and realities were obscured from the story, while the stereotype was enforced. Effectively they were culturally excluded – excluded from social production, all the while their realities remained invisible. Poor women's invisibility can be seen as an attempt to control, punish, and alienate. Their experiences and interpretation of social life finds little expression that touches the dominant culture, while that same culture imposes on the oppressed group its experience and interpretation of social life (Young, 1990).

The stereotype of "welfare bum" and "welfare mother" stigmatized the women as cheaters, liars, thieves, irresponsible, lazy, and "riding the system." The stereotype bred antagonistic public judgments that deeply affected the women's day-to-day lives. They had a heightened awareness of their low status in society and felt stigmatized and labelled as poor in many (or in some cases all) public arenas. Meanwhile, all of the women felt invisible – stereotypes obscured their real needs and experiences, and they did not fit the social fabric because of their domestic statuses and their poverty.

Experiences of Institutional Exclusion: Victimizing Policies and Practices

The following analysis examines how the practices and policies of the welfare, the health care, and community recreation systems institutionally excluded the women through viewing them as dependent, discriminating against them, and limiting their access to resources.

The Welfare System

All of the women spoke emphatically about how they were treated by their workers and the welfare system. Rene suggested that "one of the most discriminating places is welfare itself" (Rene, group meeting, April 4th, 2000). In the interviews and the Research Team meetings, the women spoke at length about their encounters with the welfare office, welfare workers, and financial aid workers (FAWs). The women said they were belittled, abused, and treated as files, numbers, and "non-persons." "The one worker I had she belittled me from the minute I went in because I was a middle-aged woman who was trying to get welfare" (Susan, group meeting, April 4th, 2000). The women described their workers as snarky, rude, high and mighty, snooty, discriminating, and low-level threatening.

> I know they have humungous case loads. But any time you leave a message you always have to include your S.I.N. number and your phone number . . . it just makes me feel like you're just a statistic. Can't you relate to me without having the nine digit number? (Elizabeth's interview, June 12th, 2000).

As well, the women believed that their workers and welfare offices changed frequently and that "good" workers did not last long in a stressful system riddled with huge case-loads, bureaucracy, and repeated paper-work.[12]

> Cynthia: That needs to change, big time, but I know that there are workers that are really helpful.
> Rene: But they're the ones that burn out and leave . . .
> Kelly: that's probably why workers change so often, because they get a few good ones in there and then change it around, they're too helpful (group meeting, April 4th, 2000).

They also reported that some workers were young and inexperienced, and as a result could not or did not relate to their struggles. "These welfare workers, they're just these young pups right out of school, and you can tell they're reading right out of the text book, they don't know a thing about real life" (Elizabeth, group meeting, April 26th, 2000). Struggles with the welfare system were raised in every Research Team meeting and interview that was conducted for my dissertation. During the Data Analysis Potluck in May 2001, when we began to discuss "systemic injustices," the women joked that we would not get beyond this topic because it was so pervasive.

The workers' mistreatment was a consequence of the negative stereotypes of poor women that are firmly embedded in the current social dogma and that fuel support for increasingly punitive social policies for poor women (Abramovitz, 1995). Stereotypes of inappropriate coping strategies and irresponsible decision-making are reflected in paternalistic policies and programs that strive to change poor women's deviant behavior, thus predisposing a moral reasoning justification for the government and various institutions to control policy and programs because poor women are considered incapable of looking after themselves or their children. Indeed, stereotypical notions of welfare recipients breed institutional surveillance and control. The welfare workers threatened and wielded power over the women. Susan explained:

It's low-level threatening is what it is. And if you go into any of the offices it tells you how
you're supposed to be treated and how you're supposed to treat the person . . . lack of integrity
comes into it for a lot of the workers (Susan, group meeting, April 4th, 2000).

All of the women spoke vehemently of the threatening, surveillance, and fear
they experienced when they interacted with the welfare system.

I hate having them (welfare workers) go up my ass with a microscope. That's kind of a rude way
to put it, but that's how I feel. I feel like I'm under a microscope all the time (Kelly's interview,
March 2000).

They were surveyed by their workers and by the system, and felt that if they did
not conform to it in ways expected of them they would not receive their welfare
payment ". . . they scare you. They say you won't get your cheque" (Kelly, group
meeting, September 27th, 2000).

Not only did the women feel mistreated and in some cases abused by their
workers, but they encountered systemic barriers to getting help. Workers did not
return their phone calls, welfare offices lined up recipients outside for public
display, and the women were rarely afforded privacy in their meetings at welfare
offices. Katharine said:

They (social workers) never say, "how would it be to be in her shoes, how would it be to be in
her pain, in her depression?" They never do that. They never return phone calls, it's not possible
to make appointments (Katharine, group meeting, April 26th, 2000).

As Katharine said, not only did the women have difficulty reaching their workers
on the phone, but it was also difficult for them to make appointments to see their
workers. At some offices, the only way to get help was to line up outside.

You have to stand out there and line up, there's no such thing as an appointment, so it doesn't
matter what the weather is, what your health is, you stand in that line and they only take the
first so many and the rest come back tomorrow (Wanda, group meeting, April 4th, 2000).

Elizabeth made the connection between the practice of lining up welfare recipients
outside welfare offices and generating negative public sentiments towards welfare
recipients: "they start lining up there about six-thirty in the morning on welfare
day and the people walking by you – you can just see their faces. They're like
'look at all those bums' " (Elizabeth's interview, March 20th, 2000). The women
felt that they were rarely afforded privacy or confidentiality in their exchanges
with their welfare workers and suggested that workers felt they did not deserve
privacy since they were "on the system." Elizabeth remarked:

If you go in and ask if you can get a food voucher, "well why didn't you judge your money
better?" And they give you such an attitude. And it's just so hard. And there's no privacy in that
place at all. You and everyone in the world can hear you. But you know all that plays on you. I
get this big knot in my stomach (Elizabeth's interview, June 12th, 2000).

Some felt that welfare recipients were not given privacy since they were supported by public money and had not earned the same respect and consideration as someone who was financially independent. Being "dependent" warrants having one's basic rights to privacy and respect suspended (Young, 1990).

Another barrier encountered by the women was a lack of information. The women believed that knowledge was important to making a change in their lives and improving their current situations – "knowledge is power" (Rene, group meeting, June 7th, 2000). They consistently encountered barriers to finding information despite the fact that important information regarding entitlements, training, and education existed. Willow said that "information is a barrier, just information in general on training projects, just information gathering" (Willow, group meeting, May 16th, 2000). Katharine commented:

> They don't tell you benefits, they don't tell you how it works, they don't tell you about your healthcare . . . they don't offer information, you have to extract it from them like, it's like doing a root canal or something. They don't explain all of it, they don't tell you your rights (Katharine, group meeting, April 4th, 2000).

Some of the women felt that their workers were trained to withhold information, both to prevent welfare recipients from accessing all possible resources, and to maintain their power and control over recipients.

> Kelly: Like it seems like when you do start asking all they do is get snotty with you and you get the run around and all you're trying to do is better yourself. You want to go back to school or you want to find out what's available to you to better yourself. And it's just crazy.
>
> Maey: They want you to get off welfare, but once you do get ahead, they penalize you (group meeting, October 19th, 2000).

The women felt that they were constantly "punished and penalized" for relying on welfare (Elizabeth, group meeting, May 16th, 2000). In one meeting when we were reviewing data Wanda explained "the one thing I think that's missing there, under 'experiences of welfare' is the fact that you're treated as a liar when you walk through the door" (Wanda, group meeting, May 16th, 2000). Katharine went as far to say that welfare recipients were hated. As we reviewed data at one meeting, she commented "under welfare, the word 'hate' is not there . . . when I deal with welfare, I deal with other people knowing I'm on welfare, automatically there's a hate . . . those people hate you" (Katharine, group meeting, May 16th, 2000).

Overwhelmingly, the women characterized their experiences with the welfare system as antagonistic and exclusionary. They reported a variety of injustices of the welfare system, including the mistreatment by welfare workers, workers' large caseloads, unresponsiveness, and under-training, and dehumanizing practices and policies. These institutional injustices excluded the women from participation in daily life through subjecting them to discriminatory practices and policies.

The Health Care System

Although government rhetoric supports the notion of universal Canadian health care, the women reported significant barriers to accessing the health care services. They suggested that the system was "two-tiered" in three ways – access to and affordability of health-promoting resources, access to health care services, and discriminatory treatment by health care professionals. All of the women said that they could not afford health-promoting resources or health care "extras," including various therapies (physiotherapy, massage therapy), vitamins and supplements, eye glasses, and non-generic medications. Alexa, a young woman with debilitating arthritis, said:

> I don't have the income so I can't take part in physiotherapy and do the exercises. Because I don't have the money I can't do all the things I would need to get myself in that healthy state of mind and everything . . . I feel I'm limited to the resources I can get to because of money (Alexa's interview, June 2nd, 2000).

Willow stated that she had not been able "to take care of medical needs, basic medical needs, necessities" (Willow, group meeting, May 16th, 2000). Seven women spoke of sacrificing essentials, such as food and paying their bills, to cover the cost of medications or therapies. Other women made the opposite choice and sacrificed their medications or therapies to buy food or pay essential bills. Susan explained her situation:

> This month I had to go off my supplements because I had to pay for other things. So I'm feeling it . . . the supplements are very expensive. They're good quality and they're what I need. But it was a choice this month to not feel very good (Susan's interview, June 2nd, 2000).

According to the Statistical Report on the Health of Canadians (1999)

> The level of income adequacy has some effect on the likelihood of having unmet health care needs. People in the lowest income level had a 9% chance of having unmet needs, compared with 5% of people in the highest income level. The lowest income group also had the greatest likelihood of unmet needs of an emotional nature (Health Canada, 1999).

The cost of health care "extras" was not the only form of exclusion within the health care system. The women reported that the health care system was two-tiered, was more difficult to access for people on low income, and as a consequence excluded poor people. When I asked the women about the notion of universal health care, the following exchange occurred:

> Colleen: I keep hearing that health care is equal to all whether you are rich or poor (vocal disagreement).

Susan: I'm yelling at them, well that's fine if you're rich, you can stay in the hospital for how many days, getting all the care that you need, because you don't need to leave because of financial reasons. If you're not well, you need to go home to your kids because you can only get a sitter for awhile, so your health care is not there, you have to leave that hospital earlier, you really can't do it. So I mean, what a farce. We all supposedly get it, and I don't put down the hospital staff, it's just we have to get out of there because, we have to take care of things.

Rene: And if your condition requires a private room you don't necessarily get it. . . it's a $100 and something a day now.

Elizabeth: When I had my big surgery (double mastectomy), I was only hospitalized for a week and then they shipped me home. . . . That's what it all comes down to.

Rene: And with homecare being what it is you're not getting that, the support when you get home. . . .

Elizabeth: Yep, at that time he (son) was only 6 months old.

Rene: Yeah, that's a lot, you have surgery, you are lifting that 6-month-old child, it is not good.

Wanda: And the load of stress you must have been under must have been unbelievable (group meeting, April 26th, 2000).

Over half of the women felt that they had been treated inequitably by the health care system, specifically regarding length of stay in hospitals, consideration and respect from health care professionals, dental care, and homecare support after surgeries and during major illnesses. The women felt that their stays in hospitals were shorter than people who had more money. Katharine explained: "because we have no money, they don't keep us long. They are like, "next". . . But if you're rich you have a private room then you can stay longer, the nurses treat you better, everybody treats you better" (Katharine, group meeting, April 26th, 2000).[13] The women also suggested that the health care system was two-tiered by virtue of how they were treated by health care professionals. Discrimination by health care professionals was raised as a major barrier to achieving good health or managing ill health and disability. "I went to Pearl Vision, and I said that I was on low-income disability, and what was the price range for my glasses, and he just pointed his finger over, and said 'the welfare glasses are over there' " (Trina, group meeting, May 16th, 2000). Indeed, some health care professionals had stereotypical understandings of welfare recipients and acted as gatekeepers who effectively excluded the women from equitably accessing the health care system. "It's like the foot specialist I went to who told me that if I lost weight and got off welfare I'd be ok. Now what that had to do with the shin splints or the pain I was having I don't know" (Rene, group meeting, April 26th, 2000). The health care system's discrimination of poor women systemically excluded them by preventing them from accessing and maintaining health and managing disability and illness.

Despite the rhetoric of the Canadian universal health care system, the women's experiences were a revealing commentary on the system and how they experienced two-tier service delivery. The poor women, who received the second-tier of health care services, were unable to access the full range of options to address their health. Health promotion discourse supports the notion that individuals must do all they can to support and enhance their health, while infusing the notion that all people are equally able to pursue their health and that education is the key to promoting good health. In a recent article in the Globe and Mail, the title headline in the feature section on women's health was "Lack of Awareness Is Biggest Threat" (The Globe & Mail, 2001). However, the women's experiences within the system excluded them from accessing what most consider the basic elements of the health care system. Their lives were not bound by a "lack of awareness"; rather, minimal resources confined them and discriminatory practices prevented them from fully participating in the complete range of services that fall under the rubric of the "health care system."

Community Recreation Departments
The hope of gaining access to community recreation motivated many women to become involved with WOAW; for varying reasons recreation and physical activity were important to many of the research participants. Yet the women reported that they faced considerable barriers to accessing market-driven forms of community recreation. These barriers included material deprivation (affordability of programs, childcare, transportation, equipment, and dress), programs and services that failed to consider transportation and childcare needs and expenses, stigmatizing policies and practices that marked the women as "poor," and the discrimination and stereotyping of community recreation workers. Virginia Dawn explained how the cost of programs was a barrier to her involvement.

> Not being able to have access to recreational activities is also a barrier too, because you don't have the money to go.... And, therefore you don't get out and you don't meet anyone else. Recreation is tied in with your social life, and if you can't afford recreation, you can't afford to be social (Virginia Dawn's interview, March 14th, 2000).

Similar to the women's experiences with the health care system, community recreation's two-tiered service delivery enforced the women's exclusion – making it uncomfortable for them to access programs because of being stereotyped and discriminated against, and making it more difficult or impossible to access services because of the cost. For those who are not a part of the consumer class in society, systemic barriers to community recreation services are prevalent, especially in local governments operating from the new public management ideology where revenue generation and efficiency take priority (Ford, 1991; Thibault, Frisby & Kikulis, 1999).

The majority of the community partners who were involved in WOAW worked in the local community recreation systems. Though the majority of the

WOAW-affiliated recreation staff members and their recreation departments were important resources for WOAW members, one particular recreation department posed consistent barriers to the women's full participation. At one point two women expressed their frustrations with their community recreation department and a particular staff member who systematically imposed barriers to programs, childcare, and room bookings.

> Kelly: We feel like we don't get any respect here. It's quite a political thing here, you know?
> Maey: (We should move out of the recreation facility) so she can't humiliate us, like treat us like dirt, low-class citizens. We're not, we're just as important as anyone else, right?
> Kelly: Let's have her step in our shoes for a day, see how hard it is (group meeting, June 29th, 2000).

At times the women discussed strategies for managing the mistreatment they encountered within the community recreation department, though they struggled with the possibility of alienating themselves from important community resources. After the meeting where the above exchange occurred, Katharine said "they're trying to get us out" (Colleen's fieldnotes, June 29th, 2000). She felt that the recreation centre did not want to be involved with poor women.

The community recreation departments in the women's communities offered subsidies for some recreation programs. "Leisure access" policies were designed to increase access to community recreation for impoverished populations and provided at most a 50% reduction in program registrations.[14] However, the requirements for accessing subsidies were humiliating and dehumanizing.

> But what's discomforting to people is that a person at Parks and Leisure will take your taxes and photocopy them and keep them in their records, so you are bringing in your tax forms and having some untrained person who has nothing to do with you seeing your taxes, not only seeing them, but having a copy of them in their files for anyone to look at (Willow's interview, March 15th, 2000).

Not only was the system for accessing a subsidy a barrier to many of the women, but the treatment they received when attempting to gain access to community recreation was a major deterrent. Several women spoke of getting the "run-around" and wondering why a subsidy was offered if it was so difficult to access. Virginia Dawn explained:

> I was trying to get some kind of swimming entry for myself and my daughter and I felt it (stereotype of welfare mother) there when I tried to get financial assistance. They were really putting me through the wringer and giving me the run-around for everything. And I felt like they had a personal vendetta against me because they were making it so hard for me to get what I needed. I didn't understand why they were even offering this if they weren't going to help. In some ways I felt stereotyped there, like I was begging basically for assistance when I heard that it was offered by them (Virginia Dawn's interview, June 5th, 2000).

The treatment the women encountered when attempting to access a subsidy proved to be as big a deterrent as the cost of the program or service. There is the widespread notion that recreation is a "fringe" benefit only to be enjoyed by those who have the disposable income and time to participate. With community recreation service provision deemed a fringe service in mainstream political and social agendas, community recreation becomes the commercial sector's responsibility and is increasingly offered on a fee-for-service basis making it inaccessible to low-income populations (Frisby, Crawford & Dorer, 1997). Policy makers, eager to ensure the economic viability of their initiatives, have essentially ignored or overlooked women on low income's issues and concerns (Anderson & Jack, 1991). Furthermore, the dominant middle class ideology espousing self-responsibility for one's health through the pursuit of an active lifestyle pervades most recreational initiatives (White, Young & Gillett, 1995). Those unable to achieve and maintain good health through recreation are considered individually responsible, thus obscuring social and material factors that mitigate against such involvements.

While leisure access policies did not come close to addressing the real costs and barriers to accessing community recreation, the discrimination and dehumanizing practices furthered women on low income's exclusion. Such exclusionary practices were rationalized since community recreation did not fall under the rubric "universal" and was a fringe market-driven service only to be enjoyed by those who had the money or sufficient desire to be active. Given the health benefits of physical activity for girls and women (Reid & Dyck, 2000), the women's exclusion from community recreation put them at a disadvantage in addressing their health and becoming socially engaged in meaningful and health-promoting physical activities.

Poor women on government assistance depend on bureaucratic institutions for support and services. Being a dependent in our society implies being legitimately subjected to the often arbitrary and invasive authority of social service providers and other public and private administrators. Institutions enforce rules to which "dependents" must comply, and restrict people's material lives including the resources they have access to and the opportunities they have or do not have to develop and exercise their capacities (Young, 1990). Not only are the rights and entitlements of the poor limited and viewed with suspicion, but they are also controlled and defined from the outside – by authorities that, by virtue of their independence, claim to know what is best for them. Women on welfare are therefore institutionally excluded in two ways – in terms of the treatment they encounter when attempting to access services and entitlements, and in terms of being materially deprived "legitimately" because of their dependency.

Material Exclusion

Unjust institutions and their threatening and surveillance reduced many women to be materially deprived and unable to afford the most essential items and services. All of the women spoke at length about their material deprivation and the challenges of budgeting and paying for food, housing, clothing, and transportation. After Elizabeth paid her rent, "I get $359 and that's to cover everything. I get child welfare and that brings it up $200" (Elizabeth, group meeting, May 15th, 2000). Wanda, who was on a seniors' pension, "went to the welfare office because I lived on $730 (a month), I had no medical, no dental, none of the extras that you don't think of as extras but they are when you don't have them" (Wanda, group meeting, April 4th, 2000). The women's material deprivation was so severe that they were never able to pay all of their bills "and it never stops, you're always thinking of how can I do this, how can I do that? Who can I not pay this month, who do I have to pay?" (Kelly, group meeting, April 26th, 2000).

Housing
Safe and affordable housing was a concern for all of the women.[15] Housing was a challenge for two reasons – there were few affordable places to live, and many landlords were unwilling to rent to people on income assistance. "I had one lady, she was just downright rude on the phone. 'Well if you're anyone from assistance I don't want you. And I won't rent to you' " (Elizabeth's interview, June 12th, 2000). For some women housing co-operatives were an alternative to high rental rates, but often there was up to a three-year waiting list to enter a co-operative. Rene spoke about her co-operative and how it made her limited income more manageable: "I've got the accommodation that's realistic to what I'm making. I only pay $300 a month here. Whereas I would be paying $500 or $600 elsewhere. And when you take that out of $789 that I get that's a big chunk" (Rene's interview, June 5th, 2000). Trina, who was also in a co-operative, spoke of being relieved in having her housing arranged and affordable "at least I can live here. I can afford the rent. I can afford the hydro, I can afford the cable and the telephone. I'm sitting real pretty. . . . I can breathe. I can breathe" (Trina's interview, June 5th, 2000). Many other women, however, did not have secure or affordable housing and were constantly worried about having a safe and dependable place to live. Several mentioned that they did not want to live in a government housing project because of the dangerous environment (drug dealing and violence) it presented to them and their children. During the 18 months of my research study over half of the women moved at least one time. Towards the end of my study, several women had become involved in various community initiatives to generate more affordable housing to seniors and other families on limited incomes.[16]

Parenting Costs

Since the women had limited support structures and very little money, most did not have access to childcare. The women with children under five years old rarely had respite from their mothering – "I raise my daughter 24-7, without holiday pay, without any time off" (Kelly, group meeting, June 29th, 2000). Their day-to-day existence was a constant struggle of providing and caring for their children. Willow explained how getting out of her house with her two small children was a challenge: "I have two little children, no car. How do you carry anything when you have a stroller and another child and a baby and a baby bag?" (Willow's interview, September 20th, 2000). School fees and childcare were expenses encountered by the mothers. Although the education system was publicly funded and theoretically accessible to all, school expenses marked their children as poor. Rene suggested that the school and welfare systems should work together to ensure that essential costs were covered for all students:

> Then give them the $50 towards clothes and stuff like that. I'm not talking want, I'm talking need. . . . The schools should be able to print out what is needed for lab fees, locks, class pictures, and all this sort of stuff, and that should be given to the welfare office and they just write a cheque (Rene, group meeting, September 6th, 2000).

Transportation

All of the women struggled with affordable and accessible transportation. Two women had bus passes paid for by the welfare system, four women had cars, and the remaining women did not have ready access to transportation.[17] Transportation arose as a barrier to accessing health care, attending WOAW meetings and activities, and generally being involved in community life. The cost and accessibility of public transportation was cited as a major cause of isolation.[18] Elizabeth said: "transportation . . . that's a big isolation thing. Because with these bus fare increases who can afford to go anywhere?" (Elizabeth's interview, June 12th, 2000). The women who owned cars often car-pooled to WOAW meetings and activities. However, all of the car-owners expressed concern over the cost of running a car and the reality that they could not afford to replace their current car once it no longer functioned. Despite car-pooling and efforts by the service providers and researchers to accommodate all WOAW women, transportation remained an ongoing barrier to the women's participation in WOAW. At various times different women said they were unable to participate in activities or attend meetings because of transportation. Julie recounted that she had not been involved in WOAW for the first six months because of transportation: "why I didn't stay involved at the very beginning was transportation" (Julie's interview, March 14th, 2000). Transportation constraints not only influenced the women's ability to participate in WOAW; such constraints also restricted their access to other community services and activities and forced many women to live in isolation.

The institutions that wielded control over the women's lives were organized to prevent welfare fraud and to ensure that no recipient lived "in the lap of luxury" (Elizabeth's interview, March 14th, 2000).[19] Yet forcing women to live in scarcity perpetuated scarcity, inhibited good health, and reinforced the juxtaposition of those dependent on the government and the morally righteous self-reliant.

> How much money is the woman on welfare raising kids living on? Less than half the poverty level. Her welfare money is divided into two parts – shelter and support. If she's not lucky enough to live in public housing or a co-op, the rest of the rent has to come from the support portion, which is for food, clothing, transport, recreation, Hydro, telephone, and so on (O'Connell, 1988, p.78).

By virtue of their dependence on the welfare system, poor women are stereotyped as cheaters, lazy, and choosing to not work. These negative stereotypes, so often publicly voiced, have permeated the institutions that control women's fates (Kelly, 1996). The welfare, health care, and community recreation systems enforced and perpetuated stereotypical notions of welfare recipients as intentionally abusing the system, being undeserving, and needing surveillance. These institutions excluded the women from fully participating in and accessing their services. They provided minimal or deficient services and programs, had discriminatory practices and policies, and forced many women to live in severe material scarcity. The women's exclusion enforced the stigma of welfare, removed rights and entitlements, perpetuated material deprivation, and made them feel invisible.

Exclusion as a Determinant of Poor Women's Health

Discriminatory policies and practices, enforced material deprivation, and the obfuscation of information excluded the women from participating in the very institutions that were meant to help them. Both the health care and the community recreation systems were "two-tiered" and provided a better range and higher quality of services to those who could pay while discriminating against and excluding the poor from the full range of options to address their health. Not only did their exclusion from these institutions prevent them from accessing important health promoting resources, but their exclusion influenced their health through being shamed and humiliated, living in material deprivation and not affording health essentials, feeling stressed and depressed as a consequence of material scarcity, and at times coping through engaging in unhealthy behaviors. In this section I describe the various ways that exclusion had an impact on the women's health.

Psychosocial Health Problems as Shame Markers

Health is powerfully affected by social position and by the scale of social and economic differences among the population (Raphael, 2001a; Wilkinson, 1992, 1996, 2000). Social position has its effect on health through psychosocial pathways and psychosocial conditions such as stress, depression, low self-esteem, and anger influence health and well-being (Brunner & Marmot, 2000; Raphael, 2001a; Wilkinson, 1996; Wilkinson, 2000). There are a number of suggestions in the psychological literature that issues to do with shame, inferiority, subordination, and people being put down and not respected are extremely important, yet largely unrecognized, sources of recurrent stress and anxiety resulting from hierarchy (Wilkinson, 1992, 1996, 2000).

The research participants discussed at length their psychosocial health concerns, particularly stress, depression, low self-esteem, and anger.[20] Yet often these terms were used interchangeably to describe their shame, humiliation, and loss of pride "Depression and stress. How is that? I thought depression was stress" (Trina's interview, March 21st, 2000).[21] The literature suggests that shame is the primary social emotion generated by the virtually constant monitoring of the self in relation to others (Scheff et al., 1989). Shame involves painful feelings that are not always identified as shame by the person experiencing them. Rather they are labelled with a wide variety of terms that serve to disguise the experience of shame – being stressed and depressed, having low self-esteem, feeling foolish, stupid, ridiculous, inadequate, defective, incompetent, awkward, exposed, vulnerable, insecure, and helpless. Lewis (1971) classified all of these terms as "shame markers" because they occurred in a context that involved a perception of self as negatively evaluated by either oneself or someone else (cited in Scheff et al., 1989). What is at stake is the sense of pride and need for self-confirmation on the one hand, and shame, humiliation, and rejection on the other. It is the unacknowledged or repressed nature of shame that "explains how shame might be ubiquitous, yet usually escape notice" (Scheff et al., 1989, p. 184).

Authorities who controlled the women's lives cast them as reprehensible through various exclusion processes. Significantly, these exclusion processes led the women to evaluate themselves and each other negatively – they were shameful and dependent clients of public charity. For instance, Elizabeth felt that she was "less of a person" (Elizabeth's interview, March 20th, 2000), and Willow said that "when someone has power over you, it can feel like they have a personal vendetta" (Willow, Beth's fieldnotes, March 7th, 2000). Susan felt that humiliating treatment was purposeful "(a welfare worker) worked on a shame factor. You know, shame to be on social services" (Susan's interview, March 24th, 2000). Not only were the women's interactions with authorities shaming, but the very nature of the services that were meant to help them were humiliating. Community recreation's "leisure access" cards, food banks, and other community services that labelled people as "poor" embarrassed many of the women. Elizabeth said:

> From October to January I had to swallow a lot of pride. I had to go to the food bank and I registered us at Christmas for a hamper. It was a really humiliating experience . . . and everyone was like 'oh you've got to think of your son first.' Well that's what I did. Of course I hid the sack from him, he doesn't need to know that (Elizabeth's interview, March 20th, 2000).

All of the women spoke of their shame, loss of dignity, and humiliation, and at times "marked" their shame with terms such as stress, depression, self-esteem, and anger. Kelly said:

> I'm just very low on the totem pole . . . there's that stereotyping again. Like you're just a single, welfare mother . . . if you don't feel like you belong and you don't feel like you're valued it's definitely going to impact you. For sure. If you feel like all your neighbors think you're a loser welfare bum it's going to impact you. I think the biggest for me with being on welfare is self-esteem. And a lot of people is the self-esteem. Like it's hard on you, right. It's really hard on you (Kelly's interview, June 6th, 2000).

And Willow commented on feeling shame and depression when she left her house:

> I feel shame. I feel a lot of shame and humility and that's where depression and anxiety (come from). I feel like everybody's looking at you everywhere you go. So I've actually been diagnosed with social anxiety disorder because I turn red all the time and I can't speak to people. Always looking down (Willow's interview, September 20th, 2000).

Alexa felt that her poor self-worth was a consequence of being judged for being on welfare "I have low self-worth because I always feel like I'm being judged because I'm on welfare. I just don't feel very good about myself" (Alexa's interview, June 2nd, 2000). Katharine referred to being "rejected" and how her health was implicated:

> It (being rejected) does affect your health. Because you're starting to question yourself. It takes quite a while to realize why they truly are rejecting you . . . and that was humiliating. That was your life, and then all of a sudden, nobody wants you anymore (Katharine's interview, June 9, 2000).

In the same interview Katharine explained how struggling with depression, which was a consequence of her exclusion, doubled-back on itself and contributed to the stigma of welfare.

> You're there because you want it. You want to stay to home. You don't want to work. You're lazy. You're not depressed. And you're not sick. . . . There's always people around who don't believe in depression. It's ignorant people. But yet the stigma is so common it's so big that they say "oh well it must be nice to stay home" (Katharine's interview, June 9th, 2000). For at least six other women, anger was a response to their shame and humiliation. Virginia Dawn said: At the time it used to really upset me when I was feeling it more. And you know doing that,

having that happen, you just you go inward. And you have a lot of anger. I used to be a very,
very angry person (Virginia Dawn's interview, June 6th, 2000).

Susan described her anger towards the dehumanizing lack of privacy at the welfare
office: "I was angry. Why should this man who I don't know know my personal life?
I wouldn't ask you, you know" (Susan's interview, June 2nd, 2000). The women
who reported struggling with anger felt that it was a consequence of institutional
and cultural exclusion and, for some, previous experiences of abuse. Scheff et al.
(1989) contend that as humiliation increases, rage and hostility increase propor-
tionally to defend against loss of self-esteem. Hostility and anger can be viewed
as an attempt to ward off feelings of humiliation and shame, and a lack of power
to defend against insults (Scheff et al., 1989). As the women said, the shaming
and victimizing of the welfare system fueled their anger. It is possible that their
anger preserved their albeit diminished sense of esteem, power, and self-worth.

While some women's shame was expressed through their anger, others felt
powerless and hopeless. Consistently encountering barriers, being stereotyped,
and feeling invisible made some women feel helpless in changing their situations
"If someone is not willing to address it, how do you stop feeling helpless about
it?" (Willow, WOAW retreat, October 20th, 2001). Many of the women explained
that they currently or had previously felt hopeless and powerless "once you get
so low you can't see beyond. You just you can't. I don't even know what I want
to be when I grow up . . . because there is no tomorrow" (Trina's interview, June
5th, 2000). The women's hopelessness often prevented them from seeking the
help they needed. Alexa explained how shame was a barrier to getting help "even
though there's resources to use, they don't see how it's going to help them, it's
just they're too embarrassed to go to them" (Alexa's interview, March 20th,
2000). Willow said that she had been turned down so often, and had so rarely
received help, that she felt isolated, hopeless, and alone. "What do you do? And
how do you feel not so alone? How do you feel like you can continue after all
these agencies and all the steps that you've been told to take are turning you
down?"(Willow, group meeting, September 27th, 2000).

Information was obfuscated by welfare workers and welfare recipient entitlements were withheld or concealed to varying degrees. Information gathering
then became a difficult and shrouded process for all of the women, some of
whom feared negative repercussions for challenging their workers or demanding
more public resources. However, welfare recipient entitlements were available
on the internet and could be accessed through a personal or public computer.
Being constantly shamed and denied information and entitlements undermined
the women's sense that information was readily available. Possibly, through the
barrage of mistreatments they assumed they had no entitlements. Some women

knew friends who had been denied certain benefits and therefore they did not request information from their own workers.

Some women felt invisible because of their hopelessness and powerlessness. Elizabeth spoke how being stereotyped bred contempt and exclusion.

> Just feeling like you get more isolated and feeling alone. You almost feel like you're getting dumped on because no one wants to be involved with you. Because you're low income a lot of people think you must be a cheap, a liar, a thief. So they don't want to get involved with helping you out (Elizabeth's interview, June 12th, 2000).

Susan explained that because she was poor she was not important and was consequently invisible.

> We're not part of society. We're not part of the running of the community. We shouldn't have say . . . because we're not putting anything into the community. That's the stigma . . . If you're on welfare you don't count. I don't mean that in a negative way, you're just not there (Susan's interview, June 2nd, 2000).

Another way that shame and "shame markers" affected the women's health was through health-related behaviours. According to Wilkinson (1996), to some degree eating comfort foods and staying at home and not exercising are attempts to satisfy what may be partly social needs. The social gradient in some behavioral risk factors may be more important for what it tells us about people's morale, stress, and the extent to which they feel in control of their lives than for its direct impact on health (Wilkinson, 1996). Maey described how the shame of poverty so significantly lowered her self-esteem that she no longer cared about herself and in turn adopted stereotyped and unhealthy behaviors.

> It'll (the stereotype of the welfare recipient) make you feel like scum. You feel rotten and then your self-esteem will go. And then when your self-esteem goes your health will go with it . . . Because you're not going to give a care about yourself. They think I'm scum so I might as well be scum. Act like scum. Dress like scum . . . if you treated a dog bad that dog is going to eventually turn on you and start peeing in the house and everything, right? Destroying stuff. It's just like if you put a person down constantly, humiliating them, their self-esteem's going to be so low, they're going to start acting out (Maey's interview, June 9th, 2000).

As Maey explained, defiant behavior was a means of asserting herself in the face of shame. The above quotation underscores the complex relationship between health behaviors and psychosocial health and illustrates the ineffectiveness of health promotion campaigns that focus entirely on health behaviors without considering a person's social and economic context. In contrast to Maey's experience of low self-esteem and unhealthy behaviors, Abood and Conway (1992) contends that high self-esteem might increase the general tendency for a person to engage in a wide variety of health-enhancing behaviors. Additionally, engaging in a wide variety of health behaviors may enhance one's perceptions of self-worth

(Abood & Conway, 1992). There is also some evidence to suggest that self-esteem and a sense of control may make it easier to keep to resolutions about giving up smoking or adopting other health-promoting behaviors. This might explain why behavioral risk factors such as body mass index, smoking, and sedentarism appear to be related to the extent of inequality (Wilkinson, 2000).

According to Frank and Mustard (1994), an individual's sense of achievement, self-esteem, and control over her life appears to affect health and wellbeing. In the Whitehall civil service study[22] a high proportion of people in the lower tiers of the civil service felt they had less control of their work than did individuals in the top tiers of the civil service. When the health of individuals was measured against their position in a well-defined job hierarchy there was a clear social gradient of health. People's position in the hierarchy of society, the degree of control they enjoyed, and their diets appeared to be important factors in determining vulnerability to a wide range of diseases (Frank & Mustard, 1994). The social hierarchy presents itself as if it were a hierarchy of human adequacy, from the most superior, successful, and capable, at the top, to the most incapable at the bottom. The health risks associated with low social status, lack of social ties, and early emotional insecurity may then all point to the same source of anxiety at the heart of social life. The possible central-ity of shame and inferiority in relation to people in superior positions is important because, according to health equity researchers, a central part of the research task is to identify the most potent sources of recurrent anxiety related to low social status (Wilkinson, 2000).

The Cost of Good Health

Being materially deprived severely influenced the women's access to health essentials such as food, clothing, transportation, and child rearing expenses. For instance, the women shared stories of sacrificing their own food so that their children could eat. At one Research Team meeting Willow appeared gaunt and thin: "there have been occasions where I have not had enough money to eat myself so that my children could . . . last month I lost almost 15 pounds" (Willow's interview, September 20th, 2000). At times the women could not afford enough food, and at others they could only afford less-nutritious and more filling food options for themselves and their families. Kelly spoke of juggling her expenses and having to decide between eating and her phone: "Or you don't get to eat. It's just that bad. It's like do I eat this week or do I pay my phone bill? It is health related for sure. For sure it is . . . because you're on such a low income you can't eat properly" (Kelly's interview, June 6th, 2000). Almost all of the women had at one time frequented a food bank, though for various reasons none of them attended regularly. Some said that the food was poor quality and often stale, and for others the foodbanks were inaccessible and either a very long walk or bus ride away (which they could not afford). Maey said that the location of the closest food bank was inconvenient: "I think there should be one (food bank) closer by. But of course there's not enough facilities for that" (Maey's interview, June 9th, 2000). As well as affecting aspects of their lives – where they live, how they eat, and where the children go to school – living on a low income makes it difficult to exercise control over family health, and as a result the health needs of parents, particularly women, are often compromised for those of children (Shaw et al., 2000).

For financial reasons the women reported that they were unable to access services or resources that could improve or manage their health – some, including food, health promoting resources, and community recreation, were too costly, while other services or resources were inaccessible due to transportation constraints. All aspects of material deprivation profoundly influenced the women's ability to connect with individuals or groups in their communities. Being isolated for financial reasons contributed to the women's exclusion: "We're excluded, because we're the poor ones. We can't afford to pay for anything. If there's a fee or whatever, forget it" (Katharine's interview, June 9th, 2000). Many of the women remarked that leaving the house cost money, which they could not afford. Isolation for financial reasons not only prevented the women from accessing community services, but it also hampered their ability to meet friends and other people in their communities. Indeed, material deprivation creates differences in individuals' exposures to the beneficial aspects of the physical world.

Material deprivation is the phenomenon by which those with lower incomes have less access to health enhancing resources and greater exposure to negative influences upon health than the income group above them and experience disease in corresponding degrees (Raphael, 2001a). Some research suggests that material conditions are the underlying root of ill health, including health-related behaviors. Poverty imposes constraints on the material conditions of everyday life – by limiting access to the fundamental building blocks of health such as adequate housing, good nutrition, and opportunities to participate in society.

The Stress and Depression of Material Scarcity

Poor women experience more frequent, threatening, and uncontrollable life events than do members of the general population. For example, inadequate housing, dangerous neighborhoods, burdensome responsibilities, and financial uncertainties, are commonplace, all of which are potent stressors (Belle, 1990). The women's lives were unpredictable and stressful because of their material deprivation. Elizabeth commented: "I know life has to have its ups and downs. But not continually having to worry 'is my hydro going to get cut off, or my cable, or my phone?' Having no food, that's a killer" (Elizabeth's interview, June 12th, 2000). Budgeting was a major source of stress – learning to juggle expenses, choosing which bills to pay and which to defer to the following month, and determining the exact amount of money to survive on each month. Kelly, who was "one cheque away from being homeless" (Kelly, group meeting, April 26th, 2000), said that she was stressed and depressed as a result. For most of the women stress was indeed ubiquitous and omnipresent "when I get stressed out, you tighten your muscles up, and you're constantly in a state of anxiety. It doesn't seem to ever leave me" (Martha's interview, April 2000).

The mothers discussed the physical stress and tiredness of parenting, the worry of adequately providing for their children, having little support and security, and the uncompromising government stipulations to find work when their youngest child turned seven years old.[23] The single mothers acknowledged that being solely responsible for their children, exhaustion, and wanting better for their children were major sources of stress.

> It's (stress) very huge. Also just being a single parent is very stressful. Knowing that you're the sole person that's responsible for your child, and then having the weight also of being on welfare and knowing that you're not going to stay there forever, which is something that you wouldn't want anyway because it's so hard to live on. But knowing that you have to get off eventually, and not having any skills to do that . . . It's like having the weight of the world on your shoulders (Virginia Dawn's interview, March 2000).

Although the women discussed their depression as a consequence of stress, anger, or social isolation, in all cases they reported that it was aggravated by the stress of living in material scarcity. Belle (1982) reported that the social and economic trends that are forcing many women and children into poverty have tremendous significance for the mental health of women. Women who live in financially strained circumstances and who have responsibility for young children are more likely than other women to become depressed (Belle, 1982).

All of the women reported that their unrelenting financial worries caused them stress and depression. Repetti and Wood (1997) cite that people living in poverty are likely to be exposed to multiple, persistent, uncontrollable demands and to live in environments characterized by "chronic burden." The experience of living on low income creates uncertainty, insecurity, and feelings of lack of control over one's life (Raphael, 2001a). Families facing chronic poverty must react immediately and regularly to constant demands, and, for this reason, their coping may be at times less planned (Repetti & Wood, 1997). Chronic economic strain may "grind away and deplete emotional reserves" (McLoyd & Wilson, 1997; cited in Repetti & Wood, 1997), possibly resulting in a diminished ability to reflect upon and develop a problem-focused plan of action. Poverty is among the chronic stressors that may require constant coping in the short term – coping that is likely to be unintentional and less action-oriented. Living in poverty does not allow time for recuperation (Repetti & Wood, 1997).

Unhealthy Behaviors

The women's health behaviors were a consequence of their living situations, coping strategies, and a choice within a range of options severely confined by material deprivation. The social conditions under which health-damaging choices occur reflect efforts at stress management, a desire to conform to peer group norms, or a minimal expression of power in the context of lives characterized by isolation, alienation, or excessive strain (Ruzek & Hill, 1986). Several research studies have found that, contrary to popular belief, women possess adequate knowledge, skills, and motivation to engage in health-enhancing behaviors, but that their unhealthy behaviors result from struggles to meet conflicting health priorities in the face of decreased resources (Anderson, Blue, Holbrook & Ng, 1996). The health behaviors that are subsequently discussed include smoking and other addictions, eating, and physical activity.

Smoking and Other Addictions
Four women on the Research Team were regular smokers. Trina explained that the only indulgence she enjoyed was cigarettes.

> The only thing I do is smoke cigarettes. I don't drink. I don't do drugs. I only smoke cigarettes. And I live in a co-op here. And there's nothing extra. Paid my taxes for my cigarettes that's for sure (Trina's interview, June 5th, 2000).[24]

Trina suggested that smoking was comforting and a small luxury. For some women, cigarettes represent one of the few purchases directed solely toward their own pleasure and one of the few luxuries in their lives (Greaves, 1996). People facing difficulties often engage in behaviors that are short-term stress reducers but that entail risks to health (Health Canada, 1997). Smoking is a way of coping or maintaining "equilibrium" (Calnan & Williams, 1991); some women smoke instead of expressing their anxiety and frustration with limited resources and decreased personal control (McDonough & Walters, 2001). The factors that predict smoking involve material circumstances, cultural deprivation, and indicators of stressful life events including marital, personal, and household circumstances (Jarvis & Wardle, 1999). Indeed, smokers are drawn disproportionately from those who are disadvantaged within their gender and class groups, and are concentrated among those who are most disadvantaged.[25]

Although addictions were rarely raised in the Research Team meetings or interviews, in passing conversations I ascertained that at least three women had previously struggled with an alcohol addiction. Several women had been raised in homes with addicted parents and siblings, and three of the women's ex-partners had been drug- or alcohol-addicted. Although smoking and other addictions were a reality for many of the women, the women rarely spoke about them as a health concern or something to address with WOAW or the Research Team. Possibly, drug and alcohol addictions were not raised because the women felt they were too private or shameful.

Unhealthy and Disordered Eating

Food and eating were raised as major concerns by all of the women. The women's material deprivation and their psychosocial health influenced how they ate. As previously mentioned, most had experienced having insufficient money to buy food for themselves and their children, and as a result had been undernourished and gone hungry. Katharine explained: "Food is a big concern. Because I don't eat well . . . because of poverty you don't eat as well . . . Nothing that you do is normal anymore. Even eating. You eat terribly. You don't have your vitamins" (Katharine's interview, June 9th, 2000). Others were not able to afford nutritious foods and sacrificed healthy options for cheaper options that would last longer and provide for more meals. Trina spoke about the illusion of choice regarding healthy foods:

> You watch on the news how wonderful it is that you should be eating all these fruits and vegetables and it shows a handful of grapes and strawberries and stuff like that. You can't go out and buy that when you're on assistance. Or even disability you can't go out and buy that. I've lost my car, lost my job, lost my health (Trina's interview, March 21st, 2000).

Trina felt that her eating behavior was a direct result of living in poverty – she managed with the few resources she had and as a consequence had "lost her health." Most people, irrespective of social position, consider food and diet a key element in the maintenance of health (Calnan & Williams, 1991). Yet good nutrition is more than an issue of knowledge of the healthiest foods; to a large degree eating behaviors are determined by the cost of food. Lower income women shop more often because they are less likely to have the money for a single large outlay and are less likely to be able to store large quantities of food. They are also more likely to shop locally[26] instead of travelling to larger discount stores since they cannot afford bus transportation in addition to the cost of their groceries. Material deprivation also forces many women to go without food in order to feed their children or partners (Walters et al., 1995).

Susan suggested that many women on low income had disordered eating – either they under-ate or they over-ate – and that many used food for comfort and to manage chronic psychosocial health problems.

(Poor women) have eating disorders. . . . Either they don't eat or they're bulimic, (or they) eat for comfort. And we do admit it. You know so it's interesting how food does play a big aspect on our emotional (health). There's another one (research project) for you (Susan, group meeting, November 9th, 2000).

Julie affirmed that stress caused people to under-eat or over-eat "if you get totally stressed out, then you don't eat, or you eat too much . . . it can go either way" (Julie's interview, March 14th, 2000). According to Walters et al. (1995), using food for comfort is an embedded social behavior. From our earliest experiences, we learn that food is a source of comfort and it is used by women as a way of coping with their lack of control over their lives, particularly if they are at home with young children (Walters et al., 1995). Bloch (1987) found that a group of poor women who were socially isolated were overwhelmed by an urge to overeat. These episodes were followed by an effort to control their socially visible body by dieting (Bloch, 1987).

Three women reported that they consistently under-ate because of the stress of living in poverty. Caroline explained "a lot of it is 'cause I'm not eating properly, not like I should. Very seldom do I eat. I eat once a day, once every couple of days. I get so much on my mind, it just turns me right off of food" (Caroline's interview, April 12th, 2000). As well, two women reported that they struggled with anorexia and bulimia nervosa. Both suggested that low self-esteem was the primary reason for their disordered eating.

I've never really felt that good about myself. So when my ex told me that the biggest two mistakes of his life – the first one was marrying me and the second one was having our son. So, you were like 'What's wrong with me? There must be something wrong with me.' And I think that was what started all my eating-type things (Elizabeth's interview, March 20th, 2000).

Poor women's eating behavior is not determined by a lack of knowledge; the women in this study were familiar with the basics of good nutrition and healthy foods. Yet contrary to common perceptions their eating behavior was influenced by both material deprivation and their psychosocial health.

Physical Inactivity
All of the women became involved in WOAW as an initial means to gain better access to community recreation; only one woman had been regularly active in community recreation prior to her involvement in WOAW. The women saw recreation as a means to improve their health, manage chronic pain, reduce stress, decrease social isolation, meet other women in the local communities, set a positive example for their children, and involve their children in physical activities. All of the women cited the cost of community recreation, the transportation required to get to a community centre, the lack of available childcare, and discriminatory practices

and policies as barriers to becoming involved. Willow explained the barriers she faced in trying to access community recreation:

> It just became impossible to do any programs that that other people have access who are in a middle income setting. It would be so easy for somebody to pick up in their car, go down with their kids, drop them off at day program and leave again. For me it's get on the bus with two children, a bag and a stroller, and you're scraping up that bit of money that you have so you can't pay for a full length swimming program, and I can't stand through a situation where I have another little child who's hanging off me and screaming and be an instructor to her, or be a watcher to her. So, it's, just everything becomes so difficult, that access to leisure (Willow's interview, March 15th, 2000).

The women said that their material deprivation contributed to their low participation levels. Trina said: "If you don't have any money, you can't get there and you can't do anything if you don't have any money. You have to have money. You need money to buy tickets. You need money to have proper apparel" (Trina's interview, March 21st, 2000). Other women saw exercise as a coping strategy for managing their psychosocial health problems. Cynthia spoke of physical activity in the following way:

> Anybody who isn't active can easily become depressed or stressed or whatever and anybody who's depressed can tell you you don't need to take medicine, you need to start some kind of exercise program. Because when your body's active it stimulates your mind or whatever. I don't know how it works, all I know is it does work. Exercise is huge for keeping your mind going (Cynthia's interview, April 12th, 2000).

Additionally, community recreation was seen as a way of becoming socially integrated, thus helping to deal with psychosocial health problems such as stress and depression.

> It's like a cycle. If you're physically inactive, obviously you're not going to go out for a walk. And if you're not going for a walk, you're not meeting anybody out there. But, I walk lots and I don't meet anyone when I'm on my walks. I think if you're socially isolated that can lead in to depression and possibly physical inactivity if you don't know anyone. I think they're all interrelated, stress is in there, too because you'd be stressed out if you were lonely and you don't know anyone. They all affect each other (Virginia Dawn's interview, March 14, 2000).

There is considerable evidence for the relationship between physical activity and health (Reid & Dyck, 2000). The women considered regular physical activity as a means to address some major health problems such as heart disease and diabetes, as a strategy for managing chronic health conditions such as fibromyalgia and back problems, and as a way of meeting other women in the community and to socially integrate in a meaningful way. Yet all of the women faced barriers to being regularly physically active – including the costs of program registrations, transportation, childcare, and discrimination.

Stigmatized Health Behaviors

Not only did the structure of the women's put them at a disadvantage in addressing and pursuing their health, but their health behaviors and physical appearance doubled-back on themselves and marked them as "poor." Some women felt that their behaviours and appearance enforced the stereotype of the welfare recipient and negative public judgments, and marked them as shamed and deviant. The women suggested that their clothes, body weight, and health behaviors (smoking, physical inactivity, food shopping) were outward markers of the stereotype of the welfare recipient. Young (1990) claims that stereotypes function by confining people to a nature which is often attached in some way to their bodies, and which cannot be easily denied (Young, 1990). Thus the women's stigmatization was branded on their physical selves. Most of the women suggested that how they dressed stereotyped them. They acknowledged that they did not have the resources to dress well, and that people could "tell" that they were on welfare. For some this judgement of their physical appearance affected their self-esteem.

> It does play on your self-esteem, too, right. Because you can't afford to buy nice clothes. Or you know like I wear rags because she (daughter) needs clothes. Then people judge you by the way you dress. And it's like who cares how I dress? Isn't it who I am? If I won the lottery tomorrow you'd like me (Kelly's interview, June 6th, 2000).

Susan explained that there was a societal expectation for people on income assistance to appear a certain way and to exhibit certain behaviors:

> People on assistance are not supposed to look good. They're supposed to be overweight because they don't do anything. So all they do is stay at home and eat . . . or they're skinny, gangly young girls who don't dress nicely. And look slobbish (Susan's interview, November 9th, 2000).

She also suggested that the women's body weight fueled stereotyping and furthered their stigmatization:

> You know, "look how fat she is." And now I'm beginning to realize that you eat such poor food, you don't have a choice. You can't afford the food that makes you healthy and thin. And you can't get the activity, the women can't get the activity because they've got the kids all the time. So most of us are overweight (Susan's interview, June 2nd, 2000).

Elizabeth felt that she was stereotyped when she went food shopping "They just judge you. You know 'look at all the junk she's buying.' They judge you all the time" (Elizabeth's interview, June 12th, 2000). Cynthia suggested that widespread notions about "wasting" money on cigarettes stereotyped poor people. Smoking fueled negative public sentiments towards people on assistance, while little was known about the difficulties of quitting. "You're burning money away, and when you have no money, and you're in such a space, it's so hard to quit, it's expensive too, expensive to quit" (Cynthia, group meeting, April 4th, 2000).

Through outward markers of the stereotype, the women were culturally excluded and shamed. They were seen as reprehensible, further stigmatized, and "justifiably" subjected to punitive treatment. According to Young (1990), our society enacts the oppression of cultural imperialism to a large degree through feelings and reactions. Such reactions of aversion deeply structure the oppression of all culturally imperialized groups. When the dominant culture defines some groups as different, as the Other, the members of those groups are imprisoned in their bodies. Dominant discourse defines them in terms of bodily characteristics, and constructs those bodies as ugly, dirty, defiled, impure, contaminated, and sick. Those who experience such an "epidermalizing" of their world discover their status by means of the embodied behavior of others: in their gestures, a certain nervousness that they exhibit, their avoidance of eye contact, and the distance they keep (Young, 1990, p. 123).

The women's health behaviours were a consequence of limited choices, material deprivation, and psychosocial health. "Choice" is always shaped by the options that exist within one's specific life circumstances, and women's choices are often more rhetorical than real (Ruzek et al., 1997). People do not have equal choices about how they live their lives or the health behaviors available to them. Several researchers have suggested that the link between social structures and patterns or styles of life can be explained by different groups having differential access to a range of resources in the management of their everyday lives (Calnan & Williams, 1991). As well, material restrictions operate through a number of processes, and "unhealthy" behaviors need to be understood in the context of the constraints on everyday life which accompany them (Shaw et al., 2000). Smoking, drinking, poor nutrition, and physical inactivity are socially patterned and represent structural challenges that women face (Walters et al., 1995). Behavior is related to the social context in which people live and is difficult to change in isolation. Indeed, if behavior was not partly determined by the social environment, there would presumably not be a social class gradient in smoking, diet, or in the amount of leisure-time exercise which people take. In other words, to change behavior it is necessary to change more than behavior (Wilkinson, 1996, p.63).

Exclusion had a major influence on the women's health. Poor women on government assistance are subjected to exclusionary institutions that prevent them from accessing the full range of health-promoting services and entitlements, both within the health care system and beyond. Being stereotyped is shaming and has a profound influence on psychosocial health, which has been shown to influence overall health and well-being (Marmot, 2002; Raphael, 2001a; Wilkinson, 1996, 2000). Exclusionary practices enforced poor women's material deprivation, influenced their ability to access health-promoting resources, generated stress and depression, and restricted their ability to pursue healthful behaviors.

Health as a Social Justice Issue

While there is substantial evidence for the "gradient of health," few researchers have employed qualitative methods to examine the ways that the experience of living in poverty influences women's health. Exclusion emerged from the data as the most significant experience of poverty – the stereotyping and invisibility of cultural exclusion, the discriminatory practices and policies of institutional exclusion, and the limited subsidies and scarcity of material deprivation. The women were stigmatized and shamed when they interacted with the welfare, health care, and community recreation systems. As a consequence some women struggled with anger, others felt increasingly hopeless, powerless, and invisible, and still others adopted unhealthy behaviors as a way to cope. Meanwhile widespread stereotypes justified the women's material scarcity, thus denying them access to important health-promoting resources, programs, and services. In these multi-faceted and interconnected ways, exclusion had a deep and serious impact on poor women's health.

Health equity researchers argue that the quality of social relations is a prime determinant of human welfare and the quality of life. As well as more egalitarian societies having a smaller burden of relative deprivation pressing down on health standards, they also seem to be more socially cohesive (Wilkinson, 1996). Yet in many societies people are systematically excluded from resources and opportunities (Raphael, 2001b). Exclusionary institutional practices and policies preserve relative and absolute disparities between the rich and the poor, while confining people's material lives including the resources they have access to and the opportunities they have or do not have to develop and exercise their capacities. Unquestioned norms and stereotypes mark poor women as deviant and reprehensible. Poor women live with shame and humiliation and are controlled by exclusionary institutions that reflect "the same patterns of control and power that are often characteristic of relationships between men and women, between parents and children" (Wall, 1993, p.285). According to Wilkinson (1996),

> To feel depressed, cheated, bitter, desperate, vulnerable, frightened, angry, worried about debts or job and housing insecurity; to feel devalued, useless, helpless, uncared for, hopeless, isolated, anxious and a failure; these feelings can dominate people's whole experience of life ... The material environment is merely the indelible mark and constant reminder of the oppressive fact of one's failure, of the atrophy of any sense of having a place in the community, and of one's social exclusion and devaluation as a human being (Wilkinson, 1996, p. 215).

While low-income people, particularly women, are cut off from the ongoing economic growth enjoyed by most Canadians, "most governments are not yet prepared to address these problems seriously, nor are they prepared to ensure a reasonable level of support for low-income people either inside or outside of the paid labor force" (National Council of Welfare, 2000, p.145). Furthermore, in attempting to recognize the association between exclusion and health, health and wellness become complex and threatening to the status quo. Doing something about exclusion, discrimination, and inequitable access to resources involves notions of planned social and economic change (Becker, 1986). Addressing these larger issues turns the concept of health into a battleground over rights and resources (Rootman & Raeburn, 1994). While theory and research evidence support the link between exclusion and ill-health, the extent to which any new program actually succeeds in empowering a community and the ultimate impact this has on its collective health remains to be demonstrated (Shiell & Hawe, 1996).

Health is widely recognized as a fundamental right of citizenship "the enjoyment of the highest attainable standard of health is one of the fundamental rights of every human being without distinction of race, religion, political belief, economics, or social condition" (WHO, 1948; cited in Hankivsky, 1999). In that vein, health is a social justice issue – "it is one of the greatest of contemporary social injustices that people who live in the most disadvantaged circumstances have more illnesses, more disability, and shorter lives than those who are more affluent" (Benzeval, Judge & Whitehead, 1995, p. 1; cited in Raphael, 2001a). According to Young (1990), social justice concerns the degree to which a society contains and supports the conditions necessary for all individuals to exercise capacities, express experiences, and participate in determining actions. Social justice requires not the melting away of difference, but the promotion and respect for group differences without oppression (Young, 1990). If there is not a sense of social justice in society, then the legitimacy of social institutions is fundamentally weakened and the moral community which makes social life coherent is lacking (Wilkinson, 1996). Numerous international platforms explicitly focus on women's right to health as an integral component of human rights protection and promotion.[27] International conventions, documents, and platforms obligate the global community, including Canada, to take concrete action to eliminate all forms of discrimination against women. Importantly, it is not enough to state or recognize human rights, rather, conditions must exist in which they can be exercised and realized (Hankivsky, 1999).

Health as a social justice issue is concerned with creating the opportunities for attaining full health potential and reducing health inequities (Hankivsky, 1999). Equity refers to conditions largely out of individuals' control that create unjust differentials in health. Lack of power at the individual, community, and societal levels is a major risk factor for poor health. Empowering the disadvantaged – or disempowering those who use their privilege to benefit themselves at the expense of the wellbeing of the community – is an important tool for health promotion. Protecting and restoring health involves a social justice ethic based on collective action and fair play that respects individual rights and experiences (Wallerstein & Freudenberg, 1998). Ultimately the decision all of us have to make is between valuing human development and all its potentials, including good health and the avoidance of illness, or living within a society that excludes the poor and furthers inequities (Raphael, 2001b).

NOTES

1. Globalization can be defined as a set of processes leading to the creation of a world as a single entity, relatively undivided by national borders or other types of boundaries such as cultural or economic. Globalization contributes to intensified human interaction in a wide range of spheres (economic, political, social, environmental) and across three types of boundaries – spatial, temporal, and cognitive – that have hitherto separated individuals and societies. It also influences the timeframe of human interaction and thought processes (Bettcher & Lee, 2002).

2. Socioeconomic status is "a composite measure that typically incorporates economic status, measure by income; social status, measured by education; and work status; measure by occupation" (Adler, Boyce, Chesney, Cohen, Folkman, Kahn & Syme, 1994, p. 15). Socioeconomic status refers to the position in the social hierarchy that gives individuals relative power and recognition due to wealth and certain forms of income (Ballantyne, 1999).

3. A series of studies in the United Kingdom document how those living on lower incomes are more likely to suffer and die from cardiovascular disease – and a number of other diseases – at every age. A recent study found significant differences in overall death rates between those in the lowest two income groups and those in the highest two income groups in England and Wales. Lower income women had a 55% greater chance of dying than those with higher incomes. In the United States, low-income Americans have a higher incidence of a range of illnesses including cardiovascular disease. In Canada, data on individuals' income and social status are not routinely collected at death, so national examination of the relationship between income and death from various diseases must use census tract of residence to estimate individuals' income. In both 1986 and 1996, those Canadians living within the poorest 20% of urban neighborhoods were much more likely to die from cardiovascular disease, cancer, diabetes, and respiratory diseases – among other diseases – than other Canadians (Raphael, 2001a). According to a Health Canada report, Canadians with the lowest income were five times more likely than those from the highest income groups to report their health as only fair or poor, two times more likely to have a long-term activity limitation, and only one-third as likely to have dental insurance (Health Canada, 1999).

4. Currently there are no universal definitions of health. Perceptions vary across individuals and cultures depending on the meaning and importance people give to it. Reviewing

the literature revealed three major themes regarding health – the absence of disease, a functional capacity, and a positive condition (Colantonio, 1988). Generally, conceptualizations of health range from narrow to broad – from the physical body to the ecosphere – and use terms such as biological, psychological, social, societal, environmental, cultural, economic, and political (Rootman & Raeburn, 1994). According to Allen (1981), health is a way of life, living, and becoming (Allen, 1981; cited in Jones & Meleis, 1993). Jones and Meleis (1993) conceptualized health as empowerment. Health is a process of growth and becoming, of being whole and maximizing the development of one's potential. Health is being empowered to define, seek, and find conditions, resources, and processes to be an effective agent in meeting the significant needs perceived by individuals (Jones & Meleis, 1993). Well-being involves improved quality of life, efficient functioning, the capacity to perform at more productive and satisfying levels, and the opportunity to live out one's life span with vigor and stamina (McAuley & Rudolph, 1995). The "emerging consensus among researchers is that the term 'well-being' implies an emphasis on the individual's perception or sense of wholeness of self, groups, or community" (Schlicht, 1993). Health is an important component of well-being, but it is not the only component (Deaton, 2002).

5. I use the terms "unhealthy," "ill health," and "the unhealthy" to represent the experiences of declining health, disability, and disease. Although I consciously use these terms as "catch-alls," in many cases the experiences of health, disability, and disease are distinctly different.

6. The term "Other" is used throughout the chapter. I distinguish it from common usages of the word "other" by capitalizing it – Other – and, when necessary, marking it with quotations – "Other." At times I have also used the terms "othering" and being "othered" to capture the process of being designated the Other.

7. Stigmatization captures what Swanson (2001) calls "poor-bashing." Poor-bashing occurs when people who are poor are humiliated, discriminated against, shunned, pitied, patronized, ignored, blamed, and falsely accused of being lazy, drunk, stupid uneducated, having large families, and not looking for work (Swanson, 2001, p. 2). To stigmatize is to characterize or brand as disgraceful or ignominious. A stereotype is a conventional, formulaic, usually oversimplified conception, opinion, or belief (Morris, 1982). It denotes something fixed or lacking in originality. In common usage stereotyping can be seen as an ideological discursive strategy which demarcates an us/them binary which functions to reinforce the dominant discourse (Gamble, 1999). To be invisible means to not be easily noticed or detected; to be inconspicuous (Morris, 1982).

8. "Culture is a matrix of beliefs, values, and norms that inform, give meaning to, and regulate experience" (Westkott, 1998, p. 816). According to Young (1990), culture includes symbols, images, meanings, habitual comportments, stories, and so on through which people express their experience and communicate with others. Culture is ubiquitous. . . . The symbolic meanings that people attach to other kinds of people and to actions, gestures, or institutions can often significantly affect the social standing of persons and their opportunities (Young, 1990).

9. It is important to note that not all authorities are paternalistic and discriminating. The majority of welfare and health care workers, whether or not they agree, are forced to comply with their institutional policies. Some attempt to resist and to use covert practices in order to help the poor.

10. This study occurred in the greater Vancouver area, in British Columbia, Canada. Monetary references are in Canadian dollars and B.C. Benefits refers to the provincial

program that offers social assistance (welfare), disability benefits I and II, and seniors' pensions. "Employable" one-parent families with one child receive $845.58 per month on social assistance; one-parent families with two children receive $935.58. Single people on Disability Benefits I receive $802.92 per month; one-parent families with one child receive $896.58. Disability Benefits II recipients who are single adults receive $981.42, and recipients who are single parents with one child receive $1 050.08.

    11. Katharine, Research Team Meeting, April 26th, 2000.

    12. This was the women's experience of B.C. Benefits. I cannot confirm that "good" workers did not last long and were pushed out of the welfare system.

    13. Although the women believed that their stays in hospitals were shorter than the stays of people who had more money, it is difficult to say whether this was in fact the case. Current public discourse contends that all people have shorter stays in hospitals due to reduced government spending on the health care system.

    14. It should be noted that leisure access policies only cover a fraction of the cost of the program itself and do not cover childcare, transportation, or other expenses (clothing, equipment) associated with participating.

    15. Five of the women lived in housing co-operatives, eleven women lived alone in apartments (some with their children), one woman lived with her parents, and three women lived with their partners in apartments or houses.

    16. Research indicates that people living in poverty are often forced to live in substandard or even dangerous housing. Health problems may be induced by substandard housing in terms of environmental hazards (location of low income units near toxic waste sites); safety hazards (dilapidated facilities, poor ventilation, infestation); physical conditions (crowding and disrepair); psychological factors (isolation, low self-worth, anxiety, depression); geographic factors (proximity to grocery store, access to transportation); discrimination by race, gender, social class, or location; and access to health care. Inadequate housing is an outcome of poverty, but it also reinforces poverty by creating conditions such as poor sanitation, increased stress levels, lack of safety; and increased rates of infection, injury, and illness, all of which make it difficult to obtain and retain employment. As well, the very structure and layout of many marginalized neighborhoods discourages mobility and fosters isolation. Public housing developments, often designed as high-rise buildings located in pockets throughout the inner city, are generally isolated from commerce and basic amenities and typically lack common areas such as benches or playgrounds where residents can socialize (Welch, 1997).

    17. The welfare cuts announced in British Columbia on January 17th, 2002 affected thousands of seniors on low income who were no longer to be entitled to bus-fare subsidies, something "that was necessary because such subsidies are not available elsewhere in Canada" (Lunman, 2002, p. A4).

    18. Transportation as a barrier for several reasons. Welfare recipients in British Columbia do not receive subsidies for transportation, therefore the cost of taking the bus comes from recipients' monthly cheques. This cost was prohibitive for many women: "Everything costs money, even the bus. There was one activity last year that I wanted to do.... I had to take the bus three times a week to go, I couldn't afford the bus three times a week" (Katharine, group meeting, April 4th, 2000). The women also suggested that the transit system did not accommodate them in terms of schedules and routes: "Trying to get anywhere on transit, especially in this area, you have to leave sometimes two hours before you want to get somewhere" (Elizabeth's interview, March 20th, 2000). The older women suggested that

transportation was a barrier in a couple of ways. The 'handi-dart' service for people on disability had restricted hours and limited service areas, and needed to be booked three days in advance. "You can't go out after a certain hour at night. I just see it as not being a very independent way for a senior to live" (Wanda's interview, June 5th, 2000). Some of the older women were concerned about taking the regular bus because of their health, difficulties climbing the bus stairs, the distance to and from the bus stops, the waiting that was required, and the possibility of not being able to sit on the bus.

19. The women said that their limited incomes forced them to become good budgeters, which often conflicts with the common stereotype of the welfare recipient as being careless with her money. According to Susan, "if anybody can stick on a budget it's someone on assistance, because you have to feed the kids, you have to eat, and you may not have enough, but you take care of that budget as good as you can" (Susan, group meeting, April 4th, 2000).

20. All of the women said that stress was a health concern, ten women reported depression, and three of the women who had depression were clinically depressed.

21. The four women who had clinical depression were notable exceptions. At times they spoke of the relationship between stress and depression, while at other times they cited their depression as a biological problem rather than a consequence of societal factors. The women's psychosocial health discourses, specifically their uses of the terms "stress" and "depression," would be a fruitful avenue for future study. A closer examination of the women's psychosocial health discourses, however, was beyond the scope of this dissertation.

22. The Whitehall civil service studies in Great Britain were groundbreaking research studies that aimed to determine the relationship between social status and health. These studies have been widely referenced and have provided a foundation for debates in the health equity field (Marmot, 1991; Marmot, Shipley & Rose, 1984).

23. Under the provincial Liberal government elected in May 2001, single mothers are now expected to return to work when their child turns three years old. According to the provincial human resources minister Murray Coell, he aims to "break the cycle of welfare dependency in B.C." and the best social safety net "is a job . . . Welfare in Canada has been an attitude of entitlement" (Lunman, 2002). In a conversation with several women in December 2001, they questioned how single mothers were expected to earn a living, pay for childcare, and cover other living expenses. This was particularly troublesome since the minimum wage for untrained workers (presumably students but also applying to many single mothers) was reduced to $6/hour. The women felt that single mothers with no previous work experience would be forced to leave their children unattended at home while working for $6/hour.

24. When Trina and I reviewed her quotations, she asked that I footnote that she rolled her own cigarettes in order to save money.

25. In a study conducted by Walters et al. (1995) with a group of women on low income, 71.7% of women who were lone parents were smokers (Walters, Lenton & Mckeary, 1995). For a thorough analysis of the context of women's smoking, consult Lorraine Greaves (1996) "Smoke Screen: Women's Smoking and Social Control" (Greaves, 1996).

26. There is some evidence to support the fact that smaller grocery stores in low-income neighborhoods in Vancouver B.C. have on average higher prices than larger grocery stores in middle-class suburbs (Baxter, 1988).

27. According to United Nations Economic and Social Council (1999), "the realization by women of their right to the enjoyment of the highest attainable standard of physical and

mental health is an integral part of the full realization by them of all human rights, and that the human rights of women and the girl child are an inalienable, integral, and indivisible part of universal human rights" (cited in Hankivsky, 1999).

REFERENCES

Abood, D. A., & Conway, T. L. (1992). Health value and self-esteem as predictors of wellness behavior. *Health Values, 16*(3), 20–26.

Abramovitz, M. (1995). From tenement class to dangerous class to underclass: Blaming women for social problems. In: N. Van Den Bergh (Ed.), *Feminist Practice in the 21st Century* (pp. 211–231). Washington: NASW Press.

Adler, N. E., Boyce, T., Chesney, M. A., Cohen, S., Folkman, S., Kahn, R. L., & Syme, S. L. (1994). Socioeconomic status and health: The challenge of the gradient. *American Psychologist, 49*(1), 15–24.

Allen, M. J. (1981). The health dimension in nursing practice: Notes on nursing in primary health care. *Journal of Advanced Nursing, 6*, 153–154.

Alvesson, M., & Skoldberg, K. (2000). Language/gender/power: Discourse analysis, feminism and genealogy. In: M. Alvesson & K. Skoldberg (Eds), *Reflexive Methodology: New Vistas for Qualitative Research* (pp. 200–237). London: Sage.

Anderson, J. M., Blue, C., Holbrook, A., & Ng, M. (1996). On chronic illness: Immigrant women in Canada's work force: A feminist perspective. *Canadian Journal of Nursing Research, 25*(2), 7–22.

Anderson, K., & Jack, D. C. (1991). Learning to listen: Interview techniques and analyses. In: S. B. Gluck & D. Patai (Eds), *Women's Words: The Feminist Practise of Oral History* (pp. 11–26). New York, NY: Routledge.

Angrosino, M. V., & Mays de Perez, K. A. (2000). Rethinking observation: From method to context. In: N. K. Denzin & Y. S. Lincoln (Eds), *Handbook of Qualitative Research* (2nd ed., pp. 673–702). Thousand Oaks: Sage Publications.

Audi, R. (General Editor) (1995). *The Cambridge dictionary of philosophy*. Cambridge, UK: Cambridge University Press.

Ballantyne, P. J. (1999). The social determinants of health: A contribution to the analysis of gender differences in health and illness. *Scandanavian Journal of Public Health, 27*(4), 290–295.

Batsleer, J., & Humphries, B. (2000). Welfare, exclusion, and political agency. In: J. Batsleer & B. Humphries (Eds), *Welfare, Exclusion, and Political Agency* (pp. 1–21). London, UK: Routledge.

Baxter, S. (1988). *No way to live: Poor women speak out*. Vancouver: New Star Books.

Becker, M. H. (1986). The tyranny of health promotion. *Public Health Review, 14*, 15–25.

Belle, D. (1982). Introduction. In: D. Belle (Ed.), *Lives in Stress: Women and Depression* (pp. 11–23). Beverly Hills: Sage Publications.

Belle, D. (1990). Poverty and women's mental health. *American Psychologist, 45*(3), 385–389.

Benzeval, M., Judge, K., & Whitehead, M. (1995). *Tackling inequalities in health: An agenda for action*. London, UK: Kings Fund.

Bettcher, D., & Lee, K. (2002). Glossary: Globalisation and public health. *Journal of Epidemiological and Community Health, 56*, 8–17.

Bloch, C. (1987). Female unemployment and knowledge of self. In: P. J. Pederson & R. Lund (Eds), *Unemployment: Theory, Policy and Structure* (pp. 339–353). New York: Walter de Gruter.

Brunner, E., & Marmot, M. (2000). Social organization, stress, and health. In: M. Marmot & R. G. Wilkinson (Eds), *Social Determinants of Health* (pp. 17–43). Oxford: Oxford University Press.

Calnan, M., & Williams, S. (1991). Style of life and the salience of health: An exploratory study of health related practises in households from differing socio-economic circumstances. *Sociology of Health and Illness, 13*(4), 506–529.

Cohen, M. (1998). Towards a framework for women's health. *Patient Education and Counselling, 33,* 187–196.

Colantonio, A. (1988). Lay concepts of health. *Health Values, 12*(5), 3–7.

Comstock, D. E., & Fox, R. (1993). Participatory research as critical theory: The North Bonneville, USA, experience. In: P. Park, M. Brydon-Miller, B. Hall & T. Jackson (Eds), *Voices of Change: Participatory Research in U.S. and Canada* (pp. 103–124). London: Bergin and Garvey.

Croghan, R., & Miell, D. (1998). Strategies of resistance: 'Bad' mothers dispute the evidence. *Feminism and Psychology, 8*(4), 445–465.

Deaton, A. (2002). Policy implications of the gradient of health and wealth. *Health Affairs, 21*(2), 1–9.

Doyal, L. (1995). *What makes women sick: Gender and the political economy of health.* London, UK: Macmillan Press Ltd.

Drew, M. L., & Dobson, K. S. (1999). The negative self-concept in clinical depression: A discourse analysis. *Canadian Psychology/Psychologie Canadienne, 40*(2), 192–204.

Fine, M., & Weis, L. (1998). *The unknown city: The lives of poor and working-class young adults.* Boston, MA: Beacon Press Books.

Ford, E. S. et al. (1991). Physical activity behaviors in lower and higher socioeconomic status populations. *American Journal of Epidemiology, 133*(12), 1246–1256.

Frank, J., & Mustard, J. F. (1994). The determinants of health from a historical perspective. *Journal of the American Academy of Arts and Sciences, 123*(4), 1–19.

Fraser, N. (1987). Women, welfare and the politics of need interpretation. *Hypatia, 2*(1), 103–121.

Fraser, N. (1997). Multiculturalism, antiessentialism, and racial democracy: A genealogy of the current impasse in feminist theory. In: N. Fraser (Ed.), *Justice Interruptus: Critical Reflection on the "Postsocialist" Condition* (pp. 173–188). New York, NY: Routledge.

Fraser, N., & Gordon, L. (1997). A genealogy of dependency: Tracing a keyword of the U.S. welfare state. In: N. Fraser (Ed.), *Justice Interruptus: Critical Reflections on the "Postsocialist" Condition* (pp. 121–149). New York, NY: Routledge.

Frisby, W., Crawford, S., & Dorer, T. (1997). Reflections on participatory action research: The case of low-income women accessing local physical activity services. *Journal of Sport Management, 11,* 8–28.

Gamble, S. (1999). *The routledge critical dictionary of feminism and postfeminism.* New York: Routledge.

Goffman, E. (1963). *Stigma: Notes on the management of spoiled identity.* New York: Simon & Schuster.

Greaves, L. (1996). *Smoke screen: Women's smoking and social control.* Halifax and London: Fernwood Publishing and Scarlet Press.

Hankivsky, O. (1999). *Social justice and women's health: A Canadian perspective.* Maritime Centre of Excellence for Women's Health, Halifax, NS. http://www.medicine.dal.ca/mcewh/oct-synthesis/hankivsky-justice.htm

Harding, S. (1987). Introduction: Is there a feminist method? In: S. Harding (Ed.), *Feminism and Methodology: Social Sciences Issues* (pp. 1–14). Bloomington: Indiana University Press.

Harvey, J. (2001). The role of sport and recreation policy in fostering citizenship: The Canadian experience. *Canadian Policy Research Networks Discussion Paper NO. F/17.* Ottawa, ON.

Health Canada (1997). Final table June 26th, 1997: Determinants and Lifespan N.D.G. *Health Canada.*

Health Canada (1999). Statistical report on the health of Canadians. *Federal, provincial, and territorial advisory committee on population health* (345 pp.).

Hooks, B. (1990). Choosing the margin as a space of radical openness. In: A. Garry & M. Pearsall (Eds), *Women, Knowledge and Reality: Exploration in Feminist Philosophy* (pp. 48–55). New York: Routledge.

Ingham, A. G. (1985). From public issue to personal trouble: Well-being and the fiscal crisis of the state. *Sociology of Sport Journal, 2*, 43–55.

Jarvis, M. J., & Wardle, J. (1999). Social patterning of individual health behaviours: The case of cigarette smoking. In: M. Marmot & R. G. Wilkinson (Eds), *Social Determinants of Health* (pp. 240–255). Oxford: Oxford University Press.

Jones, P. S., & Meleis, A. I. (1993). Health is empowerment. *Advances in Nursing Science, 15*(3), 1–14.

Kelly, D. M. (1996). Stigma stories: Four discourses about teen mothers, welfare, and poverty. *Youth and Society, 27*(4), 421–449.

Lewis, H. (1971). *Shame and guilt in neurosis*. New York: International Universities Press.

Lorber, J. (1997). *Gender and social construction of illness*. Thousand Oaks: Sage publications.

Lunman, K. (2002). Welfare reform comes to B. C. *The Globe and Mail*. Vancouver: A4.

Maguire, P. (2001). Uneven ground: Feminisms and action research. In: P. Reason & H. Bradbury (Eds), *Handbook of Action Research: Participative Inquiry and Practice* (pp. 59–69). London: Sage.

Marmot, M. (2002). The influence of income on health: Views of an epidemiologist. *Health Affairs, 21*(2).

Marmot, M. G. et al. (1991). Health inequalities among British Civil Servants: The Whitehall li study. *Lancet, 8*(June), 1387–1393.

Marmot, M. G., Shipley, M. J., & Rose, G. (1984). Inequalities in death-specific explanations of a general pattern? *Lancet, 5*(May), 1003–1006.

McAuley, E., & Rudolph, D. (1995). Physical activity, aging and psychological well-being. *Journal of Aging and Physical Activity, 3*, 67–96.

McDonough, P., & Walters, V. (2001). Gender and health: Reassessing patterns and explanations. *Social Science and Medicine, 52*, 547–559.

McLoyd, V. C., & Wilson, L. (1997). The strain of living poor: Parenting, social support, and child mental health. In: A. C. Huston (Ed.), *Children in Poverty: Child Development and Public Policy* (pp. 105–135). Cambridge, England: Cambridge University Press.

Morris, W. (Ed.) (1982). *The Houghton Mifflin Canadian dictionary of the English language*. Markham, ON: Houghton Mifflin Canada Limited.

National Council of Welfare (2000). Poverty profile, 1998. *National council of welfare*.

O'Connell, D. (1988). Poverty and the common woman. In: S. Baxter (Ed.), *No Way to Live: Poor Women Speak Out* (pp. 76–82). Vancouver: New Star Books.

Rahman, M. A. (1983). The theory and practice of participatory action research. In: O. Fals-Borda (Ed.), *The Challenge of Social Change* (pp. 108–132). Geneva: International Labour Organisation.

Raphael, D. (2001a). Inequality is bad for our hearts: Why low income and social exclusion are major causes of heart disease in Canada. *North York Heart Health Network* (71 pp.).

Raphael, D. (2001b). Communication Losing the forest for the trees: Health Equity Network. health-equity-network@jiscmail.ac.uk

Razavi, S. (1998). Gendered poverty and social change: An issue paper. *United Nations Research Institute for Social Development*.

Reason, P. (1998). Political, epistemological, ecological, and spiritual dimensions of participation. *Studies in Cultures, Organizations and Societies, 4,* 147–167.

Reid, C. (2000). Seduction and enlightenment in feminist action research. *Resources for Feminist Research, 28*(1/2), 169–188.

Reid, C. (2002). A full measure: Towards a comprehensive model for the measurement of women's health. *The B.C. Centre of Excellence for Women's Health* (35 pp.).

Reid, C., & Dyck, L. (2000). Implications: Future research, program and policy development. In: C. Reid, L. Dyck, H. McKay & W. Frisby (Eds), *The Health Benefits of Physical Activity for Girls and Women: Literature Review and Recommendations for Future Research and Policy* (pp. 201–205). Vancouver: British Columbia Centre of Excellence for Women's Health.

Repetti, R. L., & Wood, J. (1997). Families accommodating to chronic stress: Unintended and unnoticed processes. In: B. H. Gottlieb (Ed.), *Coping with Chronic Stress* (pp. 191–220). New York: Plenum.

Rootman, I., & Raeburn, J. M. (1994). The concept of health. In: A. Pederson, M. O'Neill & I. Rootman (Eds), *Health Promotion in Canada: Provincial, National and International Perspectives* (pp. 56–71). Toronto: W. B. Saunders Company Canada.

Ruzek, S. B., Clarke, A. E., & Olesen, V. L. (1997). Social, biomedical, and feminist models of women's health. In: S. B. Ruzek, A. E. Clarke & V. L. Olesen (Eds), *Women's Health: Complexities and Differences* (pp. 11–28). Columbus: Ohio State University Press.

Ruzek, S., & Hill, J. (1986). Promoting women's health: Redefining the knowledge base and strategies for change. *Health Promotion, 1*(3), 301–309.

Salk, H., Stanford, W., Swenson, N., & Luce, J. D. (1992). The politics of women and medical care. In: The Boston Women's Health Collective (Ed.), *The New Our Bodies, Ourselves* (pp. 651–698). New York, NY: Touchstone.

Sargent, C., & Brettell, C. (1996). Introduction: Gender, medicine and health. In: C. Sargent & C. Brettell (Eds), *Gender and Health: An International Perspective* (pp. 1–28). New Jersey: Prentice-Hall.

Scheff, T. J., Retzinger, S. M., & Ryan, M. T. (1989). Crime, violence, and self-esteem: Review and proposals. In: A. M. Mecca, N. J. Smelser & J. Vasconcellos (Eds), *The Social Importance of Self-Esteem* (pp. 165–199). Berkeley: University of Berkeley Press.

Schlicht, W. (1993). Mental health as a consequence of physical exercise: A metal-analysis. *The German Journal of Psychology, 17,* 88–92.

Schroeder, C., & Ward, D. (1998). Women, welfare, and work: One view of the debate. *Nursing Outlook, 46,* 226–232.

Schur, E. M. (1980). *The politics of deviance: Stigma contests and the uses of power.* Englewood Cliffs, NJ: Prentice-Hall.

Sedgewick, E. K. (1993). *Tendencies.* Durham: Duke University Press.

Shaw, M., Dorling, D., & Smith, G. D. (2000). Poverty, social exclusion, and minorities. In: M. Marmot & R. G. Wilkinson (Eds), *Social Determinants of Health* (pp. 211–239). Oxford: Oxford University Press.

Shiell, A., & Hawe, P. (1996). Health promotion community development and the tyranny of individualism. *Health Economics, 5,* 241–247.

Standing, K. (1998). Writing the voices of the less powerful: Research on lone mothers. In: J. Ribbens & R. Edwards (Eds), *Feminist Dilemmas in Qualitative Research: Public Knowledge and Private Lives* (pp. 186–202). London: Sage Publications.

Swanson, J. (2001). *Poor-Bashing: The Politics of Exclusion.* Toronto: Between the Lines.

The Globe & Mail (2001). A special interest supplement *Women's Health,* September 24th, 2001, W1.

Thibault, L., Frisby, W., & Kikulis, L. (1999). Interorganizational linkages as a strategic response to institutional pressures. *Managing Leisure, 4*, 125–141.

United Nations Economic and Social Council, Commission on the Status of Women Canada, 43rd session, March 1–12, 1999.

Wall, N. B. (1993). The beautiful strength of my anger put to use. In: L. Carty (Ed.), *And Still We Rise: Political Mobilizing in Contemporary Canada* (pp. 279–298). Toronto: Women's Press.

Wallerstein, N., & Freudenberg, N. (1998). Linking health promotion and social justice: A rationale and two case stories. *Health Education Research, 13*(3), 451–457.

Walters, V., Lenton, R., & Mckeary, M. (1995). Women's health in the context of women's lives. *Health Promotion Directorate, Health Canada.*

Welch, K. (1997). Women's health and low-income housing. *Journal of Nurse-Midwifery, 42*(6), 521–526.

Wendell, S. (1996). *The rejected body: Feminist philosophical reflections on disability.* New York, NY: Routledge.

Westkott, M. (1998). Culture and women's health. In: E. A. Blechman & K. D. Brownwell (Eds), *Behavioral Medicine and Women: A Comprehensive Handbook* (pp. 816–820). New York: Guildford Press.

White, P. (1998). Urban life and social stress. In: D. Pinder (Ed.), *The New Europe: Economy, Society and Environment* (pp. 305–321). Chichester, UK: Wiley.

White, P., Young, K., & Gillett, J. (1995). Bodywork as a moral imperative: Some critical notes on health and fitness. *Society and Leisure, 18*(1), 159–182.

Wilkinson, R. G. (1992). Income distribution and life expectancy. *British Medical Journal, 304*(6820), 165–168.

Wilkinson, R. G. (1996). *Unhealthy societies: The afflictions of inequality.* London and New York: Routledge.

Wilkinson, R. G. (2000). Putting the picture together: Prosperity, redistribution, health, and welfare. In: M. Marmot & R. G. Wilkinson (Eds), *Social Determinants of Health* (pp. 256–274). Oxford: Oxford University Press.

Young, I. M. (1990). *Justice and the politics of difference.* New Jersey: Princeton University Press.

RARIU AND LUO WOMEN: ILLNESS AS RESISTANCE TO MEN AND MEDICINE IN RURAL KENYA

Nancy Luke

INTRODUCTION

The connection between women's empowerment and health has been a growing concern among demographers and other social scientists, who theorize that empowering women – or enhancing their ability to define and make strategic life choices – will improve their reproductive health (Kabeer, 1999). The importance of empowering women became a central theme at the International Conference on Population and Development (ICPD) held in Cairo in 1994. The Cairo policy document codified the notion that women must be empowered in order for them and societies as a whole reach their reproductive health goals, including lowering fertility and population growth, stemming the spread of sexually transmitted diseases (STDs) and HIV/AIDS, and ensuring healthy pregnancy and delivery (Hodgson & Watkins, 1997; Sen & Batliwala, 2000).

Demographers have made inroads into many aspects of the study of women's empowerment and reproductive health, and a general demographic framework of women's empowerment has evolved in the literature. True to their roots, demographers have focused on defining and measuring empowerment and documenting the quantitative effects of empowerment on health outcomes. Empowerment, or agency, is usually operationalized as "decision-making power" and measured by women's ability to control or have a say in key household decisions

Gender Perspectives on Health and Medicine: Key Themes
Advances in Gender Research, Volume 7, 281–321
Copyright © 2003 by Elsevier Ltd.
All rights of reproduction in any form reserved
ISSN: 1529-2126/doi:10.1016/S1529-2126(03)07008-5

(Kabeer, 1999). Among demographers, resource theories are privileged, which emphasize that social and economic resources and information serve as key empowering agents for women. In particular, the demographic framework emphasizes the role that specific individual resources, such as education, income, and control over this income, play in increasing women's decision-making power, particularly within the household vis-à-vis husbands (Ghuman, 2001; Kishor, 2000; Malhotra & Mather, 1997; Mason, 1997; Riley, 1999).

In conceptualization of reproductive health outcomes, the demographic framework of empowerment generally perceives Western medical technologies and treatments to be superior to indigenous medicine.[1] The main focus of empowering women is to get them to visit and adopt these services, such as modern methods of contraception and visits to clinics for delivery and care of sick children (Caldwell & Caldwell, 1993). Although demographers set out to find universal ways of empowering women regardless of their social setting, many now realize the difficulty in finding such cross-cultural givens and recommend examining specific means of empowerment according to context (Mason & Smith, 2001).

Although the demographic framework of women's empowerment appears to address feminist concerns with the role that gender plays in reproductive health (Riley, 1999), the usefulness of this framework is nevertheless limited. The narrow focus on active decision-making, individual resources, conflict with husbands, and Western medical prescriptions neglects the needs and experiences of a large share of women. For example, many women continue to live in extremely gender stratified societies that provide limited access or little potential to gain the social and economic resources that ensure greater agency and better health. What happens when the recognized avenues to empowerment are constrained? In short, what happens to the least empowered? This paper calls on demographic researchers to go beyond their basic framework and, with the help of a feminist perspective and more in-depth methods of inquiry, take a closer look at women in restricted situations with few immediate options for empowerment (Greenhalgh & Li, 1995).

To accomplish this, we explore an indigenous women's reproductive illness, *rariu*, suffered by rural women among the Luo ethnic group in western Kenya. The constraints of strict gender stratification have traditionally ensured that rural Luo women cannot pose a direct, organized challenge to the gender hierarchy. Therefore, whatever challenges that are mounted need to be indirect. Illness becomes the vehicle for these indirect challenges, for quiet resistance to the patriarchy. In a context of strenuous sexual, reproductive, and productive obligations, *rariu* offers women a respite from social responsibilities, including hard work and sexual intercourse, and deflects the stigma of role deviations, such as infertility and miscarriage.

In rural Kenya, few women possess the needed social and economic resources to individually challenge their local subordination, nor can they invoke the label *rariu* individually. These disempowered women need the support and legitimation of women's illness networks – those elderly women and healers who identify and legitimate sickness – to do so. The women's community has traditional authority in the realm of women's health and reproduction, and this limited power in the rural community empowers them to orchestrate the illness *rariu*.

Although *rariu*'s symptoms are similar to other reproductive conditions, such as STDs, pelvic inflammatory disease (PID), prolapsed uterus, and obstetric complications, most women are influenced by their illness networks to label these symptoms as *rariu*. According to our household survey in the study area, 61.2% of women had suffered from *rariu*. Hence, the women's community has constructed a way for many disempowered women to resist society's most stringent demands through female solidarity in traditional healing.

Luo women also resist Western medicine's labels and treatment with *rariu*. The household survey data reveal that 72.2% of women reported seeking treatment for *rariu* from traditional healers and 27.8% went to a clinic or hospital. Conflict arises when the Luo women present at the clinic with the symptoms and label of *rariu*. From the clinicians' perspective, *rariu* is not a legitimate illness because its cluster of symptoms does not parallel any specific condition in biomedicine. Clinicians delegitimate women's illness experience, which contributes to incomplete or ineffective treatment, or even no treatment at all. Rural Luo women nevertheless use Western medicine for what they can get out of it – usually temporary relief of the symptoms – but they do not allow it to dominate their decisions. Women end up delegitimating its assistance because it does not cure them, and they return to the care of a traditional healer. This process of "mutual delegitimation" represents another type of agency on the part of disempowered women in rural Kenya.

Expanding the Demographic Framework of Women's Empowerment

The demographic framework of women's empowerment focuses on active power, individual resources, spousal conflict, and Western medical prescriptions. Based on insights from feminist researchers in particular, we wish to modify this framework in several important ways.

First, the demographic framework emphasizes individual women's active agency in making decisions and carrying them out in the face of opposition. This framework does not recognize more passive forms of resistance employed by women who lack the power to undertake direct action and decision-making. Feminist researchers have brought attention to more informal and hidden forms of agency, including deception, reflection, passivity, accommodation, and other "backstage" strategies (Armstrong, 1999; Inhorn, 1996; Kabeer, 1997, 1999; Lock & Kaufert, 1998; Malhotra & Mather, 1997; Wolf, 1992). With these quiet forms of resistance, women can maneuver within the strict confines of patriarchy, although they rarely transform the gender system.

The nature of patriarchy shapes the possible forms and sites of resistance available to women in a particular setting (Inhorn, 1996; Kabeer, 1999; Lock & Kaufert, 1998; Stein, 1997). For rural Luo women, opportunities for resistance are best informal and situated in the realm of traditional healing, where the women's community has traditionally held authority and therefore women are less subject to male control. In addition to *rariu*, secret use of family planning has been identified as an indirect form of resistance among Luo women (Green & Feyisetan, 2000; Watkins et al., 1997).

Second, demographers' focus on individual resources as the major means to empowerment disregards the importance of collective action and the contribution of women's solidarity as a resource in itself (Adams et al., 2002; Malhotra & Mather, 1997). Feminist researchers have pointed out that African women have a history of exercising power through organized cooperatives at the local level, including the production and use of performance and costume and spirit possession cults (Hodgson & McCurdy, 2001; McClain, 1989). In some contexts, less formal types of organization are more influential in empowerment (Schuler et al., 1996). Particularly relevant for our study is the role of women's illness networks, which are defined as those people whom sick persons consult about illness and who provide information and advice that influence decision-making (Anyinam, 1987; Feierman, 1985; Freund & McGuire, 1999; Kleinman, 1988, 1980; McKinlay, 1973; Pescosolido, 1992).

In Africa, informal illness networks often serve as a form of female solidarity (Donaldson, 1997). Luo women's illness networks are mainly composed of elder women and traditional healers in the community. These women have the major responsibility of identifying and labeling women's symptoms as *rariu*. Although informal, illness networks serve as a substitute for other empowering resources, such as education or income, which many women may lack (Freund & McGuire, 1999).

Third, the focus on power relations between men and women hides other conflicts that are also important in the empowerment process. We recognize the plurality of groups vying for power in social life (Collins, 1994), and in addition to the pervasive conflict between men and women, this study also examines the conflict between women, and between women and alternative forms of medicine.

Feminists acknowledge that conflict between women may contribute to further gender subordination, and a prime example is women working for men, often called the "patriarchal bargain" (Chafetz, 1990; Inhorn, 1996). In this situation, women buy into the patriarchal system and use it for their own personal security and advancement, often to the detriment of other women. For example, individual women may gain power within the family over the life course as mothers-in-law who in turn use this power to dominate daughters-in-law or younger women (Das Gupta, 1996; Entwisle & Coles, 1990). In Luo society, illness networks are sites of power struggles between women. On the one hand, elder women hold authority over women's health and reproduction and, in exchange for this power, they enforce male-defined reproductive, sexual, and productive obligations of women. On the other hand, illness networks represent solidarity among women, and both young and older women's implicit cooperation is needed to ensure the continued existence of *rariu*.

The demographic framework underscores the importance of biomedical knowledge and practice and deems the process of empowerment completed when women step into the clinic for care. On the contrary, we emphasize that conflict between patient and doctor and their competing medical models exists and influences illness legitimation and treatment. Feminists and medical sociologists have criticized the dominance of the Western medical establishment and the associated medicalization of life (Conrad, 1992; Conrad & Schneider, 1992). The (bio)medicalization of natural conditions, such as menstruation, pregnancy, and menopause, has been shown to reinforce gender subordination (Annandale, 1998; Conrad, 1992; Lock, 1998; Lorber, 1997; Martin, 1992), similar to the (traditional) medicalization of women's reproduction and illness among the Luo. Feminist researchers have pointed out that women can resist this process and have used medical labels, technologies, and practices for their own ends, such as infertility treatments or modern contraceptives (Bledsoe et al., 1998; Gill & Maynard, 1995; Greenhalgh & Li, 1995; Keilmann, 1998; Lock & Kaufert, 1998). With *rariu*, rural women use traditional medical labels for their own purposes.

In addition, biomedicine has been shown to delegitimate, or systematically disconfirm, women's own perceptions of illness (Ware, 1992). In rural Kenya, clinicians trained in Western medicine do not recognize *rariu* as a legitimate illness because it does not fit their scientific model of disease. In many Western contexts, such delegitimation would be detrimental to women, as a biomedical explanation is necessary to justify women's suffering and a biomedical cure is the accepted means of seeking health (Aronowitz, 1998). Nevertheless, Western medicine is not the medical hegemon in rural Kenya, and Luo women do not need its certification to have suffering recognized as real. Women do use Western medicine as an alternative route for treatment; when it does not cure them, women reject it the same way it rejects their illness *rariu*.

Fourth, investigation into the complexities and subtleties of illness as quiet resistance is difficult to achieve by relying solely on the quantitative data that most demographers collect (Greenhalgh & Li, 1995; Riley, 1999). Quantitative methods provide an essential view of the prevalence of illness in a population and how illness is associated with particular characteristics of individuals and communities. Combining these findings with more intensive ethnographic inquiry that listens to women's own experiences gives a fuller picture of the meaning of illness in society beyond counting symptoms (Boonmongkon et al., 2001). Our expanded empowerment framework, coupled with qualitative data collection and analysis, helps us see how the body and its condition are not just "outcomes" but rather sites of empowerment.

Subsequent to this introduction, the paper contains the following sections. The second section provides a detailed look at the gender system in rural Luo society. Here, we see how the specific culture and history of the Luo shape women's present opportunities for resistance. The third section provides a description of *rariu* and its meaning for rural Luo women. We see how *rariu* is constructed as a response to women's expected behaviors and how it fits into existing Luo concepts of the body. The fourth section examines the process of legitimation of *rariu*, focusing on women's interactions with the three powerful groups that affect illness decision-making: husbands, illness networks, and healers. We also use data from the household survey to show that the least empowered women suffer most from *rariu*. The fifth section examines women's health-seeking behavior for *rariu* and the clash between rural women's and clinicians models of illness and treatment. Before commencing with the next section, we offer a brief explanation of our data sources.

Data for this study were collected by the Kenya Diffusion and Ideational Change Project as well as the author's own field trips. The KDICP took place in four sublocations of Nyanza Province, western Kenya from 1994 to 2000.[2] The initial phase of the project conducted semi-structured interviews and focus groups with ever-married women of reproductive age, as well as informal interviews with additional women, clinic personnel, and traditional healers. The household survey data were collected from a random sample of women, about half of whom ($N = 449$) were asked questions from a module focusing on conversations about *rariu*. These respondents were asked to name a maximum of four conversational (or network) partners with whom they talked about *rariu*, where they talked, how frequently, and the characteristics of those with whom they talked. The author conducted additional semi-structured and informal interviews with women, men, traditional healers, and clinicians during three subsequent research trips to Nyanza in 1999–2001. Here, the purpose was a more focused ethnographic study aimed at understanding women's illness experience and the community's perception of *rariu*.

THE LUO GENDER SYSTEM AND EXPECTATIONS FOR WOMEN

The Luo are of Nilotic origin and compose one of the largest ethnic groups in Kenya, numbering approximately three million in 1999 (Daily Nation, 2000). They reside primarily in Nyanza Province in western Kenya. The organization of social institutions, particularly bride-wealth, polygyny, and patrilineal descent – the combination of which Parkin (1978) calls the Luo "cultural logic" – ensures male control of women throughout their lives. Luo men exercise family and property decision-making and are highly restrictive of women's sexuality and movements. Luo gender ideology holds that women must be under the guardianship of men to ensure that they do not commit deviant acts, such as adultery or mismanagement of resources (Luke, 2000). In exchange for this protection, women are expected to be respectful of their male guardians and obedient.

This combination of structural and ideological domination has remained strong over the decades (Parkin, 1969, 1978; Southall, 1973; Watkins et al., 1997) and translates into several expected roles for Luo women: (1) women should always be under the guardianship of a man and obey his authority; (2) women should bear many children, especially males; (3) women should be available for sex with husbands – and husbands only; and (4) women should work hard to support the family and domestic homestead. Following these expectations, deviance is defined as unwed, disobedient, infertile, sexually unwilling or unfaithful, and indolent. Sanctions include divorce, separation, and beatings. This section discusses each of these roles in turn and accompanying male sanctions against transgressions from these social responsibilities.

Role 1: Marriage and Obedience

The first institution comprising the cultural logic of the Luo is bride-wealth. In many sub-Saharan African societies, the kinship group is the primary social unit, which historically worked collectively to cultivate family farms on abundant land. Due to a natural shortage of labor, men were encouraged to marry numerous wives, who supplied labor as well as produced the next generation of workers. Thus, an economic value was attached to women's capabilities, which men controlled and traded through marriage arrangements (Caldwell et al., 1993). Among the Luo, bride-wealth cattle symbolize a woman's worth and continue to be exchanged between families to mark the transfer of the rights to a woman's sexuality, progeny, and labor from one lineage of men to another (Blount, 1973; Cohen & Atieno Odhiambo, 1989; Ndisi, 1974; Ocholla-Ayayo, 1976; Pala, 1980). With bride-wealth exchange, a husband's control over his wife is in principle absolute, and men expect wives to obey and respect them (Mbogoh, 1986; Potash, 1978; Watkins et al., 1997).

Polygyny is the second principle of the Luo cultural logic, and its importance to the Luo is signified by the high levels that continue to exist today. In our sample of rural Luo women, 34% are in a polygynous union. Marriage to many wives is a symbol of wealth for men, and continues to be practiced in light of competing needs for income, such as education of children (Parkin, 1978). Reasons for polygynous marriages include increasing the prestige of men but also stem from the first wife's (or wives') deviance: If a first wife is infertile, bears only girls, is lazy or too weak or sickly to carry out work, or if she becomes unattractive to her husband, an additional wife may be found.

In order to ensure that women continue to carry out their responsibilities, divorce and separation are held as realistic threats by men (Hay, 1982; Potash, 1978). Women could be divorced for reasons such as adultery, laziness, or acting with a "hard head," i.e. going against a husband's wishes. A divorced woman must leave her husband's homestead, and her children are not permitted to accompany her, as they belong to the husband's lineage (Potash, 1978). Beatings also appear to be accepted punishment for female deviance (Miruka, 1997; Potash, 1978).

The third institution is the organization of Luo society into strong patrilineages with patrilocal residence, the combination of which means that inheritance and residence are centered on the male lineage. Luos also practice exogamous marriage, which implies that wives must come from unrelated, often distant, clans. This structure ensures that women are "marginal, transient outsiders" who move into lineages of men and rankings of unrelated women (Hay, 1982, p. 113).

The relationships between unrelated women within an extended-family homestead are characterized by cooperation and conflict. Depending on age, ranking of wives, and status, some of these co-resident women are in positions of authority relative to new or younger wives. Mothers-in-law have authority over a new wife's productive activities, including cooking and farming (Hay, 1976; Ndisi, 1974; Potash, 1986; Whyte & Wanjiru Kariuki, 1997). Due to high levels of polygyny, co-wives are abundant and are often a source of jealousy between women who vie for the attentions and resources of husbands (Parkin, 1978; Potash, 1978, 1995). Senior sisters-in-law may also have authority over newer wives within the homestead. In our sample, 51.5% of the respondents had one or more co-wives or sisters-in-law[3] living in their homestead, and 12.1% had one or more mothers-in-law in their homestead.[4]

These elder women not only have some degree of power over new wives, but they may be a source of camaraderie and support as well. If relations are good, co-wives or sisters-in-law may share domestic tasks, farm work, and childrearing, for example (Mbogoh, 1986). Women seek the advice of mothers-in-law on issues that deal with married life, fertility, child care, and illness (Potash, 1995). Illness in particular appears to be an area of cooperation between women, and in addition to offering advice, resident women take over the domestic tasks of others in time of sickness (Ndisi, 1974).

Role 2: Reproduction

Luo women are expected to produce many children and births should follow at regular intervals (Pala, 1980; Shipton, 1989). Women especially need sons, to symbolically carry on the male lineage (and thereby afford women higher status) and practically to support them in old age. Producing children also assures marital stability (Hay, 1982; Potash, 1978). Infertility or subfertility, including bearing only girl children and repeated miscarriages or child deaths, are a social disgrace for a woman because it ends the genealogical line of both her and her husband (Kawango, 1995) and are also a practical dilemma, as she will have no sons to support her in old age. Barren women or women with no sons face the threats of divorce or polygynous remarriage, as a husband will search for a new wife to produce the desired offspring.

Despite the high value placed on children, successful pregnancy, delivery, and childrearing are difficult in the rural Kenyan context, and pregnancy and delivery place a woman at risk of morbidity and mortality.[5] Luo women usually keep working until the last weeks or days before delivery and often continue to perform highly strenuous tasks, such as carrying water or fuel wood on their heads and other farming duties (Ocholla-Ayayo, personal communication).

The women's community traditionally retained authority in all aspects of women's reproductive matters and ensured that women carried out their fertility expectations successfully (Geissler et al., 2000; Parkin, 1978). As mentioned, advice may be passed onto younger women by elder women or "grandmothers." This "informal" health care is something that, as our informants told us, "every mother knows" and includes numerous herbal remedies for minor illnesses (Geissler et al., 2000). Slightly more serious illness as well as the processes of pregnancy and childbirth have been relegated to herbalists and traditional midwives (Kawango, 1995). The specific type of healer is usually called a *nyamrerwa*, plural *nyamreche*. A *nyamrerwa* is a minor medicine man or woman who does not possess *bilo*, or magic power, but knows how to obtain drugs from specific plants used for curing people. *Nyamreche* specializing in women's and children's conditions are usually women (Hauge, 1974; Nyamwaya, 1986; Ocholla-Ayayo, 1976), and they continue to advise and treat pregnant women today (Moore et al., 2002). For example, *nyamreche* have traditionally prescribed daily doses of "pot medicine" – a herbal concoction kept in a clay pot – to ward off illness, and they also give advice about diet, exercise, and work patterns (Moore et al., 2002; Nyamwaya, 1986).

Nyanza has recently begun a fertility decline. In 1993, the total fertility rate for Nyanza Province was 5.8 and by 1998 it had declined to 5.0 (NCPD et al., 1994, 1999). The average number of children born per woman in our sample is 4.5. Although fertility norms remain high overall, many women wish to limit their number of children, particularly because they are "expensive." Family planning programs introduced in the late 1960s and Western medical care in general have stripped away some of the power of elders in terms of overall fertility decisions and the women's community in terms of providing birth control knowledge and methods, and alternative pregnancy and delivery services. Watkins et al. (1997) find that rural Luo women no longer seek advice about family planning from elder women, and, in fact, many women reported secretly using contraception to circumvent husbands and relatives' pressure for more children. Husbands dislike their wives' use of family planning secretly not only because it may upset their own fertility desires, but because it represents wife disobedience (Green & Feyisetan, 2000; Watkins et al., 1997).

Role 3: Sexual Availability and Faithfulness

In their survey of African groups, Caldwell et al. (1992) determined that the Luo are one of the most restrictive societies in terms of women's sexuality. According to respondents and the literature, women's sexual activities have always been restricted to marriage (Blount, 1973). A wife's adultery brought shame and tarnished a man's honor (Parkin, 1978). With respect to female power over sexuality within marriage, women can make limited sexual demands, but they are not as directly imposed or fulfilled as are the sexual demands of husbands (Ocholla-Ayayo, 1991).

Adultery is believed to affect a woman's ability to carry out her social obligations, including sexual intercourse and childbearing. For example, the Luo believe that an extramarital affair during pregnancy will lead to miscarriage, ante-partum hemorrhage, the habitual loss of children, or the indigenous illness *chira*, which is associated with breaking Luo traditions (Kawango, 1995; Nyamwaya, 1986; Ocholla-Ayayo, 1976; Parkin, 1978; Sindiga, 1995; Whyte & Wanjiru Kariuki, 1997; Wilson, 1955).

There is greater tolerance for sexual activities outside marriage for men than for women. It is a widespread belief in Africa that men need frequent sexual gratification (NRC, 1996), and as a response, it appears that Luo men are expected to have multiple partners (Watkins et al., 1997, for Africa see Adepoju &

Mbugua, 1997). Some observers point to the institution of polygyny as one way to fulfill the excess male desire, but it also can be seen as perpetuating the expectation of multiple sexual partners for men (Caldwell et al., 1991). Nevertheless, if Luo men are unable to afford numerous wives, there appears to be little sanction against extramarital partners unless it is "openly promiscuous" or "blatant" (Blount, 1973).

There is a widespread acknowledgement among Luo women that men like to "move around." Women appear to resent this freedom and disapprove of their husbands' extramarital partners. African women are mostly at risk of STDs and HIV/AIDS from their husbands (Caldwell et al., 1991), and the Luo women we interviewed believe that husbands and "other women" men sleep with are to blame for the spread of these diseases.

There are several Luo illnesses that are thought to be sexually transmitted and brought about by adultery. The illness *nyach* (mostly closely associated with syphilis and gonorrhea), *segete* (similar to menstrual cramps), and Western medical categories of STDs are all linked to promiscuity. Men usually attribute the spread of STDs to adulterous women (see Moss et al., 1999, for the Luhya, a neighboring ethnic group of the Luo). This has made STDs very stigmatizing for women in the community, whereas our observations suggest they are a symbol of potency for men.

Role 4: Production for Family and Farm

Women's productive labor is highly valued in Luo society (Hay, 1982; Pala, 1980; Potash, 1989; Shipton, 1989). The sexual division of labor in African is such that women oversee food production for the entire family, the care of children, and maintenance of the domestic sphere. Modernization of the economy has made Luos beholden to cash, which is needed to pay for expenses such as taxes, schooling, and modern goods, such as clothing, salt, and soap. Men are responsible for larger expenses, such as medical payments and school fees, and women are responsible for domestic expenditures (Shipton, 1989). Increasingly, women must earn a cash to meet these smaller expenses and contribute to the larger ones (Hay, 1982).

Women's productive power is limited structurally and ideologically, however. Women face limitations on their ownership and access to property and economic resources, which impacts their potential for entrepreneurialship and their ability to increase their own earnings and agency. For example, the rights of women to land and their rewards from it have been diminished in the postcolonial period. Under the land tenure system carried out during this time, land ownership has been transferred almost exclusively to men (Pala, 1980). In addition, the advent of cash crops, such as tobacco and sugar cane, has brought about increased monetarization of agriculture. Such crops are usually grown and harvested by family labor but subsequently sold and the proceeds controlled by men. This process has increased women's burden of labor and concentrated wealth in the hands of men, who often use newly-earned money for personal consumption, including drinking, girlfriends, and prostitution (Hay, 1982; Pala, 1980; Shipton, 1989).

Many Luo men have migrated from their rural homes in search of paid labor, a trend that has increased since colonial times (Ndisi, 1974; Pala, 1980; Shipton, 1989). In our sample, 24.6% of women said their husbands usually do not reside in the rural homestead. The result of this male out-migration on women's situation has been double-edged: on the one hand, male absence has made women largely responsible for overseeing the household and farm. This sole responsibility has brought women more autonomy and existence beyond the gaze of male guardianship (Cohen & Atieno Odhiambo, 1989). On the other hand, this sole responsibility has produced a great amount of work for women, particularly in agriculture, and little real freedom from traditional role expectations. Leaving women to tend the farm has also reinforced the notion that women should remain in subsistence farming at home and the economic opportunities of the cash economy and urban wage employment are open only to men (Pala, 1979).

Women may also migrate, but they do not appear to go as regularly as men or for as long. In our sample, 39.2% of women reported they have lived outside of Nyanza Province for six or more months since marriage, which affords them greater exposure to modern ideas and practices. Education is also recognized by the Luo as a means to increased prosperity, however education of women is especially limited. In our sample, only 13.1% of women had any years of secondary schooling and 20.0% had no schooling.

Over the past decades, serious land shortages have appeared in Nyanza along with reductions in crops yields, and farming is less likely to be a means of secure income for a family (Francis & Hoddinott, 1993; Potash, 1986). These developments, coupled with the need for cash income, has compelled women to add income-generating activities to the onerous work of subsistence agriculture and household duties (Potash, 1995). Occupations available to women in rural Nyanza are limited, however. In our sample, only 4.1% of women earned a salary, while 38.2% reported that they earn nothing. Most women in the study areas continue to undertake subsistence farming to feed their families and, if able, to grow some crops for sale. These crops include finger millet and groundnuts, whose cultivation require long hours of bending and weeding. Women's other economic activities include small trade or businesses, such as selling "something small," like baskets, fish, or woven mats (Watkins et al., 1996).

Opportunities for Resistance

The rise of the state and government institutions, including the Western medical establishment, has usurped some of the traditional power of elder men and women in sub-Saharan African over the past century, first with colonization and later independence. The result of these developments, accompanied by the advent of a monetarized economy, has afforded women access to new resources, such as education, employment, and urban residence, as well as autonomy from men and elders (Collins, 1971; Collins et al., 1993). Nevertheless, past studies and our more recent observations conclude that the structural and ideological constraints of patriarchy in Luo society continue to limit women's social and economic opportunities while maintaining firm restrictions on female sexuality and expectations for reproduction and production. Women continue to be held to realistic threats of beating, divorce, and separation at the hands of husbands if they do not carry out expected norms of faithfulness, industriousness, and submissiveness.

The contemporary organization of Luo patriarchy shapes women's opportunities for resistance. There is no history of Luo women's overt resistance at the group level (Parkin, 1978), perhaps stemming from the fact that all wives come as foreigners to the male lineage into which they have married, and there is no overarching organization of Luo women today. Parkin's (1978) study of the Luo in Nairobi and Kampala concludes that women's organized resistance is constrained by the persistence of the Luo "cultural logic," and the patriarchal bargain ensures that women will not challenge this male control. At the local level, our research finds that few Luo women possess the social and economic resources that could empowerment them to challenge men and medicine individually.

As a result of these constraints, rural Luo women's best opportunities for resistance are indirect. Their dependence on one another for friendship, advice, and assistance fosters an informal solidarity in the community. This female solidarity, combined with women's limited authority in the realm of medicine, empowers them to construct an illness that serves as quiet resistance to their enduring social obligations.

THE MEANING OF *RARIU* FOR RURAL LUO WOMEN

This section offers a detailed description of the illness *rariu* and its meaning for rural Luo women, including *rariu*'s symptoms; its relevance to Luo concepts of the body; its effects on normal functioning; and its causes and prescriptions. We also make reference to an alternative biomedical interpretation of *rariu*'s characteristics and Western medical prescription.

Symptoms of Rariu

When women talk about *rariu* they begin by placing their arm across their abdomen, often bending at the waist. The symptoms women cite are varied, but common words or idioms appear. Following are some descriptions of *rariu* from rural Luo women (common idioms italicized and sublocations and respondent's interview number are given in parentheses):

> When I'm heavy like this (pregnant), my *lower abdomen hurts* me a lot. It even makes me walk slowly (Ugina, woman 8).

> When I am pregnant I have *lower abdomen pain and it feels like that thing is coming out* of my rectum (Kawadhgone, woman 3).

> At times (*rariu*) lays parallel in the lower abdomen. *When it's blocking the lower abdomen*, then I can't walk (Obisa, woman 122).

> It was *rariu* because it *sits across your lower abdomen* and *even blocks the baby* (Obisa, woman 128).

There is a high degree of consensus on the main symptoms of *rariu*. Women agree that there is pain in the stomach or lower abdomen, which may be accompanied by pain during sexual intercourse and pain in the back, thighs, and legs or headache. Women may have difficulty urinating, defecating, or breathing. *Rariu* may cause weakness and difficulty walking, sitting, or standing erect. The *nyamreche* use similar language as the rural women to describe *rariu*: "something coming out" and "blocks" a birth; something that can be touched or felt in the lower abdomen; and something "hard in the abdomen."

Rariu is recognized as a women's illness, mostly occurring among married women. When women and *nyamreche* discuss *rariu*, they usually situate it during pregnancy. However, when asked, they also point out that all women can get it, regardless of marital or pregnancy status or parity. Men and children may also suffer from *rariu*, but less frequently, which will be discussed below. Women indicate that *rariu* may appear periodically and repeatedly, often noting they suffer "whenever I am pregnant." The high amount of inter-informant agreement about the symptoms of *rariu*, the repetition of idioms describing it, and the use of common hand and arm gestures suggest a shared understanding or cultural consensus about *rariu* among rural Luo women.

Conception of Rariu in the Body

Rural Luo women and *nyamreche* conceptualize *rariu* as a "thing" that causes illness when it is out of its normal position in the body. In its improper position, it is described as "sitting across" the lower abdomen, and it causes pain and inhibits normal functioning. We were told that *rariu* literally means "comes before the fetus" or "the one that goes across."

The perception that *rariu* is a "thing" in the lower abdomen coincides with the feeling that something is "pressing" on the lower abdomen or something "wants to come out" instead of the baby, or urine, or feces. In serious cases, *rariu* may protrude from the body as well. Following is a description of the conception of *rariu* given by a nyamrerwa. Idioms particular to *rariu* are italicized.

> *Rariu* is something that *blocks*. It affects people in two ways: During pregnancy and normal life (non-pregnancy). During pregnancy it *blocks the way of the child* just before birth. It *drops down* before birth or after, and then it must be *returned*. It is normally painful when touched, and it can be felt. After birth, it prevents blood from coming out to free the woman. Ordinarily the blood that comes out after birth makes the woman feel free. In normal life, it is a kind of *moving tumor* and prevents the sperm from reaching the eggs. It also *blocks* the eggs from dropping to the fallopian tubes. The *rariu drops down* at conception to *block the way* (Obisa, nyamrerwa 1).

Some respondents equate the "thing" *rariu* to the uterus, worms, or simply a nondescript entity in the lower abdomen. This perception coincides with other Luo concepts of the body. For example, Luos have traditionally believed that there are beneficial worms in the body that sustain life by digesting food and transforming the corpse back into soil at death (Geissler, 1998a; Ndisi, 1974). When provoked by occurrences in the natural or social environment, the worms cause illness. Herbal remedies are needed to "calm them down" and balance the inner force between the human body and independently-acting worms. Western medical treatment can be fatal if the worms are harmed or killed. It is important to note that worms are a natural, necessary part of the body and should not be killed, only appeased if they are harming an individual (Geissler, 1998a).

Just as worms are a necessary, yet potentially harmful, living part of the body, so too is the "thing" *rariu*. *Rariu* does not appear to have any specific positive functions, but it does cause harm when it is "outside" of its normal position. The measures that need to be taken to "return" *rariu* to its natural place in the body and cure the illness are discussed below.

Although *rariu* is categorized as a single, distinct illness by the rural Luo women and their healers, its broad range of symptoms may be translated into numerous conditions in Western medicine,[6] mostly associated with reproduction. Women who complain of difficulties with urination may have urinary tract infections (UTIs) or PID, and pain in the lower abdomen is associated with PID as well. A "thing" protruding from the body may be prolapsed uterus or rectum. The belief that something is "blocking" the uterus may be a reproductive tract infection (RTI), PID, a prolapsed uterus, or an STD. Women who cannot "do anything" may also be anemic. Some of the symptoms of *rariu* suggest harmless conditions defined by Western medicine, such as braxton hicks contractions during pregnancy or simply a fetus pushing on nerve endings. *Rariu* appears to be an umbrella term for most conditions in the lower abdominal region.

Rariu *and Women's Reproductive and Productive Roles*

When *rariu* leaves its normal position in the body, it impairs a woman's ability to fulfill her expected roles. Most importantly, *rariu* can affect all stages of reproduction. It can "block" or prevent conception, or nourishment to the fetus (causing miscarriage), or delivery of a baby. In worst cases, *rariu* can cause infertility.[7] During pregnancy, it wants to come out before or instead of the baby, producing pregnancy complications. Following are examples of delaying childbirth and blocking fertilization (R = "respondent" and I = "interviewer"):

> *Something settles in the abdomen* so that when it is time for giving birth, *something blocks the child's outlet*. It can delay the child's birth for another one or two weeks (Owich woman, focus group 2).

> R: And even if you want to get pregnant you will find (*rariu*) also fights there (prevents it).
> I: How does it fight?
> R: It fights in the sense that, let's say you want to get pregnant. There is a type of worm that if you hear it making a noise like "akuuuu," it can spoil (the pregnancy) at once. This means that *thing* is nearby there and can spoil it. So there is nothing that can happen (you cannot conceive). Then you hear people commenting that "so-and-so's" womb has not stood (she has not conceived) . . . because of that *rariu* (Obisa, woman 150).

Rariu not only inhibits women's reproduction; it interferes with women's sexual and productive roles as well, including completing domestic tasks, working in the fields, and being available for sexual intercourse. There is consensus among the women and *nyamreche* that when one is affected by *rariu*, it is so painful that one cannot work, walk, have sexual intercourse, or, in sum, "do anything." There are numerous stories of women who were bedridden and could not leave the house. Most women say they have *rariu* repeatedly, and it can last for days to weeks to months. Some women may be afflicted with less severe symptoms, which allow them to complete their household duties.[8]

Causes of Rariu

There is a high degree of consensus among women and *nyamreche* that the main causes of *rariu* are hard work or carrying heavy loads, sexual transmission, and ingesting modern cooking oils. Other causes mentioned include continued childbearing, bewitching, and worries. Due to these numerous origins, it appears that *nyamreche* find it difficult to locate any particular cause for a particular episode. In all the accounts we heard of *rariu* cases, a specific cause was never mentioned or established for any one case. Although some say *rariu* can be transmitted from woman to woman, its spread through this route is evidently minimal, such that *rariu* does not become an epidemic that can be blamed on women. Thus, *rariu* is not a means of group defiance by women; it retains its character as resistance to social obligations by individuals.

The cause of *rariu* attributed to the use of modern cooking oils represents an attempt by the elder healers to warn women against the new and modern ways of thinking and behaving. Traditionally, fat from cow's milk (known as *ghee*) was used for cooking (Odaga, 1986), whereas today new commercial cooking oils are used. These new oils do not "rhyme" with *rariu* and traditional conceptions of the body.

In addition to modern cooking oils, women and *nyamreche* note that abandoning the traditional health instructions for pregnant women also contributes to *rariu*. For example, the practice of drinking "pot medicine" has diminished greatly, perhaps with the advent of prenatal care and hospital delivery. Thus, some of the causes that elder women and *nyamreche* attribute to *rariu* reflect their lamentation of the "good old days," perhaps in response to their losing some authority over pregnancy and childbirth, and generational power more generally.

The causes clinicians cite for *rariu* overlap with those of the rural women: hard work, sexual transmission, pregnancy-related complications, abortion, or frequent childbearing. The clinicians' stated causes are connected to the Western medical model, however, and focus on the connection between women's everyday activities and physiological problems associated with reproductive morbidity. The physical exertion and frequency of tasks, such as procuring water and fuel wood or weeding, can lead to symptoms similar to *rariu*, including fatigue, sore hips and legs, and conditions such as prolapsed uterus (Paolisso & Leslie, 1995). Women of high parity may experience prolapsed uterus, and women may be infected by husbands or other partners with STDs. The Western medical conditions associated with *rariu*, including UTIs, which can lead to PID, or a prolapsed uterus, can also "compromise a woman's ability to achieve and sustain a pregnancy and to produce healthy children" (Erwin, 1993, p. 137). Furthermore, physical and mental abuse has been linked to chronic pelvic pain (Heise, 1994), which is also a symptom of *rariu*.

Rariu *and Responsibility for Sexual Transmission*

The stigma attached to sexually transmitted diseases weighs more heavily on Luo women than men. *Rariu* is resistance to this gender difference in stigma in two ways.

First, *rariu* is not embarrassing and deflects any suspicion of improper behavior on the part of women. *Rariu* may be sexually transmitted and share some of the symptoms of biomedically and indigenously recognized STDs; nonetheless, women readily distinguish between *rariu* and stigmatized reproductive illnesses, including *nyach* and syphilis, for example. *Rariu* is a neutral illness label, which may be an explanation for its application to a broad array of symptoms and mostly to women (see Erwin, 1993, for indigenous African labels for STDs).

> *Nyach* is very shameful because everyone will know that you have been with someone or for girls (unmarried women), you know they've been with someone. *Rariu* is not an embarrassing one because it's not necessarily brought by prostitution or "moving around" (Obisa, woman 129).

Second, women often associate *rariu* with men's extramarital sexual behavior or "movements," and we believe this signifies an attempt by women to reproach men for these bad behaviors. The fault for sexual transmission of *rariu* is usually described by women as "men bring it to women" or "men bring it to the home."

> I: What causes *rariu*? . . .
> R: Sometimes it is said that it is hard labor, sometimes it is said that the way men have many movements, he could get it from somebody and bring it to you, the woman . . . With men, you can't know his movements (Obisa, woman 150).

Women see men as "carriers," who transfer *rariu* from one woman to another, but men rarely contract it themselves. Nonetheless, most women see this means of transmission as *husbands* that bring *rariu* to innocent wives. When it was noted that women can transmit *rariu* to men, the women implicated were not married women but prostitutes, girlfriends, or young girls – other, less respected females.

Although Luo women have complaints about their *husbands'* movements, there is no punishment or stigma for men stemming from these accusations that they transmit *rariu*. This results from the myriad of causes believed to be associated with *rariu* and the difficulty of pinning down a specific cause for a specific case of illness. As one woman said, "*Rariu* is not embarrassing because you never know what caused it." If the cause of a specific case could be identified as sexually transmitted, then one's husband could be labeled an adulterer; but since a specific cause is usually unknown, he cannot be blamed for infidelity. As we will see below, men may not accept a label of *rariu* – and its cause and meaning – in the first place, thereby denying the connotation that men have committed a wrongdoing. It is important to note that women are also protected from the suspicion of infidelity due to *rariu*'s many causes.

In a society where women have little control over their husbands, we see a unsuccessful attempt by women to blame men for harming the health and welfare of themselves and potentially the family. In short, the multiple causes of *rariu* are double-edged sword: on the one hand, *rariu* deflects stigma from embarrassing reproductive conditions or actions for women, including infidelity; on the other hand, women do not have the cultural power to blame the spread of *rariu* on male transgressions either.

Rariu *and Men*

Rariu has traditionally functioned as a women's illness. However, when asked if *rariu* causes stigma for women, most women say it is not an embarrassing condition is because "it even affects men." There is agreement that it does not affect men as often as women, and many say they have not heard that it affects men. We believe the illness *rariu* has been extended to men, possibly as an attempt to legitimize it further should men balk at the high prevalence of women who have *rariu* and are excused from their obligations. When men also suffer, they become "co-conspirators" in *rariu*'s social definition.

If *rariu* is, in fact, suffered by men, what aspects would we expect it to cover? *Rariu* has similar symptoms for men and similar conceptions of what is wrong with the body. There are also similar effects on functioning, causes, and prescriptions. *Rariu* is also a legitimate excuse for men to temporarily abstain from work and sexual performance. The limited information we collected on men's experiences with *rariu* suggests that it renders them impotent. One man who suffered from *rariu* admitted, "What I know is (*rariu*) affects you so that you cannot be one with somebody (have sexual intercourse). ... I stopped, truly. It can't happen. You can't do it" (Obisa, man 2). And similar to women, the stigma from this sexual dysfunction is deflected because one is suffering from a legitimate illness.

Men, however, do not want to admit suffering from *rariu*; instead, men label their symptoms as those of STDs. STDs are seen as a sign of potency for men, whereas *rariu* is known foremost as a women's illness, which is embarrassing.

I: Why do you think (men) don't want to say (that they have *rariu*)?

R: This *rariu* was previously associated with women so if a man contracts it, at first he thinks that it is a new disease. But when he goes for help, he is told, "That is *rariu*." Other people would say that "so-and-so" got affected by *rariu*, but he himself cannot say so. The fact that it is known to be a female disease makes men not ready to divulge to others, "I have *rariu*." Besides, you also find that it was a female disease, that is why you find that those who heal it are women. It is women who know it and they are the ones to cure it (Obisa, man in *nyamrerwa* 5 interview).

Thus, men do not appear to readily recognize the symptoms of *rariu* for two reasons. One reason is because they have not likely heard of *rariu*, and they more readily recognize their symptoms as those of STDs than women do (Caraël, 1994). The more likely reason is because *rariu* is a women's illness, and the label is more stigmatizing for men than the label of an STD, such as syphilis.

Prescriptions for Rariu

The treatment offered by traditional medicine for *rariu* includes prescriptions for medicines and abstention from normal activities. *Nyamreche* prescribe medicine for *rariu* through a mixture of herbs that are drunk or rubbed on the body or by palpating the abdominal area (often with a herbal mixture). These therapies are meant to ease the pain and "return" the "thing that blocks" to its proper position in the body. *Nyamreche* also prescribe avoidance of hard work or sexual intercourse when one is sick, and women may be exempted from these obligations for the duration of the illness, which may last months.

Luo women note that *nyamreche* will come to their homes, listen to their complaints, and advise and administer treatments. *Nyamreche* are quite numerous, and there appear to be several *nyamreche* in each of our study villages or within easy walking distance. A *nyamrerwa*'s services are less expensive relative to Western medical treatment, and, unlike the clinics, they accept in-kind payment, such as a chicken, or delayed payments (Moore et al., 2002).

Each *nyamrerwa* has her own knowledge of herbal remedies. *Nyamreche* do not readily share this knowledge, except with their apprentices. This secrecy allows traditional medicine the benefit of numerous avenues to cure. For example, one *nyamrerwa* can treat *rariu* with a succession of different herbs; or a woman can go from one *nyamrerwa* to another in search of new herbal treatments. Multiple potential treatments from traditional medicine fosters a enduring faith in the legitimacy of traditional healing.

Since 1996 when I got that cure from that *nyamrerwa*, that disease had cleared until now when it recurred. I will go back to the same *nyamrerwa*, and if I fail to get well then I will consider looking for alternative *nyamrerwa* where I could seek help (Obisa, woman 133).

Treatment from biomedicine in Nyanza includes various levels of health care services: government dispensaries, health care centers, and hospitals, in addition to various private facilities. There are, however, problems of distance to and long waiting lines at health care facilities, and frequent shortages of drugs, equipment, and beds (Geissler et al., 2000; Koinange, 1996; Moore et al., 2002). In addition, staff are underpaid, overworked, and often discontented to be assigned to rural posts. Preventive care (e.g. family planning, ante-natal care, immunizations) is free from government facilities, and payment is necessary for curative services (Okoth-Owiro, 1994; Sindiga, 1990). Private facilities charge even higher fees.

Most clinic personnel prescribe Panadol for *rariu*, a common painkiller similar to aspirin, which appears to temporarily relieve the pain. They may also prescribe antibiotics if they believe a woman suffers from a UTI or an STD. Most clinicians also report that they refer women to a district hospital if they believe *rariu* is serious, if any tests are inconclusive for their specific diagnosis or for further testing, or if a patient does not respond to antibiotics. Some clinicians also refer women to a *nyamrerwa*.

The rural Luo women see Western medicine as a monolith. For example, they do not distinguish between the levels of health care (such as dispensary, health center, and hospital) when referring to treatment of *rariu* but usually use the term "hospital" in reference to any biomedical establishment. Women appear to recognize the universality of scientific pharmaceuticals, such that each nurse is equipped with the same limited battery of drugs to prescribe. Once biomedical treatment has failed, women do not appear to believe that repeat visits to the same clinic or additional visits to another clinic will help them. In contrast to *nyamreche*, Western medicine has one chance to cure a woman; if it does not, the whole establishment is dismissed as a course of therapy.

LEGITIMATION OF ILLNESS AND EMPOWERMENT

The subject of this section is the process by which *rariu* is legitimated in the rural community and the characterization of women most likely to suffer from *rariu*. We concentrate on women's interactions with the three influential groups in rural Luo society that affect illness decision-making: husbands, women in the community, and healers, both traditional and those trained in Western medicine.

Husbands' Role in Legitimation and Treatment

The initial labeling of Luo women as ill usually happens within the family homestead (Parkin, 1972). From our observations, it is evident that women commonly tell their husbands, mothers-in-law, mothers, co-wives and women friends about their symptoms. Almost all of the women who suffered from *rariu* reported speaking to their husbands about their illness, and many told their husbands before anyone else, explaining that they had to notify them. In most cases, however, husbands did not know what to do about *rariu* and referred their wives to older, more experienced women for advice.

> I: Do you talk with your husband about such problems (like *rariu*)?
> R: Yes, of course. When you are sick and in bed he has to ask you. It hurts you so that you can't wash his clothing and can't cook. He has to ask you, "How are you sick?" But even if you tell him, he can't know (what to do about it) because he also doesn't know. If I don't know it must be that he also doesn't know, and that is why I went to ask my mother-in-law (Obisa, woman 6).

Why must husbands be told about illness if they do not know what to do about it? In Luo society, men have decision-making power over the domestic household and those within it; therefore, husbands must be informed about their wives' health status, particularly if it will affect their ability to perform domestic duties or it will require money for treatment, which men are supposed to provide (Moore et al., 2002). Although almost all women reported speaking to husbands about illness, when asked with whom one talked about *rariu* in the household survey, respondents rarely reported husbands – or men in general – as network partners. Only 0.3% of the illness network partners named are spouses (see Table 1 for characteristics of *rariu* network partners). We believe this discrepancy arises because of the distinction between the requirement to "report" to or inform a husband about an illness – which is nearly universal – and "chatting" with and seeking advice from husbands, which most women do not report doing.

Despite the necessity to inform husbands about sickness, husbands are not instrumental in the legitimation process because they do not know about "women's illness." Husbands respect the expertise of the women's community and accept their wives' illness and excuse from daily responsibilities.

Husbands do not know about *rariu* and many do not know or advise how to treat it. Nevertheless, husbands act as gatekeepers for treatment because they have control over the household's resources. If a husband has limited funds, a woman may be denied treatment from Western medical facilities, which is the most expensive. If a husband has no funds available, any type of treatment may be infeasible.

All women agree that if a husband does not have the money for treatment, a woman can pay with her own money, although it is unlikely that women have enough surplus cash for the clinic. In the event that one's own funds can be used for treatment, this does not translate into complete control over decision-making, however. About half of the women said that even if one had her own money, her husband could still control the decision whether she can use it for treatment (and perhaps what kind of treatment) based on husbands' general rights

Table 1. Characteristics of *Rariu* Network Partners.

Characteristic	% of All Women's Network Partners ($N = 1,013$)
Relationship to respondent	
Mother	4.2
Mother-in-law	10.0
Sister	10.3
Co-wife/sister-in-law	32.1
Friend	19.6
Spouse	0.3
Brother/other male relative	0.8
Nurse	0.3
Nyamrerwa	5.4
Other	17.0
Residence	
Same homestead	15.3
Same village	38.7
Same sublocation	13.6
Same location	22.1
Other part of Nyanza Province	10.1
Don't know	0.2
Highest level of schooling	
Secondary	15.0
Primary	48.0
None	25.2
Don't know	11.9
Age relative to respondent	
Older	57.7
Age mate	16.6
Younger	25.7

to decision-making. Interestingly, several women mentioned that they would override a husband's decision by secretly seeking treatment. The other half of the women remarked that using their own money does translate into decision-making power, assuming that they should have their choice of treatment because it is their money and, more importantly, because they are the ones who are suffering.

In general, husbands do not appear to deny treatment outright or insist on one type of healer over another. A husband's only real power is denying treatment if he does not have the money. This may be an active denial if a husband does not want to use the money on his wife's care, but, more likely, it is merely a reflection of the household's constrained budget.

R: Can a husband feel very bad if the wife went for treatment to a place he had refused?

I: If he could give her money he may not feel bad, because maybe he was only refusing because of money. But if she had money and went with her own money, then he wouldn't feel bad. The man can only stop you when he knows his hands are empty since if you go there (for treatment), you may embarrass him by saying, "Husband, why don't you go and pay that bill?" He can only stop you if he doesn't have. If he knows you have money, he can't stop you from a place that will help you (Obisa, woman 150).

Women's Legitimation of Rariu and Treatment Advice

After informing husbands, women seek the advice of women in their illness networks to help them give meaning to their symptoms and decide on treatment options. It is evident from the conversations below that network partners are influential in these illness decisions.

Many women noted that they did not know what their symptoms were until another woman told them they had *rariu*. Young women and those experiencing their first pregnancy may not have heard about *rariu* in their natal home or experienced an episode of the symptoms previously. Older women – who have likely experienced *rariu* themselves – typically identify and legitimate *rariu*.

I: Who told you that that disease you were suffering from was *rariu*?

R: Older women. They told me that if you feel pain in your thighs, stomach pains, and something pulls the lower part of your stomach downwards then that must be *rariu* (Obisa, woman 131).

In the ethnographic interviews and on the household survey, women report that the individuals with whom they discuss *rariu* are primarily women: mothers-in-law, co-wives/sisters-in-law, mothers, sisters, aunts, friends, and *nyamreche*, the majority of whom are related by marriage or by birth (see Table 1). Overall, we find that 82.4% of women report having network partners with whom they discussed *rariu* at some time.

The survey data also show that network partners are mostly women who are older than the respondents (see Table 1). Of the network partners named, 57.7% were older than the respondents themselves, and 25.7% were younger, and 16.6% were the same age. Women also speak with network partners who have similar educational attainment as the respondents. Of the *rariu* network partners named, 15.0% had secondary education, 48.0% had primary, and 25.2% had no schooling (11.9% of the partners' education was not known).[9] The network partners also reside quite close, with 54.0% living in the same homestead or village as the respondents.

Some network partners appear to be more crucial in identifying *rariu* and offering treatment advice. The advice of mothers-in-law, mothers, and co-wives/sisters-in-law appears to be particularly important in determining if a woman was recognized as suffering from *rariu*. Over half of the women in ethnographic interviews reported telling their mothers-in-law about their symptoms, and most followed their advice about treatment.

> I: Why did you choose to tell your mother-in-law (about your case of *rariu*)?
> R: You see, when it was hurting I had not had such an experience before. But you know your (mother-in-law) is like your mother, so she is the one you have to go to (Obisa, woman 6).

On the whole, women in illness networks unanimously recommended treatment from *nyamreche* for *rariu*.

> There is no way the illness (*rariu*) can be treated at the hospital. It has to be treated at the *nyamrerwa's*. In fact, older women will straight away tell you to go to "so-and-so's" (name of a *nyamrerwa*) place for treatment (Obisa, woman 101).

Women talk to other women about illness for three main reasons. First, because labeling usually occurs in the homestead, most women are likely to speak to marital kin and neighboring women because of proximity, and some women like mothers-in-law and senior co-wives because they have to. Due to the patriarchal structure of Luo society and financial difficulties with travel, women's movements are restricted to activities close to home, including farming, fetching fuel wood, and visits. Women need permission from their husbands to venture further than this, which may inhibit conversations with other women further from home, including distant relatives. Nonetheless, it appears that visits to natal kin, particularly mothers, is sanctioned during illness.

Second, the women in illness networks are older and have experience and knowledge about illness.

> Older women suffer from *rariu* also. They know it. That is the best explanation why they are the ones who know about it and also why they are the ones who know how to treat it (Obisa, woman 101).

In many traditional societies, including among the Luo, knowledge about reproduction, bodily processes, and illness has been passed down from older, more experienced women through informal communication (Geissler, 1998b; for cross-cultural comparisons, see Manderson, 1999; March & Taqqu, 1986; Sukkary-Stolba, 1985). Women have historically had little access to formal education and outside information (for example, about the biomedical model of disease), and thus women trust the experience of elder women because "they saw the world before us."

Third, the women in illness networks offer a means of support for sick women: they attend to their duties and care for their children, bring medicine, and are sympathetic. They reinforce the legitimacy and validity of the illness to allow women to be temporarily exempted from their social obligations.

In sum, we see that *rariu* is associated with traditional concepts of the body and women's traditional normative roles. It is a rural illness. When we asked urban Luo women living in Nairobi about *rariu*, they usually had never heard of *rariu* or were uncomfortable discussing it. Perhaps they associated *rariu* not with the modern world of Nairobi or with foreigners, but with illiterate female relatives they had left behind in rural Nyanza and were embarrassed to acknowledge it. Urban women are generally more educated and affluent than rural Luo women, and they are less beholden to traditional role expectations. They are less likely to listen to the traditional illness networks, and they favor Western medical diagnoses and treatment instead. In short, urban women are more likely to have the social and economic resources to empower them, so they are less likely to need the quiet resistance of *rariu*.

Healers

There is a great contrast between traditional and Western medical healers and their place in women's networks and their roles in the legitimation process. *Nyamreche* are part of women's illness networks. They are rural Luo women themselves, living in nearby villages, and they may even know ill women as friends or relatives. In fact, *nyamreche* are not readily distinguished from other women, such that during our fieldwork, we found several *nyamreche* by accident while interviewing respondents. *Nyamreche* are in similar power positions within illness networks as the other elder women, due to their age and expertise. They may confirm the network diagnosis of *rariu* or identify it if nearby women do not know what it is. Most importantly, they offer legitimate illness status and prescriptions for deflection of stigma and cure.

Respondents reported that 5.4% of their network partners were *nyamreche* (see Table 1).[10] This contrasts to the Western medical nurses, who made up only 0.3% of women's networks. Clinicians do not recognize nor legitimate *rariu* and are of higher socioeconomic status than most rural Luo women. Thus, *nyamreche* are people women "chat" with and seek advise about for *rariu*, whereas women's relationships with clinicians appear to be less familiar and helpful.

Least Empowered and Suffering from Rariu

The household survey data show that 61.2% of women have suffered from *rariu* at some point in their lives. The qualitative evidence suggests that those most likely to suffer from *rariu* are less educated and experienced, rural women who are unable to resist the domination of husbands and are most likely to be influenced by their illness networks. In short, these women are the least empowered in society. Using the survey data, we can verify these findings with a wider, more representative sample of Luo women. We also provide a biomedical explanation for the findings. The results of bivariate associations between women's characteristics and ever having suffered from *rariu* are shown in Table 2.

According to women's reports, age does not appear to be associated with suffering from *rariu*, as *rariu* "occurs among both young and old." The results in Table 2 show that age is not significantly associated with ever having *rariu*,

Table 2. Percentage of Women who Reported Ever Suffering from *Rariu*, by Characteristics.

Characteristic	$N = 449^a$	% Reporting *Rariu*
Age		
15–24	166	60.2
25–34	170	61.8
35+	113	62.0
Education		
None	90	64.4**
Primary 1–6	136	71.3
Primary 7–8	164	53.7
Secondary	59	54.2
Lived outside of Nyanza Province for 6+ months		
Yes	176	57.4
No	273	63.7
Husband stays in homestead		
Yes	245	67.8**
No	80	51.3
Has *rariu* network partners		
Yes	370	68.7***
No	79	26.6
One or more mothers-in-law in homestead		
Yes	53	67.9
No	312	59.6
One or more sisters-in-law in homestead		
Yes	191	68.6**
No	180	52.2

[a] Several categories do not add up to 449 due to missing responses.
**$p < 0.01$.
***$p < 0.001$; chi-squared test.

and younger women are as likely to have suffered from *rariu* as older women in the sample. This suggests that beliefs about illness are passed down from older women, and younger women embrace them. From a biomedical perspective, women of all reproductive ages may suffer from conditions that are associated with *rariu*: Younger women are particularly vulnerable to RTIs (Manderson, 1999) and are more likely to be pregnant, when many of the symptoms of *rariu* usually appear. Other conditions with which *rariu* is associated, such as prolapsed uterus, may be more frequent among older and high-parity women.

Women with lower levels of education and who have not lived outside of Nyanza Province are more likely to have ever suffered from *rariu*, although the relationship with migration is not statistically significant. Those with lower educational attainment and less exposure to the world beyond the rural area may be more likely to hold traditional beliefs about illness, possibly because they have not been exposed to the biomedical model of disease through schooling or outside influences (Fosu, 1981; Geissler, 1998b; Kleinman, 1980). Those with lower levels of education also have less bargaining power relative to their husbands and rely on the advice and influence of their illness networks. Regarding a biomedical explanation, education and urban exposure may lead women to behave in ways that are less likely to produce *rariu*, such as do less carrying of heavy burdens or adopt more hygienic habits (Bhatia & Cleland, 1995; Boonmongkon et al., 2001; Caraël, 1994).

Women whose husbands usually stay in the homestead and have not migrated are significantly more likely to suffer from *rariu*. Husbands' presence may be interpreted as a direct restraint on women's freedom, and it poses a greater burden on them to fulfill husbands' desires – productive, reproductive, and sexual. In addition to these physical demands, women are also pressed to conform to the Luo ideology of obedience and submissiveness when husbands are in the homestead. These situations may bring about marital stresses and quarreling. From a biomedical perspective, women with husbands usually at home may be more likely to suffer from physical and sexual abuse, which have been linked to chronic pelvic pain, STDs, pregnancy complications, and miscarriage, all of which are associated with *rariu* (Heise, 1994; Inhorn, 1996).

Finally, there are several variables in Table 2 that reflect the influence of illness networks on suffering from *rariu*. Women who have talked about *rariu* with network partners and have mothers-in-law and co-wives/sisters-in-law residing in the homestead are more likely to suffer from *rariu* (although the relationship with mothers-in-law is not statistically significant).

Overall, the quantitative evidence underscores that the least empowered women are more likely to suffer from *rariu*. The biomedical interpretation of the associations argues that the least empowered are more likely to suffer from reproductive symptoms in the first place. We believe that these women are also more likely to have their suffering labeled and legitimized as *rariu* instead of biomedical diagnoses. This legitimation by the women's community provides a temporary means of respite from the strict domination of patriarchy, which is felt most greatly by the least empowered.

HEALTH-SEEKING BEHAVIOR FOR *RARIU*

Women's illness networks overwhelmingly advise treatment from a *nyamrerwa* for *rariu*. Because the networks legitimate *rariu*, and its meaning is rooted in the rural Luo culture, we would expect women to follow the networks' advice. Husbands influence decisions as well because they oversee household resources and the money needed for treatment, and it appears many deny care at the clinic because of the potential costs involved. In addition, we saw that structural deficiencies of clinics in rural Nyanza dissuade women from seeking care there. Nevertheless, some women visit the clinics for *rariu*. As noted above, 72.2% of women reported seeking treatment for *rariu* from a *nyamrerwa* and 27.8% went to a clinic or hospital.

Health-seeking behavior does not involve a simple dichotomous decision whether to seek treatment from traditional medicine or Western medicine, however. In the in-depth illness narratives, patterns of treatment emerged (Feierman, 1985; Green, 1992), where many rural Luo women visit numerous healers consecutively for *rariu* (see also Kawango, 1995; Sindiga, 1995 for patterns of treatment for other illnesses among the Luo).[11] Most women try traditional medicine first, based on advice of their illness networks. When they are not cured or if the pain persists, they try Western medicine in place of or in addition to another *nyamrerwa*. About half of the women said they went to the hospital at some point for *rariu*. As noted earlier, women do not appear to make consecutive trips to Western medical care for *rariu* from the same or different clinics, but they readily seek help from numerous *nyamreche* or return several times to the same *nyamrerwa* for treatment.

Thus, despite the influence of others, some women go to the clinic instead of or, more likely, in addition to the *nyamrerwa*. Why is this? We believe that seeking treatment from biomedicine is not a rejection of traditional medicine and networks' advice, but simply a means to alleviate suffering – employing "considerable pragmatism" to find relief from distress (Erwin, 1993, p. 145; Last, 1992; Obeyesekere, 1978; Osero, 1990). Because illness is serious and the pain is personal, women use their own discretion when choosing Western medicine as an alternative. Following is an example of one woman's desire for "hospital" treatment after she used traditional medicine and it did not help her. She wanted to go to the clinic over her husband's and network's objections.

> I: If all these days – six months – you were so sick that you could only be dragged to the sun (you could not walk yourself), were you not taken for any other treatment?
>
> R: I could not be taken for any other treatment because they said if she goes for injections (at the clinic) it will make it worse. . . . That thing (*rariu*) doesn't rhyme with injections.
>
> I: And how did you feel yourself? Or what was your husband's feeling?
>
> R: You know, people differ (in opinion), and according to him only traditional medicine could cure this disease. But I was telling him, "Just take me to the hospital so that even if I die, I can die in the hospital because this thing is hurting me. I can feel this thing is hurting me" (Obsia, woman 136).

There is a general conviction among the Luo that Western medical interventions relieve pain faster than those of traditional medicine (Geissler et al., 2000; Osero, 1990; Sindiga, 1995). When the *nyamrerwa*'s treatment has not worked or is slow to act, women may search for more rapid relief from the clinic.

After initial advice, women appear to make decisions about treatment on their own. Networks and *nyamreche* have the power to legitimate *rariu* but they do not have the power to enforce treatment from traditional medicine. This disconnect between legitimation and treatment decision-making appears at first at odds (Feierman & Janzen, 1992). Nevertheless, African healing traditionally placed paramount importance on the identification of an illness and its related causes; treatment for the physical ailment could be procured from a number of sources, including Western medicine (Beck, 1981; Last, 1992). Intervention by the women's community is crucial to legitimize a woman's suffering in the rural community, while seeking relief from the physical pain appears to involve more individual choice, where women can promote their own notions of appropriate treatment.

Rariu *does Not "Rhyme" with Western Medicine*

Although women seek relief from Western medicine, after evaluation of treatment at the clinic, the overwhelming majority of women have the impression that the clinic cannot cure them of *rariu* (see also Moore et al., 2002). Almost all women reported they were cured by traditional medicine, whether for one episode or if it recurs. Why is traditional medicine viewed as best? Besides the structural problems with Western medical facilities noted above, there is also a social side to healing that biomedicine lacks: First, rural Luo women and clinicians clash over understanding of the body and the meaning of *rariu*. Second, the clinics offer poor quality of care. Each of these aspects will be seen as we contrast the perspectives of the clinicians and women's view of treatment.

Clinicians' Perceptions of Rariu

There is a large "social distance" between *rariu* patients and biomedical healers (Rutenberg & Watkins, 1997). Although most clinic personnel are Luo, some are trained locally and the higher-level nurses have national training, and they are of a relatively higher socioeconomic status than rural Luo women. Clinicians have worked hard to become skilled medical personnel, and they wish to maintain their distinction as an educated elite. One way of doing this is to show their commitment to the scientific model of disease.

When rural women present at the clinic, they have been labeled by their illness networks with *rariu* and this diagnosis may have little to do with biomedical reality (Feierman, 1985; Waxler, 1981). Nevertheless, the power of clinicians over rural women ensures that their view of medical reality must be accepted inside the clinic. Because of the mismatch between *rariu* and Western medical diagnoses, most clinicians delegitimate women's experience with *rariu*. This delegitimation occurs in several ways. At one extreme, clinicians may reject *rariu* as legitimate suffering altogether. Many clinicians we interviewed express doubt that the symptoms of *rariu* are "real" or they say that *rariu* is "mainly psychological." They believe that women with *rariu* are malingerers who "just want to get out of work." At the opposite extreme, other clinicians may reject the label *rariu*; they tell us that *rariu* is "not in English" or "there is no medical term for it" – which means that it has no equivalent Western biomedical classification. They attempt to fit the condition to a specific diagnosis they recognize and can try to treat.

Any condition is hard to diagnose with the lack of equipment and clinical expertise of rural personnel (Christakis et al., 1994; Moore et al., 2002), but a *rariu* patient presents an "additional layer" of difficulty. A complaint of "*rariu*" is a red flag that the patient is a "rural, ignorant" woman who believes in traditional things like *rariu*. We saw from the discussion surrounding Table 2 that women with *rariu* are those least empowered in rural society and most influenced by their illness networks. Therefore, clinic personnel may perceive them as difficult to elicit proper information from, compel to follow a treatment regimen, and therefore heal.

We recorded numerous strategies that clinicians use to treat *rariu*, including convincing women *rariu* does not exist and they are not ill; explaining that *rariu* is another illness, such as an STD; or dissuading women from using traditional herbs[12] and recommending a new course of treatment (Luke et al., 2001). Many of these strategies are incompatible with women's concept of *rariu*, and often fail; as a result, many clinicians become frustrated and minimize their treatment of future *rariu* cases. In the end, most clinicians repeatedly prescribe Panadol, do not examine women completely, or refer them to the hospital or *nyamrerwa*. Most clinicians do not deny women treatment or referral for *rariu*; their measures, however, may be a means of declining responsibility if the women are not effectively healed. As a result of their interactions at the clinic, rural Luo women do not readily revise their belief in *rariu*, and clinicians and women remain at odds in their understanding of the illness.

Contrasting Treatment From Nyamreche

In contrast to Western medical treatment, rural women note that *nyamreche* understand the meaning of *rariu* and their quality of care is superior. There is little social distance between the *nyamreche* and rural women, and *nyamreche* offer personal support, understanding, and specific treatment for *rariu* (Moore et al., 2002).

Nyamreche know how to "return" *rariu* to its normal position and therefore restore normal functioning, including rectifying infertility. In contrast, Western medicine can only temporarily relieve the pain of suffering. This conviction is echoed in numerous studies of African healing, where traditional medicine is believed to eliminate the root cause of an illness while biomedicine only addresses the symptoms (Geissler et al., 2000; Green, 1992; Mbiti, 1990; Moss et al., 1999).

> (*Rariu*) is mainly treated by *nyamreche*. But if you go to the hospital as well they can inject you and give you drugs that reduce it (reduce the pain). But it doesn't reduce it the same way as the *nyamrerwa* would (Obisa, woman 136).

Western medicine may also cause more harm than good. Incorrect treatment of *rariu* by clinicians can be detrimental or even fatal, as several biomedical procedures do not "rhyme" with *rariu*. For example, if a woman is suffering from a prolapsed uterus, clinicians recommend an operation in order to reattach the ligaments that hold it in place. Luo women believe if *rariu* is operated on (and therefore cut), the patient could die or be rendered infertile. Traditional medicine is therefore less risky and superior; for example, it can cure infertility from *rariu*, not cause it.

Overall, biomedicine can only offer women a relief from suffering; it does not cure women and more importantly it does not offer all the functions provided by the traditional system, such as legitimation for a respite from social obligations and reintegration into society (Kunstadter, 1978). The biomedical diagnoses clinicians pin on *rariu* are not accompanied by a certificate of legitimate illness in the rural community – in fact, a diagnosis such as an STD would be stigmatizing and unfavorable for rural women instead of validating their suffering. One respondent summarized the differences between the two types of treatment.

> R: Now that you have gone to the clinic and you have gone to the *nyamrerwa*, how can you compare the welcome you received from the clinic to that you received from the *nyamrerwa*?

I: I could see the one I got from the *nyamrerwa* was good. The reason it was good is that she can advise you in a good way on how you can use the medicine and the times you should use them, and how you can go back to her, meaning she deals with you in love. But if you go to the hospital and explain, you may find the nurse there and maybe she has many people and you go to her place there. She could probably just tell you to go and buy such and such a drug and leave you like that. Now you don't understand well.

I: So the *nyamrerwa* is better?

R: She is better (Obisa, woman 150).

CONCLUSIONS

This study enhances the benefits of a demographic framework of women's empowerment with a feminist perspective that emphasizes greater attention to women's voices and experiences regarding gender inequality and illness. Using quantitative survey data, we have revealed the high prevalence of *rariu* in the rural community and have confirmed the statistical relationship between women's disempowerment and illness. Our major task has been to illustrate how rural Luo women are able to resist the constraints on individual agency in ways that are less obvious to conventional demographic analyses.

This study demonstrates that illness can act as a quiet response to the social control mechanisms of the powerful. *Rariu* serves as a covert form of resistance to rural Luo women's contemporary social position. For those whose symptoms are labeled as *rariu*, it offers them a temporary respite from their daily obligations, be they hard work, sexual intercourse, or continued childbearing. Unlike other illnesses, such as *nyach* or other STDs that reprimand women for their transgressions, *rariu* deflects the stigma of incomplete role expectations. With *rariu*, women who are infertile, subfecund, or need a rest from work are not stigmatized. Their bodies are not deficient, because the illness is at fault. Had women deliberately committed these offenses, these would be justifiable reasons for husbands to reprimand them. With *rariu*, the women's community has granted a certificate of illness, and this serves as a defense from threats of sanction, including divorce and physical abuse.

Rariu represents considerable resistance to men's expectations of women. But in order to ensure its continued existence, the women's community must not become suspect in the eyes of men. The symptoms that define *rariu* do not cause death and are usually temporary. *Rariu* does not extend beyond the women's realm of authority, for example, by becoming so serious that it needs the assistance of more prestigious male healers. If *rariu* were too blatant a protest, it would threaten men's authority, and men could delegitimate *rariu* as means of suffering and sanction women for becoming ill.

The women's community has the cultural power to identify, legitimate, and treat *rariu*. It is noteworthy that most of the symptoms of *rariu* are subjective, such that women suffering from them could be labeled by men as malingerers feigning illness. Instead, men trust the women's community, which has supported high fertility and the health of mothers and children traditionally. Thus, for the legitimation of *rariu*, the power of ill women and their networks is just as important if not more so than the power of men.

The process of legitimation does not occur without conflict between women. The most disempowered women are compelled to listen to those in their networks because they have authority over illness, and because the may be the only people available to talk to. In exchange for this deference, ill women get what they need from the networks: support, experience, and legitimation.

Our study concentrates on Luo women's perceptions of care and cure as determinants of treatment choice. We uncovered two aspects that deter women from treatment by biomedicine for *rariu*: The clash between clinicians' and Luo women's understanding of illness, and the poor quality of care received at the clinic. Clinicians, who are dedicated to the biomedicine model of disease, do not focus on these social aspects in their healing; indeed, they are likely to dismiss *rariu* as not "real" and minimize their treatment of it. We conclude that women's experiences inside the clinic, combined with the lack of equipment and drugs and high costs, leads to their conviction that Western medicine offers ineffective treatment. Rural Luo women use Western medicine for relief from suffering and delegitimate it when it does not cure them.

Our study suggests that improving the social interactions surrounding treatment could go a long way to improve care from Western medicine. More consideration should be given to understanding lay definitions of illness and the meaning of *rariu* for rural women (Erwin, 1993; Moore et al., 2002; Osero, 1990). Combined with improved client-patient interactions, clinicians can place biomedical explanations in terms understandable to rural women and help them make informed choices about treatment (Murphy, 2000; Sherwin, 1998). In addition, illness networks, and traditional healers in particular, should be involved in treatment consultations and spreading health education messages (Moore et al., 2002).

We believe that *rariu* is a bundle of complaints similar to reproductive health conditions, and these are precisely the sorts of conditions the Cairo conference aims to target. We doubt that the clinic will ever offer the same degree of legitimation and support as the women's community, but biomedicine can go a long way to cure *rariu*. Rural Luo women have garnered their collective power resist the constructs of men and Western medicine; perhaps a greater sensitivity to local illnesses that may not "rhyme" with biomedicine can help clinicians to deliver improved care.

NOTES

1. We use the term "Western medicine" and "biomedicine" to refer to allopathic medicine, which is distinguished from "traditional" or "indigenous" African medicine. We use the term "clinic" to refer to facilities that offer allopathic medical treatments and "clinicians" to refer to personnel trained in allopathic medicine who work there.

2. When KDICP began, the four sublocations of study were all part of South Nyanza District, which has subsequently been divided into numerous districts in Nyanza Province. All transcripts, survey data, and field notes from KDICP are available from the Population Studies Center at the University of Pennsylvania, http://www.pop.upenn.edu/networks

3. Because the same Luo word is used for a woman's co-wife (another wife of her husband) and sister-in-law (wife of her husband's brother), the research team suspects that the interviewers sometimes confused them. Therefore, we combine the categories in the analysis.

4. Multiple mothers-in-law can occur if a woman's father-in-law has multiple wives, all of whom are considered her mothers-in-law.

5. The maternal mortality ratio for Kenya is 590 per 100,000 live births, applicable to the period 1989–1998 (NCPD et al., 1999). This figure is comparable to other low-income African countries but high in comparison to the industrialized West. For example, the maternal mortality ratio for the United States was nine and for Canada two (most recent estimate for the 1980–1985 period) (World Bank, 1996).

6. Although it is not possible to diagnose *rariu* without clinical examinations, we asked Kenyan Western medical personnel, as well as numerous other Western medical experts working in developing countries on reproductive health issues, to translate the symptoms of *rariu* into what they believe are its Western medical equivalents.

7. *Rariu* is associated with pain and suffering, but not mortality; few women believe *rariu* can kill a person.

8. It appears that most women are in great pain when suffering from *rariu*, and we do not believe women are actively labeling their symptoms as *rariu* or feigning sickness in goal-oriented behavior aimed at seeking the "benefits" of the illness. Although there is the possibility that individuals invoke *rariu* complaints as a means to avoid work or sexual relations, our observations suggest that this is not the case for the majority of women (see Boonmongkon et al., 2001, for similar discussion on the illness *mot luuk* in Thailand).

9. Recall that 20.0% of women had no schooling and 13.1% had at least some secondary schooling.

10. The survey question regarding the relationship of network partners to the respondent included a category of "CBD/*nyamrerwa*." Community-based distributors (CBDs) are unpaid, trained distributors of contraceptives in rural areas, and may also be traditional healers.

11. The data from the household survey are problematic with regard to discovering women's patterns of treatment. The survey does not ask information on concurrent or consecutive treatment, and the responses permit only one treatment option to be reported. Data from the ethnographic interviews, however, provide more information on treatment patterns.

12. We are unable to conclude whether women are truly cured from *rariu*. The efficacy of herbs specific for *rariu* is not known, although some clinicians say they work for certain cases and *nyamreche* obviously believe in them. Some nurses also believe that particular

herbs will make a condition worse or nullify Western medical prescriptions. The symptoms associated with *rariu* may be temporarily eliminated or clear up on their own (such as those of an STD or premature labor pains, for example) (Green, 1992), and thus women may believe they have been cured by herbs. Nevertheless, our purpose is not to discern the physiological nature of the treatment from either the clinics or the *nyamrerwa* but rather women's perception of cure.

REFERENCES

Adams, A. M., Madhavan, S., & Simon, D. (2002). Women's social networks and child survival in Mali. *Social Science and Medicine, 54*, 165–178.

Adepoju, A., & Mbugua, W. (1997). The African family: An overview of changing forms. In: A. Adepoju (Ed.), *Family, Population and Development in Africa* (pp. 41–59). London: Zed Books Ltd.

Annandale, E. (1998). *The sociology of health and medicine*. Cambridge, UK: Polity Press.

Anyinam, C. (1987). Availability, accessibility, acceptability, and adaptability: Four attributes of African ethno-medicine. *Social Science and Medicine, 25*(7), 803–811.

Armstrong, K. (1999). Introduction. In: K. Armstrong (Ed.), *Shifting Ground and Cultured Bodies*. New York: University Press of America.

Aronowitz, R. A. (1998). *Making sense of illness*. Cambridge: Cambridge University Press.

Beck, A. (1981). *Medicine, tradition, and development in Kenya and Tanzania, 1920–1970*. Waltham, MA: Crossroads Press.

Bhatia, J. C., & Cleland, J. (1995). Self-reported symptoms of gynecological morbidity and their treatment in south India. *Studies in Family Planning, 26*(4), 203–216.

Bledsoe, C., Banja, F., & Hill, A. G. (1998). Reproductive mishaps and western contraception: An African challenge to fertility theory. *Population and Development Review, 24*(1), 15–57.

Blount, B. G. (1973). The Luo of South Nyanza, Western Kenya. In: A. Molnos (Ed.), *Cultural Source Materials for Population Planning in East Africa* (Vol. 3). Nairobi: East African Publishing House.

Boonmongkon, P., Nichter, M., & Pylypa, J. (2001). Mot Luuk problems in Northeast Thailand: Why women's own health concerns matter as much as disease rates. *Social Science & Medicine, 53*, 1095–1112.

Caldwell, J., & Caldwell, P. (1993). Women's position and child mortality and morbidity in less developed countries. In: N. Federici, K. Oppenheim Mason & S. Sogner (Eds), *Women's Position and Demographic Change*. Oxford: Clarendon Press.

Caldwell, J., Caldwell, P., Maxine Ankrah, E., Anarfi, J. K., Agyeman, D. K., Awusabo-Asare, K., & Orubuloye, I. O. (1993). African families and AIDS: Context, reactions and potential interventions. *Health Transition Review, 3*(Suppl.), 1–16.

Caldwell, J. C., Caldwell, P., & Orubuloye, I. O. (1992). The family and sexual networking in sub-Saharan Africa: Historical regional differences and present-day implications. *Population Studies, 46*, 385–410.

Caldwell, J. C., Orubuloye, I. O., & Caldwell, P. (1991). The destabilization of the traditional yoruba sexual system. *Population and Development Review, 17*(2), 229–262.

Caraël, M. (1994). The impact of marriage change on the risks of exposure to sexually transmitted diseases in Africa. In: C. Bledsoe & G. Pison (Eds), *Nuptiality in Sub-Saharan Africa*. Oxford: Clarendon Press.

Chafetz, J. S. (1990). *Gender equity*. Newbury Park, CA: Sage Publications.

Christakis, N. A., Ware, N. C., & Kleinman, A. (1994). Illness behavior and the health transition in the developing world. In: L. C. Chen, A. Kleinman & N. C. Ware (Eds), *Health and Social Change in International Perspective*. Boston: Harvard School of Public Health.

Cohen, D. W., & Atieno Odhiambo, E. S. (1989). *Siaya: The historical anthropology of an African landscape*. London: James Currey.

Collins, R. (1971). A conflict theory of sexual stratification. *Social Problems*, *9*, 3–21.

Collins, R. (1994). *Four sociological traditions*. New York: Oxford University Press.

Collins, R., Saltzman Chafetz, J., Blumberg, R. L., Coltrane, S., & Turner, J. H. (1993). Toward an integrated theory of gender stratification. *Sociological Perspectives*, *36*(3), 185–216.

Conrad, P. (1992). Medicalization and social control. *Annual Review of Sociology*, *1*, 209–232.

Conrad, P., & Schneider, J. W. (1992). *Deviance and medicalization: From badness to sickness*. Philadelphia: Temple University Press.

Daily Nation (2000). We're 28 million. Daily Nation (Kenya). February 17th.

Das Gupta, M. (1996). Life course perspectives on women's autonomy and health outcomes. *Health Transition Review*, *6*(Suppl.), 213–231.

Donaldson, S. R. (1997). Our women keep our skies from falling: Women's networks and survival imperatives in Tshunyane, South Africa. In: G. Mikell (Ed.), *African Feminism: The Politics of Survival in Sub-Saharan Africa*. Philadelphia: University of Pennsylvania Press.

Entwisle, B., & Coles, C. M. (1990). Demographics surveys and Nigerian women. *Signs*, *15*(2), 259–284.

Erwin, O. J. (1993). Reproductive tract infections among women in Ado-Ekiti, Nigeria: Symptoms recognition, perceived causes and treatment choices. *Health Transition Review*, *3*(Suppl.), 135–149.

Feierman, S. (1985). Struggles for control: The social roots of health and healing in modern Africa. *African Studies Review*, *28*(2/3), 73–147.

Feierman, S., & Janzen, J. M. (1992). *The social basis of health and healing in Africa*. Berkeley: University of California Press.

Fosu, G. B. (1981). Disease classification in rural Ghana: Framework and implications for health behaviour. *Social Science and Medicine*, *15B*, 471–482.

Francis, E., & Hoddinott, J. (1993). Migration and differentiation in Western Kenya: A tale of two sub-locations. *The Journal of Development Studies*, *30*(1), 115–145.

Freund, P. E. S., & McGuire, M. B. (1999). *Health, illness, and the social body*. Upper Saddle River, NJ: Prentice-Hall.

Geissler, P. W. (1998a). Worms are our life, Part I: Understandings of worms and the body among the Luo of Western Kenya. *Anthropology and Medicine*, *5*(1), 63–79.

Geissler, P. W. (1998b). Worms are our life, Part II: Luo children's thoughts about worms and illness. *Anthropology and Medicine*, *5*(2), 133–144.

Geissler, P. W., Nokes, K., Prince, R. J., Achieng' Odhiambo, R., Aagaard-Hansen, J., & Ouma, J. H. (2000). Children and medicines: Self-treatment of common illnesses among Luo schoolchildren in Western Kenya. *Social Science and Medicine*, *50*, 1771–1783.

Ghuman, S. J. (2001). *Employment, autonomy, and violence against women in India and Pakistan*. University of Pennsylvania, mimeo.

Gill, V. T., & Maynard, D. W. (1995). On labeling in actual interaction: Delivering and receiving diagnoses of developmental disabilities. *Social Problems*, *42*(1), 11–37.

Green, E. C. (1992). Sexually transmitted disease, ethnomedicine and health policy in Africa. *Social Science and Medicine*, *35*(2), 121–130.

Green, S. R., & Feyisetan, B. J. (2000). How secret is secret? A qualitative study of men's views of covert contraceptive use in Western Kenya. Paper presented at the Annual Meeting of the Population Association of America, Los Angeles, CA, March 23th–25th.

Greenhalgh, S., & Li, J. (1995). Engendering reproductive policy and practice in peasant China: For a feminist demography of reproduction. *Signs 1995 Spring, 20*(3), 601–641.

Hauge, H.-E. (1974). *Luo religion and folklore*. Oslo: Universitetsforlaget.

Hay, M. J. (1976). Luo women and economic change during the colonial period. In: N. J. Hafkin & E. G. Bay (Eds), *Women in Africa*. Stanford, CA: Stanford University Press.

Hay, M. J. (1982). Women as owners, occupants, and managers of property in colonial Western Kenya. In: M. J. Hay & M. Wright (Eds), *African Women and the Law: Historical Perspectives*. Boston: Boston University Papers on Africa, VII.

Heise, L. L. (1994). Gender-based violence and women's reproductive health. *International Journal of Gynecology & Obstetrics, 46*, 221–229.

Hodgson, D. L., & McCurdy, S. A. (2001). Introduction. In: D. L. Hodgson & S. A. McCurdy (Eds), *Wicked Women and the Reconfiguration of Gender in Africa*. Portsmouth, NH: Heinemann.

Hodgson, D., & Watkins, S. C. (1997). Feminists and neo-malthusians: Past and present alliances. *Population and Development Review, 23*(3), 469–523.

Inhorn, M. C. (1996). *Infertility and patriarchy*. Philadelphia: University of Pennsylvania Press.

Kabeer, N. (1997). Women, wages and intra-household power relations in urban Bangladesh. *Development and Change, 28*(2), 261–302.

Kabeer, N. (1999). Resources, agency, achievements: Reflections on the measurement of women's empowerment. *Development and Change, 30*, 435–464.

Kawango, E. A. (1995). Ethnomedical remedies and therapies in maternal and child health among the rural Luo. In: I. Sindiga (Ed.), *Traditional Medicine in Africa*. Nairobi, Kenya: East African Educational Publishers.

Keilmann, K. (1998). Barren ground: Contesting identities of infertile women in Pemba, Tanzania. In: M. Lock & P. A. Kaufert (Eds), *Pragmatic Women and Body Politics*. Cambridge: Cambridge University Press.

Kishor, S. (2000). Empowerment of women in Egypt and links to the survival and health of their infants. In: H. B. Presser & G. Sen (Eds), *Women's Empowerment and Demographic Processes*. Oxford: Oxford University Press.

Kleinman, A. (1980). *Patients and healers in the context of culture*. Berkeley: University of California Press.

Kleinman, A. (1988). *The illness narratives: Suffering, healing and the human condition*. New York: Basic Books.

Koinange, W. (1996). *Towards better health in Kenya*. Nairobi: Kenya Litho.

Kunstadter, P. (1978). The comparative anthropological study of medical systems in society. In: A. Kleinman, P. Kunstadter, E. Russel Alexander & J. L. Gate (Eds), *Culture and Healing in Asian Societies*. Cambridge, MA: Schenkman Publishing Company.

Last, M. (1992). The importance of knowing and not knowing: Observations from Hausaland. In: S. Feierman & J. M. Janzen (Eds), *The Social Basis of Healing in Africa*. Berkeley: University of California Press.

Lock, M. (1998). Situating women in the politics of health. In: S. Sherwin (Coordinator), *The Politics of Women's Health*. Philadelphia: Temple University Press.

Lock, M., & Kaufert, P. A. (1998). Introduction. In: M. Lock & P. A. Kaufert (Eds), *Pragmatic Women and Body Politics*. Cambridge: Cambridge University Press.

Lorber, J. (1997). *Gender and the social construction of illness*. Thousand Oaks, CA: Sage Publications.

Luke, N. (2000). *Rariu* and Luo women: Illness as resistance in rural Kenya. Unpublished Dissertation. University of Pennsylvania.

Luke, N., Warriner, I., & Cotts Watkins, S. (2001). *Rariu* doesn't rhyme with western medicine: Lay beliefs and illness networks in Kenya. In: C. Makhlouf Obermeyer (Ed.), *Cultural Perspectives of Reproductive Health*. Oxford: Oxford University Press.

Malhotra, A., & Mather, M. (1997). Do schooling and work empower women in developing countries? Gender and domestic decisions in Sri Lanka. *Sociological Forum, 12*(4), 599–630.

Manderson, L. (1999). Social meanings and sexual bodies: Gender, sexuality and barriers to women's health care. In: T. M. Pollard & S. B. Hyatt (Eds), *Sex, Gender and Health*. Cambridge, UK: Cambridge University Press.

March, K., & Taqqu, R. (1986). *Women's informal associations in developing countries: Catalysts for change?* Boulder: Westview Press.

Martin, E. (1992). *The woman in the body*. Boston: Beacon Press.

Mason, K. O. (1997). Gender and demographic change. In: G. Jones et al. (Eds), *The Continuing Demographic Transition*. Oxford: Clarendon Press.

Mason, K. O., & Smith, H. L. (2001). Thinking about, measuring, and analyzing women's empowerment/autonomy: Lessons from a cross-country comparative studies. Presentation at the Annual Meeting of the Population Association of America, Washington, DC, March 29th–31th.

Mbiti, J. S. (1990). *African religions and philosophy* (2nd ed.). Oxford: Heinemann International.

Mbogoh, S. G. (1986). Production systems and labour. In: G. S. Were, B. E. Kipkorir & E. O. Ayiemba (Eds), *South Nyanza District Socio-Cultural Profile*. Nairobi: Ministry of Planning and National Development, Government of Kenya, and Institute of African Studies, University of Nairobi.

McClain, C. S. (1989). Reinterpreting women in healing roles. In: C. S. McClain (Ed.), *Women as Healers: Cross-Cultural Perspectives*. New Brunswick, NJ: Rutgers University Press.

McKinlay, J. B. (1973). Social networks, lay consultation and help-seeking behavior. *Social Forces, 51*, 275–292.

Miruka, O. (1997). Gender perspectives in Luo proverbs, riddles and tongue-twisters. In: W. M. Kabira, M. Masinjila & M. Obote (Eds), *Contesting Social Death*. Nairobi: Kenya Oral Literature Association.

Moore, M., Copeland, R., Chege, I., Pido, D., & Girffiths, M. (2002). A behavior change approach to investigating factors influencing women's use of skilled care in Homa Bay District, Kenya. Draft report from The CHANGE Project. Washington, DC: Academy for Educational Development/The Manoff Group.

Moss, W., Bentley, M., Maman, S., Ayuko, D., Egessah, O., Sweat, M., Nyarang'o, P., Zenilman, J., Chemtai, A., & Halsey, N. (1999). Foundations of effective strategies to control sexually transmitted infections: Voices from rural Kenya. *AIDS Care, 11*(1), 95–113.

Murphy, E. (2000). Client-provider interactions in family planning services: Guidance from Research and program experiences. *MAQ Papers 1*(2). Boston, MA: Management Sciences for Health.

National Council for Population and Development (NCPD), Central Bureau of Statistics (CBS) (Office of the Vice-President and Ministry of Planning and Development (Kenya)), and Macro International Inc. (MI) (1994). Kenya demographic and health survey, 1993. Calverton, MD: NCPD, CBS, and MI.

National Council for Population and Development (NCPD), Central Bureau of Statistics (CBS) (Office of the Vice-President and Ministry of Planning and Development (Kenya)), and Macro International Inc. (MI) (1999). Kenya demographic and health survey 1998. Calverton, MD: NCPD, CBS, and MI.

National Research Council (NRC) (1996). Preventing and mitigating AIDS in sub-Saharan Africa. Washington, DC: National Academy Press.

Ndisi, J. W. (1974). *A study in the economic and social life of the Luo of Kenya*. Lund: Berlingska Boktryckeriet.

Nyamwaya, D. (1986). Medicine and health. In: G. S. Were, B. E. Kipkorir & E. O. Ayiemba (Eds), *South Nyanza District Socio-Sultural Profile*. Nairobi: Government of Kenya, The Ministry of Planning and National Development and the Institute of African Studies, University of Nairobi.

Obeyesekere, G. (1978). Illness, culture, and meaning: Some comments on the nature of traditional medicine. In: A. Kleinman, P. Kunstadter, E. Russell Alexander & J. L. Gate (Eds), *Culture and Healing in Asian Societies*. Cambridge, MA: Schenkman Publishing Company.

Ocholla-Ayayo, A. B. C. (1976). *Traditional ideology and ethics among the Southern Luo*. Uppsala: Scandinavian Institute of African Studies.

Ocholla-Ayayo, A. B. C. (1991). *The spirit of a nation*. Nairobi: Shirikon Publishers.

Odaga, A. (1986). Food and drink. In: G. S. Were, B. E. Kipkorir & E. O. Ayiemba (Eds), *South Nyanza District Socio-Cultural Profile*. Nairobi: Ministry of Planning and National Development, Government of Kenya, and Institute of African Studies, University of Nairobi.

Okoth-Owiro, A. (1994). Traditional health systems: Issues and concerns. In: A. Islam & R. Wiltshire (Eds), *Traditional Heath Systems and Public Policy*. Proceedings of an International Workshop, International Development Research Centre, Ottawa, Canada, March 2nd–4th.

Osero, J. O. (1990). *Health seeking behaviour in a rural setting: The case of Ukwala division in Siaya district*. M.A. thesis. Nairobi: Institute of African Studies, University of Nairobi.

Pala, A. O. (1979). Women in the household economy: Managing multiple roles. *Studies in Family Planning*, *10*(11/12), 337–343.

Pala, A. O. (1980). Daughters of the lakes and rivers: Colonization and the land rights of Luo women. In: M. Etienne & E. Leacock (Eds), *Women and Colonization*. New York: Praeger.

Paolisso, M., & Leslie, J. (1995). Meeting the challenging health needs of women in developing counties. *Social Science and Medicine*, *40*(1), 55–65.

Parkin, D. (1969). *Neighbors and nationals in an African city ward*. Berkeley, CA: University of California Press.

Parkin, D. J. (1972). The Luo living in Kampala, Uganda, and Central Nyanza, Kenya. In: A. Molnos (Ed.), *Cultural Source Materials for Population Planning in East Africa* (Vol. 3). Nairobi: East African Publishing House.

Parkin, D. (1978). *The cultural definition of political response: Lineal destiny among the Luo*. London: Academic Press.

Pescosolido, B. A. (1992). Beyond rational choice: The social dynamics of how people seek help. *American Journal of Sociology*, *97*(4), 1096–1138.

Potash, B. (1978). Some aspects of marital stability in a rural Luo community. *Africa*, *48*(4), 380–397.

Potash, B. (1986). Wives of the grave: Widows in a rural Luo community. In: B. Potash (Ed.), *Widows in African Societies*. Stanford: Stanford University Press.

Potash, B. (1989). Gender relations in sub-Saharan Africa. In: S. Morgan (Ed.), *Gender and Anthropology*. Washington, DC: American Anthropological Association.

Potash, B. (1995). Women in the changing African family. In: M. J. Hay & S. Stichter (Eds), *African Women South of the Sahara*. New York: Longman Scientific & Technical.

Riley, N. E. (1999). Challenging demography: Contributions from feminist theory. *Sociological Forum*, *14*(3), 369–397.

Rutenberg, N., & Watkins, S. C. (1997). The buzz outside the clinics: Conversation and contraception in Nyanza, Kenya. *Studies in Family Planning*, *28*(4), 290–307.

Schuler, S. R., Hashemi, S. M., Riley, A. P., & Akhter, S. (1996). Credit programs, patriarchy and men's violence against women in rural Bangladesh. *Social Science and Medicine, 43*(12), 1729–1742.

Sen, G., & Batliwala, S. (2000). Empowering women for reproductive rights. In: H. B. Presser & G. Sen (Eds), *Women's Empowerment and Demographic Processes*. Oxford: Oxford University Press.

Sherwin, S. (1998). A relational approach to autonomy in health care. In: S. Sherwin (Coordinator), *The politics of Women's Health*. Philadelphia: Temple University Press.

Shipton, P. (1989). Bitter money: Cultural economy and some African meanings of forbidden commodities. *American Ethnological Society Monograph Series*, No. 1.

Sindiga, I. (1990). Health and disease. In: W. R. Ochieng' (Ed.), *Themes in Kenyan History*. Nairobi: East African Educational Publishers.

Sindiga, I. (1995). Managing illness among the Luo. In: I. Sindiga (Ed.), *Traditional Medicine in Africa*. Nairobi, Kenya: East African Educational Publishers.

Southall, A. W. (1973). The Luo of South Nyanza, Western Kenya. In: A. Molnos (Ed.), *Cultural Source Materials for Population Planning in East Africa* (Vol. 3). Nairobi: East African Publishing House.

Stein, J. (1997). *Empowerment and women's health*. Atlantic Highlands, NJ: Zed Books Ltd.

Sukkary-Stolba, S. (1985). Indigenous fertility regulating methods in two Egyptian villages. In: L. Newman (Ed.), *Women's Medicine: A Cross-Cultural Study of Indigenous Fertility Regulation*. New Jersey: Rutgers University Press.

Ware, N. C. (1992). Suffering and the social construction of illness: The delegitimation of illness experience in chronic fatigue syndrome. *Medical Anthropology Quarterly, 6*(4), 347–361.

Watkins, S. C., Rutenberg, N., Green, S., Onoko, C., White, K., Franklin, N., & Clark, S. (1996). Circle no bicycle: Fieldwork in Nyanza Province, Kenya, 1994–1995. University of Pennsylvania. Unpublished notes.

Watkins, S. C., Rutenberg, N., & Wilkinson, D. (1997). Orderly theories, disorderly women. In: G. W. Jones, R. M. Douglas, J. C. Caldwell & R. M. D'Souza (Eds), *The Continuing Demographic Transition*. Oxford: Clarendon Press.

Waxler, N. E. (1981). The social labeling perspective on illness. In: A. Kleinman & L. Eisenberg (Eds), *The Relevance of Social Science for Medicine*. Dordrecht, Holland: D. Reidel Publishing.

Whyte, S. R., & Wanjiru Kariuki, P. (1997). Malnutrition and gender relations in Western Kenya. In: T. S. Weisner, C. Bradley & P. L. Kilbride (Eds), *African Families and the Crisis of Social Change*. Westport, CT: Bergin & Garvey.

Wilson, G. M. (1955). *Luo customary law and marriage laws customs*. Nairobi.

Wolf, D. L. (1992). *Factory daughters: Gender, household dynamics, and rural industrialization in Java*. Berkeley: University of California Press.

ABOUT THE AUTHORS

Erica S. Breslau, Ph.D., M.P.H. is a scientific program director in the Applied Cancer Screening Research Branch, in the Behavioral Research Program within the Division of Cancer Control and Population Sciences at the National Cancer Institute. Dr. Breslau's research interests focus on women's oncology issues in general, and specifically as they pertain to the social, behavioral, and psychological influences associated with breast, gynecological and colorectal cancer screening. Recent efforts include ensuring that research is able to inform and improve the quality of health services among women disproportionately affected with breast and cervical cancer through the dissemination of evidence-based intervention approaches. She has conducted population-based research in the area of infectious diseases, including HIV/AIDS and sexually transmitted diseases in military populations, and has implemented large-scale health promotion approaches to improve the adoption of prevention practices. Dr. Breslau received her Ph.D. in Public Health from The Johns Hopkins Bloomberg School of Public Health, and her Master's in Public Health from Tulane University, School of Public Health and Tropical Medicine.

Vasilikie Demos is a Professor of Sociology at the University of Minnesota-Morris. She has studied ethnicity and gender in the United States and is currently completing a monograph on her study of Kytherian Greek women based on interviews in Greece and among immigrants in the United States and Australia. With Marcia Texler Segal, she is co-editor of the Advances in Gender Research series and *Ethnic Women: A Multiple Status Reality* (General Hall, 1994). She is a past president of Sociologists for Women in Society and of the North Central Sociological Association, and has been an Honorary Visiting Professor at the University of New South Wales in Australia.

Heather Hartley is an Assistant Professor of Sociology at Portland State University. Dr. Hartley's research interests include the sociology of health and medicine, the sociology of gender, the sociology of sexualities, and political sociology. Within these general specialty areas, her work focuses on the politics of women's health, the pharmaceutical industry and the changing distribution of power within the health care system.

Beth E. Jackson is a Doctoral Student in Sociology at York University in Toronto, Canada. Drawing on the traditions of feminist epistemologies and critical social studies of science, her dissertation research puts questions of epistemic authority and the nature of evidence into the specific context of public health and epidemiology. Specifically, she explores the conditions, contexts, tools and processes through which public health knowledge claims are made, by focusing on a particular technology of "population health" i.e. the National Population Health Survey (NPHS) (a longitudinal, biennial survey of the mental and physical health of Canadians and their use of health care services). Her research also speaks to policy implications of "situated" data and evidence – in this case, the implications of how "women's health" is defined, and the extent to which a gendered analysis of health is considered in the construction and analysis of the NPHS.

Jennie Jacobs Kronenfeld is a Professor in the Department of Sociology, Arizona State University. She conducts research in the areas of health policy, health across the life course, health behavior including preventive health behavior, and research into AIDS in geographically mobile populations. She has recently authored *Health Care Policy: Issues and Trends* (Praeger, 2002). She has conducted research in a variety of topics related to child health, including recruitment into CHIP (child health insurance program) and has published a book on the impact of school based health clinics, *Schools and the Health of Children* (Sage, 2000). She is a past president of Sociologists for Women in Society and past chair of the Medical Sociology Section of the American Sociological Association.

Nancy Luke is an Assistant Professor of Research in the Population Studies and Training Center at Brown University and a Research Fellow in the Center for Population and Development Studies at Harvard University. Her primary research interest is the impact of social organization on health and well-being, particularly among women and adolescents. She is presently co-Principal Investigator of two research projects, both of which include collection of household survey and ethnographic data. A project in Kenya studies the influence of marriage and economic transactions on sexual behavior in an area of high HIV/AIDS prevalence, and a project in India examines women's empowerment in a context where norms sanction intimate partner violence. She has also collaborated with numerous non-governmental organizations on research projects pertaining to reproductive health and gender equity in developing countries. Dr. Luke has a Ph.D. in Demography and Sociology from the University of Pennsylvania and an M.A. from Johns Hopkins School of Advanced International Studies.

Deborah Parra-Medina, Ph.D., M.P.H., is Assistant Professor at the University of South Carolina with joint appointments in the Department of Health Promotion, Education and Behavior (HPEB) and Women's Studies. She received her Ph.D. in Epidemiology at the UC San Diego, an M.P.H. in Health Promotion at San Diego State University and a B.A. in Social Science at UC Berkeley. She has extensive experience working with under-served communities, having worked in several chronic disease prevention and control efforts including cancer screening, tobacco control, weight loss and nutrition. Her research based on a participatory action model emphasizes the intersections of race, class and gender and the influence of socio-cultural environment on adaptive and maladaptive health behaviors. This perspective is exemplified in her current research. She is Principle Investigator of the SC American Legacy Empowerment (SCALE) Evaluation Project that is examining how to effectively engage youth as agents for social change within the context of tobacco prevention and control. Dr. Parra-Medina was recently awarded a pilot study grant from NCI, the broad goal of this project is to foster individual and organizational empowerment among the emerging Hispanic population in South Carolina in relation to cancer prevention and health promotion through the development of the South Carolina Hispanic Health Coalition: Partnership for Cancer Prevention (PCP).

Colleen Reid recently completed her Ph.D. in Interdisciplinary Studies in health promotion research at the University of British Columbia in Vancouver, Canada. Her doctoral dissertation was a feminist action research project with a group of women on low income. Together they examined the relationship between exclusion and health, the women's varied discourses of poverty and health, and the promises and challenges of engaging in feminist action research. Dr. Reid has also been involved in community health research projects with organizations including the Vancouver YWCA, AIDS Vancouver, Literacy B.C., and the B.C. Centre of Excellence for Women's Health.

Elianne Riska is von Willebrand-Fahlbeck Professor of Sociology at Åbo Akademi University, Finland since 1985. She has been Chairperson of the Department of Sociology 1985–1997 and Director of the Institute of Women's Studies at Åbo Akademi University 1986–1993. Elianne Riska received her Ph.D. in Sociology at the State University of New York at Stony Brook in 1974. She was an Assistant Professor and an Associate Professor of Sociology in the Department of Sociology and College of Human Medicine at Michigan State University from 1974 to 1981. She was Academy Professor of the Academy of Finland 1997–2002. She is currently the President of the Research Committee of the Sociology of Health (RC15) of the International Sociological Association (2002–2006). Her most recent books are *Gender, Work and Medicine* (Sage, 1993), *Gendered*

Moods (Routledge, 1995) and *Medical Careers and Feminist Agendas: American, Scandinavian, and Russian Women Physicians* (Aldine de Gruyter, 2001).

Marcia Texler Segal is Associate Vice-Chancellor for Academic Affairs, Dean for Research and a Professor of Sociology at Indiana University Southeast. Her research and consulting focus on education and on women in Sub-Saharan Africa and on ethnic women in the United States. With Vasilikie Demos, she is co-editor of the Advances in Gender Research series and *Ethnic Women: A Multiple Status Reality* (General Hall, 1994). She is a past president of the North Central Sociological Association and past chair of the American Sociological Association Sections on Sex and Gender and Race, Gender and Class.

Lynn Weber is a Director of the Women's Studies Program and Professor of Sociology at the University of South Carolina. For the 2002–2003 year, she is Visiting Professor in the Consortium for Research on Race, Gender, and Ethnicity and the Department of Women's Studies at the University of Maryland. Her research and teaching explore the intersections of race, class, gender, and sexuality particularly as they are manifest in women's health, in the process of upward social mobility and work, and in the creation of an inclusive classroom environment. In 2001 and 2002, she published two books, *Understanding Race, Class, Gender, and Sexuality: A Conceptual Framework* and *Understanding Race, Class, Gender, and Sexuality: Case Studies* (NY: McGraw-Hill) which are intended to move the field of intersectional scholarship ahead by serving as a guide to facilitate intersectional analyses and to foster more integrative thinking in the classroom. Dr. Weber is also co-author of *The American Perception of Class*.

INDEX

adultery/infidelity, 287–289, 291
agency, 1, 36–38, 40, 50, 122, 164, 234,
    237, 281, 282, 284, 290
androgen
    deficiency syndrome (see FADS), 91,
        103, 105
    replacement therapies, 91, 103, 105
anorexia nervosa, 3, 261
attention deficit/hyperactivity disorder
    (ADHT), 2

biomedical
    model of healthcare, 6, 7
    research, 6, 92, 110, 115, 182
biomedicine, 36, 61, 63, 65, 77, 151, 154,
    158, 163, 169, 191, 283, 285, 300,
    309, 310, 312, 314, 315
breast cancer, 66, 67, 132–135, 137, 138,
    140–142, 144, 145, 148–150,
    152–157, 160, 162, 164–171

Canada/Canadian, 4, 7, 27, 38, 53, 54
Centers for Disease Control and Prevention
    (CDC), 2
childbirth/delivery, 62, 66, 69, 94, 152,
    204, 289, 286, 297
chronic fatigue syndrome (CFS), 64, 69,
    146, 152, 157
class (also see social class), 6, 27, 42, 49,
    183, 190, 191, 195, 199, 200–203,
    207, 219, 268, 273
clinical drug trials
    bias in
    trends in
commercial drug networks, 100
Continuing Medical Education Conference
    (CME), 91, 93
contraception, 94, 282, 290

coping, 29, 40, 131, 132, 134, 136–138,
    140, 141, 143, 148, 159, 161, 245,
    255, 262, 263, 265, 266

Daily Wellness Company, 120
(de)legitimation of illness, 301,
Diagnostic and Statistical Manual of
    Mental Disorders (DSM), 91, 95
determinants of health, 28, 30, 36, 37, 39,
    40, 42, 50, 195
diagnosis, 1, 4, 8, 22, 34, 59, 76, 95, 96,
    104, 105, 131, 133–135, 137–141,
    145, 147, 148, 149, 151–156, 158,
    162, 165, 168, 170, 301, 306, 311, 312
Direct-to-consumer (DTC) advertising, 107
disease(s)
    cardiovascular (CVD), 181, 194, 206,
        207, 271
    diabetes, 2, 81, 181, 195, 266, 271
disease-specific advocacy, 169
disparities, 3, 6, 181–192, 195–198,
    200–203, 206, 207, 214, 217–219,
    221, 223, 231, 269
distress
    as response, 168
    psychological, 133, 139–141, 143, 145,
        149, 150, 152, 159
divorce, 8, 287–289, 313
drug prescribing practices and trends, 1, 4,
    73, 78, 79
    off-label prescribing, 103, 109, 124, 126
drugs, 1, 4, 5, 66, 71, 75, 89–91, 97, 98,
    100–102, 113–115, 118, 120,
    123–125, 149, 150, 154, 263, 289,
    301, 312, 314
dysfunctions, 91, 111

ecological epidemiology, 33, 36

empowerment, 30, 72, 272, 281–286, 313,
    325
Erectile Dysfunction (ED), 75, 89
EROS-CTD, 90, 125
epidemiology, 4, 6, 11–15, 17, 19, 20,
    22–37
epistemology, 2–15, 17, 51, 53
evidence, 11–13, 15–17, 22, 23, 31, 33, 38,
    41, 43, 46–53, 71, 96, 99, 106, 110,
    123, 132, 146, 154, 155, 157, 161,
    165, 195, 196, 215, 221, 260, 266,
    269, 270, 274, 306, 308, 324
exclusion
    invisible, 7, 22, 43, 71, 74
    isolation, 24, 183, 239, 254, 255, 261,
        263, 265, 268

family planning, 68, 284, 290, 301
Female Androgen Deficiency Syndrome
    (FADS), 91, 103, 122
Female Sexual Dysfunction (FSD), 89, 100
feminist critiques of biomedical
    perspectives ???
Food and Drug Administration (FDA), 90,
    163

gay men, 5
gender, 1, 2, 4–7, 31, 38, 47, 54, 64–69,
    71–76, 78, 79, 82, 83, 159, 164, 182,
    183, 184, 186–190, 192, 193, 195,
    200, 201, 203, 205, 207, 214–217,
    220–222, 233, 234, 263, 273, 282,
    284, 285, 286, 287, 298, 313, 323,
    324, 326
    biased, 66, 67, 69, 80, 159
    roles, 168, 193, 194
    symmetry, 74, 75
genetic essentialism
    medicine, 63
genomania, 62
germ theory, 23–27, 52, 63
Gulf War syndrome, 146

hardiness, 73
health, 1–8, 11, 12, 15, 18, 20–22
    population, 3, 19–23, 28
    women's, 6, 7

health-care services
    comodification of, 29, 164, 165, 170,
        184
health-seeking, 144, 161, 286
healthicization, 62
healthism, 62
HIV/AIDS, 167, 181, 281, 291
homosexuality (see gay men, lesbians), 3,
    63

ICOS, 100, 125
illness
    networks, 283–285 305–309
infertility, 282, 285, 289, 296, 312
intersectional approach/intersectionality,
    186, 187, 194, 214, 222
invisible, 7, 22, 27, 43, 71, 74, 77, 186,
    234, 235, 239, 242–244, 255, 258,
    259, 269, 272

Kenya, Nyanza Province, 286, 287, 290,
    292, 303, 307, 308, 315

labeling 65, 133, 136, 143, 234, 284, 301,
    305, 315
lesbians, 3, 192, 194, 196
low income, 75, 199, 202, 207, 208, 232,
    233, 238, 239, 248, 249, 252,
    259–262, 264, 270, 271, 273, 277,
    315, 325
Luo, 8, 282, 295, 297, 298, 300–302,
    305–315

managed care, 3, 4, 80, 92, 135, 154, 164,
    167, 170, 171
marginalization, 82, 237
marriage/bridewealth, 8, 28, 234, 287–290,
    292, 304
masculinity (ies), 5, 72–75, 78, 82, 194
matrix of power, 7
medical
    education, 91, 102, 159
    practitioner, 1, 102, 159
medicalized/medicalization, 2, 3, 5, 6,
    64–67, 69, 71–74, 80, 82, 89–94, 97,
    104, 107, 122, 123, 133, 152, 154,
    156, 157

medicine
  behavioral, 61, 63, 73, 208
  corporate, 80
  genetic, 62, 81
  high tech, 61–63
  traditional, 8, 300, 309, 310, 312
  Western, 8, 283, 285, 295, 296, 301,
    309, 310, 312, 314, 315
men's health studies, 78, 83
menopause, 2, 67, 71, 76, 94, 285
miscarriage, 282, 289, 290, 296, 308
models of disease causation, 24
monopolization thesis, 59, 64
mortality, 11, 18, 19, 21, 22, 24, 25, 40, 44,
    53, 61, 181, 183, 191, 192, 195, 233,
    289, 315
morbidity, 18, 22, 24, 40, 61, 135, 141,
    183, 192, 194, 227, 289, 297

Nastech, 100, 103, 125
National Institutes of Health (NIH), 98,
    112, 117, 120, 121, 183, 191, 198, 219
neo-liberal(ism), 2, 4, 5, 8, 50, 51
NexMed, 100, 125

obesity, 2, 63, 82, 207–209, 211
ovarian theory, 82

patriarchy, 8, 43, 94, 206, 282, 284, 293,
    309
patriarchal
  bargain, 285, 293
  control, 80
pelvic inflamatory disease (PID), 283
Pentech, 100, 103, 125
Pfizer, 99, 100, 113, 114, 120, 125
pharmaceutical industry (also see specific
    companies), 5, 65, 89, 91, 92, 95, 97,
    98, 102, 106, 109, 112, 121–125, 324
poor, 2, 3, 7, 21, 23, 37, 40, 51, 53, 68, 80,
    125, 150, 162, 186, 187, 191–193,
    196, 199, 202, 215, 217, 219, 231, 232
positivist, 4, 13–16, 21, 22, 32, 35, 36, 183,
    197, 203, 206, 219–221
poverty (see poor), 21, 22, 25, 183, 212,
    213, 231–236, 239, 242, 244, 255,
    259, 261, 262–265, 269,
    273, 325

prescription medications, 2
Proctor & Gamble, 104, 125
Pharmaceutical Research and
    Manufacturers of America (PhRMA),
    93, 100, 101
polygyny, 287, 288, 291
productive roles/expectations, 296
prolapsed uterus or rectum, 283, 295–297
public health, 1, 4, 11–14, 18, 19, 21–26,
    28–33, 37–39, 43, 48–53, 77, 172,
    182, 195, 207, 208, 210, 221, 233,
    323, 321
public hygiene movement, 20

race, 1, 2, 4–7, 31, 38, 49, 54, 74, 77, 78,
    90, 164, 182–230, 273, 325, 326
rariu, 8, 281–321
reductionism, ???
reproductive
  health theory, 82
  roles/expectations, 296
research
  education, 97
  industry, 99
  medical, 62, 63, 92, 97, 197, 323
research funding streams
  government, 100, 114, 117, 122, 123
  industry, 94, 97, 100, 101, 105, 109,
    111–126
research methods
  feminist action, 198, 232
  qualitative, 3, 7, 8
  quantitative, 39, 198
resistance, 16, 52, 76, 77, 116, 188, 281,
    282, 284, 286, 293, 297, 298,
    306, 313
resources
  economic, 194, 209, 217, 292, 283, 306
  education, 124
risk-factor(s), 12, 61, 62, 64, 82

scientific knowledge, 4, 11, 14, 49, 50, 52,
    154, 155, 158, 159
scientific research, 52
sex-role
  expectations, 193
  theory, 75, 82, 83

sexual problems – women
  arousal, 95, 106, 110–115, 117,
      120–122, 125
  desire, 95, 105, 106, 113, 115, 118, 121,
      122
  orgasm, 95, 104, 105, 124
  pain, 95, 110, 119, 148, 297
sexual problems – men, 94, 119, 124
sexuality, 1, 5, 6, 7, 67, 69, 75, 76, 81, 83,
      95, 104, 109, 111, 114–116, 119, 121,
      123, 182, 185–189, 194, 196,
      199–204, 217, 221–223, 287, 290, 293
sexually transmitted disease (STD), 108,
      281, 283, 291, 296–301, 310, 312,
      313, 316
situating knowledge, 8
social construction of disease, 153
social class (also see class), 6, 27, 42, 49,
      183, 190, 191, 194, 195, 200, 201,
      203, 207, 209, 213, 219, 220
social inequality, 28, 185, 187, 189, 192,
      199, 200, 214, 215, 218, 220, 222
socioeconomic status
  education, 184
  income, 184, 191, 193, 214, 271
  occupation, 271
Solvay, 100, 104, 125
somatization, 6, 8, 131–133, 140, 141,
      146–149, 151, 152, 155, 156, 159,
      160, 162, 166, 170, 171
statistics, 3, 12, 17–25, 31, 34, 43–47, 50,
      51, 53
stigma, 3, 234, 237, 241, 255–257, 259,
      298, 299, 306, 313

strategies, 22, 31, 36, 49, 70, 77, 79, 111,
      137, 168, 188, 195, 203, 211, 217,
      219, 222, 245, 251, 263, 284, 311
stress, 4, 40, 62, 73, 75, 131, 132, 135, 136,
      138, 140, 142, 151, 169, 170
syphilis, 291, 298, 300
symptoms, 2, 4, 6, 8, 19, 63, 64, 69, 71, 77,
      78, 79, 81, 105, 124

traditional healing, 283, 284, 300
treatment
  clinical, 142, 151
  interpersonal, 135
  theory, ???
technology, 152, 154, 160, 162–164, 167,
      169, 171, 326
Type A personality, 2, 4, 72, 73, 82

Urometrics, 125

Viagra, 5, 75, 82, 89, 90
viagracization, 76, 81, 82
victimization model, 66, 75, 82, 83

"web of causation", 26, 27, 33, 36, 42, 52
women's health movement, 67, 70, 74, 77,
      81
Working Group for a New View of
      Women's Sexual Problems, 95, 98,
      126, 127

Zonagan, 125